Dear Dad, אבינו,

Thank you so much for everything you have taught and given me, and for the opportunity that you have given me to learn in Israel for the year.

I hope that this book will be as much of an inspiration to you as you have been to me.

חן חלקי יהי שלך אמן!

With love always,
Shira

"All for the Boss"

an affectionate

family chronicle

of Yaakov Yosef

Herman

---

a Torah pioneer

in America

---

by **Ruchoma Shain**

"All for the Boss"

FELDHEIM PUBLISHERS *Jerusalem / New York*

Picture credits

Pages 32 and 134: Library of Congress, Washington, D.C.
Page 101, left: SHMUEL GORR PICTURE ARCHIVES, Jerusalem
Page 173: courtesy Rabbi Aryeh Carmell, Jerusalem

First published 1984
ISBN 0-87306-346-5

Phototypeset at the Feldheim Press

Philipp Feldheim Inc.
200 Airport Executive Park
Spring Valley, NY 10977

Printed in Israel

Foreword

Among the untold stories of Jewish heroes is the saga of the legendary Mr. Herman.

If America has produced Jewish notables, he was indeed one of the greatest.

It was my privilege to know him personally, and although fifty years have elapsed since I last saw him, he still stands before my mind's eye in the full radiance of his unique personality.

The biography of this servant of Hashem is long overdue. He was active in many original and ingenious ways in numerous aspects of Torah, *avodah* and acts of kindness. And his thoughts, words and deeds were saturated with a fiery love of Hashem and His people.

He was an independent thinker, and he was learned in Torah; he was fearless, energetic, prudent, unselfish, and altogether lovable.

Our generation can profit from the biography of this great soul, the results of whose efforts are still very much alive and exercise their influence among us even today.

Rabbi Avigdor Miller

Acknowledgments

Rabbi Yaakov Haber, a former *talmid* of Yeshiva Torah Ore (Yerusholayim) and now a rabbi in Buffalo, New York, related this to me:

A man once asked the Chofetz Chaim if he should write the true experiences and events in the life of his ancestors. He was afraid it might make him appear to be haughty.

The Chofetz Chaim, however, told him to go ahead, and he cited, to support his answer, a verse from the Written Torah: "Remember the days of old, understand the years of the many generations. Ask your father and he will inform you; your elders, and they will tell you" (Deuteronomy 32:7).

I followed the advice of the Chofetz Chaim, and of many other learned men, who requested that I perpetuate the authentic history of my father's life.

I was able to undertake the task, however, only because I did not have to face it alone:

Rabbi Avigdor Miller (who kindly wrote the Foreword) aided me more than he knew. In addition, may I offer my deep appreciation to those who helped and encouraged me to meet the "lifeline" of the "birth" of this book, which I completed in nine months:

First, there are Papa's *talmidim* who supplied me with tapes in which they relived their relationship with him:

> * Rabbi Boruch Kaplan, founder of the Bais Yaakov Seminary in America.
> * Rabbi Noson Wachtfogel, *mashgiach* of the Bais Medrash Govoha in Lakewood, New Jersey.
> * Rabbi Shachne Zohn, *rosh yeshiva* of the Institute for Advanced Talmudic Scholars, in Yerusholayim.
> * Rabbi Shmuel Shechter, Torah scholar and educator, resident in Yerusholayim.

My nephews Rabbi Moshe Aaron Stern, *mashgiach* of the Kaminetz Yeshiva in Yerusholayim, and Rabbi Shmuel Yitzchok Stern, a director of Bayit Lepletot and the Girls' Town Jerusalem Orphan Homes, earned my thanks by their kind assistance.

One of the dividends I gained from writing the book is my friendship with Yaakov Feldheim, the publisher. He became personally involved, and invested time and effort. By his invaluable constructive criticism and editorial thought this volume was greatly enhanced.

Rabbi Yehoshua Leiman first published some of my material in his *Light*, and this was certainly encouraging.

Finally I must mention my good friends Rochel Landsberg, who gave me a helping hand; Rivka Kirzner, who lent me a listening ear; Penina Zelivansky, who helped with the translation of two articles from Hebrew into English, and Nellie Douek Rubin, who assisted with part of the typing.

My thanks to them all.

R.S.

Contents

Preface

Dearest Papa,

This past year has been one of the most difficult yet inspiring periods of my life. I tried, in some small measure, to recreate your life of intense devotion to Hashem and sacrifice for Him.

Please forgive me, Papa, if I could not do full justice to you in the book. It is almost impossible for me to find words sufficient to describe you, with your great leadership and love of the Jewish people.

Never did you swerve from your duty as a "soldier of the Boss." You obeyed His every commandment, against overwhelming odds. You were not daunted by the jeers from every side that ridiculed your "one-man battle."

With your indomitable courage and your impassioned loyalty to the "Boss" as your only weapons, almost single-handedly, you blazed a trail through the dense, dark thickets of ignorance that pervaded Jewish life in America at the turn of the century — so that many lost souls could find an illuminated, enlightened way to return to their religion.

Out of the raging oceans of secularism and materialism you plucked many drowning victims, as you fought the engulfing waves that flooded the American shores, to bring them to the sure haven of our age-old faith.

In those times of atheism and agnosticism you braved the parched desert bereft of Torah, to plant seeds in its scorched earth, which have transformed it into a garden of growing blossoms and sturdy trees spreading forth their branches and disseminating their fruit of the spirit far and wide throughout the Jewish world.

You used your life to climb insurmountable mountains, to reach higher and ever higher, in order to gain the "front lines" and be as close to the "Boss" as humanly possible.

I hope you know that your large army of followers, whom you trained with patience, devotion and love, walk in your well-trodden path. Even today recruits are continuously swelling its throngs, because many of your cadets became, in turn, captains and majors.

Sweet, gentle Mama stood by your side through every hardship, penetrating your armor to reach straight into your heart with her words of comfort and encouragement, to ease your turmoil and stress.

This book is my loving tribute to you, Papa, and to you, Mama. I pray that both of you are looking down from your exalted places in heaven and taking pride in it.

I am truly blessed to be your daughter.

Ruchoma

6 Elul 5742
August 25, 1982

1

In Retrospect

1

The pinch

I reread Papa's letter. The thread of longing to see me that I detected of late in his letters was evident in each line. Since Mama's death, almost ten years earlier, this longing was intensified, even though Papa had remarried.

True, Papa had several loving grandchildren living near him in Yerusholayim, but as Papa once wrote, "Grandchildren are not children."

Fifteen long years had passed since I'd last seen Papa. There were always valid reasons for not being able to make the trip: The Second World War, the births of my two younger children, The War of Independence in Eretz Yisroel. Yet I always had it in mind and kept the hope in my heart—next year I shall surely visit Papa. . . .

An overwhelming desire to see Papa engulfed me. I wanted to feel the warm clasp of his hands, see his penetrating steel-gray eyes soften with affection as he gazed at me. I wanted to talk to him, bare my troubled thoughts and questions which his wisdom could clarify and answer. . . . I burst into tears.

....

Yerusholayim: Jerusalem / **Eretz Yisroel**: Land of Israel

Moshe came home from yeshiva to find me red-eyed. "Racoma, what's happened?" he asked anxiously.

"Moshe, I want to visit Papa. I can't wait any longer. I long to see him." He saw Papa's letter on the table and understood.

I called a travel agent. The agent informed me that the round trip fare cost $987. Flight time was approximately forty hours, with five stopovers: Labrador, Shannon, Paris, Rome, Athens and finally Tel Aviv. (There were no jets in the early 1950s.) There was a flight at the end of June. I immediately made reservations to leave on June 29 for a month's stay.

Fortunately, we had United States war bonds, which we were able to cash in to pay for the plane fare. I notified Papa, "I am flying to visit you. In six weeks we shall be together. Wait for me. . . . Love, Ruchoma."

His answer came in record time, "I am waiting. Your 'Pinch' awaits you also. Papa."

The "Pinch." I touched my cheek. It was an integral part of my childhood. Even when we were very young children, Papa never kissed us. His religious principles of child-training were so firm and unyielding that he subdued his paternal emotions.

However, he showed his approval of me, his youngest, by, every so often, giving me a pinch on the cheek when I was an especially good girl or when he enjoyed a quip of mine. Sometimes, the pinch left a slight black-and-blue mark on my skinny cheek, which I wore as a "badge of honor."

I thrust the flitting memories of my childhood out of my mind. I would have enough time to think about them on the long plane flight to Papa.

I plunged into a whirlwind of activity. Mashi and Yitzchok, our younger children, had to be readied for camp, their first experience away from home. There was shopping, sewing name tapes on their clothes, washing, ironing, moth-proofing the closets, and inoculations for me. I also prepared meals in advance for Moshe and our oldest son, Yisroel Meir, who would fend for themselves during my absence, with our close relatives lending a helping hand.

The phone rang incessantly. Each relative and friend had a different comment, ranging from "Racoma, how wonderful that you are finally going to see your father after so many years," "You must be terribly excited to be traveling on a plane for the first time," "I have a cousin in Tiberias. Can you bring him a small gift from me?" to "Take along suntan lotion. I heard the sun is fiery there during the summer," "How I envy your going."

The day of my departure finally arrived. Mashi and Yitzchok left for their camps the day before in a flurry of hugs, kisses and tears. I boarded the plane Tuesday evening with thumping heart, waving a last farewell to my dear ones.

The last-minute instructions were announced: "Fasten your seat belts." The plane with fifty-eight passengers aboard zoomed towards the sky. The clouds parted respectfully to allow this strange flying bird to usurp some of their sky space. The plane gathered momentum. The soothing droning sound of the whirring engines relaxed me for the first time in weeks. I adjusted my seat to a reclining position. I raised my hand to wipe the beads of sweat from my face and touched my cheek . . . the pinch!

Vivid memories of my childhood flashed on the screen of my mind.

When Mama was pregnant with me, Papa decided that this time she would present him with a second son. Esther, Frieda, Nochum Dovid, and Bessie had preceded me.

As Papa hurried home from *shul*, he was greeted by his sister, Molly. "*Mazel tov*, Aidel just gave birth to a girl."

Papa stared at her unbelievingly. "Are you absolutely sure?" He rushed up the steps two at a time. Doctor Bluestone, our family doctor, came out of Mama's bedroom. (In those days, the customary place of birth was in the home.)

"Reb Yaakov Yosef, you have a fine, healthy little girl." He shook Papa's hand warmly. Papa was crestfallen. "Do not

shul: synagogue

worry," the doctor comforted him, "in due time she will bring you a son when she marries."

It was the eighteenth day of Kislev (December 6, 1914). The First World War, which started in August, 1914, had already unleashed havoc on many European countries. The dead and wounded mounted each day.

Papa chose my name, Ruchoma, meaning pity—which he took from the Prophet Hosea (2:3): "Say unto your brethren, Ammi; and to your sisters, Ruchoma. . . ."—as a symbol for our Father in Heaven to have pity on the entire world. And, as an added hope, I guess, to have pity on Papa and bless him with more sons. However, it was destined not to be, for I remained the youngest in the family.

Papa showed his partiality for me as a child, which I attributed to his guilty conscience for being so disappointed when I was born. When I was a very young child, he enjoyed holding me on his lap, allowing me to stroke his beard, the special privilege given only to me.

When Papa registered me for the first grade in P.S. 42 on the Lower East Side, he showed the registrar my birth certificate, which had my name listed as "Ruchoma." Papa was told that there is no sound in English corresponding to the Hebrew letter *ches*. Then and there, Papa created my English name, Racoma (pronounced Rakoma). Papa and Mama always called me by my Hebrew name, but almost everyone else used my English name.

During my school years, my English name elicited much curiosity in my teachers and school friends. I proudly gave everyone a lengthy explanation on its origin, stressing that my name was taken from the Bible.

Papa had definite ideas for every phase of our lives. We lived in an apartment heated only with a coal stove in the kitchen, although Papa could have afforded a much more expensive and warmer home for us. He was sure that this would immunize us against respiratory diseases. His theory seems to have worked, as we rarely suffered from colds or the flu.

Castor oil was the medication for a multitude of ills, ranging from headache to stomach ache. There was a battle royal when Papa administered it to me. Mama hovered nearby with an orange. (To this day the sight of an orange revives the taste of castor oil.)

Papa could be harsh and strict with us children, but Mama tempered his discipline with her warmth and understanding. However, despite Papa's punitive measures to teach and direct us in the ways of the Torah, his intense devotion to our every need took precedence over his fur business, or any other activity except for his religious duties. Though as a young child I feared Papa, he instilled in me the feeling of great emotional security that he could protect me from any harm that loomed ahead.

Once I had a severe earache on Shabbos. When Papa returned from *shul*, Mama said worriedly, "Yankev Yosef, I just don't know what to do for Ruchoma. She is in such pain." My sobbing could be heard throughout the house.

Papa came over to me. "Ruchoma, place your ear on my *tallis* and lie down. Your earache will get all better," he assured me with conviction. Mama tucked me into bed with my ear on Papa's *tallis*. I fell asleep. When I awoke, my earache had vanished.

One winter day, when I was six years old, I became feverish. My body was covered with a deep red rash. Dr. Bluestone was called.

"Ruchoma has scarlet fever. She will have to be in bed for at least six weeks. It is very contagious, so keep her isolated." The doctor wrote a prescription for medication to lower the fever. (There were no antibiotics in those days.)

The red blotches itched terribly. Mama watched over me with deep concern to prevent me from scratching myself. Papa took over my care for the nights, so Mama could have some rest.

....
tallis: Prayer shawl

"Yankev Yosef, do not allow Ruchoma to scratch her face. It could leave marks," Mama warned Papa over and over again. I remember that as I lay in a daze of fever and itching, Papa gently held my hands all through the nights, telling me little stories of the Bible while he half-dozed. I recovered without any telltale signs.

"Ruchoma, give me your doll," Papa said firmly. I crept under the dark recess of my bed and slowly pulled out the shoe box I had converted into a bed for the doll.

I took the dolly and held her close to my heart. It was a present from Aunt Fanny. I had hidden it during the entire week. Then on Shabbos, I played with it in full view of Papa, knowing very well that on that day he would not hurt my dolly.

Now it was Saturday night. The die was cast. Papa took the doll from my reluctant hands. Smash! The doll's nose was broken. I screamed. Mama drew me into her arms. "It did not hurt the doll," she soothed me. My flowing tears soaked the doll's pink dress, as I clutched her tightly to my heart once more.

"Ruchoma, come here," Papa said gently. "Even though you are a little girl, you must learn to obey the Torah. It says there must not be an idol in a Jewish home. Your doll is like an idol. When you become a big girl, you will understand."

Papa showed his concern for us by tenderly ministering to our foot problems all through our childhood. Where he ever acquired the art of chiropody, I never discovered, but the results were excellent.

Papa was in his element. Mama had given birth to "his" son—the first boy after two daughters, Esther and Frieda. Though his joy was boundless, he controlled his emotions with great effort because it was *erev* Tisha b'Av.

....

erev: eve of / **Tisha b'Av**: Ninth day of Av; fast day commemorating the destruction of the Temple

In fact, he did not inform Zeidy and Bobie Andron, Mama's parents, until after the fast. Papa decided to name his son Nochum Dovid, which indicated the period in which he was born.

When Zeidy and Bobie Andron visited Mama, Zeidy said to Papa, "I would very much like to have the baby named after my father."

"I have already chosen his name," Papa answered. It turned out that Zeidy's father's name was Nochum Dovid. In his excitement, Papa had forgotten.

Davie received the brunt of Papa's strictness. At the age of four, Papa wrapped him in a large *tallis* and carried him to Yeshiva Tiferes Yerusholayim to begin his Hebrew studies.

Each morning, I awoke to cries of protest emanating from his room, as Papa pulled him sleepily out of bed and carried him to *shul* for the morning prayers. Davie had little time for games or other pastimes, as a *rebbe* awaited him daily when he returned from the yeshiva.

However, Mama cushioned the blow, as Nochum Dovid was her favorite. In her eyes, he could do no wrong, and she yielded to his whims. Surprisingly enough, though I was the "baby" of the family, I had no feeling of jealousy where Davie was concerned. It was only natural that the *ben yochid* should receive extra benefits. I liked the *pulke* of the chicken; however, throughout my childhood, whenever Davie was home, the *pulkes* were his. I accepted this as a matter of course.

Papa had no problem with the girls' getting up in time for school, especially on the cold wintry mornings. He walked into our bedroom, removed the heavy down quilts, and stalked out of our room with them. Four shivery girls flew into the kitchen to warm themselves by the glowing coal stove Mama had ready for us.

Papa's method of punishment was unique. When I was

Zeidy: Grandfather / Bobie: Grandmother / *rebbe*: teacher
ben yochid: only son / *pulke*: drumstick

naughty, he escorted me into the bedroom, took off his leather strap, and brought it down heavily on the iron bedpost. Though the strap was nowhere near me, I screamed loudly at each strike Papa gave.

Mama stood outside the closed door pleading, "Yankev Yosef, enough. Let Ruchoma go. She will be a good girl from now on." I ran out of the bedroom, crying hysterically, into Mama's soothing arms.

Somehow, I think that this was a pre-planned act, which Papa and Mama played to perfection. However, I rarely needed such "severe" punishment. One glare from Papa's steel-gray eyes was sufficient to squelch any thought of misbehavior on my part.

Another way of keeping us children obedient was Mama's admonition, "I'll tell Papa." After we misbehaved, we had to kiss Papa's hand to show that we accepted his rebuke.

When Papa walked into the house, we always stood up for him. We were supposed to do the same for Mama, but unless we were prodded by Papa, we forgot.

Once, while I was doing my homework, Papa came over to me suddenly and sharply slapped my hand. I cried out in protest. Mama called from the kitchen, "I did not mean Ruchoma."

Papa, not disconcerted, responded, "Most probably Ruchoma deserved this for some other wrongdoing for which she received no punishment."

On one hot summer day during my school vacation I was playing "potsy" with my friends in the street. Papa hurried over to me and said, "Ruchoma, you are *bas mitzva* already. Go up to the house and change into long stockings."

I ran up the stairs and into the house. "Mama," I cried out, "Papa won't let me wear my knee socks any more because I am twelve years old. I have no light-weight stockings," I complained, as I searched through my drawer. I pulled out my

bas mitzva: girl 12 years old—considered adult in Jewish law

heavy winter hose and looked at them with distaste.

"Wear them in the meantime," Mama advised, "I will buy you summer stockings as soon as I get the chance."

I returned to my potsy game with all my friends casting pitying glances at my heavy winter hose.

Osna was my best childhood friend. Her father, Alter Winevsky, had arrived in America with very little funds, leaving his wife, Chana, and their two sons in Russia until he could send for them.

Papa found him in *shul* one night, alone and distraught. He had no close relatives or friends to turn to, so Papa invited him to stay at our house. Papa, who was in the fur business, taught him the fur trade and helped him earn enough to bring his family over. When they arrived, Papa rented an apartment for the Winevsky family in the building where we lived. Mama and Chana soon became very close friends.

Mama and Chana were both expecting at the same time. After Osna was born, Chana waited impatiently for Mama to give birth. Three weeks later, Esther ran down to Chana to announce excitedly, "I have a new baby sister. Her name is Ruchoma."

Osna's mother was delighted. She commented, "Now my daughter will have a good friend."

Osna spent most of her spare time in our house. Her parents were busy trying to make ends meet, so they had little time to cater to her. Papa and Mama treated her like one of us, and she became part of our family.

Osna had an innate fear of darkness and would tremble if the lights went out for a moment. "The black hand will get you in the dark," she warned me.

However, Papa's oft-repeated statement, "You must never fear anyone but the Boss," engendered in me such a sense of emotional security that Osna's threat did not have any effect.

Papa sought to cure Osna of her fear with his best childhood psychology. "Ruchoma and Osna, come with me," Papa ordered one Sunday afternoon. We followed Papa dutifully down the steps to our cellar. He unbolted the heavy door and turned on the switch. The cellar was bathed in a yellow light.

There stood all our Pesach appliances and other household equipment, our *sukka* boards and ladder. The Pesach gas stove and table occupied one wall. Our Pesach pots, pans and dishes were packed in different-sized cartons, covered with large sheets. A giant trunk was pushed into an empty corner.

"Osna, touch each thing and tell me exactly what they are," Papa instructed her. Osna ran, touching the items and calling out, "Table, gas stove, cartons, boards, ladder, trunk." She enjoyed the attention Papa gave her.

Suddenly, without notice, Papa switched off the lights. The cellar became pitch-black. Osna uttered a desperate cry. Papa held her hand tightly and propelled her to the different shapes and sizes, which appeared like grotesque figures in the darkness. "Touch them," he commanded. Osna whimpered. Papa turned on the switch. Once again the cellar was suffused with light. "See, there is nothing to fear," Papa calmed her. Over and over again, he repeated this procedure until Osna touched everything in the dark.

I am not sure if Papa's psychology cured Osna completely of her fear of darkness; however, before Pesach, when I went down to the cellar to help bring up our dishes, I knew with my eyes shut where each carton stood.

I was an avid reader, and books kept me spellbound. However, Papa did not approve of our reading library books, so I hid the books in various places. I had one in the cutlery drawer, and as I dried the spoons I would read it. Under my pillow, I hid another book, which I read whenever Papa was late coming home at night. The bathroom shaft was another good hiding place. But it didn't always work.

....

Pesach: Passover / *sukka*: hut used during Feast of Tabernacles

"What are you reading, Ruchoma?" Papa caught me red-handed.

"Just a boo . . . book," I stammered. He grabbed the book from my hands and glanced at the first and last pages.

"This fills your head with nonsense. Come, I am returning this book to the library."

I dreaded going with Papa, but his word was law. I cried softly, as I walked towards my doom, but Papa was never cowed by our tears.

"Do not lend my daughter any library books," Papa told the startled librarian, as he handed her the book. I hid my face in shame.

A few weeks later, when I visited the library, I made sure that a different librarian would be on duty.

Papa was in a state of excitement that was contagious. Charles Lindbergh was about to make the first non-stop solo flight from New York to Paris. The year was 1927. We anxiously awaited every bit of news.

"He made it!" Papa ran into the house waving the newspaper with the glaring headlines: "Lindbergh lands in France."

Papa sat down in his armchair, caught his breath and exclaimed, "This is a preview of *Moshiach*'s times when Hashem will gather the Jews from all parts of the world and fly them over the oceans to Eretz Yisroel. As it says in *Shmos* (Exodus 19:4), 'How I bore you on eagles' wings . . .' "

Papa pointed to the picture of the plane. "Doesn't it resemble a flying bird?"

I peered closely at the photograph. Then I looked at Papa with wonder and thought, "Would I ever fly into the sky?"

Mama once told me that when she was engaged to Papa, he took her to a boxing match. She almost fainted. That was the

---

Moshiach: the Messiah / **Hashem**: God

first and last time she went, and it dampened Papa's enthusiasm for this sport.

One Sunday morning Mama took Davie, Bessie and me to visit Bobie Herman (Papa's mother), who lived in Harlem. We loved to go there. She fussed over us and always prepared special treats for us.

Bobie and Mama got along very well. Though Mama called Bobie "*shvigger*" (mother-in-law), it was more of a mother-daughter relationship.

As we left the elevated train on our way home, Davie straggled behind us. Suddenly, there was a piercing scream from him. His jacket had caught on the iron grating of the gate of the moving train, which was pushing him along the platform. In another moment, he would be thrown to the street below.

Mama cried out in great alarm, and Bessie and I wailed loudly. Fortunately, the motorman heard our cries and the train stopped abruptly. Davie was sheet-white. Mama clasped his trembling body in her arms and sat down with him on the nearest bench to catch her breath.

We returned home to find Papa red-eyed, reciting *tehillim*. Mama poured out an account of the near-tragic event. "A short while ago, I felt a terrible premonition of tragedy," Papa said with deep emotion. "I immediately started to pray. The Boss answered my prayers."

Going to the movies was our favorite treat. Papa, of course, discouraged us. One Sunday morning, after we had pestered Mama endlessly, she finally yielded to us. "Yankev Yosef, let the children go to the movies. They have nothing else to do today."

Papa glanced at Mama with surprise. She usually went along with Papa's dictates, especially when they concerned any

---

tehillim: Psalms

facet of our religious upbringing. Bessie and I awaited Papa's verdict with trepidation.

"Did you say your prayers today?" Papa asked us. We nodded our heads. Papa assumed that by reciting our prayers our desire for this necessary evil should automatically vanish. Papa could not give his definite approval. He left the room, which did not mean "No."

Mama hurriedly prepared a large bag of food, handed us each five cents—the price of the movie—and whispered, "Stay as long as you can." She was relieved to get rid of us for a few hours.

We flew on a magic carpet to the movie theater. Bessie and I read the titles out loud. (There were no talkies in those days.) If I could not understand a word, Bessie explained it to me.

The seats all around us emptied, as the other patrons were distracted by our loud talking. However, we were oblivious to all except the movie, which captivated us.

By the third time around, we knew all the titles by heart. Several hours later, after we had finished all the food Mama had given us, we reluctantly left the dark movie-house, blinking in the bright sunlight.

We rushed home to hug and kiss Mama and tell her all about the wonderful movie we had seen. Papa showed his disapproval. "No movies for three months." I carefully made a small notation on our calendar.

Once Mama received a free pass to the movies from our corner candy store. It was conditional that it be used only during school hours. "Mama, go; you will love it," I encouraged her.

I could not concentrate on my schoolwork that day. Imagine, Mama going to the movies! I ran home and burst into the house to find Papa and Mama home. "Mama, what movie did you see?" I asked eagerly.

"I saw a cowboy riding on a horse down a dusty road."

"What else?" I prompted.

"Well, it was so cool and comfortable that I fell asleep right away. When I awoke, I saw the same cowboy on the horse returning. That was the end of the movie," Mama finished. I gaped!

Papa had his ears tuned to Mama. "Aidel, the movies are good for you. Whenever you receive a free pass, you can go." Papa smiled broadly at Mama, who looked refreshed and rested.

My sisters and I attended the neighborhood public school. We mingled with the other children of diverse nationalities — Italian, Polish, Russian, Chinese — and we were friendly with all of them.

In fact, many of my non-Jewish schoolmates came to our house to do their homework with me. Papa and Mama always treated them respectfully. However, there was a strict, standing rule that we obeyed scrupulously: We were not allowed to visit the home of anyone else, other than a few very close friends whose parents Papa and Mama knew very well.

Still, that never prevented me from having friends. On Shabbos, ten to fifteen girlfriends usually visited me. Papa related stories of the Bible and discussed any problems they had. And Mama always served her delicious coffee cake and drinks.

When we graduated public school, Papa searched high and low for an all-girls high school. There was an excellent high school in the vicinity, but it was co-educational, and Papa would not hear of it.

Papa finally discovered a private girls high school on East Fourteenth Street, Manhattan, that met his demands. The tuition was costly. All our textbooks had to be purchased, and the carfare added to the expense. However, Papa never considered money when it conflicted with his religious convictions.

The high school offered a two-year accelerated program, with no vacation during the hot summer months, except for a few days off here and there. Papa was impressed with the excellent curriculum and the physical fitness course, which included swimming, basketball, tennis, and special physical exercises.

In order to enter the high school, we were required to pass an entrance examination. Esther, Frieda and Bessie were accepted without any problem. However, when my turn came to register, Papa had difficulty. The required age of entry was fourteen, and I was only thirteen and a half.

Papa did his best to persuade the school authorities to accept me. Finally, because the Herman girls had such a good reputation, Papa was told that if I would pass the entrance examination with a high average, they would make an exception in my case.

I tossed and turned the night before I was to take the exam with the disturbing thought, "If I fail, or do not receive a high mark, I will bring shame to the Herman family."

Trembling, I went to take the test, with Papa's and Mama's blessings ringing in my ears. My application was approved.

The teachers took a personal interest in their students, and I enjoyed my studies immensely. The entire student body wore green uniforms over white blouses and gym bloomers.

The physical fitness program enticed me, and Papa was all for it. In no time, I was diving, floating, and performing varied swimming strokes in the large pool. I was chosen to be "forward" on my basketball team. Each day I hurried home from school to share my experiences with Papa and Mama.

Mama made sure that we took along nutritious lunches to school. Each morning, she prepared them painstakingly, not trusting us to do it. Before we left for school, her parting words were, "Don't forget your lunch." But I did forget it one morning.

At recess, I received a message from the office. I quickly descended the large stone stairs, wondering why I was being summoned. Mama was seated in the office. She jumped up when I entered.

"Ruchoma, you forgot your lunch. I brought it for you."
Not one word of reproach. I discovered later that Mama had
walked to and from my high school, a matter of several miles, in
order to save the carfare. Papa was facing difficult financial
setbacks in his fur business, and she had not wanted to spend
the extra money.

*Immigrants from Eastern Europe on an Atlantic liner, coming into the
New York harbor in 1906. When Papa arrived with his family in 1888,
it might have been under similar conditions.*

2

Recollections

PAPA'S YOUTH

In the late afternoon, when we returned from public school, we studied Hebrew and Bible at the Talmud Torah. When Papa discovered that some of the teachers were not strict Sabbath observers, he withdrew us.

He hired a Hebrew teacher for us. However, no teacher lasted very long with the lively Herman girls. So Papa took to teaching us himself. During these sessions, he kept us fascinated with stories of his family and childhood.

Papa was eight years old when he emigrated from Slutsk, Russia, with his parents and younger sister, Molly. The year was 1888.

Zeidy Yitzchok Isaac married Bobie Minna Rivka when he was eighteen years old, and she a year or two older. He was a *yeshiva bochur.* After their wedding, they lived on the farm of Bobie's parents, outside of Slutsk.

Zeidy Herman could not eke out an income sufficient to

---

yeshiva bochur: Talmudic Academy student

sustain his growing family. He decided that America was the golden opportunity for him. When they arrived in the United States, Zeidy first sought employment as a private *rebbe*, to give lessons, but he quickly found out that few were interested. Papa remained his only student.

Zeidy tried to obtain work even in menial jobs or in factories, but when he did not show up on Shabbos, the following Monday he was out of work. The fact that he also did not work on *chol hamoed* Pesach and Sukkos compounded his difficulties in retaining employment.

He was ridiculed by his fellow Jews for not wanting to shave his beard nor lessen his religious principles by one iota. "In America, you cannot be the same as you were in the Old Country, or you will never make a living for your family," his acquaintances advised him.

After five years of struggle, he realized how correct his friends were. He decided to return to his hometown in Russia, so as not to lower his religious standards.

Zeidy was able to muster enough money to purchase two-and-a-half tickets—for himself, for Bobie, and for Molly, who was still able to travel on a child's half-fare. However, since Papa was already *bar mitzva*, he needed a full ticket. Zeidy and Bobie had no alternative but to leave him with distant cousins until they could find the means to bring him home.

The cousins agreed to provide Papa with room and board for the price of one dollar a week. Papa worked as a handy-boy for the salary of one and a quarter dollars a week at a fur shop. It was one of the rare ones that was Sabbath-observant.

When Papa returned from the pier after bidding farewell to his parents and sister, he was a forlorn lad. Suddenly, he thrust his hands in his pocket and felt his treasured pack of marbles. He squared his frail shoulders, pulled the marbles from their bag and threw them to the curb. As the gaily colored marbles

....

chol hamoed: Intermediate Days of a Festival / **Sukkos**: Feast of Tabernacles / *bar mitzva*: boy 13 years old—considered adult in Jewish law

rolled down the dusty street, the last vestige of his childhood followed them. "No more playing games for me. I have to be a man now," he said to himself.

Though he valiantly tried to become a "man," it was no easy task for a thirteen-year-old boy to grow up overnight. Pangs of lonesomeness overwhelmed him, and his pillow was often soaked with tears.

However, instead of bearing a grudge against his parents for leaving him, Papa determined to work with greater effort and save enough money to bring them and his sister Molly back to America and help towards their support.

Several weeks after Papa had started boarding with his cousins, he was told, "If you want to remain with us, you must pay $1.25 a week."

Papa felt a terrible sense of betrayal. With choking sobs, he ran from their house. It was *erev* Shabbos. The sun was soon setting, and Shabbos was fast approaching.

Papa resolved not to return to his cousins' house even if it meant spending Shabbos in the street. He hurried to a bakery and bought three little *challos.*

The sun set. Shabbos came and found a lonely, forsaken boy sitting on a hard bench in deserted Hester Park. There was no place for a young, confused, broken-hearted lad to go to in the vast city of New York.

Papa made *kiddush* over two *challos* and hungrily gulped down one of them. All through the long night he sat huddled on the hard bench, half-dozing and half-awake.

When dawn finally broke, Papa made a vow that when he would marry and have a home of his own, he would never sit down at his Shabbos or Yom Tov table without having *orchim* gathered around him. He would even search in the parks for lonely, hungry people to feed.

....

challos: Sabbath bread / *kiddush*: ritual of ushering in the Sabbath
Yom Tov: holiday / *orchim*: guests

Saturday night, Papa withdrew his few belongings from his cousins' house and found different lodgings.

Most of the week, Papa existed on delicatessen food for his main meal. However, Papa was physically very strong, and his years of deprivation did nothing to weaken him in the least. In fact, even in the coldest winter weather, he never wore an overcoat. (After Papa and Mama were married, she complained to him, "Yankev Yosef, people will think you can't afford a winter coat." To appease her, he bought a very expensive one, but he seldom wore it.)

Although there was no one to teach or admonish him, Papa scrupulously observed all the *mitzvos* Zeidy had taught him. During the few times he allowed himself the luxury of playing ball with his friends, when it came time for his afternoon and evening prayers, he dropped the ball in the middle of the game and rushed off to *shul*.

Papa advanced steadily in the fur shop where he started as a handy-boy. He developed from apprentice into an experienced worker with furs. His salary grew, and with it his savings, which he hoarded carefully.

Four years after Papa bade farewell to Zeidy, Bobie and Molly, he sent them enough money to purchase tickets. By that time, another ticket was needed for his little brother, Chatzkel, whom he had never met. (His youngest sister, Sarah, was born in the United States.) It was a joyful day for the Herman family, and especially for Papa, when they were finally reunited.

Papa rented an apartment for them. With his salary, he was able to support them, so that Zeidy could have the luxury of being a *rebbe*, his specialty, on the small salary he earned.

---

mitzvos: religious commandments

△Papa at 18, in a studio photo with Zeidy Herman (seated).

◁ Papa aged 7, with his mother and his sister Molly, in the Old Country.

ZEIDY & BOBIE
HERMAN

Zeidy and Bobie Herman were loving, devoted grandparents, who were very close to us throughout their lifetimes. We adored Bobie Herman. Her chocolate bars came together with her whenever she visited us. During the summer months, we children took turns staying at Zeidy and Bobie's house for a week's time. This was the highlight of our vacation. We reveled and basked in the personal attention Bobie showered on us.

They lived in Harlem, near Central Park, and Bobie took us on picnics to the park. We visited the famous zoo, which fascinated us. When Bobie brought us home, we were washed, combed and bow-bedecked girls, with bright rosy cheeks.

Bobie's pride and joy was Papa, her oldest son. He, in turn, revered her. Late one night, we were all riding home by subway from a wedding. As we neared the steep staircase leading up to the street level, Bobie said quietly, "I am so tired."

Suddenly, Papa scooped her up in his arms and raced up the high flight of steps, with Bobie's little feet kicking back and forth in protest. "Yankev Yosef, put me down," she pleaded. By that time Papa had already safely stood her up at the top of the staircase.

In 1926, Zeidy Herman decided to leave for Eretz Yisroel. He had his heart set on settling there. He set out on a freighter, which took over a month to arrive there. His letter describing his harrowing trip brought us to tears and laughter simultaneously.

Papa arranged for Zeidy to live in the Anshei Maimod in Yerusholayim, an organization where elderly men board and study Torah. So Zeidy became a *yeshiva bochur* once again.

He enjoyed life in Eretz Yisroel and became acquainted with many of the *rabbonim* living in Meah She'arim. Zeidy became close to a brilliant Torah student, Reb Yosef Sholom Elyashiv (who is today the very well-known *dayon* in Yerusholayim). Zeidy suggested an excellent *shidduch* for him. The girl was the daughter of Reb Aryeh Levin (*A Tzaddik in our Time*), who was already known in those days for his *tzidkus* and *chesed*. Zeidy was very friendly with him. The *shidduch* was successfully concluded, and the young couple were married, much to Zeidy's satisfaction.

During the time Zeidy was living in Eretz Yisroel, Bobie came to stay with us. We were delighted. When we returned from school, she would hold us spellbound with many tales of her childhood, which came to life with her presentation.

Bobie pitched in to help Mama with all the chores of the house. They got along very harmoniously. "Aidel, you work too hard. Tell Yankev Yosef to get you help." Or on another occasion, "Why don't you buy yourself some new clothes?" Bobie advised Mama.

....

rabbonim: rabbis / *dayon*: judge / *shidduch*: match / *tzidkus*: piety
chesed: loving-kindness

Zeidy and Bobie Herman

The standing joke in our home was Papa's calling Bobie *shvigger* whenever she defended Mama. However, he showed his mother great respect. When she entered the room, Papa arose from his chair and stood up until she sat down. Bobie and Mama were the only ones permitted to sit in Papa's armchair.

When Zeidy had been in Yerusholayim for over a year, he wrote Bobie asking her to join him. However, by then, Bobie did not want to part from her children. A few months later, Zeidy returned to the United States. We were happy to have Zeidy back, but very sad when Bobie left our home.

After they had lived in New York for a number of years, Zeidy and Bobie accepted a proposition to manage a *Hachnosas Orchim,* a free hostel, supported by the Jewish Community in Jersey City. Bobie prepared all the meals, baked the *challos* for Shabbos and kept the premises clean.

One *erev* Shabbos, a short while before lighting the candles, when Bobie was finishing washing the kitchen floor on her knees, she suffered a heart attack. It was too late for Zeidy to notify Papa.

After *havdolo* Zeidy called to tell Papa that Bobie had passed away. It was Rosh Chodesh Menachem Av. Papa did not break down, but Mama and I did. (I was the only one of the children home, as all the others were married.) We were inconsolable.

Bobie Herman was gone. Her bright spirit had illuminated our lives with her wisdom and sage advice. She was gentle, yet firm; she was helpful, but gave us self-reliance. Above all, she was my loving Bobie, whom I would miss.

There was a great deal for Papa to arrange. All the preparations for the funeral and burial had to be taken care of. Papa was a bulwark of strength.

The first day of *shiva*, right after the morning prayers, Papa closed the door to our living room. Suddenly, Mama and I were transfixed. Heartbreaking, anguished sobs were coming forth from the closed room. It was Papa.

Papa, the brave, courageous, dauntless soldier was weeping — a son grieving for his lost mother.

It was the first time I ever heard Papa cry.

In time, Zeidy Herman remarried. We became attached to his wife, Tante Rivka, who was devoted to us.

After ten years of marriage, Zeidy passed away on *isru chag* Pesach. We children took care of the arrangements of his funeral and burial because Papa and Mama were already settled in Eretz Yisroel.

Zeidy Herman left us a rich heritage of good deeds. My memory of him is of a person who was always kind and considerate, with a cheery word for everyone.

....

havdolo: literally, separation: ritual of ushering out the Sabbath
Rosh Chodesh Menachem Av: the first day of the month of Av — a minor holiday / *shiva*: seven days of mourning / *tante*: aunt / *isru chag*: day after the holiday

3

Mix and match

By the time Papa was twenty-one years old, he was a handsome, dashing, wealthy young man, the owner of a flourishing fur business. It was time for him to get married. The *shadchonim*, who were waiting for his cue, descended upon him *en masse*.

Papa explained to each of them that he was interested in a truly Orthodox girl from a family of culture and Torah education. Of course, each of the *shadchonim* had "The Girl" who met all of his qualifications. In addition, she was extremely wealthy, with many other fine attributes that Papa would surely discover once he met his prospective bride. So he was assured.

Papa soon found out that there was no exaggeration as to the wealthy home, for no *shadchen* would dare introduce a girl to Papa who could not offer him the dowry suitable for such a rich, handsome young man. However, they definitely magnified "the truly religious girl from a fine Orthodox home."

In order for Papa to be convinced that the girl was a strict

shadchen: matchmaker / *shadchonim*: matchmakers

Sabbath observer, he arranged his visits for Friday night, even though it meant walking great distances to the girl's home. (In the early 1900s, formal Jewish education for girls was non-existent. Consequently, the girls' training was a product of the home.) On more than one Friday night Papa kept his appointment only to be disappointed. On one occasion, Papa noticed the girl placing the tea kettle from the table back onto the stove. Papa stood up and announced, "It seems the *shadchen* gave me the wrong address," and out he stalked.

On another occasion, when it was impossible for Papa to meet the girl on Friday night because the distance to her home was too great to walk, he came during the week. While in her home, she responded to a knock at the door. A poor man stood there, and she handed him a large donation. Papa noticed that her parents were perturbed by her extravagance. He never returned. He would not consider marrying into a family which did not give charity with open hands.

At last, one of the matchmakers, who refused to surrender, knowing he would receive a substantial fee if he could find the right girl for Papa, said timidly, "I have just the girl for you who will meet all your demands. However, I must confess that she is penniless and has no dowry whatsoever."

Papa was astounded. A girl without a dowry! No reputable young man would consider her for marriage. However, he was intrigued by the *shadchen*'s courage and asked, "Who is she?"

"Her name is Aidel Andron. Her father, Reb Shmuel Yitzchok Andron, is a great *talmid chochom* and a very learned man," the *shadchen* concluded bravely.

Papa went there Friday night. The candles burned brightly on the table, which was set with a spotless white cloth. Reb Shmuel Yitzchok, a stately person with a graying beard, and his wife, Fruma Rochel, wearing a wig, sat at the head of the table. Their five sons were gathered around listening to a *dvar Torah* from their father. Aidel was busy serving everyone tea,

---

talmid chochom: learned man / **dvar Torah**: short Torah discourse

cake and fruit. There was a warm Shabbos atmosphere that permeated every corner of their house.

Rabbi Andron was the only one who did not inquire of the *shadchen* about Papa's earning potential, but instead dwelled on his learning capabilities. Papa was immediately captivated by the Androns and their lovely, charming daughter, Aidel.

Papa told Zeidy and Bobie Herman that he had finally found the girl he was looking for. He added, "She has no dowry, but it really does not matter. I do not need any money from her."

"What!" Bobie exclaimed. "Will you marry a poor girl when you have so many offers to marry rich, fine girls? I refuse to permit you to go through with this *shidduch*." Bobie was adamant.

Papa tried every way to convince his mother to change her mind. When he realized he could not, he had no recourse but to tell the matchmaker that he could not marry the Andron girl. He would not disobey his mother's wishes.

Months passed. Papa met other girls but none to compare with Aidel or her family. Depressed, he hid his feelings from his parents.

One morning, as he was walking along, he met Yankev Leib Andron, Aidel's oldest brother. Yankev Leib greeted Papa warmly and asked him frankly, "Why did you stop seeing my sister? We were all so sure that you were interested in her."

Papa poured out his woes. "I still want to marry your sister, but my mother absolutely refuses to allow me to because there is no suitable dowry."

Yankev Leib thought for a moment and then asked, "Do you have two thousand dollars in the bank?"

Papa answered quickly, "I have even more than that."

"I have an excellent way to solve the problem satisfactorily for all concerned. Give me the two thousand dollars as a present. On the night of your engagement I will return it to you as Aidel's dowry," Yankev Leib advised. (Two thousand dollars was considered a very handsome dowry.) Papa was delighted.

He went with Yankev Leib to his bank and withdrew the money.

The engagement party was a joyous one. Uncle Yankel Leib spoke a few words, and with a grand flourish, he handed Papa the dowry.

Zeidy and Bobie Herman were very happy that Papa was marrying a lovely girl from such a distinguished family. Bobie was especially ecstatic with the substantial dowry that she felt Papa deserved. Zeidy and Bobie Andron were pleased that their daughter, Aidel, was marrying a fine, Jewish young man who was willing to accept her without any money. But most radiant were the glowing young couple — Papa and Mama, who had at last found each other.

After Papa's engagement, he discovered how very illustrious Mama's family was. Zeidy Shmuel Yitzchok had emigrated from Dvinsk, Latvia, in the year 1892, with his oldest son, Uncle Yankev Leib. Bobie Fruma Rochel, my other uncles — Yechiel Michel, Yisroel Isser, Feitel, Feivish — and Mama, who was the only daughter then (the third child in succession), had arrived a year after them. (Aunt Fannie, the youngest, was born in the United States.)

In Dvinsk, Zeidy Andron was known for his great erudition. Before his twentieth birthday, he was ordained as rabbi by the great Rabbi Meir Simcha Ha-Kohen (known as the Ohr Somei'ach, after a *sefer* which he wrote), who was the rabbi in Dvinsk at that time. Zeidy was renowned as a brilliant Talmudist, and he was a master of eight languages. He occupied an important position in the community, and the Andron family lived comfortably. As my five uncles grew older, Zeidy faced the persistent fear that they would be conscripted into the army, which could endanger not only their Torah studies, but also their future as Orthodox Jews. His only solution was emigration to the "Golden Land" — free America.

....

sefer (plural *seforim*): book(s)

Mama and Papa, when they were a young lady and a young gentleman.

Their wedding invitation was in Hebrew only, something revolutionary at the time.

שמואל יצחק אנדראן ורעיתו

אייזק הערמאן ורעיתו

מתכבדים לבקש את כבודו וביתו לבא לקחת חלק בשמחת כלולת בניהם,

איידלא אנדראן

עב"ג

יעקב יוסף הערמאן

אשר תהיה בשעה מוצלחת ביום ב', כ"ט כסלו (29 דעצעמבער)

תרס"ג, בשעה 6 בערב,

בפראגרעסם אסעמבלי רומס. 28־30 עוועניו A, נויארק.

בית מגורי הכלה:

195 קלינטאן סט., נויארק.

Zeidy and Bobie Andron

Papa and Mama in 1909, with Esther and Frieda standing, and Nochum Dovid on Papa's lap.

Zeidy soon discovered, much to his dismay, that no yeshiva existed where my uncles could continue their Torah learning. He'd sacrificed everything to save his sons from one danger, only to be confronted with an equal danger in America. He therefore spent much of his time teaching them himself.

He faced the additional problem of acquiring suitable employment, in accord with his status, that would provide adequate support for his large family. Zeidy secured a position as a Hebrew teacher in a Talmud Torah. However, he soon gave up his teaching, disillusioned. He felt that the students were not receiving the proper Jewish education by attending only two hours daily. His salary was also nominal, so that there was little reward in his teaching. The only alternative that enabled him to observe the Sabbath and Holidays was self-employment, so he became an insurance agent.

One evening, the Slutsker Rabbi, known as the Ridbaz (an acronym of his name, Reb Yaakov Dovid ben Z'ev), who had recently arrived in New York from Russia, delivered a stirring speech in the Pike Street Shul on the Lower East Side of Manhattan. He drew a very large audience, as he was known as one of the great rabbis of the era. Zeidy Andron was among the audience and listened intently to every word he spoke.

The Ridbaz quoted Proverbs 23:6: "A *mitzva* is compared to a candle—the Torah to a torch. Both diffuse light in a dark room. However, while the candle will be extinguished in a strong wind, the torch will grow even stronger, with its light spreading over a large area. Unless there will be yeshivos to propagate Torah in America, religion will be buffeted by the strong winds of secularism and disappear altogether," the rabbi warned.

Zeidy Andron was very moved by his talk. He went home to tell Bobie Andron how troubled he was. However, a few days later, when Uncle Feivish, a young lad, returned home from public school one afternoon in late December, asking Zeidy for money towards a Christmas party, he was electrified.

He immediately withdrew Uncle Feivish from school.

Zeidy persuaded some of his clients from his insurance business to have their sons join Uncle Feivish. With ten boys at the outset, Zeidy engaged a Hebrew teacher to teach them religious subjects from nine in the morning until two in the afternoon. Then he hired a public school teacher to teach them secular subjects from four to six o'clock. He paid the teachers with his own money.

Zeidy rented space in an Orthodox synagogue on Hester Street, and named the yeshiva in memory of the late Chief Rabbi of New York, Rabbi Jacob Joseph, a personal friend of his.

Each Shabbos, the students came to Zeidy's house so that he could check on their progress. He also interviewed each Hebrew and English teacher he hired to make sure they were capable of imparting true Jewish values to their students. Of course, Zeidy could not concentrate very well on his insurance business. Instead of canvassing for customers, he and Bobie Andron spent their time trying to recruit people to interest themselves in helping finance the yeshiva and gain new students.

Understandably, his insurance business suffered and was a source of little income. The family struggled. No wonder there was no dowry for Mama. Trying to interest people in a yeshiva at that time was no easy task. The concept of an all-day Jewish school was unheard of in the early twentieth century.

However, Zeidy and Bobie Andron persevered. The yeshiva grew slowly but steadily. In time, "The Mother Yeshiva" as it is known, was relocated in its own building at 156-165 Henry Street on the Lower East Side of Manhattan.

The Rabbi Jacob Joseph School grew to great proportions, which included a kindergarten, elementary school, high school, and post-high school leading to ordination. It had a registration of well over a thousand students. Both Uncle Yankev Leib and Uncle Yisroel Isser were principals at different times. Through Zeidy's keen foresight, the torch of Torah was kindled in America, as the Ridbaz had predicted.

4

Papa corners the market

During Papa's engagement period, he told Mama the story of his childhood and the vow he'd made as a young boy sitting all alone in Hester Street Park on Shabbos.

He requested that Mama be willing to have *orchim* at their Shabbos and Yom Tov table. Mama agreed immediately. The "Herman business of *hachnosas orchim*" had its roots then and there.

My sister Esther related the following incident about this "business." It best describes Papa and Mama's devotion to it and Papa's manner of teaching and impressing upon his children the great *mitzva* of *hachnosas orchim*.

Let me tell it to you in her own words.

"You know what was doing in our house. Since I was the oldest I got the full brunt of all the work. Mama never had a moment's time. She was either busy with you children or with the *orchim,* who came in morning, noon or night, without any advance notice.

"I never went any place. I was glad if I could go downstairs

hachnosas orchim: taking in guests

in the street for a little while just to jump rope or play 'potsy' with the other girls my age.

"Once, when I was almost ten years old, Mama whispered to me, 'I have a great surprise for you. Because you are such a good girl and always help me, I will take you to see Uncle Yankev Leib leave for Europe.' He was leaving the next day, and Mama would take me to the boat to see him off.

"I was beside myself with joy and anticipation. I would see a big boat; I would have Mama all to myself. I was so excited I could not close my eyes the whole night.

"From early in the morning, I began pestering Mama. 'When are we going? What should I put on?'

"Mama kept shushing me, 'Don't let the other children hear, or they too will want to tag along. It is still early. The boat only sails at three in the afternoon.'

"I chose my nicest dress and prepared my Shabbos shoes. I made Mama so nervous that she finally gave me permission to dress. I could not eat my lunch from excitement. You would think *I* was sailing that day.

"Finally, Mama started to get dressed. Aunt Sarah was called to watch you children. She had her hands full, because you understood that something was up if Mama was taking me someplace.

"After what seemed like hours to me, Mama was ready. She whispered, 'Esther, sneak outside the door when the children are not watching.' I barely made it to the door, when it was thrown wide open. In walked Papa with an *orech*.

" 'Get busy,' he said. 'We have an *orech*.' Papa had that certain gleam in his eyes that was always there when *orchim* came to our house. I cannot explain it exactly, but young as I was I had learned to recognize it.

"For me, it was the end of all my dreams. My world collapsed. I realized we would not be able to go to the boat. Mama tried to appease me, but I was beyond comfort.

***

orech: guest / *orchim*: guests

"I hated everyone in the world. I just wanted to run away from the *orchim* and the house. I was afraid to say a word to Papa. I ran into the bedroom and cried my heart out.

"Papa followed me, and with blazing eyes he said, 'Esther, now is not the time for tears. Mama needs your help. I will talk to you later.'

"When the *orech* was fed and left our house, it was late in the afternoon. Papa took me into the last bedroom and closed the door. He took my hand and squeezed it tightly.

" 'Listen, *Tochter*, and I will explain to you why you had nothing to cry about. In fact, you should really have felt that today you are the luckiest girl in the whole wide world.

" 'Do not think that when we give *orchim* food to eat we are doing them a favor. No, they are really doing us the biggest favor. Do you know how much we earned today? We are one of the richest families in all of America.

" 'Look at all your friends' homes. Do they always have poor people eating there? No! There are very few homes in America which make a business of feeding poor people and guests. There are hundreds of *mitzvos* that people observe, but the *mitzva* of *hachnosas orchim* is neglected by almost everyone.

" 'Do you know what Mama and I are doing, Esther? We "cornered the market" on this great *mitzva*! All the many "dividends" that we shall earn from it will remain with our family forever and ever. You are a very rich girl, for you help Mama with the *orchim*. Your children and grandchildren will also be wealthy because of our outstanding "business of *hachnosas orchim*."

" 'You will go with Mama someplace another time, but when you can earn millions within a short while, you grasp the opportunity. You do not allow it to slip through your fingers.'

"I did not understand everything Papa was telling me — especially the business angle of 'cornering the market.' How-

tochter: daughter

ever, something stirred deep within me and said that I was witnessing a great and wonderful occurrence.

"Suddenly, my intense disappointment vanished. I truly felt that I was one of the richest girls in the world."

Esther was very ill. Dr. Bluestone, our family doctor, shook his head after his examination. Papa and Mama, worried and frightened, awaited his verdict. "Reb Yaakov Yosef, your little girl's condition is critical. She has diphtheria. You must rush her to the hospital immediately."

Esther lay in the hospital, hovering between life and death. Mama sat near her bedside day and night reciting prayers from *tehillim*. All our loved ones joined Mama in prayer.

Papa went with a *minyon* to the graveside of the late Chief Rabbi of New York, Rabbi Jacob Joseph, to pray and add the name "Chaya" to Esther's name, so that she would be called "Chaya Esther."

Thursday afternoon came. Papa said to Mama, "Aidel, I want you to go home and prepare Shabbos for the *orchim,* as we do each Shabbos. I want nothing missing. In the *zechus* of Shabbos and our *orchim,* I hope the Boss will answer our prayers and Chaya Esther will recover."

Mama did not argue. She left Esther's bedside, with one last heartbroken glance, as Esther lay in an unconscious state.

The entire Shabbos Papa did not show his great anxiety in any way. The house was filled with *orchim.* The hot Shabbos meals were served. Papa sang *zemiros* and discussed Torah topics.

However, our relatives and friends did not share Papa's faith. Aunt Molly, his sister, stood watch in the street awaiting the tragic news she knew would be arriving momentarily. (Diphtheria was almost always fatal in those days.)

---

minyon: religious quorum (ten adult men) / *zechus*: merit
zemiros: table songs

On Shabbos morning the news came in the form of a telegram, which Aunt Molly intercepted. She became hysterical and ran to the neighbors. All of them cried together the entire Shabbos. Of course, they decided not to break the tragic news to Papa and Mama until after *havdolo*.

When Papa finished *havdolo* and just before Aunt Molly could blurt out the terrible news, a messenger hurried into the house with a telegram which read: "Esther Herman alive and out of danger."

The first telegram that had arrived Shabbos morning was a case of mistaken identity by the hospital staff. Another child, who shared the room with Esther and was also ill with diphtheria, was the victim.

When Papa and Mama were told what had occurred on Shabbos morning, Papa said, "You see, Aidel, how Shabbos and our *orchim* protect us from harm."

When Papa and Mama were first married, they moved into a third-floor, three-room apartment at 58 First Street in Manhattan. When our family grew and the *orchim* increased, they exchanged it for a five-room apartment that became vacant on the same floor.

Fortunately for them, Mr. and Mrs. Waldman, their two grown daughters, Fannie and Gussie, and their son, Bennie, occupied an apartment one floor below. Mrs. Waldman, a pious and kind-hearted woman, promptly adopted Papa and Mama as her own. She became our third "Bobie" and Fannie and Gussie our "tantes."

It was from Mrs. Waldman that Mama sought advice for every womanly problem. She was a most willing helping hand and a sympathetic ear. It was also Mrs. Waldman who attended Mama through all five births, since Bobie Andron and Bobie Herman lived quite a distance from us.

Fannie and Gussie shopped with us for clothes, polished our white shoes, prettied us up, and listened patiently to our childhood tales and complaints.

Mrs. Waldman readily assisted Mama with the *orchim*. She always prepared the *lokshen* for the Friday night chicken soup, and helped with the baking of the small *challos*.

Mama baked all the *challos* for the Shabbos *orchim*. In addition, she baked small *challos* that we distributed to three *shuls* for *sholosh seudos*.

When I became of age, it was my duty each *erev* Shabbos to deliver the *challos* to the Tiferes Yerusholayim, Anshei Maimod and the Makover *shuls*. I proudly carried this out, for Papa impressed upon me that many Jews would make a blessing over these *challos*, and I would share in this *mitzva*.

My friends deemed it an honor when I chose any of them to help me carry the *challos* to the *shuls*.

When I was three-and-a-half years old, we moved from 58 First Street to a second-floor, five-room apartment at 108 East Broadway. Papa wanted to live closer to the Tiferes Yerusholayim Yeshiva and *shul*, and the Rabbi Jacob Joseph School.

However, our close contact with the Waldman family continued. In fact, it was Papa who introduced Fannie to her husband, Reb Avrohom Lipshitz, who frequented our house. Their wedding was celebrated in our 108 East Broadway apartment. Papa also introduced Gussie to one of his *talmidim*, Reb Yaakov Halpern, whom she married.

We remained the Waldmans' loving adopted family throughout the years.

Mama and Mrs. Schroit were busily scraping the potatoes and carrots for the *cholent* and *tzimmes* for Shabbos. Mrs. Schroit came every Thursday afternoon to help Mama. She was a whiz at peeling potatoes. I watched, fascinated, as she deftly peeled without once looking at the potato.

Papa burst through the door carrying a large bulky

....
lokshen: noodles / *sholosh seudos*: the third meal on Sabbath afternoon
talmidim: disciples / *cholent*: hot bean stew / *tzimmes*: carrot stew

package. "Aidel, look what I just bought. It will make all your kitchen tasks simpler."

He made space on the dining-room table, unwrapped the package and proudly displayed the wares. There was every imaginable kitchen gadget: potato peelers, scrapers, mashers, graters, shredders and juicers, all in different sizes and shapes.

Mama and Mrs. Schroit stared at them in amazement. "Yankev Yosef, it must have cost a fortune. Where did you buy all this?" Mama queried.

"As I was walking in the street, I found a ten-dollar bill. It was a gift from Heaven. I went to the Woolworth Five and Ten Cent Store and bought all this to save you time and effort," Papa concluded with satisfaction.

"Here, take the scraper and try it, Aidel," Papa urged. He also handed Mrs. Schroit the potato peeler. Both took the gadgets as if they were potentially lethal weapons.

Mama took the scraper and attacked the carrot. The peel would not budge. In the meantime, Mrs. Schroit was struggling with the potato peeler, which kept slipping out of her hand.

After several minutes of intense concentration with their new devices, Mama threw up her hands. "Phew, this is a toy for children, Yankev Yosef." She grabbed her discarded knife, and with a few swift strokes the carrot was scraped to perfection. Mrs. Schroit took her cue from Mama, dropped the potato peeler as if it were a hot coal, and snatched up her knife. The potato peels vanished in a moment.

Papa was chagrined. For the first time that I could remember, he was at a loss for words.

Papa also wanted to make my lot easier. He bought a special pail with a wringer on top to squeeze out the mop. It had a foot pedal that opened the wringer. Papa patiently taught me the intricate steps of getting the mop wrung out. However, each time I stepped on the pedal and clumsily pushed the dripping wet mop through the wringer, the pail tipped over and the sudsy water cascaded all over the floors.

When Papa realized I would never become a good

"mopper," he zestfully washed the floors himself each *erev* Shabbos, using his mopping device with gratification.

But it was Saturday night, after *havdolo*, that the "fun" really began. The kitchen tables were stacked high with dirty, dried-out dishes from Shabbos. Mama lit the boiler for hot water.

We children took turns washing the dishes. When I was very young, I had to stand on a stool in order to reach the sink, but I still had to pitch in and do my share. Mama scoured the tremendous pots. They were so gigantic that I used to play "hide-and-seek" in them.

Once when Mama was out shopping, she slipped on a banana peel and broke her arm. It was a catastrophe. With her arm in a cast she would need someone to take her place in caring for the children and the *orchim*.

Papa hired a servant. She was an elderly woman who was constantly bemoaning her fate. However, in our house, she was accorded royal treatment.

She awoke very early in the morning and hurried off to *shul* for her morning prayers. Mama was left to take care of us and get us ready for school as best as she could with the cast on her arm. When Mrs. Reese returned from *shul*, she ate her breakfast slowly, with great relish. Her afternoon prayers were also recited in *shul*. Each time Mama needed her desperately, she was conveniently praying, but Mama never complained, and treated her with the greatest respect.

When bedtime came, Papa made sure to prepare Mrs. Reese's bed.

As soon as Mama's arm healed a bit, she begged Papa. "Yankev Yosef, I do not need a servant any longer. I do not have the time nor the strength to take care of her."

Of course, the servant was not anxious to leave our house. When she did, she parted with a sorrowful good-bye. Mama sighed with relief.

When "cornering the market," Papa chose a good partner to help him run the "business." Mama did her share with devotion and dedication.

Once, a man came from abroad, and after inquiring for a kosher place to eat, he was directed to the Herman household. It was Friday morning when he knocked at our door and found Mama busy preparing for Shabbos.

"Excuse me," he said timidly, "I would like to eat at your home for a few days as I have to be in New York. I want to make sure that I will have kosher meals and was advised to come to you. Of course, I will gladly pay whatever you wish."

"You can eat your meals here and stay as long as you need. Do not worry about the payment. When you leave, we will discuss it," Mama said graciously.

The *orech* ate all his meals at our home until Tuesday morning. As he was preparing to leave, he took out his wallet and said to Mama, "Mrs. Herman, I want to thank you very much for your hospitality and the very good meals you served me. Please tell me what I owe you."

Mama looked at the *orech* quizzically, "Do you expect me to sell the *mitzva* of *hachnosas orchim* for money?"

"Mrs. He-e-er-man," he stammered, "you said we would discuss the payment when I leave."

Mama smiled at him. "Oh, that was only said to make sure that you would eat to your complete satisfaction."

It was two o'clock in the morning when an *orech* knocked softly at our door. Papa heard his knock and quickly jumped out of bed to admit him. Mama also awoke.

The *orech* was tired and hungry. His train had been delayed and his trip took hours longer than he had expected it would. Mama immediately prepared a meal for him, while Papa spoke kindly, interesting himself in the man's journey.

Our *orech* had come "home."

Papa tiptoed over to the bed of one of our *orchim*, thinking him to be fast asleep. The *orech* was touched to see that Papa had prepared a jug of water in a pan near his bed to be used for *negel vasser* and then gently tucked the covers around him.

Rabbi Eliezer Yudel Finkel, Rosh Yeshiva of Mirrer Yeshiva in Poland, and Rabbi Avrohom Kalmanovitz, Rabbi of Tiktin, came to America in the early 1920s to raise money for the yeshiva. Of course they were our *orchim*. Not only did they eat their meals on Shabbos and Yom Tov at our home, but also during the week whenever they were in New York.

Since my Yiddish left much to be desired, I spoke mostly English to our *orchim*. Once when Reb Lezer Yudel engaged me in conversation, I noticed that he did not understand what I said to him. It troubled me. "Rebbe," I suggested, "I will teach you English." Each afternoon I hurried home from public school to give him a lesson.

"Rebbe, say 'One.' " I held up one finger to denote the number one.

Rabbi Finkel said, "Von."

"Rebbe, you have to say 'Wu-u-n,' " I corrected him.

Mama's voice called from the kitchen. "Ruchoma, stop bothering the Rebbe." Rabbi Finkel, however, always defended me, realizing that even though I was a young child, I took the teaching seriously.

When my sister Frieda gave birth to her oldest child, Avremal, she came from her stay in the maternity hospital to recuperate in our house. A large baby carriage was delivered to our home for the new baby.

After they had been with us for several weeks, it came time for Frieda and her baby to leave. It was late afternoon. We needed two men to carry the cumbersome carriage down the two flights of stairs to the street.

Papa was not at home, so Mama ran to our neighbors to

---

negel vasser: water to wash the hands upon awakening
rosh yeshiva (plural *roshei yeshiva*): head(s) of yeshiva

seek help with the carriage. As soon as she walked out the door, Reb Lezer Yudel Finkel and Reb Avrohom Kalmanovitz each took hold of one side of the carriage and proceeded down the large flight of stairs. As Mama came hurrying up the stairs, she spied both *rabbonim* carrying the heavy carriage. She threw up her hands in protest. "Please, please, Rebbes," she begged them, "it is not *kovod* for you to carry the carriage down. Leave it on the first landing. Someone else will carry it down from there." However, they kept going until they had the carriage safely standing in the street outside our house.

When Mama took Avremal into her arms, she whispered to him, "Avremale, you had the great honor to have two outstanding *talmidei chachomim* carry your carriage down. May it be a *zechus* for you to grow up to be a true *ben Torah*."

Papa rushed through the front door waving the Yiddish newspaper in his hand. "Aidel," he called, "come quickly." Mama came running from the kitchen, wiping her hands on her apron.

"Look what it says in the paper," Papa said excitedly. He read aloud, " 'The great Gaon and Rosh Yeshiva of Kaminetz, Poland, Rabbi Boruch Ber Leibowitz, and his son-in-law, the Gaon Rabbi Reuven Grozovsky, are arriving today. Many notables, among them renowned *rabbonim*, influential *baalebatim,* and other dignitaries will be on hand to welcome them when the ship docks at 11:00 AM. They will be staying at the Broadway Central Hotel on Second Avenue in Manhattan.' "

Papa glanced at our big clock over the mantelpiece. "It is after three o'clock. I missed going to the boat." His voice ended on a note of great disappointment.

"Nu," Mama said, "there will be plenty of people to greet them without you."

....
kovod: honor / *ben Torah*: literally, son of Torah: God-fearing, learned Jew / *talmidei chachomim*: learned men / *gaon*: luminary
baale-batim: householders

Papa looked at Mama in amazement and exclaimed, "How could you say that, Aidel? If we have an opportunity to invite such *gedolim* to be *orchim* in our house, should we allow a golden opportunity to slip out of our hands? I am riding right over to the hotel to invite them," Papa said emphatically.

"Listen, Yankev Yosef, with all those well-known *rabbonim* and wealthy business people, do you really expect them to come to us?" Mama looked at our old, worn-out mahogany table and the cracked leather chairs. "Just look at our furniture; it is practically falling apart."

Papa spied me sitting in the kitchen drinking warm cocoa and eating the chocolate bun that Mama always prepared for me when I returned from school. "Ruchoma, go get your coat. We are going to meet great *tzaddikim*."

I swallowed my bun in one bite, gulped down the rest of the cocoa, and put on my coat. "Hurry, it's getting late," Papa urged.

As we hurried out the front door, Mama called out, "Go with *hatzlocho*."

Papa practically flew down the the two flights of stairs. I barely kept up with him. We ran down the street to catch the Avenue B trolley car that would take us near the Broadway Central Hotel.

During the ride to the hotel, Papa did not say a word. He held on to my hand, squeezing it every once in a while. This was his way of telling me that he loved me. I felt a deep sense of joy. It was not very often that Papa and I went somewhere, just the two of us.

We alighted from the trolley car about two blocks from the hotel. Papa walked with his long strides. "Papa," I said breathlessly, "I can't catch up to you. You are running so fast."

Papa stopped in his tracks. "Ruchoma, when you are going to do a *mitzva*, you *must* run, or the *mitzva* can run away from you—especially, the *mitzva* of *hachnosas orchim*."

....
gedolim: great men / *tzaddikim*: pious men / *hatzlocho*: good luck

I clutched Papa's sleeve, and we ran all the way to the hotel. When we got there, a large crowd of people was milling about. We caught snatches of conversation: "The Rosh Yeshiva cannot see anyone today," a bearded man said. "He is very tired," another man added. "His room is on the second floor, but you cannot get in," a third person whispered.

"Papa," I said disappointedly, "we will not be able to meet the *tzaddikim*. They say no one is allowed in."

Papa did not answer but edged his way through the crowd. I pushed after him. We finally made it into the hotel, found the staircase, and walked up the two flights of carpeted stairs.

There was a large number of people talking and walking about in the corridor as well. Papa and I reached the room. He asked one of the men stationed outside the door if he could have just a few words with the Rosh Yeshiva. "It will only take a few minutes," Papa assured him.

"I am sorry, but no one can see him today. Perhaps, if you return tomorrow, you will be able to have a few minutes with him."

Suddenly, another man, overhearing the conversation, hurried over to Papa. "Excuse me, what is your name?" he asked.

"Herman," Papa answered.

"Herman? Reb Yaakov Yosef Herman, the *Machnis Orech*?" he queried.

Papa answered, "I am Herman from the East Side."

Without another word, we were ushered into the room. Reb Boruch Ber sat in an armchair. He raised his penetrating deep-blue eyes to look at us. I gazed spellbound at his radiant face. Reb Reuven, his son-in-law, who was conversing with some people, stopped talking to stare at us.

The man who ushered us in said quickly, "Reb Yaakov Yosef Herman is here."

....

machnis orech: one who takes in guests

Papa welcomed Reb Boruch Ber and Reb Reuven. "I came to invite you to my house," he said graciously.

"*Boruch Hashem* that you came. We have been waiting for you," Reb Boruch Ber said with relief.

"It will only take a few minutes for us to get ready," Reb Reuven added.

I cast a wondering glance at Papa, whose face showed no surprise at all. It glowed with joy.

A little while later, we filed out of the room, rode down the elevator, and headed for the cars parked in front of the hotel. We entered a car where a chauffeur was seated at the wheel. Reb Boruch Ber, Reb Reuven, another man, Papa and I rode together. Several other cars quickly filled up with people and followed our car.

As we rode along, Papa excused himself to our esteemed *orchim,* "I had no idea you were arriving today; otherwise I would have been at the boat to meet you. I found out just a short while ago."

During the ride, I discovered that the other man riding with us, the owner of the car, was the well-known millionaire who owned the Rokeach factories. As we neared our house, Papa whispered to me, "Ruchoma, the minute the car stops, run up quickly and tell Mama to get everything ready."

I flew up the stairs and burst through the door yelling, "Mama, Mama, they are here! The great *tzaddik,* his son-in-law, and many other people are coming up. Papa said to get everything ready."

Mama's face showed her pride in Papa. "What Papa can do, no one in the world can do," she said proudly.

I noticed the dining-room table was covered with a spotless, white tablecloth. Sliced bread was heaped up in the bread basket. On the stove, a large pot of food was cooking.

"Mama, do you know who else is coming up? Mr. Rokeach, the very rich one. We rode in his car." I ran to our cupboard and

---

boruch Hashem: blessed be God

Two photos of Reb Boruch Ber Leibowitz (of the Kaminetz Yeshiva), one of our most distinguished orchim. *(At left, with three* talmidim.*)*

pulled out the boxes of Rokeach's dishwashing powder that were stored there and placed them in prominent places all over the kitchen. I hoped he would notice them as he passed through on the way to our dining room.

In a matter of minutes, our house was crowded with people. Reb Boruch Ber and Reb Reuven sat on our cracked leather chairs, eating a delicious hot meal at our worn-out mahogany table.

Several weeks later, when Mama could not contain her curiosity any longer, she finally asked Reb Reuven, "How is it that you chose our humble home, when, no doubt, many great *rabbonim* and wealthy people invited you to their houses?"

Reb Reuven explained, "The last few years have been very difficult ones financially for our Kaminetzer Yeshiva. Things were going from bad to worse. We were deeply in debt. The depression in America affected our income to such an extent that we were afraid the yeshiva would have to close, *chas v'sholom.*

"Our old *meshuloch* was not well. He could not continue to raise money for the yeshiva. We saw no way out unless the Rosh Yeshiva himself journeyed to America to rescue the yeshiva.

"When the Rosh Yeshiva first heard of this idea, he shook his head in dismay. How could he leave his *talmidim* for such a length of time? Where could he find a home in America on whose *kashrus* he could rely one hundred percent?

" 'As far as eating,' the old *meshuloch* said with assurance, you have nothing to worry about. There is a man who lives in New York, a great *tzaddik* and *y'rei shomayim*, who is known as the *Machnis Orech*. All the *meshulochim* eat at his house. You can rely upon him fully. His name is Reb Yaakov Yosef Herman.'

" 'Well,' said Reb Boruch Ber, 'we must write him immediately to ask if we can eat at his house.'

" 'You do not even have to write him,' the *meshuloch* advised. 'He will surely come to you as soon as you arrive and beg you to come to his house. I am sure of that.'

"You know," concluded Reb Reuven, "when Reb Yaakov Yosef did not appear at the boat or at the hotel when we arrived, we were very worried. We did not even know your address. But the *meshuloch* was right. We really had nothing to worry about. Reb Yaakov Yosef, the *Machnis Orech*, came himself to invite us to his house. May it be blessed."

Reb Reuven told us of an interesting incident that happened to him in a hotel in Paris when he was on the way to the United States. Shabbos morning, he entered one of the men's rooms. To his great consternation, the electric bulb went

---

chas v'sholom: God forbid / *meshuloch*: fund raiser / *talmidim*: disciples
kashrus: adherence to dietary laws / *y'rei shomayim*: God-fearing

on automatically. He understood that by his walking out of the room, the electric bulb would be turned off.

Meanwhile, Reb Boruch Ber was very perturbed not knowing where his son-in-law had disappeared. After intensive investigation, the mystery was solved. However, Reb Reuven spent the entire Shabbos locked in.

For almost two years, Reb Boruch Ber and Reb Reuven lived with us. Whenever they were in New York they stayed in our house from early morning until night, going to the hotel only to sleep.

Although I was a young girl, Reb Boruch Ber's actions made a very deep impression on me, and his presence gave me spiritual contentment. In fact, I used to hurry home from school hoping he would be in our house and not away on a trip.

Reb Boruch Ber kept an unlighted cigarette in his mouth for much of the day. When questioned about it, he told us that his father had once said to him, "I would be happier if you did not smoke." From that day on, he never lit a cigarette again.

Reb Boruch Ber's blessings over food were wondrous to behold. Each time he started a *brocho*, I watched breathlessly as he stammered, "B-b-b-b-b" until the word *Boruch* was finally spoken. This was caused by his intense concentration on what a blessing to Hashem means.

Both Papa and Reb Boruch Ber brought out the true spirit of Shabbos when they sang *zemiros*. As Papa sang, his voice was filled with emotion, his cheeks a shiny red, his eyes alight with the love of the Boss. Reb Boruch Ber's face shone with a spiritual light. His voice brought rapture into our home. I thought, "This must be how an angel sounds singing *shira*."

Many people came from near and far to hear him sing

shira: heavenly song

zemiros. When there was no more standing room in our house, the visitors overflowed into our hallway and even down the stairs.

Papa awakened Nochum Dovid one Friday night. "I want you to see how a *tzaddik* sleeps," he said to him. Reb Boruch Ber slept with his hands above his waist. His appearance was angelic.

My nephew, Moshe Aaron, told me that Reb Boruch Ber was given the honor of receiving the "key" to the City of New York by Mayor Jimmy Walker. At the presentation, Mayor Walker remarked, "Rabbi Leibowitz disproves Darwin's theory of evolution. A holy person like him could only be created by God."

One very rainy day, Reb Boruch Ber was ready to leave our house. His rubbers were nowhere to be found. I crept under our large china closet to search for them. They were pushed into the far corner, and I fished them out.

Reb Boruch Ber blessed me with exuberance. "May you be blessed with your true *zivug.*"

The fervent blessing I received from such a great *tzaddik* was a reward far above my insignificant action.

Reb Boruch Ber once became ill. On doctor's orders he was confined to bed. He therefore could not travel to his sleeping quarters at the Broadway Central Hotel.

"Rebbe," Papa assured him, "we have ample room. You will sleep in our home until you completely recuperate."

"Ruchoma," Papa whispered to me, "until Reb Boruch Ber gets well, he will sleep in your room."

"Where will I sleep, Papa?" I asked.

"Don't worry, I'll find a place for you," Papa said confi-

---

zivug: match

dently. For the next few nights, I was bedded on the living-room floor.

It was at the time that Reb Boruch Ber was staying at our house that the *roshei yeshiva* from different yeshivos in Europe and America decided to organize the *Vaad Hayeshivos.* There already was such an organization in Europe dedicated to help the yeshivos and their *talmidim* financially.

Erev Shavuos (1929) ten *roshei yeshiva* gathered around our mahogany table in the dining room. Among those present were Reb Boruch Ber, Reb Reuven, Reb Shimon Shkop from Grodno Yeshiva, Reb Elchonon Wasserman from Baranowitz Yeshiva, Reb Boruch Halevi Horowitz from Slobodka Yeshiva, Reb Yosef Kahaneman from Ponievezh Yeshiva in Bnei Brak and several others.

I understood then why Papa always maintained that our old table was worth its weight in spiritual "gold."

Reb Boruch Ber and Reb Reuven were returning to Kaminetz. In our house, we already felt a sense of loneliness at the thought of their departure.

Thousands gathered to say good-bye. The streets were teeming with people. Each one hoped to receive a blessing from this great *tzaddik* and a last look at him.

Papa called me, "Ruchoma, come quickly, Reb Boruch Ber wants to bless you." Amidst all the tumult he did not forget to call for me. I hurried into the living room with Papa, where Reb Boruch Ber blessed me with intense feeling. I am sure his blessing brought me significant dividends.

Rabbi Yaakov Moshe Zimmerman, brother-in-law of Reb Boruch Ber Leibowitz, arrived in New York with his teenage son, Chaim. His wife, Rebbetzin Esther Gittel, their daughters, Rochel and Toby, and a younger son, Hershel, remained in Russia.

Rabbi Zimmerman immediately negotiated for the necessary documents to enable the rest of the family to join them. In the meantime, Rabbi Zimmerman and Chaim were welcomed in our home for the period of almost two years that was required to arrange for the family's immigration.

Chaim was a brilliant boy, full of zest. His pranks with the *orchim* dismayed his father, who tried his utmost to control his exuberance. However, Chaim livened up our house considerably.

He helped to serve the food to our *orchim* on Friday nights and Shabbos afternoon. However, Mama did not trust him with the hot chicken soup. One Friday night, Chaim took one of our newborn kittens (our large cat had just given birth to them) and placed the kitten squarely on the head of the *orech* who was serving the hot, noodle soup. The cries of the *orech* and the mewing of the kitten brought Papa and Rabbi Zimmerman rushing into our kitchen. Chaim was soundly rebuked. Since I was a teenager also, I enjoyed the rumpus.

Mama usually served cooked prunes for dessert. There was one *orech* who insisted that he be given one prune and one prune only. Week after week, he reiterated his request to Chaim, who followed his instructions. Finally, one Shabbos, Chaim took our largest round tray, placed one solitary prune in the center and served it to our *orech*. The tray occupied almost half of our table. The *orech* protested. Chaim was loudly reproved by his father, but he took it all in stride.

Mama looked on with motherly tolerance at Chaim's escapades, pitying him because his mother was not close by.

One day, Rabbi Zimmerman came bearing good tidings. His wife and two daughters were arriving shortly from Russia. His younger son would be coming at a later date.

At the last moment, much to everyone's disappointment, word was received that Rebbetzin Zimmerman was refused a visa as she had developed a contagious eye condition. Therefore, Rochel and Toby Zimmerman would be coming by themselves.

By that time, I was engaged to Moshe. Rabbi Zimmerman asked us to meet his daughters at the port, since he had an

*Rabbi Yaakov Moshe Zimmerman dancing at the wedding of his
daughter Rochel to Abraham Pernikoff, who is seated between Rabbi
Reuven Grozovsky (left) and Rabbi Eliezer Silver (1943).*

important meeting and would not be able to get there in time.

Moshe and I took the subway to the port. The ship had
already docked, and most of the passengers had disembarked.
Rochel and Toby stood alone on the large deck of the boat
peering anxiously down at the people below.

We inquired from the customs officer regarding their
release and were informed that they would first have to be
processed at Ellis Island, where all the new immigrants were
stationed. That could take days. We were perplexed. Under no
circumstances could we return home without the Zimmerman
girls; their father would be very perturbed.

Moshe and I were finally able to reach the chief of customs.
With as much authority as we could possibly muster, we told
him, "We are the guardians of these girls. We cannot allow

them to be sent to Ellis Island. We guarantee their care and all their needs." The customs officer gazed at us condescendingly. We hardly looked like suitable guardians for young teenagers, as we were not too much older ourselves. However, something in our demeanor impressed him. He issued the proper papers for their release.

Rochel and Toby accompanied us to our house for a joyful reunion with their father and their brother Chaim. They all stayed in our house until they were able to rent an apartment and get settled.

It was a very happy day when Rebbetzin Zimmerman arrived to be reunited with her family.

(It should be noted that today Rabbi Chaim Zimmerman is one of the most outstanding Talmudists of our generation and at present resides in Jerusalem.)

Rabbi Yitzchok Shmidman arrived in the United States in December, 1926, to accept a position as rabbi in Newport, Rhode Island. He left his expectant wife and three small children in his hometown, Simyatich, Poland. As a young man, he had learned in Novarodok Yeshiva and later in Mir, where he became known for his scholarship.

After residing in Newport for a short time, he decided he would rather live in New York. He undertook to raise funds for the Mirrer Yeshiva, and for the next three years, he was our *orech* whenever he was in New York, until his wife and four children were able to join him.

At night, our large dining room was converted into a bedroom for our *orchim*. The table and chairs were shoved to one side of the room, and the cot beds took over.

One night, when Reb Yitzchok came in late, it seemed as if all our available beds were already occupied for the night. Reb Boruch Ber, who was then an *orech* in our house and occasionally slept over, insisted that Reb Yitzchok sleep in his bed. Of course, Reb Yitzchok would not hear of it. Papa came to the rescue. He went down to the cellar and returned breathlessly with another cot bed to accommodate Reb Yitzchok.

Rabbi Shmidman told me that words cannot suffice to describe adequately Papa's and Mama's devotion to the *mitzva* of *hachnosas orchim.* "I was fortunate to be one of the recipients of the warmth and care given in the Herman household." He remarked that it alleviated the lonesomeness of our *orchim* for their families and helped them surmount the many obstacles they encountered in a foreign country under difficult circumstances.

Rabbi Shmidman went on to found Yeshiva Toras Chaim in the East New York section of Brooklyn, where he was Rosh Yeshiva for forty-five years. He also provided for the financial needs of the yeshiva, which eventually reached an enrollment of five hundred students.

Rabbi Shmidman immigrated to Eretz Yisroel in 1972. He organized a branch of Toras Chaim, known as the Yeshiva Tze'irim Toras Chaim—Pri Yitzchok, which is part of Itri Yeshiva in Yerusholayim, whose founder and Rosh Yeshiva is Rabbi Mordechai Elefant, son-in-law of my brother, Reb Nochum Dovid.

In an address Rabbi Shmidman delivered many years ago at the installation ceremony at which Nochum Dovid became the rabbi of Gates Avenue Shul in Brooklyn, he said, "If leaders of the *lamed-vovniks* were to be appointed, then Reb Yaakov Yosef would surely be elected its president and Reb Avrohom Horowitz [Nochum Dovid's father-in-law] would be vice-president."

Rabbi Avrohom Yitzchok Faivelson came to the United States from Kovno in 1924. He left his wife and two young children in his hometown, where he was already known as a man learned in Torah. He was one of our special *orchim*, who

....

lamed-vovniks: thirty-six righteous Jews in each generation who remain anonymous

not only ate in our house on Shabbosim and Yomim Tovim, but also lodged with us during the week.

At that time, Papa was fighting, almost single-handedly, the uphill battle of spreading *yiddishkeit* in New York. Rabbi Faivelson realized the need of organizing a *vaad horabbonim*, which also furthered Papa's efforts.

He founded the well-known *Vaad Horabonim* of New York, which he headed as its president and executive secretary. Its task was to oversee *kashrus* in slaughter-houses, butcher stores, and grocery shops which sold Pesach products, because there was little supervision in these areas. The *Vaad* also built and supervised *mikveh*s in many vicinities of New York. The *Vaad Horabonim* raised large amounts of money to help the needy. In addition, they distributed *maos chittim*. Rabbi Avrohom Yitzchok Faivelson remained the inspiring force behind this vital organization and its varied activities throughout his life.

Rabbi Dovid Ber Kreiser, a tenth-generation direct descendant of the Taz (an acronym of the title of his *seforim, Turei Zohov*), was one of our most beloved *orchim*. He carried the name of his forefather, the Taz, Reb Dovid ben Shmuel Halevi.

As a young man, he was rabbi in Greiver, Poland. He was married at eighteen and then lived in Slutsk, where he gave a *shiur* in the yeshiva founded by Rabbi Isser Zalman Meltzer. Rabbi Meltzer was Rosh Yeshiva, together with his renowned son-in-law, Rabbi Aaron Kotler. After the First World War, when Russia became Communist, the Slutsker Yeshiva was transferred over the border to the first city on the Polish side, Kletsk. Rabbi Kreiser became one of the *roshei yeshiva*.

When the yeshiva found itself in dire financial straits, Rabbi Kreiser came to the United States to raise money. He

yiddishkeit: Judaism / *vaad horabbonim*: committee of Rabbis
mikveh: ritual bath / *maos chittim*: Passover charity fund (literally, money for wheat)

Rabbi Dovid Ber Kreiser

was our *orech* for over a year, and during this time he became close to our family.

One day, he returned from one of his extended trips outside of New York exhausted. He had caught a very bad cold en route. Papa and Mama took care of him, but the cold not only persisted, it grew steadily worse. The doctor who attended him recommended that he be taken to the hospital.

Papa visited him regularly. Each time Papa returned from the hospital, Mama and I anxiously inquired about his condition. Though he received adequate care in the hospital, Rabbi Kreiser passed away from the pneumonia that had developed. He was forty-eight years old.

Papa made the arrangements for the funeral, and he was buried near the great *talmid chochom,* the Meitcheter Iluy. It was a cold, dreary day (the sixteenth day of Teves, 5691 — 1931) when Papa, Mama and I sorrowfully attended the funeral of our beloved Rabbi Kreiser. We felt his loss keenly, for he had become one of our family.

The tragedy was intensified because Rabbi Kreiser had been preparing to leave the United States to attend the wedding of his oldest daughter, Tzipora, who was to be married to Rabbi Dovid Povarsky (presently, one of the *roshei yeshiva* in Ponievezh, Bnei Brak). In fact, when Rabbi Kreiser had become ill, he had sent word to his family not to postpone the wedding.

His younger daughter, Rebbetzin Yaffa Ebner (formerly married to the late Rabbi Leib Malin, Rosh Yeshiva of Beis Hatalmud in Brooklyn), told me that she recalls that the letters her father sent the family were often filled with details of the devotion shown to our *orchim* and Papa's original and strict manner of carrying out *mitzvos.*

Rabbi Kreiser was so impressed with the invitation he received to my brother Nochum Dovid's wedding which had the added note (unheard of then), "Ladies are please requested to come dressed according to the Jewish law" that he sent the invitation to his family in Kletsk.

One of the incidents I remember best about Rabbi Kreiser is the following.

"Yankev Yosef, we need a new couch. This one should be thrown out," Mama complained.

Papa carefully examined our brown leather couch in the living room, which had seen better days. The leather was cracked, and the springs were trying their utmost to push their way through. "It is comfortable for our *orchim,*" he decided.

One weekend, Rabbi Kreiser was invited to the home of a very wealthy family in upper Manhattan. As he was leaving, Mama commented, "Rabbi Kreiser, after tasting such wealth, I am sure you will not wish to return to our humble home."

Saturday night, Rabbi Kreiser returned. He placed his little valise on the floor and hurried into our living room. He quickly lay down on our torn, brown leather couch, stretched out his feet with his shoes on, and emitted a great sigh of satisfaction.

"Mrs. Herman," Rabbi Kreiser said emphatically, "you cannot imagine how much I missed Shabbos in your house. True, the house where I spent Shabbos is elegantly furnished:

rugs on all the floors, couches only to look at, china dishes I feared to touch lest they break. All I waited for was to return to your house. This couch is *gan eden*," Rabbi Kreiser added, as his eyes closed sleepily.

Papa looked at Mama with a smug "I-told-you-so" look. The couch remained.

Uncle Yisroel Isser, Mama's brother, announced to Mama, "Aidel, Helen and I are buying a new dining-room set. Our old one is in perfect condition. You can have it. Yours is so worn-out." He eyed our old-fashioned mahogany table with deep scratches in the wood grain and our leather chairs which were in need of re-upholstering.

Mama was delighted. When Papa returned from *shul,* she excitedly told him the good news. "Yankev Yosef, we are getting a dining-room set: a large table, six chairs and two armchairs. It is a used set, but in excellent condition. My brother, Yisroel Isser, said we can have his, as he is buying a new one."

Papa frowned for a moment. "Aidel, I don't agree to it."

Mama looked askance at Papa. "It won't cost us a penny. I'm sure Yisroel Isser will even pay for the shipping," Mama argued.

"It's not the money at all. You see, Aidel, our table and chairs are very precious. Think of all the great *talmidei chachomim* who sat around our table. Here sat Reb Boruch Ber, here Reb Lezer Yudel Finkel, here Reb Moshe Mordechai Epstein, here Reb Avrohom Kalmanovitz, here Reb Reuven Grozovsky." Papa walked around the table touching each place with reverence. "How can we part with this holy treasure?" Papa asked Mama. For a minute Mama showed disappointment, but as she watched Papa eyeing the table as something sacred, our scratched, old mahogany table became an "antique" to be cherished forever.

....
gan eden: Paradise (literally, Garden of Eden)

Papa always impressed upon me that we must treat the *orchim* as if they were part of our family. I tried very hard, but it was not always easy.

One of our *orchim* enjoyed his tea piping hot. After the Shabbos meal, Reb Berel would call to me, "Ruchoma, a glass of hot tea." I brought him a steaming glass of tea, which he gulped down quickly, much to my amazement. As soon as he finished one cup of tea, he would repeat his call for another one. This went on until he drank seven or eight cups of tea.

One Shabbos, when my friends were impatiently waiting for me, I took a large tray, filled eight cups with hot tea and served it to our *orech*. "Quick, Reb Berel, drink your tea, or they will cool off," I advised him, as I slipped out the door.

The next Shabbos, Reb Berel wagged his finger at me, "Ruchoma, do not bother to serve me tea. I will take it myself."

One Thursday late in the afternoon, as I was playing jump-rope with my friends, a shiny, black car with a uniformed chauffeur in the driver's seat stopped in front of our house. A smartly dressed lady alighted from the car. She asked to be directed to the Herman apartment. I hurried up the stairs with her following me.

"Mama," I called out, "there is a lady who wants to see you." Mama greeted her courteously. She introduced herself as Neche Golding and explained to Mama that she had heard a great deal about the Herman *hachnosas orchim* from some of our *orchim* who found their way to her house.

Mama recognized her name. Some of our *orchim* had told Mama of the impressive Shabbos they had spent in her luxurious home with many servants in attendance. Mrs. Golding was a very wealthy lady, who lived on the West Side of Manhattan. She was known for her many charitable contributions to yeshivos, institutions and to the needy.

Mrs. Golding had a "special" request. She was anxious to have a little share in Mama's *mitzva* of *hachnosas orchim* and had come especially in order to help for Shabbos.

Mama gazed with surprise at Mrs. Golding and asked her, "How do you want to help me?"

"Well," she answered, "I could even wash your floors."

Mama looked at the stylish, immaculate outfit Mrs. Golding was wearing and smiled at her. "Do you think I would allow you to wash my floors?" Mama asked in amazement.

"I could help with the cooking," Mrs. Golding offered.

"First let me serve you a drink," Mama said graciously. I prepared a bowl of fruit, while Mama placed the kettle on the stove and filled our cake dish with slices of apple pie.

Soon Mama and Mrs. Golding were enjoying each other's company. Mrs. Golding did not wash our floors, nor help with the cooking, but a very close friendship developed between her and our family.

Added note:

Years later, due to Papa's influence, Mrs. Golding sent her sons, Abba Shaul and Moshe, to study in the Mirrer Yeshiva in Poland.

Rabbi Isaac Sher, son-in-law of the Alter of Slobodka, Rabbi Noson Tzvi Finkel, was Rosh Yeshiva of Slobodka Yeshiva. When he was visiting the United States, Papa met him in *shul* one day and greeted him warmly.

"Rebbe, I need an *orech* for Shabbos. Please do me the honor and eat with us this Shabbos." Rabbi Sher agreed. He had heard all about Papa.

After the Friday night prayers, Papa escorted him to our home. When he entered our house, Rabbi Sher was amazed to see about twenty-five *orchim* sitting at our table.

After Shabbos, Rabbi Sher questioned Papa, "Reb Yaakov Yosef, I do not understand. You said to me that you need an *orech* for Shabbos. I thought that you surely had no one eating at your house for this Shabbos, but you had more than two *minyonim*. Why did you need me?"

Rabbi Shmuel Greineman

"You see, Rebbe, my wife works very hard the entire week preparing for our *orchim* for Shabbos. When a person of your greatness graces our table, we feel doubly rewarded," Papa explained.

Rabbi Shmuel Greineman, one of our *orchim*, became a close friend and confidant of our family. His wife was the sister of the renowned Chazon Ish of Bnei Brak, Rabbi Avrohom Yeshaya Karelitz.

In his early years, Rabbi Greineman learned in the Radun Yeshiva and was a *ben bayis* in the Chofetz Chaim's house. He wrote a *sefer* on the Torah based on the sayings of the Chofetz Chaim.

Afterwards, he learned in Mirrer Yeshiva and became executive secretary of the yeshiva office. Whenever he came to America to raise money for the yeshiva, he stayed at our house.

It became difficult for him to be separated from his family for extended periods of time. He therefore brought his family to New York, where he was offered the position of principal of Yeshiva Tiferes Yerusholayim.

His daughter, Rebbetzin Esther Finkel, wife of Rabbi Beinish Finkel, told me that when her father returned to Poland from his trip to America, they were fascinated by the interesting stories about the Herman family and their *orchim*. One fact that stands out clearly in her mind is that each *orech* was given *lechem mishneh*. Papa did this especially to make our *orchim* feel at home. Mama baked a great many *challos* to provide for each Shabbos and Yom Tov meal.

Among our *orchim*, there were three *geirim*. The first one was a former minister who had been married and had three children. He was recommended to Papa. Papa personally supervised his learning and helped him financially. He lived with us until he was settled.

He was a highly intelligent person and before long had a good knowledge of what it meant to be a Torah Jew. Papa's encouragement and help in the first years after his conversion to Judaism stood him in good stead for his entire life. Avrohom married a fine Jewish woman and raised a generation of Torah Jews.

....

Chazon Ish: name of work / **ben bayis**: member (literally, son) of the house / **lechem mishneh**: double bread / **geir(im)**: proselyte(s)

Our first *geir* brought a second one to Papa. Here, too, Papa took over the teaching of the laws of Judaism and their meaning. This *geir* ate at our Shabbos table and was a frequent guest of ours during the week as well.

One Friday, late in the afternoon, Avrohom (the second) was driving his large truck (he worked for a trucking company) through the very busy Times Square thoroughfare. The traffic was stalled. He glanced at his watch, checked his little calendar for the time Shabbos would make its entry, and realized that if he did not leave his truck immediately, he would be late for Shabbos. Without a moment's hesitation, he alighted from his truck, left his wallet and all his possessions in the truck and just walked off.

It took him some time to walk from mid-Manhattan to our house on the Lower East Side. We were already finishing our chicken soup when Avrohom walked in. When he had not shown up as usual for *kiddush*, we had been worried, so now we were relieved to see him. He did not elaborate, but just mentioned that he had been stuck in traffic.

Saturday night Avrohom finally located his truck. The police had carted it away, and several summonses were attached to the windshield. Papa went with Avrohom to court to plead his case. The judge demanded that Avrohom's trucking license be revoked. Papa defended Avrohom, explaining to the irate judge that had Avrohom not left his truck at that time, he would have desecrated the Sabbath, a very grave transgression against our Jewish religion. Of course, Papa added, Avrohom would pay his fine. The judge was impressed and placated.

This Avrohom also married a Jewish woman and lived a life of *yiddishkeit*.

Our third *geir* surprised Mama and me. Friday night, Papa walked in from *shul* with a young man, black as ebony, with a deep Southern accent. Papa sat down next to him, so he could explain the Torah to him in English, as well as the general conversation at the table.

Under Papa's wings, he gained stature as a true Jew. He looked forward to being with us each Shabbos, where Papa accorded him respect and Mama and I showed him special attention.

Zelig Heller, a young man in his early twenties, was a glazier by trade. He became friendly with Avrohom (our first *geir*). They began to study together every *erev* Shabbos in Tiferes Yerusholayim.

Zelig related to me that once, as he sat engrossed in his studies, a total stranger walked over to him and said, "It will soon be Shabbos. I would like you to be my *orech*." Zelig was astounded. No one had ever interested himself in him or invited him for Shabbos. He decided to accept the invitation.

"In Reb Yaakov Yosef's house, I first became aware of what *hachnosas orchim* and the holiness of Shabbos really mean. From the moment your father made *kiddush,* sang *zemiros* and said a *dvar Torah,* I was in a new world—a *gan eden.* Your mother, Aidel, was truly an *aidele* woman. She served the *orchim* with graciousness and made me feel at home. I savored each moment of Shabbos and wished it would not end."

Zelig became a regular *orech* and a friend of our family. He joined one of Papa's Torah groups and studied nightly at his table. "Only Reb Yaakov Yosef could give me the willpower to be able to learn Torah after a day of hard labor at my work, without feeling a sense of tiredness," Zelig said.

"One night, Reb Yaakov Yosef said to me, 'Zeligel, Reb Boruch Ber needs someone to spend the night with him in the Broadway Central Hotel.' I felt elated that he gave me the honor to accompany this great *tzaddik* to his sleeping quarters. Late that evening, Reb Boruch Ber asked if I could get him a glass of tea. 'Be sure the water is poured only from the samovar into a paper cup. Do not allow a spoon to touch it. Keep the tea bag and sugar separate.' Reb Boruch Ber gave me explicit

....

aidele: refined

instructions. To this day, I feel blessed that I was given the *mitzva* of serving Reb Boruch Ber Leibowitz, thanks to Reb Yaakov Yosef.

"When the news got out that Reb Yaakov Yosef was leaving America to settle in Eretz Yisroel, all his *talmidim, orchim,* and friends felt a sense of impending loss — like a ship without a captain. There was no one at all who could replace him. He was our *rebbe,* our mentor, the loyal and wise adviser of the entire East Side.

"Reb Yaakov Yosef Herman remains alive for me. If only I could once more be in his *daled amos,* hear his teachings, and be part of his *hachnosas orchim,* it would give me the greatest happiness in life. I could ask for nothing more."

Papa's fur business was tottering. The entire week Papa and Mama scraped together every available penny to cover the expenses of the Shabbos *orchim.*

One Friday afternoon, Mama realized that she hadn't baked enough *challos* for our *orchim.* She was very upset. "Don't worry, Aidel," Papa comforted Mama, "I will see what I can do."

Papa hurried to the bakery which was still open. "Have you any *challos* left over?" Papa asked anxiously.

"Reb Yaakov Yosef, you are fortunate. Someone ordered a very large *kitka* for a *bris.* They were supposed to pick it up early this morning, but they never showed up. Since it's almost Shabbos, you can have it for very cheap. No one else can use such a very large *challa,*" the baker said.

Papa counted out the few pennies he had in his pocket. The baker understandingly accepted the ten cents.

Papa ran home carrying his treasure. He proudly unwrapped the tremendous, well-baked *kitka* and explained to Mama how he had bought it for ten cents.

....

daled amos: within his four cubits / **kitka**: challa, bread
bris: circumcision

"Yankev Yosef," Mama exclaimed with adoration, "I've always known that you're capable of doing miracles, but such a miracle as this I have never witnessed. It is surely the *zechus* of our *orchim.*"

One night, Papa could not fall asleep. His wholesale fur business was gone, with most of his savings, which he had lost in the 1929 crash.

Since he did not want to declare bankruptcy because he did not want his creditors to lose any of their money, he went into deep debt. Papa was doing his utmost to try to sell fur on the retail market, but there were few customers because of the Depression.

Mama realized how very disturbed Papa was, something unusual for him. The only time Papa lost his equilibrium and showed anger or frustration was when he was thwarted from carrying out his religious principles, but never in financial matters.

"Yankev Yosef, I do not understand why you are so terribly upset. It is true, you lost your business and a great deal of money. However, what did you do with all your money? You spent it for charity, for *mitzvos,* for our *hachnosas orchim.* Do we have a steam-heated apartment? Do we have fancy

Business card: The printed announcement when Papa moved his fur business from Downtown to Midtown.

Telephone Connection

JACOB J. HERMAN
Dealer in
FURS and SKINS
of
41 BLEECKER STREET
will remove to 8 West 29th Street, New York
Near Fifth Avenue

furniture? Do we ever go for a vacation? Never! If Hashem does not want us to do all these *mitzvos,* that is His business, so why worry? As for our food and rent, I am sure Hashem will not forsake us."

Mama's simple but profound words found their mark. Papa perked up immediately. "Aidel, you are so very right. I cannot understand why I should have worried even for a moment," Papa said gratefully to Mama.

Within minutes, Papa fell fast asleep.

However, the problem of providing for our *orchim* was a serious one. One day, Papa and Mama discussed it at length. "Yankev Yosef," Mama asked tearfully, "how can we invite so many *orchim* when we are deeply in debt and have very little for our daily expenses?"

Papa sat engrossed in his thoughts. Of late, his smooth face showed wrinkles; his beard had new streaks of gray.

"Aidel, I think you may be right. This Shabbos I will tell the *orchim* that we cannot invite them for the time being," Papa said disconsolately.

It was a very sad day in the Herman household. Shabbos without *orchim*? How could that possibly be? I, too, shared the gloominess that pervaded our once happy home.

Thursday at dusk, Mama was kneading the dough for the *challos* for Shabbos. There was a knock at our door. Mama ran to open it. A stranger stood in the shadowy hall. "Is this the house of Reb Yaakov Yosef Herman where *orchim* eat on Shabbos?" he asked.

"Yes," Mama answered without hesitation. "You can eat with us on Shabbos." He disappeared quickly down the steps.

On Shabbos, Papa and Mama waited for the stranger to appear. No new *orech* came.

After the Shabbos meal, Papa said nothing to the *orchim.* When all our *orchim* had left, Papa said to Mama, "Aidel, I was thinking. Maybe the stranger who came on Thursday was sent to deliver the message to us that we must not give up our *hachnosas orchim,* even temporarily."

"I was thinking the same thing," Mama agreed.

From that time on, there was never a thought or word mentioned about discontinuing our *hachnosas orchim*.

When our *orchim* reached the "over-thirty" mark, and the extra folding tables extended almost into our living room, Papa would say animatedly, *"Boruch Hashem,* business is booming!" Mama always cooked enough food for as many *orchim* as came. Our *orchim* who came Saturday night for *melaveh malka* finished up whatever food remained from Shabbos.

Yes, Papa and Mama "cornered the market" on the business of *hachnosas orchim*.

---

melaveh malka: literally, accompanying the Queen: festive meal eaten Saturday night

5

An undertaking of sacrifice

When Papa was thirty-three years old, he began fasting daily. He didn't confide the reason for this undertaking to anyone.

He consulted our family doctor for medical advice. "I've started to fast daily and need an adequate diet to maintain my health," Papa said matter-of-factly. Papa's statement did not elicit any surprise or comment from the doctor. He knew Papa well.

"Your diet must contain carbohydrates, protein, fat and iron." Dr. Bluestone jotted down the nutrients on his prescription blank.

"Thank you, Doctor." Papa handed him some money.

"No charge, Reb Yaakov Yosef." He patted Papa on his back.

After investigating the different foods, Papa decided that his evening meal, after fasting all day, would consist of canned sardines for the protein and fat and a pear for the iron. Bread, and sugar in his coffee, would supply the carbohydrates.

Shabbos, Yomim Tovim, and Rosh Chodesh were excluded from his fasting.

Mama did everything possible to persuade Papa to

discontinue his fasting, but to no avail. She enlisted the aid of Zeidy and Bobie Herman to influence him, but although he always showed his parents great respect, Papa was adamant.

After his evening prayers and teaching a *blatt gemora* to a group of men, Papa would come home to break his fast. In the long, summer days, he would often eat his meal after ten o'clock.

A heavy snowstorm raged. Mama kept peering out the streaked window. Suddenly she put on her heavy winter coat, wrapped her head and shoulders in a large woolen scarf and said, "Children, I will be back soon."

"Where are you going, Mama, in such a terrible snowstorm?" I asked anxiously.

"I have to buy something." She hurried out the door.

Bessie and I pressed our faces to the window. We could hardly see the street as the large snowflakes fell thicker and thicker.

An hour went by. It seemed endless. Finally, we heard Mama climbing the steps. I ran to the hall. She was covered with icy snow. She shook out her coat and scarf, which made a mound of snow on the floor of our kitchen.

"What did you buy?" I asked curiously. From her coat pocket, she drew out a damp, brown paper bag. She carefully took out a large green pear and held it up like a treasure. "I didn't have a pear for Papa's supper tonight. He fasts the entire day and needs it. It cost fifteen cents," she explained.

I gasped. I could buy a box of chocolate for that much money. Mama picked up the pear again and proudly examined it as if it were an *esrog*. She placed it on the table.

"Don't tell Papa that I went out today to buy it," Mama admonished us.

When Papa ate his meal that night, I watched him intently

....

esrog: citron

as he bit into the precious pear, little realizing the large expense and great effort Mama had expended to obtain it for him.

Papa had been fasting for many years when he prepared to leave for Europe on business. One of his anticipated stops was a visit to the Chofetz Chaim, who lived in Radun, Poland.

Mama still had not given up hope of convincing Papa to stop fasting. She approached Rabbi Shmuel Greineman, a *talmid* of the Chofetz Chaim and an *orech* of ours at that time, and asked him to intercede with the Chofetz Chaim to dissuade Papa from fasting. Rabbi Greineman immediately penned a letter to the Chofetz Chaim detailing the problem and informing him of Papa's intended visit.

When Papa got to the Chofetz Chaim's house, he invited Papa to a meal. Papa answered quickly, "Today it is *ba-hab*."

After Papa's visit with the Chofetz Chaim, Rabbi Greineman received a reply to his letter. He hurried to tell Mama its contents. "Mrs. Herman, the Chofetz Chaim writes that he discussed Reb Yaakov Yosef's fasting with him and advises us not to bother him about it."

Mama heeded the Chofetz Chaim's advice, but from time to time, she greeted Papa when he came home after a long day of fasting, "Look how pale you are, Yankev Yosef, actually yellow." Her sigh could be heard throughout the house.

Papa flexed his muscles. His skinny arm bulged. "Try to move me," Papa dared. No one took him up on that.

Papa's fasting did not have any ill effect on his physical health, nor detract in any way from his multitude of religious activities. In fact, when Papa left for Eretz Yisroel in 1939 and was checked by the doctor, he said to him, "Mr. Herman, you are an excellent specimen of good health." Papa was fifty-nine years old and had been fasting for over twenty-five years.

....

ba-hab: literally, two-five-two: i.e. Monday, Thursday and the next Monday soon after Passover and Sukkos when some pious people fast

The Chofetz Chaim

Zeidy Herman passed away on *isru chag* Pesach and Bobie Herman on Rosh Chodesh Av—days when fasting is prohibited. Papa therefore undertook, instead, not to speak on their *yahrzeit*.

Papa remarked ruefully, "My father and mother, *zatzal*, got even with me for fasting. I find it no hardship at all to fast from food, while fasting from talking is a very difficult chore for me."

After Papa had been living in Eretz Yisroel for many years, he awoke one morning with an agonizing pain in his lower back and limbs. He could hardly walk. Professor Adler, a renowned neurologist from Hadassah Hospital, was consulted. After a thorough examination, he diagnosed Papa's condition as acute sciatica. He thought it might be a result of Papa's fasting for forty years. It seems the lack of nutrients in his diet, especially fat, had taken its toll. He advised Papa to stop fasting immediately.

Papa was not convinced until Dr. Nochum Kook, a renowned surgeon in Yerusholayim, related the following story to him. "I once had to visit an old *chasidisher rebbe* who was very ill, to notify him that he was not allowed to fast on Yom Kippur. I trembled when I thought of his reaction.

yahrzeit: anniversary of death / *chasidisher rebbe*: hassidic Rabbi

"I finally mustered enough courage and said to the *rebbe* firmly, 'According to your physical condition, I am compelled, as a doctor, to tell you that you must not fast at all on Yom Kippur.'

"The *rebbe* jumped from his bed and, with as much strength as he could gather, began to dance. 'Hashem, Hashem,' he cried out with fervor, 'I served you by fasting on Yom Kippur for over seventy years. Now I shall serve you by eating.' "

From that day on, Papa fasted only on Mondays and Thursdays. His condition improved greatly with a supplementary diet.

6

Esther had passed her sixteenth birthday. "It's time to think about Esther's getting married," Papa said to Mama. There was an outstanding young man on whom Papa had his eye.

Yom Tov Lipman Stern was one of the many young men of a group to whom Papa taught various religious subjects after the evening prayers. He lived on the East Side with his parents, Rabbi Yosef and Cheyene Stern, and his older brother, David Zussman, eight years his senior.

His father and grandparents had emigrated from Europe just before the turn of the twentieth century. Reb Yosef was a respected student of the Chofetz Chaim, who had sanctioned his settling in America. Though the Chofetz Chaim did not advocate such a step for most Jews at that time, he was confident that Reb Yosef would not be influenced by the irreligious atmosphere prevailing then in the United States.

He chose Reb Yosef to be his emissary to collect funds for the Radun Yeshiva. The Chofetz Chaim refused to accept any donations gratis for the yeshiva and sent along his *seforim* to be distributed to the donors.

A short time after arriving in New York, Reb Yosef met his

wife, Cheyene, who had recently arrived from Russia. Their three sons, David Zussman, Avrohom Shmuel and Yom Tov Lipman, grew to be brilliant young men. Sadly, Avrohom Shmuel passed away at the age of nineteen after a seemingly simple appendectomy.

Rabbi Dr. David Zussman Stern became spiritual leader of the Young Israel of the East Side. Every Shabbos afternoon, rain or shine, he walked across the Williamsburg Bridge (which separates Brooklyn from Manhattan) to deliver lectures on various Torah topics to the young members. He also taught Bible classes twice a week to the fifteen-to-seventeen-year-old group. Thanks to his devoted efforts, given without remuneration, many young men and women became steadfast in their religious observance.

Yom Tov Lipman attended New York University and majored in accounting. He, too, was well versed in the Talmud. His home was filled with an impressive library of religious books.

Papa sent a close friend to talk to the Sterns about their son, Yom Tov Lipman, as a possible suitor for Esther. They were pleased with the proposition, having heard of Papa's reputation.

After a few meetings with Lipman, Esther was engaged to be married, the first in the Herman household. The wedding was scheduled for December 19, 1922, at the Beethoven Hall on East Fifth Street and Third Avenue in Manhattan.

Each day I rushed home from public school to be part of all the excitement. Mama busied herself shopping for clothes for the bride, setting up Esther's new apartment, buying the rest of the family new outfits for the wedding and greeting all the relatives and friends who came to offer their congratulations.

Papa was occupied with the preparations for the wedding itself. The invitations he ordered were different from any that had ever been printed before.

"Mr. Herman, are you absolutely sure you want this added

to the invitation?" The printer's voice trembled as he read what Papa had written, "Ladies, please come dressed according to the Jewish law."

"Print it just as it is. I want no change at all," Papa said decisively. "I also want separate cards printed with the following wording: 'Men and women are asked to dance separately.' "

The printer shook his head disapprovingly. "People will laugh at you."

"Let them laugh," Papa was unabashed. "I want to follow the Torah's commandments.

"I also want to order a large cardboard sign." Papa wrote the wording in bold capital letters: "ALL THE FOOD BELONGS TO THE LORD; AFTER THE *BROCHO*, TO YOU."

From the printer, Papa proceeded to the caterer. "I want to *kasher* all the pots and pans before my daughter's wedding. I also want all the dishes to be new."

"What is wrong with the pots and pans and dishes?" the caterer asked Papa in amazement. "All my religious customers used them until now without any question."

Papa placed a large bill in the caterer's hand. "This is just a deposit," Papa assured him.

"It's your money, Mr. Herman. Everything will be done as you wish."

A few days before the wedding, Papa contacted the caterer once again. "I want to be at the slaughterhouse when the chickens are being slaughtered." This time the caterer clucked his tongue in disapproval, without uttering a word.

And so, the wedding day arrived—a cold, clear wintry day in December. Esther, at seventeen, was a glowing bride. Mama looked lovely, but jittery. I was prettied up in my pink, ruffled dress and new black patent-leather pumps. Papa was most impressive in his Prince Albert suit and stovepipe hat.

kasher: make kosher (by immersing in boiling water)

As we rode to the wedding hall, Papa coached me on how to carry the large sign that would remind the guests to recite the proper blessings before the wedding dinner.

We entered the hall with Papa striding ahead, prepared for battle. One of our relatives was stationed at the entrance with the shawls Papa had prepared for any woman coming improperly attired. Another relative handed each guest the card which requested men and women to dance separately.

The invitations and cards made an uproar among the hundreds of guests. The ladies stood in groups discussing the added requests, which were unheard of at that time. Some were openly hostile. "Where does he get the nerve to tell us what to wear?" one woman asked sarcastically.

"I had to buy a special jacket to wear over my evening gown," another complained.

The men's discussions were no less scathing. "Can you imagine? I can't dance with whomever I want!"

Papa was not having an easy time of it. The soft music was inviting, and already some insolent couples were gliding on the polished floor. Papa marched over to each couple. "I must ask you to stop. The Torah prohibits men and women from dancing together."

The sign I proudly displayed also caused some caustic remarks: "I do not have to be told to wash my hands before meals or make the blessing," an elderly man exclaimed.

We came home from the wedding tired and sleepy, but Papa was elated. "You see, children, when one fulfills the commandments of the Torah, he must act proudly and without shame."

Papa set the precedent, and what he insisted on then has become accepted procedure at religious weddings nowadays.

The following are excerpts taken from Uncle Yankev Leib's letter to Zeidy and Bobie Andron in Eretz Yisroel the day after Esther's wedding. This is my translation of it from the Yiddish.

Seventh Day of Chanuka
December 20, 1922
MAZEL TOV! MAZEL TOV!

Dear Parents,

I am writing this letter the morning following the wedding of my niece Esther, the first of your grandchildren to be married. I want to give you a report of the wedding.

A wedding! Oh, what a wedding!

I've attended many weddings, but this wedding was a true, fine *yiddishe* wedding in every detail. Hashem should bless us with many such joyous occasions.

The hall is situated at Fifth Street and Third Avenue. It is not an aristocratic hall like the Astor or the Waldorf Astoria, but inside it is spacious. The dining hall is also very convenient.

Tuesday evening at seven o'clock my wife, children and I arrived at Aidel's house. In the dining room, the table was set with drinks and other delicacies. Around the table sat *rabbonim,* learned men, who were discussing Torah topics.

In the other room, the women were busy putting last touches to the *kalla*'s attire. My daughters, Esther and Yehudis, joined the others in helping in this *mitzva*. In truth, Esther looked beautiful, like a shining star — *shtern* — which is her married name.

A little while later, the *choson* and his parents arrived. He looked very handsome in a "full dress suit."

In a *mazeldikke shoh* we finally got into the automobiles to ride to the wedding hall. Upon entering, each one received a card in English requesting men and women to dance separately. Yankev Yosef busied himself seeing that all his demands would be carried out.

There were many guests when we arrived, but more and more kept coming: *rabbonim*, learned men, important *baalebatim*, young men, all wearing hats or yarmulkes. No one had his head uncovered.

....

kalla: bride / **choson**: groom / **mazeldikke shoh**: lucky hour
yarmulke: skullcap

Men danced with men—women with women!

At eleven PM the ceremony started. My wife and I were the escorts walking behind the *kalla* and her parents.

Rabbi Reimer and Rabbi Sillman of Tiferes Yerusholayim performed the wedding ceremony. After the breaking of the glass, the *mazel tov*s resounded throughout the hall.

Then all the men joined hands and danced in a circle. The women did the same. It was a wonder to behold the old and weak dancing with such enthusiasm. It was evident that the dancing stemmed from a spiritual joy. The old became young. The weak became strong. They danced without stop until a quarter to twelve.

At midnight, we went to the dining hall. As we entered, Ruchoma carried a sign in English in large print, which read: "All the food belongs to the Lord; after the *brocho*, to you." This was a "gentle hint" to wash your hands and say the blessing over the *challa*. The dinner was elaborate, as in the times of King Solomon.

I feared the speeches might last for the entire seven days of the *simcha*. However, the *kalla* asked that there should not be too many speeches, and on this Yankev Yosef yielded to her. Only two *rabbonim* and I spoke.

Yisroel Isser read the many congratulatory telegrams. Yours was read first, and received the greatest applause.

The guests were asked not to leave the hall until after the *sheva brochos*, and everyone remained.

All the guests recited the blessings after the meal with great fervor. At about three AM the happy guests began to leave, blessing the *choson* and *kalla* with joy and long years.

Your son, Yankev Leib

After his marriage to Esther, Lipman worked as a book-keeper and continued his accounting course at night. Within a

....
simcha: literally, joy: i.e. joyful time
sheva brochos: seven blessings recited at wedding feast

short time, he graduated college with a degree in accounting.

When Lipman was twenty-six years old, he developed chronic nephritis, a kidney disease which is often fatal. He was confined to bed for many months. Doctor after doctor was consulted.

Finally, the famous Professor Loeb issued the frightening verdict. Lipman had six months to live at the most. It was a sad and trying time for the Herman and Stern families. They undertook the support of Esther and her children and also paid the huge medical expenses incurred by Lipman's illness. Miraculously, Lipman recovered from his serious illness.

Thirty years later, when Rabbi Dr. David Zussman Stern was sitting *shiva* for his younger brother, Yom Tov Lipman, he related this unusual incident:

"My father, Rabbi Yosef Stern, was understandably very upset by the professor's prognosis. He found no respite day or night.

"Finally, he wrote a letter to his *rebbe*, the Chofetz Chaim, pouring out his deep anguish and asking him to pray for his son's recovery. My father added a note asking the Chofetz Chaim if he was permitted to grant his remaining years to his son. The Chofetz Chaim replied in the affirmative."

Rabbi Stern concluded, "As you know, my brother, Yom Tov Lipman, recovered completely from his dreaded and fatal illness. A few months later, my father became ill with cancer, and he passed away a year and a half later."

Yom Tov Lipman was granted thirty additional years. During that time, he and Esther brought up a family of Torah scholars and true Jewish daughters. He was a man who quietly, without fanfare, did many acts of *chesed* and gave charity to hundreds of people.

For many years, Lipman also devoted a few hours each Shabbos afternoon to teach *mishnayos, Ein Yaakov,* and *Shulchon Oruch* to a study group.

Frieda was my favorite sister. She was eight years older

than I, and I looked up to her as all-wise. We shared a double bed at night. Before dropping off to sleep, Frieda told me wondrous fairy tales and recited poetry that kept me entranced.

When I was six years old, she made a surprise birthday party for me and invited my young friends. Papa entered in the midst of the celebration. "What's this?" he asked.

Frieda explained, "Papa, it's Racoma's sixth birthday. She's a good girl and deserves to have a party."

Papa was not convinced. I trembled at what would follow. Papa caught my eyes and his softened. "Ruchoma, you are now a year older. If this birthday party will make you understand to be a year better, then it is worthwhile and will accomplish its purpose."

I sighed with relief as Papa left the room. Papa's words left their impact, whether I realized their deep meaning at that time or not.

Once, when I was playing jacks on the dining room floor, Frieda hurried by and accidentally stepped hard on my little finger. It swelled up and turned black and blue, but I didn't cry. Frieda cuddled me and said guiltily, "Racoma, I didn't mean to hurt you. I'm so very sorry."

With quivering lips, I answered, "Frieda, I love you so much that it doesn't hurt me."

At eighteen, and still not engaged to be married, Frieda was considered an "old maid" in our family. Though she had met several fine young men, she was not interested in any of them.

One of the young men she met was from a very reputable family of rabbis, and he, himself, was an ordained rabbi. Papa and Mama were very satisfied and hoped that Frieda would choose this young man as her husband.

One night, Frieda returned from her meeting with him sorely troubled. "I don't think I will see him again," she said to Papa and Mama. When they queried her for the reason, she told them, "We were walking off the curb of the sidewalk, and a pussy-cat brushed against his foot. He kicked the kitten brusquely. I feel that a person who would do that to a helpless kitten does not have a kind heart. You taught me not only to be considerate of people, but also of animals."

Mama tried to persuade Frieda that this was only an isolated incident and might not have any bearing on his general character. Papa, however, sided with Frieda and said to Mama, "Aidel, I don't feel that Frieda should be pressured in any way."

The Kaufman family moved into the building next to ours. Reb Aaron Tzvi Gershon Kaufman had emigrated from Dvinsk, Russia, in the 1880s. His father, Reb Yosef Kaufman, was a good friend of my Zeidy Andron, who also came from Dvinsk. Reb Aaron Tzvi Gershon married Tobia Zizmore, who had arrived in the United States at about the same time he had. They brought up their five children to observe and respect *yiddishkeit*.

Their oldest son, Philip, attended the Rabbi Jacob Joseph Yeshiva and was a student in the first elementary school graduating class. As a young man, Philip worked in a men's clothing shop during the day and, together with his father, attended Papa's *shiurim* at night.

Frieda became close friends with Bessie, Philip's younger sister, and visited her quite often. Philip became very interested in Frieda, and before long she showed an interest in him.

She told Papa that she would like to go out with him formally, and Papa consented. Frieda became engaged to Philip just before her nineteenth birthday and was married shortly after. I was very forlorn at the thought of my beloved Frieda forsaking me in favor of Philip. Though he tried his utmost to win me over to his side, it took a long time before I became reconciled.

Frieda's wedding was a replica of Esther's. There was still opposition to Papa's demand for men and women to dance

....
shiurim: classes, lectures

separately. And Papa faced an added difficulty. Since the wedding took place on a hot day in August, his card requesting: "Ladies, please come dressed according to the Jewish law" was being interpreted very liberally by some of the lady guests. Papa came prepared with shawls, scarves and light sweaters, which the guests accepted grudgingly.

Frieda and Philip moved into an apartment across the street from our house, so that I remained very close to Frieda until I got married.

When Nochum Dovid was fifteen years old, Papa took him to New Haven Yeshiva in Connecticut. The yeshiva was founded under the direction of Rabbi Yehuda Hershel Levenberg, Chief Rabbi of New Haven, and he became its Rosh Yeshiva. Rabbi Sheinkoff also gave *shiurim* there. The yeshiva's course of study was structured after the European yeshivos, with no secular studies—the first of its kind in America.

For Mama, it was a difficult adjustment, but she accepted Davie's leaving home without demurring. When Davie came home during vacation or for Yom Tov, Mama lavished her pent-up love and attention on him. She prepared all his favorite dishes. I looked forward to his coming home because of the holiday atmosphere that prevailed from the minute he entered the house.

Whenever he was in New York, Rabbi Moshe Mordechai Epstein, the Rosh Yeshiva of Chevron Yeshiva in Eretz Yisroel, was one of our *orchim*. He ate his daily dinner in our home. Papa consulted with him and then decided to send Nochum Dovid to Eretz Yisroel to study in the Chevron Yeshiva. He was then seventeen years old.

This time Mama objected, but with Papa, it was "Objection overruled." Off Davie sailed to Eretz Yisroel, one of the first American boys to travel to a foreign country to study in a yeshiva. The year was 1925.

Davie had been studying in Chevron for several years when

Rabbi Moshe Mordechai Epstein

Nochum Dovid at the Chevron Yeshiva in Hebron, photographed during the "Three Weeks"— hence slightly bearded.

the following incident prompted Papa to send for him.

In my sleep, I heard Mama sobbing. I awoke to see the first light filtering through my window. I jumped quickly out of bed, shivering in the cold dawn of that morning in the last days of autumn.

I ran into the kitchen to find Papa and Mama sitting there. Mama was wrapped in her warm robe, and her eyes were red from weeping. "Mama, what is the matter? Why are you crying?" I asked anxiously.

"It is nothing, Ruchoma. Go back to bed. You still have plenty of time until school."

"Papa, tell me what's the matter with Mama. I cannot go back to sleep unless I know why Mama is crying."

Papa answered, "Mama is upset by a dream she had."

"Mama, please tell me the dream," I begged.

Papa urged Mama, "Tell Ruchoma the dream. Let her hear it."

"I dreamt that I heard heart-rending sobs coming from a room. I found the knob of the door, softly opened it, and peered inside. The room was vast and empty except for an immense casket on the floor. On a chair, near the casket, sat a woman dressed in a long, black dress with a black kerchief covering her head. Even though she was seated, I realized that she was the tallest woman I had ever seen. It was she who was weeping uncontrollably.

"Suddenly, I heard a whisper in my ear, 'In the casket lies Avrohom Ovinu, and sitting near him is Soroh Imeinu mourning his death.' "

"Mama," I interrupted, "I learned in the *chumosh* that Avrohom Ovinu was mourning Soroh Imeinu. In your dream it's just the opposite."

"True," Mama answered, "but this is how I dreamt it." Mama continued with her dream. "As soon as I heard who they were, I rushed into the room and also began to weep and cry. In my hysteria, I ripped my clothes and shrieked, 'I will not leave this room until you promise me that my prayers have been answered.'

"As I stood there, the top of the casket slid open. Avrohom Ovinu's face appeared with eyes closed, but with tears coursing down his cheeks onto his long, white beard. Soroh Imeinu grasped my hand and said to me, 'You can go now. Your prayers have been answered.'

"I awoke then, but the dream is still so vivid and frightening that I cannot stop weeping." Mama lapsed into silence. Papa sat in deep thought. The tick-tock of our big clock over the mantelpiece mournfully ticked the time away. I shivered, and Mama looked at me. "Ruchoma, go put on something. You will catch cold. I will start the stove and prepare hot tea and milk."

Then turning to Papa, she asked, "Nu, Yankev Yosef, you are always so accurate at interpreting a dream — what does my dream mean?"

I could see that Papa was deeply disturbed. He sat near the kitchen table with both elbows on it. His hands were touching

---

Avrohom Ovinu: literally, our father: (the Patriarch) Abraham
Soroh Imeinu: literally, our mother: (the Matriarch) Sarah
chumosh: Pentateuch

his cheeks. Finally, Papa cleared his throat and said, "Aidel, it's a very good dream. Whenever you see *gedolim* in a dream, it's always a promising sign. That you saw Avrohom Ovinu and Soroh Imeinu is a *gevaldigge zechus*. Your prayers, whatever they may be, will surely be answered."

Mama, comforted, busied herself kindling the kitchen stove, and placed the kettle on it.

"You know, Aidel, I have been thinking about Nochum Dovid since his twentieth birthday. I think it is time for him to come home to find a *shidduch*."

Mama looked queerly at Papa and exclaimed, "What did you say?"

"I mean it, Aidel. I want Nochum Dovid to come home," Papa repeated with emphasis.

"Yankev Yosef, I just don't understand you. He's learning so well. We receive such wonderful letters from him and excellent reports from the Rosh Yeshiva. Why should you insist that he return? He's young. He can certainly wait a year or two to get married."

Mama continued, "I think this is the first time that you want Nochum Dovid to return home from a yeshiva, while I'm the one to encourage him to remain, even though I long very much to see him. You know how much I opposed your sending our *ben yochid* to the other side of the world when there are such good yeshivos now in America. It was you who insisted that he go to Eretz Yisroel and learn in Chevron Yeshiva."

Papa was listening to Mama but still seemed far away in his thoughts. "Aidel, it is written in the *gemora*, 'Eighteen years to the *chupa*, and you can wait until twenty.' I never look for *heteirim*, and I do not want to start now.

"I want Nochum Dovid home." There was finality in Papa's tone of voice.

"I have an idea," Mama said. "Let us ask the advice of Reb

gevaldigge: great / *gemora*: Talmud / *chupa*: wedding canopy
heteirim: lenient rulings

Boruch Ber, who should be coming soon to eat his breakfast. Whatever he advises, we shall accept."

"All right," Papa agreed.

We waited impatiently for Reb Boruch Ber's arrival. About an hour later, and still before my school time, he came with his son-in-law, Reb Reuven. Mama prepared breakfast for them.

When they finished, Mama said to Reb Boruch Ber, "Rebbe, I dreamt a dream last night that I would like you to hear." She then repeated her dream to him. He sat with averted head, as he never faced a woman directly. However, it was obvious that he concentrated on every word Mama spoke.

When Mama finished narrating the dream, she added quickly, "Now Yankev Yosef wants Nochum Dovid to return from Chevron to find a *shidduch* because he has just reached the age of twenty. I feel that since he is in the midst of learning so well, he can still wait."

Reb Boruch Ber did not say anything for a long while. Then he spoke, "The dream is a very good dream. About Nochum Dovid's coming home — if Reb Yaakov Yosef wants him to come home, he should do so. I do not like to oppose the words of a *tzaddik*."

That same morning Papa wrote Nochum Dovid informing him of his decision. He would send him a steamship ticket shortly, and he advised him to make preparations to leave Eretz Yisroel as soon as possible.

Nochum Dovid read Papa's letter with mixed emotions. "To see Papa, Mama, the family . . . but what about my learning — *shteiging* — a *shidduch*?? The boys will laugh at me."

He took the letter to his *rosh yeshiva*, Reb Moshe Mordechai Epstein, and read it to him. His reaction was similar to Reb Boruch Ber's, as he, too, knew Papa very well.

"Nochum Dovid, you must obey your father," he advised

shteiging: progressing

him. With letters going back and forth, it was early February before Davie was ready to leave Chevron.

Before he departed, his friends surprised him with a lively *tzeisschem l'sholom* party. Several of his American friends grabbed his hat, initialed their names on the inner hatband, and etched out the words: "May you be learning again in a yeshiva overseas within the year." Nochum Dovid left Yerusholayim after a tearful parting from Zeidy and Bobie Andron, who had settled in Givat Shaul.

He traveled by train through the Sinai desert to reach Port Said, from where his boat was scheduled to depart. When he finally reached there, the boat had already left. A Chinese freighter was about to depart. Since he had to reach France in time to catch the steamship crossing the Atlantic Ocean, he had no alternative but to ask the captain if he could book passage across the Mediterranean Sea. The captain allowed him to board, charging a nominal fee.

He was the only white man among several hundred Chinese. His sleeping quarters were on a lower deck, which he shared with a young Chinese. The first morning out to sea, when Davie put on his *tefillin,* the Chinese boy stared fascinated at this strange spectacle.

Davie was aboard two days, when a raging storm erupted on the high seas. It was *erev* Shabbos. The boat lurched back and forth, with the angry waves smashing against its sides, trying to conquer it and send it to a watery grave.

Davie huddled in his tiny cabin, praying to Hashem. The ship was about to capsize when the captain, with several other sailors, rushed into his room and in broken English ordered Davie, "Put on your black boxes and straps and pray to your God." Davie immediately put on his *tefillin.* A few hardy sailors carried Davie up to the heaving, swaying, wave-swept deck.

With his *tefillin* on, he called out loudly to Hashem, "It

....
tzeisschem l'sholom: farewell in peace / *tefillin*: phylacteries
menucha: rest

is almost Shabbos, a day of *menucha*. Let the sea have rest."
As the day ended and Shabbos began, the sea miraculously
calmed.

The captain and sailors kissed Davie soundly on both
cheeks. For the rest of the trip, Davie was accorded every honor.
At meals, even though he only ate fruit, he sat near the captain
and was called "the holy one."

It was a joyous day when we received Davie's telegram
telling us the time of his arrival. Papa prepared us all. "Now
remember, Nochum Dovid is a full-grown man and a *ben
Torah*. No kissing. You, too, Aidel; he's not a little boy any
more."

We started for the pier at least an hour before the boat was
scheduled to dock. It was the first time that we had gone any
place so early with Papa. We could hardly control our excitement. I kept thinking of Davie as I had known him almost four
years earlier. Would he be very different now? He was my big
brother, whom I adored. He always gave me special attention as
the baby in the family. But now I could not run and hug him
any more as I used to.

We were all engrossed in our thoughts, as we waited with
thumping hearts. Finally, there were the blasting horn and the
bustle and rush of the dockmen as they anchored the boat. We
got as close to the edge of the pier as was permitted and waited
with upturned faces.

Then we spied Nochum Dovid walking down the gangplank. The boy who had left us was now a handsome, mature
young man who waved to greet us. At last he was in our midst.

Papa gave him *sholom* like a general awarding the medal of
honor to his prize soldier. I was suddenly shy and tongue-tied.
Mama forgot all Papa's instructions and clasped Davie close to
her heart, hugging and kissing him, as tears of happiness rolled
down her flushed cheeks.

....
gave him *sholom*: greeted him

Nochum Dovid acted the role of the *ben Torah* to perfection. He did give me, however, that special look and smile that said he was still my beloved big brother, and whispered quickly, "I have a present for you." The world looked beautiful to me.

The "word" was out! Reb Yankev Yosef's son had returned from Chevron and was ready for a *shidduch.* The *shadchonim* came thick and fast. Each one had an extra-super special girl for him.

One had a millionaire's daughter with every *maale.* Another had a girl whose family came from generations of *rabbonim*—such *yichus.* A third had a businessman's daughter, whose father was willing to write over half of the business in Davie's name. A fourth had a very educated girl, a school teacher, earning high wages.

All this, besides our well-meaning relatives and friends who had either a daughter, sister, cousin or acquaintance who was perfect for Davie. I had never realized that there were so many hundreds of super-special young girls in America.

Nochum Dovid sailed through the sea of prospective matrimony impervious to it all. Mama accepted it as only natural. "Who would not want to marry a young man as special as our Nochum Dovid?"

Papa answered each one with a noncommittal, "We will see." For Papa already had set his heart on the girl for Nochum Dovid.

A few months earlier, Papa had advertised in the Yiddish newspaper that he was interested in starting an *Agudas Baale-Batim* to promote *yiddishkeit* in New York. The first to answer the advertisement had been Reb Avrohom Horowitz.

From the first meeting, they became close friends, and worked together on many projects: *shmiras Shabbos,* building

maale: good quality / **yichus**: distinguished lineage / **Agudas Baale-Batim**: league of laymen (literally, householders) / **shmiras**: observance

Nochum Dovid with Zeidy Herman, on a visit to kever Shmuel Hanovi *(Nebi Samuel) at Ramah.*

Reb Avrohom Horowitz, who became Nochum Dovid's father-in-law.

new *mikvehs*, checking the *kashrus* of butcher stores, and encouraging other *baale-batim* to join them in their efforts.

Reb Avrohom had his own special pet project: *shmiras haloshon,* to which he adhered in every detail. And he did his utmost to recruit new adherents to observe this great *mitzva.* During the entire month of Elul, he himself did not utter one word, other than Torah or prayers.

Reb Avrohom Horowitz had emigrated from Malch, Russia, in 1911. He left his wife, Soroh, and his one-year-old daughter, Chaye Dube, with his in-laws. He hoped that in the United States he would find suitable employment, and then he would send for them.

....

shmiras haloshon: literally, guarding the tongue: i.e. observance of laws concerning speech

He found work in a factory, machine-sewing knee pants. The owner, a Jew, was so impressed with Reb Avrohom's diligence in never wasting a minute from his work that he allowed him the privilege of not working on Shabbos and Yom Tov and even on *chol hamoed.*

His beard and *peyos,* which had never been touched by a pair of scissors, and his religious principles made him the target of the ridicule and scoffing of the other workers. An Italian worked alongside of Reb Avrohom. One morning, when the other workers teased Reb Avrohom with no letup, the Italian shouted angrily, "The next one who bothers this holy Jew again will get every bone in his body broken." From that time on, Reb Avrohom had peace.

The First World War intervened. It was almost nine years before his wife and daughter were able to be reunited with Reb Avrohom, by then a wan, tired, gray-bearded man, who was a stranger to Chaye Dube.

Soroh, his wife, was most perturbed that her learned husband was a simple factory worker. During the nine years, Reb Avrohom had managed to save $2,000 from his wages. Soroh bought a small house on Blake Avenue, in the East New York section of Brooklyn. She opened a small business of bedding and linens in her home and later renovated the downstairs premises into a dry-goods store. Reb Avrohom happily returned to his Torah studies, but also kept a careful eye on the business.

The customers who entered the Horowitz dry-goods store were given a blow-by-blow description of every conceivable damage the merchandise might possess. "I cannot guarantee the wool in the quilt." "Better check the sheets carefully. They might have a little tear," Reb Avrohom cautioned whenever he was on hand. Consequently, the little store was crowded. However, the profit was small, because each customer ultimately discovered a far-fetched damage that lowered the price.

....

peyos: earlocks

Much to the delight of Papa and Reb Avrohom, they discovered that one had a son and the other a daughter. A silent pact was made.

It was Chaye Dube whom Papa had chosen for Nochum Dovid. At Papa's request, it was she whom Nochum Dovid went to see first. She won his heart, and they were engaged on Rosh Chodesh Nisson.

Those were happy, exciting days in the Herman family as we prepared for Davie's wedding, which was scheduled for the end of Sivan. Hundreds of invitations were mailed, as everyone was anxious to attend this wedding.

Mama bought me an orange silk dress trimmed with dainty lace, and black patent leather slippers with silver buckles on them. I kept my new clothes near my bed, so I could peek at them each morning before hurrying to school.

A few days before Nochum Dovid's wedding, Reb Boruch Ber was expounding a difficult piece of Torah to him. To prove his point, Reb Boruch Ber pounded his hand hard on his silk high hat, which was lying on a chair near him. It folded like an accordion. Reb Boruch Ber eyed his smashed hat ruefully. Papa, of course, saw to it that he had a new silk hat in time for Davie's wedding.

Davie, however, quietly took the damaged hat to a hatter and asked him if he could restore it. He did an excellent job, and Davie proudly wore Reb Boruch Ber's silk high hat to his wedding.

The wedding day finally arrived—a mild, lovely day in June. With happy hearts we set off for Nochum Dovid's wedding. Reb Boruch Ber officiated. It was a joyous, *yiddishe* wedding, with Davie and Chaye Dube a radiant *choson* and *kalla.*

At Nochum Dovid's wedding, Papa introduced the distribution of a little prayer book of Grace and Blessings After the Meal. It was soon copied by many others for their weddings.

After Davie's wedding, the Herman household went back to normal—as normal as it could be with our "open-door policy of *hachnosas orchim.*" Mama once more apportioned the *pulkes* of the chicken to me, which Davie had "usurped" while he was home.

From the moment Nochum Dovid returned from Chevron, he had hoped to go back to Eretz Yisroel to learn in the yeshiva. During his engagement, he broached the subject several times to Chaye Dube, but it was a difficult decision for an only child to make. It meant living thousands of miles away from her beloved parents.

Without arriving at any conclusion, they temporarily moved into a little apartment right over the store, in the two-family house the Horowitzes owned. Nochum Dovid went daily to Yeshiva Toras Chaim (Rabbi Shmidman's yeshiva) to continue his Torah studies.

On a Friday night, a week after Tisha b'Av, when I was helping Mama serve the *orchim*, our dining room dimmed as one of the large bulbs from our three-bulb fixture suddenly burnt out. Reb Boruch Ber, who was in the midst of singing *zemiros* in his melodious voice, stopped for a moment. Mama whispered under her breath, *"Zoll zain tzu guten"* (May it be a good omen). After several minutes, we became accustomed to the dimmed lighting, but it brought a sense of foreboding.

It was right after *havdolo* that the terrible, tragic news came through that the city of Chevron had been attacked by hordes of rioting Arabs on Friday night and Shabbos. Hardest hit of all was the Chevron Yeshiva, where many yeshiva boys were butchered.

It was Tisha b'Av all over again in our house. Reb Boruch Ber, whose son was a student in Chevron Yeshiva, together with parents of Papa's students who were learning in Chevron, congregated in our house worriedly awaiting news of their loved ones.

Nochum Dovid and Chaye Dube came running into our house, with Davie virtually in a state of shock. He already knew of several of his very close friends who were among the victims.

Boruch Kaplan's mother burst into our house wild-eyed; she had a newspaper in her hand which listed her son among the killed.

Papa exclaimed, "I do not believe it. Boruch is surely alive."

When Papa was questioned, "How can you be so positive?" he answered simply. "I sent Boruch [one of his most beloved *talmidim*] to study Torah in Chevron Yeshiva. I did it one hundred percent *l'sheim shomayim*, so I am sure no harm has befallen him."

Then Reb Boruch Ber asked Papa, "Reb Yaakov Yosef, what about my son?"

Papa answered him, "Rebbe, I feel that your son is also alive."

An hour later a telegram came from Boruch Kaplan, "Alive-well," and a while later another one from Reb Boruch Ber's son that he, too, was among the living.

Late Sunday night, when our home was quiet, Papa, drawn and haggard, and Mama, red-eyed and pale, sat silently in our dining room. Papa looked at Mama and said quietly, "Aidel, do you remember the dream where you dreamt about Avrohom Ovinu and Soroh Imeinu, which prompted me to send for Nochum Dovid?"

"I have been thinking about it all day," Mama softly answered.

"Aidel, we were on trial 'Upstairs.' Our son's life was at stake. Because we are devoted followers of the *mitzva* of *hachnosas orchim,* which Avrohom Ovinu and Soroh Imeinu first taught to the world, they came as our advocates, pleading in our defense.

"With such holy *neshomos* pleading our cause, what could the Boss do but acquit us. Our *mitzva* had paid us a great dividend — the life of our son was spared."

After Sukkos, Nochum Dovid and Chaye Dube set sail for

----

l'sheim shomayim: for the sake of heaven / *neshomos*: souls

the Mirrer Yeshiva in Poland, the first American couple to do so. And so, he honored the wishes of his fallen comrades, who had inscribed on his hatband, "May you be learning again in a yeshiva overseas within the year."

Added note:
I am sure you noted in this remarkable story that Nochum Dovid's father-in-law's name is Reb *Avrohom* ben Reb *Yaakov* and his mother-in-law's name is *Soroh* (Leah) bas Reb *Yosef*.

I always felt that their prayers, albeit unknown to them, were also enlisted "for the defense" of their son-in-law to be.

Another interesting note:
When Reb Avrohom, *zatzal,* passed away, he was in his seventies; yet he had never had any serious dental problems or extractions. I can only attribute this unusual fact to the merit he earned by his scrupulous observance of *shmiras haloshon,* never letting any evil gossip escape his mouth.

Papa rushed into the house with that look of expectation which indicated he had news to impart. "Aidel, I have a jewel of a boy for Bessie."

Mama stared at Papa in surprise, since Bessie was all of twelve years old, a lanky pre-teenager. Bessie perked up her ears and her eyes gleamed. She mothered all the children of the block, who hovered around her; she wiped their running noses, tied their shoelaces, and combed their unruly hair.

There was sibling rivalry between us because she excluded me from her mothering. Mama soothed me, "Ruchoma, though you are the baby of our family, you are a big girl already."

Mama asked Papa curiously, "Yankev Yosef, who is this *choson* you've already prepared for Bessie?"

Boruch Kaplan, one of Papa's *talmidim*, had introduced Chaim Scheinberg to Papa when he was fourteen years old. He had recently graduated from Rabbi Jacob Joseph Yeshiva. Papa was very impressed with Chaim's great desire for Torah learning and with his mind which was keen to absorb. Papa therefore took him under his wing.

To ensure that Chaim would continue to advance in his Torah studies, Papa advised him to attend New Haven Yeshiva. At that time, Davie and some of Papa's *talmidim* were already studying there through Papa's influence.

Without receiving prior permission from Chaim's parents, because Papa feared they would veto the idea, Papa put him on the train with only his *tefillin*, a bag of food and the fare for the trip. Then Papa went to Mr. Scheinberg's tailor shop to notify him of the *fait accompli*. When Papa introduced himself, Mr. Scheinberg recognized the name, for Chaim had told his father about his *rebbe*.

Of course, Mr. Scheinberg did not take too kindly to the idea of his son's leaving without his even being consulted. He demanded that Papa get Chaim back from New Haven on the next train.

But it was not that simple. Mr. Scheinberg had not only Papa to reckon with, but also his son Chaim who was a strong-willed boy. Chaim had decided that New Haven Yeshiva was exactly the right place for him to pursue his studies.

For three weeks, his father refused to send him his clothes and other belongings, although Chaim's mother, who sided with her son, tried her utmost to convince her husband. Finally, when he saw that Chaim was adamant, he capitulated.

This was the "jewel of a boy" Papa had chosen for Bessie.

When Chaim returned from New Haven Yeshiva at the age of seventeen, he attended the Rabbi Yitzchok Elchonon Yeshiva, which was then located on East Broadway. He learned under the greatest *geonim*: The Meitcheter Iluy — Rabbi Shleima Polachek, Rabbi Moshe Soloveitchik, and Rabbi Shimon Shkop from Grodno, Poland. Rabbi Shkop had come to raise money for his yeshiva and was persuaded to remain in New York for a year's time to deliver *shiurim*.

Papa was in close contact with Chaim throughout his adolescence and constantly encouraged him.

When Chaim was nineteen years old, Papa approached him about marriage to Bessie, who was then seventeen. He agreed. By that time, Mr. Scheinberg had forgiven Papa, and he and his wife were good friends of ours.

At their wedding, Chaim received a special wedding gift—his *smicha*—which was presented to him by the dean Rabbi Dr. Bernard Revel. Chaim and Bessie were married in March. Right after Pesach, they set out for the Mirrer Yeshiva in Poland, where Chaim continued his Torah studies for five years.

Added note:

When Bessie was sixteen, a very wealthy young man, who frequented our home, expressed his desire to marry her.

He suggested to Papa, "As your son-in-law, I could be of great financial help to you, Mr. Herman. Especially now, when you are having difficulties in your business."

Papa's answer was direct and concise, "My daughter is not for sale."

---

smicha: Rabbinic ordination

7

One man's army

Papa's favorite expression was, "I am a soldier of the Boss, and I obey His commands."

He was concerned with every phase of Jewish religious life in America. Papa's indomitable courage, and his willingness to take up the defense of *yiddishkeit* uncompromisingly, earned him ridicule and derision, but this did not deter him from his unswerving path.

I recall when Papa came home from *shul* one Shabbos morning with the familiar gleam in his eyes that spelled a fighting mood. "Aidel, I will be back soon. See that the *orchim* start eating."

Mama gave Papa a worried look and quickly motioned to me, "Ruchoma, go with Papa and see where he is going. If anything happens to him, at least I will know."

I hurried after Papa and caught up with him. He smiled at me. "I see, Ruchoma, Mama sent you after me."

I could hardly keep pace with Papa as he strode down East Broadway. At the Young Israel Synagogue, he stopped and said, "Wait for me."

Curiosity impelled me to follow Papa. I entered the

corridor and peeked inside. The synagogue was packed to capacity. The reading of the *parsha* had just finished.

Papa stood for a moment at the rear of the synagogue; then he suddenly ran over to the pulpit, banged his hand on the table, and called out loudly, "You have a sign outside that advertises, 'Young Israel Dance Tonight.' The Torah forbids boys and girls to dance together. Either erase the words, 'Young Israel' or the word 'dance.' Both cannot be on the same sign."

There was an uproar. "Throw him out." Two husky young men picked Papa up bodily and unceremoniously set him down in the street.

"Papa, don't you feel ashamed that you were thrown out of *shul?*" I cried out.

"Not at all," Papa shrugged it off. "I do not know if they will take heed of what I said, but I had to register my protest."

Papa straightened his shoulders and clutched my hand tightly as we marched home to Mama and the *orchim*.

Only years later was Papa's admonition heeded, when yeshivos increased with the influx of great *roshei yeshiva* and *rabbonim* from many European countries during the Second World War.

Papa was a specialist on *shatnez*. Many people found their way to our door to ask him to check their suits and coats. However, Papa was not content with that alone.

One evening a chemistry professor came to our home with a friend of ours. Papa took one look at the well-dressed professor and said, "Would you please remove your jacket?" The man stared at Papa in amazement. "I would like to check your suit for *shatnez*," Papa explained. Since the professor had never heard the word *shatnez*, he was even more confused than before.

Papa took his sharp knife, slit open the lining of the jacket collar and pulled out some threads. He examined them care-

parsha: weekly portion / *shatnez*: forbidden mixture of wool and linen

fully. *"Shatnez,"* Papa exclaimed. "You are not allowed to wear this suit until it is completely removed."

The bewildered young man stammered, "I—I—do not understand all this." Papa patiently expounded the laws of *shatnez* to him. "Do not worry; I have a special tailor who removes the *shatnez* expertly. It will be as good as new." Papa then went to his closet and took out a jacket. "You can wear this jacket to go home," Papa said kindly. As the disconcerted professor stood up to leave, Papa added, "Bring me all your suits and overcoats so that I can check them for *shatnez.*"

Added note:

The professor returned to Papa time and time again until he became learned in the laws of the Torah. Papa encouraged him to spend his sabbatical in Mir, Poland, where he progressed further in his Torah learning.

One Shabbos, on a summer day, a woman knocked at our door. "I would like to speak to Mr. Herman." I ushered her into our dining room where Papa was drinking tea with some of our *orchim.*

"I would like to ask your advice on an important matter," she said courteously.

Papa noticed the pocketbook she carried on her arm and exclaimed loudly, "It is Shabbos. I must ask you to put it down immediately."

The confused woman dropped her pocketbook as if it were loaded with dynamite.

Then Papa said gently, "Please come into the other room, and I will gladly discuss your problem with you."

When they returned, Papa explained the laws of Shabbos to her. "You are welcome to stay in our home until Shabbos ends, and then you can take your pocketbook."

She spent an enjoyable afternoon with Mama and me. Mama served her *sholosh seudos.* When she left Saturday night, we had gained a friend who came to visit us often.

One Friday night, a policeman came to our door. "Mr. Herman, I just received word that there is a fire in your fur store. The fire department has been alerted and is doing its best to extinguish the flames. It is advisable for you to get there as soon as possible."

Papa thanked the police officer and then said, "It is our Sabbath. I cannot be there until after it ends tomorrow night."

The policeman stared at Papa in amazement. "Mr. Herman, your store is burning down, and you won't even go there to see what is happening?"

The entire Shabbos, Papa showed no anxiety. He sang *zemiros,* said his *dvar Torah* at the table, and did not hurry to make *havdolo* after Shabbos.

Saturday night, Papa rode over to Seventh Avenue, where his fur store was situated, expecting to see it in shambles. It was the adjoining fur store that had gone up in flames.

Papa was forced by the insurance company to install the Holmes protection unit against theft for his fur store. After it was installed, Papa went to the back of the store and left the window slightly open. "I cannot place my faith on this protection. The Boss protects, but I am obligated to make the normal *hishtadlus.*"

School was out, and I was in—that is, in the house, pestering Mama.

All through the last exciting weeks of school, mingled with the final exams, report cards and promotion, my friends and I had made plans to go to Coney Island on every sunny day.

That morning, my first day of vacation, I awoke very early to prepare my bathing clothes. Then Mama broke the news, "Papa says that you cannot go to Coney Island any more

hishtadlus: effort, human striving

because you are already twelve years old. You are *bas mitzva* and considered a young lady."

I looked at myself in the dresser mirror. A scrawny twelve-year-old, with short black hair and a skinny face with defiant dark eyes, stared back at me. Hardly the description of a blossoming woman.

"Mama," I wailed, "why must I always be different from all my friends? They are also religious, and they can go bathing. Why can't I?"

"You're different because your Papa is different from everyone else," Mama said simply. There was no fighting such logic. It was fact.

"Mama, what am I going to do all through my vacation? Papa does not want me to go to the movies, he does not like it when I go to the library, and now he won't let me go to Coney Island. I'll go crazy; that's what.

"Didn't you always tell me that swimming is so healthful? The sun is so good for me."

"Ruchoma, Papa will soon come from *shul*. He will talk to you," Mama said hurriedly, as she grabbed the pot of soup that was about to boil over.

Papa hurried into the house with *tallis* and *tefillin*. "Yankev Yosef, Ruchoma is driving me crazy. She wants to go to Coney Island."

Before Papa could say anything, I started, "Papa, I'm really not a lady yet. I don't even look my age. Everyone says so. Why can't I go bathing? You always said it's important to learn how to swim. How can I swim if I can't go bathing at Coney Island?"

Papa sat down in his large armchair and pulled over another chair for me, "Sit down, Ruchoma. I will explain to you why it is wrong to go bathing in Coney Island.

"If you saw a sign which read, 'Danger! No bathing allowed! By order of the Police Department,' you would surely not bathe there. First, you would be afraid something might happen to you. Secondly, you would not want to break the law.

"This is exactly why you cannot bathe at Coney Island. Though it might not be dangerous for your body, it is surely dangerous for your *neshomo.* It's against the Torah to be dressed immodestly. A *yiddishe tochter* becomes a *yiddishe* mother. Without *tznius* you cannot be either. This is the basis of our Jewish heritage.

"Soroh Imeinu, our first *yiddishe* mother, taught us what *tznius* means. If our Jewish daughters will not keep this *mitzva,* then we will not be different from the *goyim.* Now that you have turned twelve, you are obligated in all the *mitzvos.* I realize that it is difficult for you to understand this now; especially, when all your friends are going bathing at Coney Island, but someday you will thank Mama and me for not allowing you to go." Papa's words reached my ears but did not penetrate my mind or heart. "I will never thank Papa and Mama for not letting me go to Coney Island," I thought.

I did not give up. "Papa, Mama went bathing in Coney Island when she was a girl. She told me so herself."

"Listen, Ruchoma, when Mama went bathing, her bathing suit covered her from head to toe."

"How right you are, Yankev Yosef. In fact, it weighed me down so much that I could hardly move in the ocean."

"Papa, my bathing suit is not cut out so much." I ran and got it out of the shopping bag where I had prepared it in anticipation of going to the beach.

I placed the candy-striped bathing suit on the table in front of Papa. Papa examined it closely. "It exposes your arms and legs, and it is cut out at the neckline. You are not going. That's it. Not another word." Papa's eyes blazed angrily.

The tears rolled down my face. Mama looked at me with a pitying glance. "Do something, Yankev Yosef. There must be some place for Ruchoma to go bathing." Mama was of the opinion that Papa could do anything he set his heart on. We children shared that view.

....

tznius: modesty as required by Jewish law (or) the Torah / *goyim*: gentiles

Papa didn't answer for quite a while. Then he said. "I have an idea. I will ride over to City Hall and see if I can talk the mayor into setting aside a special beach for women."

I stared at Papa, hardly believing my ears. Papa was going to the mayor? "Aidel, get out my good suit and Shabbos shoes." Papa got his brush and brushed his black beard that was turning gray. I sat quietly watching him, the tears drying on my face.

Papa marched out of the house like a soldier going to battle, with Mama's usual blessing, "Go with *hatzlocho.*"

I climbed out on our fire escape, overlooking hot, parched East Broadway. I spied my friends hurrying toward my house. They looked up. "Racoma, aren't you ready?"

I peered down at them through the iron bars of my fire escape prison. "I can't go; my father won't let me go bathing in Coney Island."

My friends looked up at me pityingly but didn't question me. They knew that I couldn't do all the things they could. I watched enviously as they turned the corner towards the subway station.

Suddenly my imagination carried me along with them. There I was running down the subway steps, carrying my shopping bag with my bathing paraphernalia and lunch in one hand; clasped tightly in the other hand was my precious purse with my spending money. I heard the clink of my nickel in the turnstile, and I was out on the crowded subway station.

The train roared in like a giant whale thrashing its way through the deep seas. It opened wide its jaws and swallowed up the mass of sweating humanity like a school of sardines. I pushed my way to a little open space and stood holding onto the white pole. The whirring fans overhead tried courageously to cool us but to no avail. The train gathered momentum, hurtling through the dark tunnel, with all the passengers swaying to its rhythm. Over and over it screeched to me, "I am going to Coney Island. . . ." It was music to my ears.

The train suddenly emerged from the darkness. It took a

minute for me to get accustomed to the bright sun that blazed through the windows. Just a few more stations, and I'd be there. My excitement mounted. Then the conductor bellowed the magic words, "Cooooooooney Island, last stop, all out." The giant whale belched us out, relieved of its heavy burden.

I flew down the stairs. The cool, salty smell of the ocean greeted me. From afar, I could see the giant ferris wheel with its swinging seats touching the sky. The carousel, with its dancing ponies keeping tune to the lilting music, went round and round. The inviting aroma of roasted peanuts tickled my nose, as the peanut vendor passed by. I was in Fairyland.

Onto the boardwalk I sped. I stopped at the sign that read, "Ten Cent Lockers." It took me only a few minutes to get out of my sweat-drenched clothes and into my bathing suit and robe.

The hot sand scorched my feet as I raced to the ocean. The cool, foamy waves greeted me with a spray of salt water. Like a mermaid, I plunged into its midst. "Look at me: I can float," I sputtered to my friends, my mouth filled with ocean water. This was heaven on earth, as the sky and ocean became one in the distant horizon.

"Come eat; come eat." I ran along the crowded, hot beach and found my shopping bag. I pulled out my soggy sandwich. I washed my hands to eat from the little thermos bottle of water I had brought from home, and made a *brocho*. I took big, hungry bites from the gritty salmon sandwich that Mama had prepared—delicious . . .

"Come eat; come eat." Mama poked her head out onto the fire escape and punctured my fantasy. "Ruchoma, are you deaf? I have called you at least ten times already."

"I'm not hungry." I could still feel the sand between my teeth. My head pulsed from the hot ball of fire that had been baking me on the fire escape during my daydream.

"Hungry? Who has to be hungry to eat what I prepared for you?" Mama exclaimed. I climbed through the window into the coolness of the house. On the kitchen table was a fresh, crisp buttered roll, a plate of strawberries with whipped cream, and a cold glass of malted milk.

Without being the least bit hungry, I finished the roll to the last crumb, licked the plate clean of strawberries and cream, and gulped down the malted milk. Sweet, gentle, wise Mama, who always sided with Papa, yet understood us children so well.

"Mama," I said worriedly. "What is taking Papa so long?"

Mama looked up at me from the potatoes she was deftly undressing. "Don't you worry. Papa will get to see the mayor," she said confidently.

Her words did not quiet my fears. Maybe the mayor would refuse to see Papa. But Papa would surely insist. I could visualize Papa behind bars, with his accusing finger pointed towards me, "Just because you wanted to go to Coney Island . . ."

What seemed like hours later, I heard Papa's hurried tread on the stairs. I rushed to the door. Papa came in carrying a large box under his arm.

Mama and I looked at him expectantly. He sat down, took off his hat, and put on his yarmulke. He mopped his sweated forehead with his large handkerchief and cleared his throat.

"I finally did see Mayor Jimmy Walker, but it was not easy to get to him. First I saw his secretary, then his deputy mayor, who refused to admit me since I had no appointment. However, when I impressed on them the importance of my mission, they consulted with Mayor Walker, and he consented to give me a few minutes of his time.

"He was most courteous and listened attentively to what I had to say about the problems confronting our youth. When I suggested that there be separate bathing areas set aside for men and women, he seemed to understand the problem very well.

"But do you know what he answered me?

" 'Rabbi, you are the first person in New York City to suggest such an idea. You can well understand that I cannot set aside a beach just for you.' "

All my hopes vanished. I could never go bathing at Coney Island again.

Then Papa looked at me with a twinkle in his eyes. "Ruchoma, since you have set your heart so much on going to Coney Island, I have another idea."

He untied the large box he had brought home with him. Among the thick layers of tissue paper lay a navy-blue-and-white bathing suit with a high neckline, three-quarter sleeves, and long pantaloons to match.

One Sunday morning Papa mysteriously disappeared. He usually spent time with the family on Sunday telling us interesting stories from the Bible.

Many hours later Papa came home. His face was sunburned and he was carrying a large sign.

"Where were you all day, Yankev Yosef?" Mama asked anxiously.

"There is a serious problem with our Jewish youth," Papa said worriedly. "They do not know that the Torah forbids mixed bathing. I had this sign printed, and I strapped it to my shoulders and marched back and forth on the boardwalk of Coney Island."

We all peered at the sign which was emblazoned in large red letters: "Jewish sons and daughters, our holy Torah forbids mixed bathing."

"Yankev Yosef, who is going to heed you? All you accomplished was to become fatigued," Mama said with pity.

"Someday, I will have to give a reckoning in Heaven, where they will ask me, 'What did you do about this transgression?' At least I did my duty," Papa said emphatically.

Papa was one of the founders of Yeshiva Tiferes Yerusholayim, and he took a keen personal interest in the progress of both the yeshiva and its synagogue.

One Shabbos morning, one of the newly hired teachers was called up to the Torah. Papa noticed that he did not look directly into the *sefer Torah* during the *leining,* but kept his head averted. When *davening* ended, Papa decided to follow him. He walked after him for several blocks, and then saw him enter a candy store, where he bought cigarettes.

Papa immediately accosted him. "A *rebbe* teaching Jewish children is a desecrator of Shabbos! Don't ever show your face in the yeshiva again," Papa angrily told him.

From that time on, each *rebbe* was carefully screened.

Later, when Papa was asked, "Reb Yankov Yosef, how did you recognize that the young man was a Sabbath desecrator?" Papa answered, "A Jew who does not look directly into the Torah at the time of the *leining* is certainly an object of suspicion to me. He was as cold as ice. I followed my intuition, which proved correct."

Our Shabbos *luach* (Jewish calendar), that each home possesses, is so readily available that we tend to take it for granted. However there was a time in the early 1920s when it was non-existent. The *shuls* each had a large *luach,* and most people checked with it to ascertain the correct time for lighting the candles for Shabbos and Yom Tov.

Papa's business was faltering. His bank account had dipped to an all-time low. He had $128 in the account. Papa decided this was the time to put his money to good use.

He contacted a rabbi he knew and said to him, "I know a man who wants to donate one hundred dollars for some worthy cause to further *yiddishkeit.*" At that time a hundred dollars was a considerable sum of money.

The rabbi consulted with some other rabbis, and with Papa's assistance they formed an organization which they called "*Chizuk Hadas.*"

Their first undertaking was to print small Jewish calendars for the home. Papa gave them the one hundred dollars

sefer Torah: Torah scroll / *leining*: reading / *davening*: praying
Chizuk Hadas: strengthening the faith

toward the printing without their ever realizing that it was he who had donated this money.

Papa never spared himself when it came to imparting Torah learning to others. On Friday night after the Shabbos meal, when he could have rested, he spoke for over an hour on the *parshas hashovua* at the Madison Street Shul. A large crowd of men was present, and the gallery was filled with women. Often, I took my friends to listen to Papa's lectures. Though we did not understand Yiddish well, watching his radiant face as he spoke enthralled us.

Each night after *mairiv*, Papa gave a *shiur* on a *blatt gemora*, *mishnayos* and *Shulchon Oruch* to a group of men at the Bais Medrash Hagodol on Norfolk Street.

Of course, all this was done without any thought of remuneration.

Papa was concerned because most of the Jewish boys who attended public school received no religious training. After school, they were out in full force playing ball in the street. He tried to fill the vacuum by seeking ways and means to "woo" them.

Each afternoon, summer or winter, before *mincha* time Papa closed his fur shop and took the subway to Tiferes Yerusholayim. He brought a basket of chocolate wafers with him.

At first, he had to encourage the boys to stop their games, but after several weeks there was no problem. The distribution of the chocolate wafers spread Papa's fame far and wide. By the time he arrived at East Broadway, the boys were lined up waiting for him, and of course, their wafer.

After handing each boy his snack, Papa marched them into the *shul* to recite their prayers. Many of them could not even

....

parshas hashovua: portion of the week / *mairiv*: evening prayer
blatt gemora: page of Talmud / *mincha*: afternoon prayer

read the Hebrew prayers, and those boys received special tutoring from Papa.

After *mincha,* Papa gathered them around a table in the synagogue and related interesting stories of our great men and their Jewish heritage, until it was time for *mairiv.*

One day, a new lad joined the line. "What is your name?" Papa asked.

"Antonio," he answered.

"Where do you live?" Papa questioned further.

"Down the block." He averted his eyes from Papa's penetrating gaze.

It did not take long for Papa to discern that the young boy was Italian, intent upon receiving the chocolate wafer.

Papa was able to communicate with his lads. He understood their slang, their games, and their problems. He encouraged many of them, who came from non-religious homes, to discontinue public school. Much to the dismay and despite the negative attitude of their parents, Papa registered them in the yeshiva. He inculcated in these young boys such a love for *yiddishkeit* that they became truly religious men who followed his teachings all through their lives.

A doctor parked his expensive car in front of our house and bounded up the stairs. He dashed through the door, not bothering to knock.

"Where is Mr. Herman?" he demanded.

Papa approached the ruffled man. "Can I help you?" Papa asked him.

"My son just went on a rampage and broke all the china dishes in our home, saying they are *treif.* He told me that you are the one who is teaching him all these stupid laws. I shall kill you for that!" The doctor brandished a revolver and pointed it at Papa.

Papa did not flinch. He opened his shirt and said, "Shoot!"

....
treif: non-kosher

The doctor trembled, threw down his gun and collapsed into a chair. It took Papa quite a while to calm him, while Mama served him hot coffee and cake. He later admitted, "I have never met a man as brave as Mr. Herman. No wonder my son listens to his every word."

Bessie noticed that Papa's hand was bruised. "Papa, how did you hurt your hand?" she asked concernedly.

"As I walked down the street, a brick from a building that was being renovated fell on my hand and bloodied it. But I have an explanation for it," Papa quickly added. "Someone asked me to write a letter for him, and I postponed it for a day. So I guess this is my punishment."

There was a gathering of relatives to which Papa was invited. Davie, who was a young boy at that time, arrived before him.

Suddenly, there was a commotion. One of the relatives came panting up the stairs and into the house. "Quick, J. J. [some of our relatives called Papa by the initials of his name, Jacob Joseph] just walked out of the subway and is heading here." There was a mad dash as some of the bare-headed relatives ran to get their hats and cover their heads.

When Papa entered, everyone sat docilely in his seat, head covered, and greeted Papa with great respect.

Mr. Peretz Sheinerman had come to the United States from the "old country" as a young man. He married and settled in Washington, D.C., where he owned a wholesale dry-goods store. He was a fine, religious man who tried his best to bring up his growing family in the strict Orthodox tradition. However, it was a difficult undertaking, as Washington in the 1920s was a barren region as far as Orthodoxy was concerned.

His business often took him to New York. It was on one of these business trips that he realized he could not possibly make it home in time for Shabbos. Someone suggested to him that he stay in our house.

During the Shabbos he spent with us, Papa questioned Mr. Sheinerman about his family in Washington. "How can you bring up a family of Jewish boys and girls in a city like Washington, D.C., where there are no yeshivos or religious friends for your children? How will you marry them off?" Papa asked him incredulously.

Mr. Sheinerman agreed with Papa and shook his head sadly. "But what can I do? I have to make a living for my wife and children. My business is set up there."

"If you want to save your family, to have them remain steadfast Jews, move immediately to New York. The Boss provides *parnoso* wherever you are, so leave it up to Him," Papa advised Mr. Sheinerman.

Mr. Sheinerman took Papa's words to heart and went home to discuss them with his wife, a very clever woman. With her impetus, it wasn't long before the Sheinermans and their nine young children were moving to New York. Papa not only helped them rent an apartment, but both Papa and Mama also gave them encouragement in every way until they became firmly settled.

The Sheinerman family became very attached to us and remained fast friends of ours. Each Friday night, Mr. and Mrs. Sheinerman and some of their children came up to our house to enjoy the spiritual warmth of our home.

Many a time, Reb Peretz Sheinerman was heard to say, "It was only Reb Yankev Yosef's wise advice that saved my family."

To this day, Mrs. Sheinerman says, "I remember so well when I came to visit Mrs. Herman during the week. She always greeted me with her warm smile, the kitchen filled with a delicious aroma of cooking, and her inviting words, 'Go wash to eat, and have a bite.' "

Papa was one of the respected members of the Pike Street Shul on the Lower East Side.

parnoso: livelihood

During the month of Elul, a renowned cantor was hired to lead the Shabbos prayers. Tickets were sold for the occasion to further the activities of the *shul*, which was in difficult financial straits.

Shabbos morning, after Papa finished *davening* in Tiferes Yerusholayim, he walked over to the Pike Street Shul.

He stood watching some people enter, when, to his great consternation, he noticed that a man was selling tickets for entrance into the synagogue.

When Papa attempted to enter the *shul*, the man at the door refused him admission unless he presented his ticket. Papa asked the man to summon the president of the synagogue. Within minutes, the president saw to it that Papa was allowed entrance, not realizing that Papa had more in mind than just getting in.

As soon as the cantor stopped for a few moments between prayers, Papa ran to the front of the *shul* and shouted in fury, "You want to raise money for this *shul*'s existence by being *mechallel Shabbos*—rather let the *shul* be closed."

Papa stirred up a hornet's nest. The president and other important members of the *shul* were very embarrassed. The congregation was disconcerted because the cantor refused to continue. However, no more tickets were sold that Shabbos.

Papa left the *shul* with many an insult hurled at him, but this did not fluster him. His obligation was to the Boss.

Added note:

One of the important members of the Pike Street Shul was incensed at Papa's action and decided to take revenge. Papa always led the congregation of Tiferes Yerusholayim in the prayers of *shachris* on Rosh Hashona and Yom Kippur. This person persuaded many members of the congregation to pray in some other synagogue on Rosh Hashona. Papa had much heartache from this occurrence.

....

mechallel Shabbos: desecrating the Sabbath / **shachris**: morning prayer

A few days after Rosh Hashona, this man became critically ill. A messenger was sent immediately to Papa to beg his forgiveness. Though Papa forgave him, the man succumbed to his sickness and passed away within a short time.

The daughter of a close friend was getting married at a well-known wedding hall. We were all invited. It was a short while after my engagement to Moshe Shain, and it was the first time we were to make a public appearance as *choson* and *kalla*.

I wore a beautiful wine-colored dress for the occasion, and Moshe his new Oxford gray suit. Papa, Mama, Moshe and I went by taxi to the hall. When we arrived, the band was already playing, and many couples were dancing to the lilting music.

Papa's eyes flashed. He snatched a chair, jumped on it, and called out loudly, "The Torah forbids men and women to dance together. I beg you to stop." There was a sudden hushed silence as the band abruptly stopped playing. The couples stood like frozen statues at this unexpected assault. In a few minutes pandemonium reigned. Most of the guests had never met up with a person like Papa. His demand was preposterous to them.

The bridegroom's parents came over to Papa, who was busily arguing with some excitable guests. "Mr. Herman, you are disturbing the wedding. We want you to leave." The bride's parents were in a quandary, not knowing how to react. They looked at Mama and me apologetically.

Papa marched out, with Mama, Moshe and me following like soldiers behind the general. When we reached the street, Mama complained, "Yankev Yosef, I can never go any place with you and enjoy my evening. The children looked forward to this affair." Her face showed how sorry she was for us.

"Aidel, you know very well that we cannot stand by without protesting when the commandments of the Torah are being desecrated in public," Papa answered decisively. "Not attending the wedding is little to pay for upholding the *kovod* of

Hashem." His words reached home. Mama gave Papa that special look of pride reserved only for him.

After our initial embarrassment and disappointment at leaving the wedding so unceremoniously, Moshe and I went home with Papa and Mama, feeling a sense of spiritual uplift.

Orchard Street, on the Lower East Side, was a hubbub of activity on Friday night and Shabbos. The pushcart peddlers, selling everything from housewares to fruits, vegetables, fish and meat products, lined the streets for blocks on end.

Papa was terribly troubled by this great desecration of the Shabbos and racked his brain on how to prevent it. He advertised in the Yiddish paper for *baale-batim* who were interested in furthering *yiddishkeit* in New York City. Several men turned up. After he and a few other men organized the *Agudas Baale-Batim*, Papa and several cohorts from the organization decided to demonstrate against the *chillul Shabbos* on Orchard Street one Friday afternoon. Mama told me to follow Papa, as she knew how very rough and tough some of the Orchard Street peddlers could be and she feared that Papa might be harmed.

With Papa at the head, they marched down Orchard Street, stopping at each pushcart and explaining courteously that Shabbos was nearing and it was a great transgression of Jewish religious law to keep their pushcarts open on Shabbos. A very few of the peddlers took these words to heart and closed up, but most of them hurled insults at Papa and the others, and almost bodily pushed them away.

Papa did not give up. Each *erev* Shabbos, he strode down Orchard Street exhorting the peddlers to close their pushcarts, until he became a familiar figure to be ridiculed and assaulted.

When the *Agudas Baale-Batim* was able to raise enough funds, Papa said to each peddler, "How much will you earn during the Shabbos? I will give you the full amount if you close up your pushcart right now." This worked.

Within a few months, even the diehards capitulated. Papa's initiative and obstinacy closed the pushcarts on

Orchard Street, from Canal to Delancey Streets, on Shabbos. Instead, Orchard Street became a walking thoroughfare for people to stroll along on Shabbos and Yom Tov.

Laundry hung on clotheslines over the courtyard between two rows of tenement buildings: Part of the Lower East Side scene, where Papa grew up and lived.

8

Recruits to Papa's army

Rabbi Boruch Kaplan, the founder of the Bais Yaakov movement in America, was a close and dear *talmid* of Papa's.
"Rebbe," as he always called Papa, was the guiding force in his
life that inspired him to become the great *ben Torah* and *y'rei
shomayim* he is.

Reb Boruch's tape regarding his relationship with Papa
speaks for itself.

"My family arrived in New York from Europe before my
bar mitzva. My father sought a yeshiva for me, and Tiferes
Yerusholayim was chosen. Since it was the year of my *bar
mitzva*, in the evening I was in a group of students who were
taught *hilchos tefillin* by our principal, Rabbi Aaron Meister.

"I noticed that a man was teaching a group of young boys
Ein Yaakov and *Tanach* in the Tiferes Yerusholayim synagogue. My interest was aroused, and I went over to listen. His
teaching was so enjoyable that I soon joined the group and
became one of Reb Yaakov Yosef's steady *talmidim*.

"Reb Yaakov Yosef had such an attraction to his *talmidim*

....
y'rei shomayim: God-fearing / ***hilchos tefillin***: the laws of phylacteries

that we were drawn ever closer to him. He warmed our hearts with the love for Torah and *mitzvos*. He injected such fervor that after learning with him for an hour, I continued to study in the Montgomery *shtibel* until midnight.

"What impressed me most was that his teachings and his actions were synonymous. He was a holy man.

"After a year under his tutelage, Reb Yaakov Yosef encouraged me to transfer to the New Haven Yeshiva, where his son, Nochum Dovid, and a few of his other *talmidim* were already studying. There, he felt, I could make greater progress.

"Now, looking back, I marvel that he sent me away to New Haven. The normal approach of a teacher to a beloved student is to try to keep him nearby as long as possible. Reb Yaakov Yosef, however, was primarily concerned with the progress of his *talmidim*.

"New Haven Yeshiva was a stepping stone for me. Living in one building where I slept, ate and studied gave me additional hours for learning. The incentive to advance in Torah which had been instilled by my *rebbe* was still having its effect on me.

"The adminstration ordered all lights out at eleven PM so that the boys would get enough sleep. A few *talmidim* and I wanted to continue our learning. We quietly entered the kitchen, which had a gas jet that supplied us with sufficient light. There we studied until we heard the hoofs of the horses pulling their wagons delivering milk before dawn.

"When I came home on Sukkos after having learned at New Haven Yeshiva for a year and a half, I visited my *rebbe*. This time he advised me to go to Chevron Yeshiva in Eretz Yisroel. He had already sent Nochum Dovid there a few months earlier. He helped me with my traveling expenses.

"After the 1929 riots in Chevron, where my life was miraculously spared, I returned to the United States. My

---

shtibel: prayer room

parents, you can readily understand, were overjoyed to have me home. My *rebbe*, also, was elated to see me.

"I decided that I wanted to continue my Torah learning in Mirrer Yeshiva in Poland. It was a difficult decision to leave my family once again, and I needed much encouragement.

"In my *rebbe*'s house, each Shabbos afternoon there was a *minyon* for *mincha*. He wanted his personal *sefer Torah* to be read from at least once a week. My *rebbe* gave me an *aliya*.

"After the prayers, he quoted from the portion of the Torah that was read for me: Deuteronomy 12:9, 'For you are not as yet come to the rest and to the inheritance, which the Lord your God giveth you.'

" 'You see, Boruch, these words are a sign that you should go to Mir, where you will reach higher attainments in your learning.'

"Thanks to my *rebbe* and his great encouragement and influence, I studied in Mir and other European yeshivos, where I advanced greatly in Torah.

"I want to mention several of my *rebbe*'s actions to give just an idea of what a *tzaddik* he was. He was not interested in material things. He sought only to do the will of Hashem and to obey His commandments.

" 'What more does the Boss expect of me?' he questioned himself time and time again. The Torah tells us that one who loves doing a *mitzva* is never satisfied that he has done enough. My *rebbe* demonstrated this to a very high degree.

"For instance, in the early morning on his way to prayers, he passed a bakery. He would hurry inside and toss a log of wood into the blazing stove. Since a non-Jew manned the stove, the bread would have been considered *pas akum* (bread baked by a non-Jew). By his action my *rebbe* removed that stigma.

"Once as he rode on the subway to his business, he chatted with another Jew, who mentioned that he needed to arise at

----

aliya: call to read from the Torah / *tzaddik*: very pious man

four AM in order to get to work on time. From that moment Reb Yaakov Yosef could not rest.

" 'Imagine,' he said, 'this man awakens so early for material reasons. Surely, I should arise at that hour to accomplish more *mitzvos* and learning.'

"I wondered how he could expect more from himself. He fasted each day. After evening prayers, he gave several *shiurim* to the young boys and to older men. At about ten at night he went home to eat the first meal of the day.

"My *rebbe* repeated to his *talmidim* the important creed of being *mezakeh es harabbim* (helping the many to do *mitzvos*). 'The Satan is constantly undermining the Jew to cause him to sin. It is a daily battle, which we must seek to overcome. It is written in our Torah that one who makes the many gain merit will not come to sin. It is an insurance against sinning.'

"My *rebbe,* Reb Yaakov Yosef, lives on forever in my heart and mind."

Rabbi Shachne Zohn, a former *rosh yeshiva* in Torah Vodaas in Brooklyn, New York, and presently *rosh yeshiva* of a *kollel* in Yerusholayim, is a product of Papa's special care.

At thirteen years of age, he was attending public school on the East Side. After school, his father sent him to the Mordechai Rosenblatt Talmud Torah, at 134 Henry Street, where he received religious training for an hour and a half.

Mr. Zohn had a little cap business that kept him occupied all week. The few hours on Shabbos which he was able to spare for his son were too few to instill in Shachne the love for Torah learning.

His father, therefore, was concerned about his son's religious education. He knew Papa and had heard of his deep influence on young boys. He brought Shachne to Papa and placed him under Papa's guidance. Papa immediately withdrew him from public school and registered him in Rabbi Jacob Joseph Yeshiva.

Shachne joined the group of forty-five boys to whom Papa

taught *Ein Yaakov* in English each evening at Tiferes Yerusholayim.

A short while after Shachne began studying at the yeshiva, Papa used his tactful pressure to convince Shachne to go to the New Haven Yeshiva, where Nochum Dovid, Chaim Scheinberg, Boruch Kaplan, Reuven Epstein and a few of Papa's other *talmidim* were already studying at Papa's urging.

Papa checked up on all of his *talmidim*. He was in constant touch with Rabbi Levenberg, founder of New Haven Yeshiva, and the other *roshei yeshiva* on the progress of his "boys." When they returned home for the Yomim Tovim, he inquired into every detail of their lives and learning.

When Shachne had completed four years of study in New Haven Yeshiva, Papa advised him to go to Mir, Poland. Papa was traveling to Europe on business, and Shachne and a few of his other *talmidim* accompanied him.

Reb Shachne told me the following: "Had it not been for Reb Yaakov Yosef, I and countless other young Jewish boys would have been crushed under the wheels of mundane society and remained 'street boys' our entire lives. The year I sat at your father's table listening to his teachings built the sound foundation of my Torah learning and life.

"His teachings were from the heart and reached our hearts."

Rabbi Shmuel Shechter is a Torah educator both in America and in Eretz Yisroel. He was originally from Montreal, Canada, and was a *talmid* in Yeshivas Rabbi Yitzchok Elchonon in upper Manhattan.

He first met Papa as a teenage boy, when Papa was delivering *shiurim* in the yeshiva on the famous *mussar sefer Mesillas Yeshorim*, written several centuries ago by Rabbi Moshe Chaim Luzzatto.

These *shiurim* were given regularly every Sunday night for

....

mussar sefer: book on ethics

half a year to a group of about fifty boys who crowded into one of the dormitory rooms. The *talmidim* felt a need for spiritual elevation and inspiration, and these *shiurim* filled that gap.

They were clandestine *shiurim* because Papa was spirited into Yeshivas Rabbi Yitzchok Elchonon without the knowledge of the administration. Much to the regret of these young men, Papa's lectures were discontinued when the administration became aware that a stranger, who was not on their staff, was teaching some of their students.

The administration assured the *talmidim* that another *rebbe* would be engaged to continue these lectures; however, the new teacher could not meet Papa's high standard and the boys soon lost interest.

One of the *talmidim* was Rabbi Avigdor Miller, an outstanding influence on the Jewish scene today whose books and tapes are an inspiration to many. During this short but concentrated contact, Papa infused him with much of the spiritual vigor that remains with him until today.

Rabbi Shechter avers, "Many outstanding *bnei Torah* and personalities certainly owe your father a great debt of appreciation. Your father nurtured our Torah aspirations, which ultimately led many of us to travel to European yeshivos to advance our studies.

"This, in turn, was the nucleus of the Torah movement in America, which has such far-reaching effects to this very day."

Added note:

Papa himself sent approximately fifty young men to Mir and other European yeshivos over a period of time. In addition to them, a substantial number of young men also went to these yeshivos as a result of the example set by Papa's *talmidim*.

Papa also gave financial assistance to some of his *talmidim* — paying for their travel expenses and helping toward their support.

Rabbi Noson Wachtfogel, the *mashgiach* of Lakewood

Yeshiva, was one of Papa's staunch followers and still refers to him as "Rebbe." He met Papa in 1929, when he and Rabbi Yehuda Davis decided that they wanted to go to a European yeshiva to pursue their Torah studies. It was a new idea, and they sought encouragement.

Reb Noson had heard about Papa, his *hachnosas orchim,* and his many other religious activities, which included a deep concern for Jewish youth. They decided to spend a Shabbos in our house and meet with Papa personally.

As Reb Noson tells it, they needed no invitation or reservation. They put in their appearance Friday night after *davening.* They were quite surprised to find a conglomeration of about twenty-five *orchim* of different ethnic origin — Sephardi, Yemenite, European and American. During *sholosh seudos* Papa's *dvar Torah* dealt with *middos tovos,* stressing the importance of humility.

Reb Noson had never met a person of Papa's caliber, from whom the special glow of the holiness of Shabbos radiated. His Shabbos in our house and his meeting with Papa made such an impression on him that it gave him enough impetus to want to remain a true *ben Torah,* and not just an observant Jew, his entire life.

Reb Noson and Reb Yehuda had a lengthy discussion with Papa regarding their desire to go overseas to study Torah. Papa applauded their endeavor so heartily that after just one talk with him, they embarked for Europe.

Reb Noson had occasion to meet with Papa once again, at Nochum Dovid's home in Mir, when Papa made a trip to Europe in 1931. He recalls that Papa mentioned that he felt it important to speak to the *mashgiach,* Reb Yeruchem, of the need to strengthen the yeshiva boys to abstain from talking during the entire prayer services. The *mashgiach* heeded Papa's

----

mashgiach: supervisor / *middos tovos*: good qualities
ben (plural *b'nei*) *Torah*: literally, son of the Torah

suggestion, and the Mirrer Yeshiva students soon heard a long *shmuess* on this topic.

Seven years later, when Reb Noson returned to the United States, a few *bnei Torah*, including Reb Noson, Rabbis Boruch Kaplan, Shmuel Shechter and Moshe Gordon, invited Papa to attend a meeting for the express purpose of spreading Torah in America. During this meeting, Papa, who was much older than the others, was asked his opinion, and he expressed himself: "I am sitting among outstanding *bnei Torah*. I do not have to offer suggestions. Just tell me what I have to do and I am ready."

Several ideas were presented, which later came to fruition. Rabbi Boruch Kaplan was advised to organize a Bais Yaakov. Reb Noson and Reb Shmuel founded the first *kollel* in White Plains, New York, known as the Beth Medrash Govoha. Subsequently, Rabbi Aaron Kotler became the *rosh yeshiva* and transferred the Beth Medrash Govoha to Lakewood, New Jersey. It is now one of the greatest, world-renowned Torah centers.

Rabbi Mordecai Yoffe grew up in Baltimore. As a young man, he went to Europe to study, at the encouragement of one of Papa's followers. He spent six years diligently studying Torah in the yeshivos of Lomza, Mir and Kaminetz.

When he returned to the United States in 1938 and settled in New York, he became a frequent visitor to Papa's house and grew attached to him. It was time for Mordecai to get married, but it was not easy in those days to find a suitable girl who was interested in marrying a *ben Torah*.

One day as he was walking along Norfolk Street on the East Side, he met Papa. Papa realized that Mordecai was very discouraged because all his attempts to meet the "right girl" seemed to be headed in the wrong direction.

Papa grasped his hand as they walked together and said to him, "Reb Mortchi, let me tell you a story. There was a rich

....
kollel: institute for advanced study by young married men

Jew in Warsaw, Poland, who had a very profitable business. When he passed on, his son inherited the business. Though the son followed the same procedures as his father, he met with no success. After a period of time, the business was close to failure.

"It was then that the son sought the advice of his *rebbe*. He confided to the *rebbe* his deep concern about the deterioration of the business. The *rebbe* listened carefully to the son's discouraging tale and asked him, 'Tell me, what did your father do when there were no customers in the store?'

"The son answered, 'Whenever my father had a moment to spare, he engrossed himself in Torah learning or recited *tehillim.*'

" 'And what do you do when the store is empty?' the *rebbe* questioned the son.

" 'I am not like my father. I read a newspaper or talk to a neighbor.'

" 'Now I have the answer to give you,' said the *rebbe.* 'When Satan saw your father busy learning Torah or reciting *tehillim,* he was troubled. He therefore sent many customers to make sure that your father should not occupy himself with Torah studies. Of course, the business flourished. In your case, Satan is quite content when no customers appear, as you are busy with mundane activities.' "

Papa finished his story and said to Reb Mortchi, "You also are pleasing Satan. He notices that you cannot concentrate on your Torah studies and keeps you occupied trying to find your *zivug,* but he does all in his power not to allow her to reach you. Start your Torah learning in earnest, and Satan will see to it that your partner will put in her appearance very quickly."

Reb Mortchi heeded Papa's advice and once again became dedicated to his Torah studies. Not long after that, he met his wife, Hannah. Reb Mortchi said to me, "I followed your father's excellent advice through different phases of my life, and it always proved to be correct."

Reb Mortchi further said to me, "As Abraham, our father, brought Hashem down to earth and made many people become believers in God, so your father brought Hashem down to America and inspired many young men to follow the path of Torah."

Rabbi Mordecai Yoffe and his wife, Hannah, brought up a generation of *bnei Torah*. He is the *rosh yeshiva* of Bais Torah in Monsey, New York.

Every Shabbos, after *sholosh seudos* Papa gave *hashkofo* talks to Hashomer Hadati, a group sponsored by Hapoel Hamizrachi, which had its quarters in a basement on Henry Street near Rabbi Jacob Joseph Yeshiva. About forty to fifty young boys gathered to listen to Papa's inspirational talks.

One of the group leaders was Louis Gertz. He told me, "Your father actually hypnotized the boys with his stimulating lectures. They listened wide-eyed and open-eared as he thundered his message to them and aroused them to an everlasting love for Hashem. The group leaders were also influenced by Mr. Herman's wise counsel."

Some of these counselors and young boys became prominent rabbis and important laymen who propagated Papa's words, "Come to the call." Mr. Louis Gertz is one of the well-known laymen on whom Papa's Shabbos talks left a permanent impression. His charity is widespread, to the needy in general and to yeshivos in particular. His children are all *bnei Torah*.

Since Zeidy Andron had founded Rabbi Jacob Joseph Yeshiva, Papa took a special interest in its welfare. One morning, he entered the office to find an elderly woman crying. Near her sat a young boy.

When Papa asked the principal the reason for the woman's tears, he was told that she had been coming daily to the yeshiva to plead that her grandson be enrolled. However, the boy, who was now twelve years old, had had no previous Hebrew

----

hashkofo: Torah outlook

education. As the principal explained to Papa, "Reb Yaakov Yosef, there is no class appropriate for him. I cannot place a twelve-year-old with beginners who are six years old."

Papa motioned to the discouraged woman to follow him. As they left the office, the old woman broken-heartedly said to Papa, "Within a year my grandson will become *bar mitzva*, and he will not even know how to recite the blessing on the Torah. I do not have the money to hire a special teacher to prepare him. I cannot sleep nights worrying about my grandson, as the entire burden is on me."

Papa comforted the grandmother, assuring her that he would prepare her grandson so that he could be eligible for a class in the yeshiva appropriate for him. The woman brightened perceptibly at this encouraging news from a total stranger.

From that day on, Papa not only set aside time to acquaint the boy with religious concepts, but also hired a special *rebbe* to teach him, beginning with the basics.

Within six months, the boy was placed in a suitable class in the yeshiva. At his *bar mitzva*, he recited all the blessings, much to the pride of his grandmother, who blessed Papa with many additional *brochos*.

Papa kept an eye on him, and in time, this boy grew to be a true *ben Torah*, who now occupies a prominent position in his community.

One afternoon, a middle-aged woman came seeking Papa. "I have something very important to discuss with him," she said nervously. Papa was not at home. I told her to return in the evening.

That evening, when Papa came home from giving his *shiur,* the woman was waiting for him. "Mr. Herman, I was recommended to you by someone who said that you are the one who could help me with my problem.

....
brochos: blessings

"I have an only child, a son, who is nearing twenty. He works in a grocery store as a clerk and is forced to work on Shabbos; otherwise, he will lose his job. He is my only support, since my husband passed away, but I want him to be a religious Jew." She broke down into sobs.

Mama ran over to comfort her. "Don't worry," Mama said, "my husband will help you." I ran to get her a cup of tea.

"I want to meet with your son as soon as possible. Can he be here tomorrow night?" Papa asked. The next night Mrs. E. and her son, "Martin," were in our house.

Papa had a long conversation with the young man. Afterward, Papa told him, "I will help you in every way, but the first thing you must do is to stop working on Shabbos and Yom Tov."

"I do not like to work on Saturday," Martin said. "But where will I find a job without working Saturday?" he asked.

"Don't worry, the Boss will provide for you and your mother," Papa assured him.

The next morning, Martin informed the owner of the grocery store that he could not work late any more on Friday afternoon, or on Saturdays and holidays. The owner was most disturbed, since it was just a few days before the High Holy Days.

"Martin," the owner begged him, "just work past the holidays, and then I will allow you to be free on Saturdays." Of course, Martin told him emphatically that it was not possible for him to ever work again on Saturdays or holidays. Once the owner was convinced that his employee was willing even to lose his job, he yielded, because Martin was a very diligent and honest worker.

From that time on, Martin became another of our adopted sons. Each night after work, he came to our house where Papa taught him the basic laws of Torah. His mother was our frequent guest also, delighting in the knowledge that her only son was following the path of Torah. For the first time since she had become a widow, she had peace of mind, knowing that her son was under the guidance of Papa, who took a personal interest in his every footstep.

About a year later, Martin confided in Papa that a presentable girl frequented his grocery store to shop, and that he was interested in her. Papa asked him to bring her to our house. He brought the young lady to visit us. She was a lovely, graceful girl, who won our hearts immediately. She expressed the desire to become a religious woman, who would undertake to follow the commandments of the Torah.

Several months later, they were married in our house. It was a happy day for all concerned, and Mrs. E. was relieved that her son had married a fine, Jewish girl.

Martin and his wife are an ideal couple, who became firm, staunch Jews. Their children and grandchildren are a pride to our Jewish nation. They remained part of our family.

Benny lived on our block. He went to public school and was far from *yiddishkeit*. As a young lad, he was undisciplined. Whenever I saw him coming my way, I tried to avoid him.

Papa did his best to coax him to come up to our house on Shabbos, but he was no easy target. Finally, Papa gained his confidence and succeeded in getting him to come. Mama stuffed Benny with all the goodies possible. He became a steady customer at our house.

Slowly, Benny not only digested Mama's good food, but also Papa's subtle teachings, and he responded to the warmth and interest they showed him. Papa encouraged him to leave public school and attend a yeshiva.

When Benny was a young man, Papa convinced him to go to Mir, where he developed into a real *yeshiva bochur*. Though Benny's family was not enthusiastic about Papa's Orthodox ways, they were proud of their son, whom they respected for his strict adherence to the principles of religion and Torah.

He married into a well-known religious family, and his offspring are following in his footsteps.

Once when Papa was teaching his group of young boys in Tiferes Yerusholayim, a young man entered. "Can I help you?" Papa asked him.

"I read an advertisement in the newspaper that an evening class is being started to teach young men Torah studies in Yavne Yeshiva on Henry Street. I just went to the address listed in the ad, but found it closed, with no sign of anyone there. As I walked by, I noticed this yeshiva and hoped I could get some information," the young man said inquiringly.

"Why don't you sit down and wait until I finish my teaching? We can then discuss it further," Papa advised him.

The discussion that followed revealed that Chaim Michel Warshavsky had arrived in New York several years before, from Europe. He had received some religious training before his immigration to the United States. Now he was employed in a bookbinding shop. He very much wished to take up his Torah learning once more, and he was seeking someone to help him.

Papa became the "someone." He soon discovered that Chaim possessed great potential, and he spent much time teaching him the laws of the Torah and its moral aspect. He aroused in Chaim a fervent desire to pursue his Torah studies further.

Chaim was drawn to Papa as to a magnet and spent every spare moment in our house. Mama treated him like a son, and, to me, he was the big brother to replace Davie, who was rarely home.

His parents and family did not see much of Chaim, for even on many Yomim Tovim he walked from his house in the Bronx (a two-and-a-half-hour walk) to celebrate with us.

On the subway, riding to and from his work, he used the time to good advantage to become well-versed in the Talmud. Every night, when Chaim returned at six o'clock from his job, he continued his studies—many times until well after midnight. There came a time when he had mastered the entire *shas*.

Eventually, Chaim opened his own bookbinding business.

Reb Chaim Warshavsky (who became afterwards Chaim Warshaw). He maintained a bindery in the Chelsea district of New York City (in the building he owned), and remained a liberal dispenser of charity.

As it prospered, he became known for his open hand in dispensing charity. Many of our *orchim* found their way to Chaim's shop to receive financial aid for themselves, or for the yeshiva or other institution they were representing. He also helped Papa with the expenses needed to send Papa's *talmidim* to various yeshivos overseas.

After his marriage, Chaim continued his Torah studies and his support of *bnei Torah.* His son-in-law is Rabbi Yeruchem Kaplan, grandson of Rabbi Yeruchem Levovitz, who was the Mirrer *mashgiach.* Reb Chaim's children and grandchildren follow in his holy footsteps, the path shown to him by Papa.

One day, Chaim Warshavsky confided in me that Papa was sending him on a very important mission to Europe with an urgent message to the Chofetz Chaim in Radun. Of course Chaim aroused my curiosity to a high pitch.

I always felt that I could approach Papa about anything that bothered me. This time, when I questioned Papa about Chaim's impending trip, he answered shortly, "Ruchoma, this is something I cannot tell you." Even Mama seemed to be in the dark. At the last minute, Papa changed his mind and Chaim did not leave.

It was many years later that Nochum Dovid revealed what this very urgent message to the Chofetz Chaim was. I asked him to allow me to include this extraordinary experience in this book, and I received his permission.

A Jew was plowing his field in Eretz Yisroel. As he dug deeper, he suddenly felt the earth give way, revealing a deep cave below. He lowered himself into the cave by means of a long rope. Though the cave was pitch dark, the wondrous golden treasures he beheld brightened the cave as if the bright rays of the sun were within.

When he had regained his composure a bit, he examined the golden objects more closely. The full realization of what these treasures were awed him into immobility.

They were assuredly the sacred vessels of the *Beis Hamikdosh* that must have been buried during the destruction of the Temple, almost two thousand years before.

He covered the cave with earth, so that in no way was it evident that there was an opening below. The fearful discovery weighed heavily on the Jew's heart and mind. He sought a wise and learned man to whom he could unburden himself. However, he did not want to divulge this secret to anyone in Eretz Yisroel for fear it might leak out. He decided to travel to the United States.

When he arrived in New York, he made subtle inquiries regarding a person who could help him with a religious issue. He was advised to see Papa.

For a few days he came to Tiferes Yerusholayim and listened to Papa giving *shiurim*. He then approached Papa and told him exactly what he had witnessed in Eretz Yisroel.

When Papa was completely convinced that the Jew was telling him the truth, Papa decided that the only person in the world to be entrusted with this fearful discovery was the Chofetz Chaim.

....

Beis Hamikdosh: Holy Temple (in Jerusalem)

At first, Papa wanted to send Chaim Warshavsky to the Chofetz Chaim, but for reasons unknown, he changed his mind. Instead, Papa sent a registered letter to Nochum Dovid, who was studying in Mir, Poland. He enclosed a sealed letter to the Chofetz Chaim and instructed Nochum Dovid to take it to him immediately, without opening it.

Nochum Dovid left for Radun right away, carrying with him Papa's message. Since Papa's handwriting was not very legible, the Chofetz Chaim asked Nochum Dovid to read the letter to him. The Chofetz Chaim listened very intently as Nochum Dovid did so. He then took some *seforim* from his bookcase and became deeply engrossed in them.

After a while, he said to Nochum Dovid that according to the description of the discovery site, these golden vessels could very well be the holy vessels of the *Beis Hamikdosh.*

The Chofetz Chaim then lit a match and burned Papa's letter to ashes. He advised Nochum Dovid not to reveal anything to anyone about this matter, and added, "As long as this Jew lives, the secret will be kept."

Many years later, when Nochum Dovid settled in Yerusholayim, Papa and he suddenly recalled this remarkable happening. Papa said to Nochum Dovid, "The Jew must have passed away without revealing the secret, as the Chofetz Chaim prophesied."

As I write this, I am sure that all who read this most unusual and authentic experience will gain new faith and hope that our Jewish nation will be redeemed. May we live to see the rebuilding of our holy Temple with its holy vessels safely within its inner sanctuary.

....

seforim: books

9

Papa's business of mitzvos

Papa was involved in several "business" enterprises besides his fur business: *hachnosas orchim* (see "Papa Corners the Market"); the business of *mezakeh es harabbim*, and the Yomim Tovim business.

When Prohibition was enacted by federal law, the manufacture, transport and sale of alcoholic beverages were forbidden. Papa was concerned that it would be difficult to obtain kosher wine for sacramental purposes. He immediately got busy; he converted one of our bedrooms into a winery and learned the fine art of manufacturing wine. There was a steady stream of customers requesting Papa's kosher wine.

Before long, he was discovered preparing wine and was summoned to court. He asserted that the Prohibition Act did not apply to him, since his wine-making was solely for religious purposes, without thought of personal profit. He pleaded his case so convincingly that the judge dismissed it. Papa continued his wine business until the Prohibition Act was finally repealed.

Cholov yisroel was sold only in a few grocery stores. It was of prime importance to Papa that it be made readily available to every Jewish household.

He negotiated with the Balsam Farms and hired a young man with a small truck to initiate a *cholov yisroel* delivery route. The demand for *cholov yisroel* grew. In time, many other religious Jews started their own *cholov yisroel* delivery businesses.

The careful preparation of "eighteen-minute machine matzo" for Pesach was not in practice. Papa went to several well-known matzo factories and asked to be allowed to supervise and inspect the baking of matzo, stopping the machines every eighteen minutes to have them cleaned thoroughly.

Of course, the owners of the factories did not take kindly to such an odd request. Finally, Goodman Brothers accepted Papa's proposition.

Papa was completely absorbed in his Pesach business. By word of mouth, it was advertised throughout the East Side. Papa decided to add other Pesach items as well: prunes, for which he sent a *mashgiach* to Oregon to supervise the drying and packing process; freshly ground coffee, which was carefully watched from the picking of the coffee bean through the packaging; and spices—cinnamon, pepper and ginger—which had a special *mashgiach.*

Papa wanted Jews who lived in different parts of New York to be made aware of his special kosher products for Pesach. In the late evenings, he took time to ride to friends he knew to spread the word.

Rabbi Alexander (Sender) Linchner (founder of Boys' Town, Jerusalem) was a close friend of our family. As a young boy, he studied together with Nochum Dovid in New Haven Yeshiva. Reb Sender was originally from South Norwalk, Connecticut, and each time he traveled to New York, our house

....

cholov yisroel: milk produced under Jewish supervision

was one of his first stops. He enjoyed the friendly atmosphere of the Herman household, and always looked forward to meeting some important *roshei yeshiva* and *rabbonim, orchim* of ours.

One night, quite late, when he had been married for only a short while and was living in East New York, Brooklyn, he was very surprised to open the door to Reb Yaakov Yosef Herman. He immediately invited Papa into his home, honored by the visit.

Papa soon clarified his mission. Would Reb Sender be interested in purchasing supervised matzo and other food products for Pesach?

Reb Sender could not believe his ears. Since he could only buy a small order for himself and his wife, the profit would be in pennies. In Sender's boyhood, he remembered Papa as the wealthy furrier. He marveled that Reb Yaakov Yosef took the time and effort to come especially to his home. When Papa realized what Reb Sender was thinking, he explained, "Whether the profits are in the thousands of dollars or in pennies, we must do our share, and leave the rest up to the Boss." Rabbi Linchner never forgot this incident, which left a deep impression upon him.

Reb Sender told me of another remarkable aspect of Papa's personality. He knew Papa through different stages of his life: as a young and rich man, when he lost his fur business and most of his money, and when he lived in Eretz Yisroel in his latter years. He never saw Papa moody, sad, worried or distraught. Papa was always satisfied with his lot, busy with his "business of *mitzvos*," and above all, a true soldier of the Boss.

On Purim, our house abounded with *orchim* and resounded with joy. The house overflowed with all the *mishlo'ach monos* we received from our relatives, friends and Papa's *talmidim*. Papa treated each *orech* to special drinks, while Mama plied them with delicious food. When the *orchim* left late at night,

....
mishlo'ach monos: gifts of food sent on Purim

each one carried with him a large bag of goodies that Mama had prepared.

Each Thursday morning Mama went shopping for fish. When I was free from school, I went along. The pushcarts on Hester Street were filled with every type of fish. As Mama proceeded down the street, the peddlers would call out to her, "Mrs. Herman, give me your business today."

Mama made sure to divide her purchases among several pushcarts. She picked up a large carp, opened its head and smelled the gills. Often, she would turn up her nose and exclaim, "Pfew, this fish smells from kerosene," or "This fish lived many years ago." She was an expert, and the peddlers never fooled her.

When two large baskets were filled to capacity with different varieties of fish, we headed home. Mama allowed me only to grasp a handle of one of the baskets, while she grasped the other handle in one hand, and carried the second basket in her other hand.

In time Mama became round-shouldered from carrying such heavy loads. However, she never uttered a word of complaint.

Mama did her shopping as close as possible to Shabbos and Yom Tov so the food would not spoil. (There were no refrigerators in those days.) Every other day, the iceman delivered a large block of ice. We could never leave our house for too long a time, as the basin under the icebox had to be emptied at regular intervals; otherwise, it would flood the kitchen.

One Thursday in the early morning, a few days before Pesach, Uncle Feivish (we called him Uncle Frank), Mama's youngest brother, came running into our house. "Aidel, I'm glad I caught you before you went shopping. I have a day off from my office and I am taking you shopping today. I have my car parked downstairs."

"Feivish," Mama asked him smilingly, "how will it look if I

ride down Hester Street in your fancy large car?" However, Uncle Frank would not take "No" for an answer.

Mama and I got into the car. It had soft, velour plush seats, and I sank into one of them. Mama sat up front with Uncle Frank. It was not easy for him to maneuver his large car down Hester Street, where the street was narrowed because of the pushcarts lining either side.

As we rode slowly down Hester Street, the peddlers and vendors looked on in surprise, which turned into open amazement, as Mama got out of the car. They treated her with new respect.

Mama took advantage of the fact that she would not have to carry her heavy baskets home, and she shopped for her quota of fish and for as many other fruits and vegetables as she could buy. It took quite a while.

However, Uncle Frank was having a difficult time. All the kids on the block flocked over to view the car. Soon they were climbing all over the dashboard, peering into the windows and smearing their dirty hands over the shiny blue exterior. All Uncle Frank's threats of punishment did not frighten or drive them away.

When he finally arrived home, Mama was smiling broadly, but poor Uncle Frank was a total wreck, as was his car. He never offered to take us shopping again.

Before Pesach, our house was usually painted. When the job was completed, Papa took the ladder, climbed up to the open doorway of our dining room with a large hammer in his hand, and the *zeicher l'churbon* ceremony began.

He pounded the newly painted wall over the doorway until there was no trace of paint left. Mama pleaded, "Yankev Yosef, not such a big *zeicher*," but her words never helped.

Papa descended from the ladder with a gleam in his eyes, as he examined his handiwork.

....

zeicher l'churbon: remembrance of the destruction (of the Holy Temple)

Papa prepared a huge bowl of *charoses* for the Pesach *seder*, which he distributed to the entire community. *Erev* Pesach, the door constantly was opened for the many who came to partake of this special consideration. Papa even prepared little white paper containers for the *charoses.*

We did a record business with *orchim* for Pesach and added extra tables to accommodate them. The sparkling white tablecloths did not remain white very long. As soon as *kiddush* started, inevitably, one of our *orchim* overturned his cup of wine and stained the cloth. Mama gazed at the red-stained tablecloth and whispered softly, "Now I know Pesach is really here."

Since I was the youngest, I was given the honor of asking the "Four Questions." Papa prepared me well in advance. Mama dressed me in my new holiday clothes. For me, it was the main event of the *seder.* I felt like a performer on the stage, with so many *orchim* listening.

Of course, many of our *orchim* did not understand my recital in English, and Papa had to translate the "Four Questions" into Yiddish.

The "Three Weeks" were an ordeal that I dreaded as they approached. From the seventeenth of Tammuz until Tisha b'Av, our house was a somber place to live in. Every laugh or giggle elicited a reproving glance from Papa.

The tragic destruction of our Holy Temple was a living occurrence which pervaded every corner of our house and affected every facet of our life. The "Nine Days" before Tisha b'Av were a time of real mourning. Papa did not allow us to go any place, or to pay any visits. In fact, he even discouraged our friends from visiting us.

charoses: mixture of chopped fruit, nuts and wine into which the bitter herbs are dipped

Papa's shoulders sagged from the weight of his sorrow. His face grew lined. The destruction of the *Beis Hamikdosh* was not a happening of some time in the distant past, but right here and now. When Tisha b'Av ended, I sighed with relief, though it took a few days longer until the Herman household returned to its normal liveliness.

Rosh Chodesh Elul brought a different reaction from Papa. He led us to understand the solemnity of the days ahead. Papa talked to us at length about examining our actions and improving them. "You have to greet the Boss on the New Year as a 'new' person."

On Rosh Hashona and Yom Kippur Papa was the *chazen* for *shachris* in the Tiferes Yerusholayim *shul*. His ringing, pleading voice praying to Hashem to forgive our sins and grant us a good year inspired the congregants to penitence. The women's section was bathed in tears while Papa *davened.* "Only Reb Yankev Yosef could open our hearts to repentance," the women used to say to each other.

On Rosh Hashona, our house with its many *orchim* was filled with the Yom Tov spirit. Mama prepared different varieties of honeyed food, which our *orchim* ate down to the last morsel.

Erev Yom Kippur, Papa took his cot bed to *shul*. He did not leave the *shul* during the entire fast day. After the fast, when Papa came home carrying the cot bed, Mama remarked, "Nu, Yankev Yosef, did you close up the *shul* already?" Our *orchim* were almost through with their meal by then. Papa looked pale, but his eyes were aglow with a special spiritual brightness. He still wore his white *kittel* and looked like an angel.

I could hardly wait to welcome the joyous days of Sukkos. Right after the fast, when the last of our *orchim* had departed, Papa said with his customary sprightliness, "It is time to build

---

chazen: cantor, prayer leader / *kittel*: prayer coat

our *sukka*. Let's get busy." From that moment there was a complete metamorphosis in our house.

With Papa in the lead, we scrambled down the two flights of stairs. He unlocked the cellar door, and we felt our way down another flight of stairs to the dark, damp cellar below. All our Pesach tables and cartons stood patiently on one side, while on the other side, waiting expectantly for us, were all the boards of our *sukka,* the benches and folding tables.

Papa lugged the heavier boards, and we carried the lighter ones, chattering with excitement. Up we climbed to the top floor, then up another rickety staircase that led to our roof.

Papa started building the *sukka* that same night. It was a spacious one, with enough room to seat all our *orchim*. It was also large enough for Papa and a few of our *orchim* to sleep there.

We children had a free rein in decorating the *sukka*. Mama had special brocaded material to cover the walls. A large tapestry, depicting an ancient palace, covered one wall and gave our *sukka* an air of antiquity. From the *sechach*, we hung bunches of large purple grapes, bright yellow *esrogim,* red-cheeked apples, green pears, and lavishly colored decorations to fill the gaps.

When Papa finally made *kiddush* in his clear, resounding voice on the first night of Sukkos, he did so in a sweet-scented, picturesque garden.

It was a giant undertaking for a one-woman team to prepare food for all our *orchim*. Though we helped Mama as much as we could, she bore the brunt of it all. Mama had to be a master mathematician to figure out how much food to buy, because there was no way of knowing exactly how many *orchim* would show up. Papa often invited extra *orchim* from *shul* at the last minute. This meant dozens of trips to the chicken market and to the Hester Street pushcarts for the fish, fruits

------

sechach: roof covering made of tree branches or other plant materials
esrogim: citrons

and vegetables. Fortunately, we ordered such large quantities of grocery products that they, at least, were delivered.

Our house was so crammed with food *erev* Yom Tov that it resembled a miniature supermarket. Mama did all her own baking of *challa* and cake. She also opened all the chickens and *kashered* them herself. Her hands were chapped and sore from soaking, salting and rinsing the chickens and the meat.

Papa provided a hoisting apparatus which brought up the food from below and inevitably brought down the mound of dishes to be washed. Mama trusted no one with the hot chicken-and-noodle soup, and she climbed up to the roof to serve it herself. We had a serving table right outside the *sukka.*

Once I complained to Mama, "I wish the cord would snap, so I would not have to wash so many dishes." A few days later, a mishap occurred and the hoisting apparatus dumped some of the dishes down the stairs, where they broke. Mama looked at me accusingly, "Ruchoma, you must never wish for something bad to happen." For a few days, I had a guilty conscience.

I really did not mind washing the dishes, for the joy of Yom Tov permeated our house. On *chol hamoed* a steady flow of relatives and friends ate their dinners in our *sukka.* Mama cooked from morning to night. I had to run up and down so many times, helping to serve, that at night when I went to bed my feet were painful with charley horse.

Once our *sukka* was discovered by a fire inspector who declared it a fire hazard. Papa was given a summons to appear in court the next morning. Papa, dressed in a long *kapota* and a black velvet round hat entered the courtroom. He feigned a lack of English (which was common in those days), and an interpreter was brought in.

"Mr. Herman, you are charged with building an illegal wooden hut on your roof. It is a fire hazard and must be torn

kapota: coat

down immediately." The interpreter translated the judge's decree into Yiddish.

"Tell the judge I will comply with his order, but I have to hire someone to help me. It will take at least two weeks," Papa explained.

The judge heard Papa's request through the interpreter. "Sorry, I cannot allow a two-week period of time to elapse. I give you eight days to tear it down, or you will be fined heavily," the judge said severely.

In eight days, Papa heeded the order, and our *sukka* was dismantled.

Papa built a *sukka* in the back yard of his fur shop. Though he never did any business on *chol hamoed*, he kept his shop open in order to make a *sukka* available to the many Jews who worked in his vicinity.

On Simchas Torah in Yeshiva Tiferes Yerusholayim, Papa took part in every *hakofo*. With his own *sefer Torah* clasped in his hands, he danced and jumped with such fervor that most of the people in *shul* had their eyes glued on him.

"How does Reb Yankev Yosef keep on like that?" I overheard some of them asking. I, too, asked the same question, as I watched Papa dance without a stop. He showed no sign of fatigue, his face radiant.

For the last days of Sukkos, Mama prepared not only the main meals, but also a giant *kiddush* on Simchas Torah for all the congregants of the Tiferes Yerusholayim *shul*, who crowded into our house to sing, dance and eat her delicious *teiglach* and other delicacies.

Mama took all this in her stride. Only on one occasion do I recall Mama losing her composure.

It was the night of Hoshana Rabba. Papa went to *shul*,

---

hakofo: circuit / *teiglach*: honey cookies

where he remained the entire night, learning. It was almost midnight, and Mama was still busy *kashering* twenty-four chickens in relays of six.

I sat on a high stool watching Mama salt the chickens. It was a work of art. She sprinkled the salt so evenly into every crevice and nook of each chicken that it flowed like silvery rain drops falling from the sky.

The warm, quiet kitchen and the constant motion of Mama's hand almost lulled me to sleep. I emitted a deep yawn.

"Go to sleep, Ruchoma. You helped enough today." I was happy to obey Mama and ran off to bed.

In my sleep, I felt a tugging and heard an insistent voice from afar, "Get up, Ruchoma! Get up!"

I struggled through to consciousness to see Mama bending over me. "What time is it?" I asked drowsily.

"It's the middle of the night," Mama answered.

I sat up abruptly. "What's the matter, Mama?"

"I was just putting away all the *pupiklach* of the chickens I had finished *kashering,* and I noticed that on one *pupik* there seems to be a *shaileh.*" Mama's words ended in a stifled sob. "They are all mixed up now, so if this *pupik* is *treif,* all the chickens will be considered . . ." Mama did not finish the sentence, afraid to voice the horrible thought.

"Oh, Mama, what are we going to do?" I rushed into the lighted kitchen to look at the *pupik.* Mama pointed to the soft, wet *pupik,* which had a very slight swelling and discoloration on one side.

"Run quickly to Papa in Tiferes Yerusholayim and tell him to go right now to Rabbi Skinder to ask a *shaileh.* Don't forget to tell Papa that I have no idea from which of the twenty-four chickens this *pupik* comes," Mama cautioned.

I dressed hurriedly. Holding the *pupik* in a soggy little bag, I sped through the dark, gloomy streets, my footsteps echoing my inner anxiety. (In 1930, Mama had no qualms about send-

---

pupik (plural *pupiklach*): gizzard(s)/ **shaileh**: question of law ing me, a young teenager, out all alone in the middle of the night. Our East Side streets were completely safe.)

As I neared the brightly illuminated *shul*, I heard many voices raised in learning. I rushed into the corridor and poked my head through the swinging door. Papa was sitting up front with an open *sefer* before him.

One of the men recognized me and hurried over. "What is it, Ruchoma?" he queried anxiously.

"I have to tell my father something," I answered quickly. He went over, tapped Papa gently on the shoulder, and whispered something to him.

Papa ran over to me with a questioning glance. "Oh, Papa, Mama just finished *kashering* all the twenty-four chickens, and she mixed up all the *pupiklach*, and she found a *shaileh* on one of them, and she doesn't know from which chicken it is, and she says you should go right away to Rabbi Skinder to ask a *shaileh*." It came out all in one breath.

Papa grabbed his hat, and we both flew through the sleepy, silent streets. We reached Henry Street in a few minutes. Papa looked up to the first floor where Rabbi Skinder lived. There was a light shining from his dining room window.

We tiptoed up the stairs, and Papa knocked gently on the door. Rabbi Skinder opened the door himself. "*Sholom aleichem*, Reb Yaakov Yosef." He clasped Papa's hand warmly.

"My wife was *kashering* a chicken and found a *shaileh* on this *pupik*," Papa said matter-of-factly. I gazed at Papa in amazement and opened my mouth to speak. Papa's warning look choked back the words into my throat.

And so, while Rabbi Skinder poked and probed the defenseless *pupik* under the light of his lamp, the fate of twenty-four chickens hung in the balance.

I trembled as I stood there. What if it were *treif*? All Mama's hard work would have been in vain. What would all of our *orchim* eat on Yom Tov? It cost so much money. Mama's tired, wan face swam before my eyes and clouded my vision.

Then I glanced at Papa. He stood straight and tall, like a soldier awaiting the verdict of his general. After what seemed an eternity, Rabbi Skinder looked up and announced, "Kosher, kosher." The words of reprieve rang in my ears.

Papa then said, "Rebbe, if you had pronounced the *pupik* '*treif*,' I would have thrown out twenty-four chickens. My wife does not know from which of the chickens this *pupik* comes."

Rabbi Skinder looked at Papa reprovingly, "Ach, ach, Reb Yaakov Yosef, why did you not tell me? When there is a great *hezek* involved, I examine the *shaileh* differently."

"I never look for *heteirim*," Papa answered with his oft-repeated and oft-practiced maxim.

With the kosher *pupik* wrapped up again in the wet, little brown bag, Papa and I rushed down the stairs. "Run home quickly, Ruchoma, and tell Mama that the *pupik* is one-hundred-percent kosher. See that she gets to bed. I'm going back to *shul*."

Like a winged bird in flight, I flew through the tranquil streets, my footsteps in tune with the rhythm of Kosher, Kosher, Kosher.

When I burst into our front hall, I could not control myself and called out loudly, "Mama! Mama! The *pupik* is kosher! It's kosher!"

Mrs. Friedman, our first-floor neighbor, came running out of her apartment. "Ruchoma, what's the matter with you? Why are you making such an unearthly racket at this time of night, waking everybody?" she asked peevishly.

"The *pupik* is kosher," I babbled.

Mama heard me and rushed down to greet me. I threw myself into her arms and almost threw her off her balance. "It's all right, Mama; it's one-hundred-percent kosher!" Mama burst out crying.

By that time, our other neighbors heard the commotion

---

hezek: loss / *heteirim*: lenient rulings

and hurried into the hall, curious to know what had occurred. Over hot, sweet cocoa and Mama's delicious raisin cinnamon cookies, I told our neighbors the entire episode of the kosher *pupik.*

Our building at 108 East Broadway was ordered demolished to make way for a post office.

Papa, Mama and I were very disturbed. Our address had become known far and wide in the thirteen years we had lived there. Hundreds of *orchim* and others found their way to our home for every imaginable kind of help and advice.

Papa found an apartment at 217 East Broadway. The moving was a monumental task. The new apartment had one great advantage. It had a refrigerator. Mama and I did not get to sleep the first night we moved in. We just kept opening the refrigerator door to see if it was "real."

No more ice—no more emptying the basins of accumulated water, which left a wet trail through our entire kitchen. Now Mama could buy fish, chicken and meat for the *orchim* well in advance without having to wait for the last day before *erev* Shabbos and Yom Tov.

This luxury was short-lived. The rent was exorbitant and Papa could not afford it. In six months' time we moved again, to an apartment at 30 Rutgers Street.

Once more we had an icebox.

10

Dedication to prayer

Papa went to *shul* morning and night to *daven shachris, mincha* and *mairiv* with a *minyon*. Neither heat nor cold, rain nor snow, not even illness deterred Papa from performing this *mitzva*.

The following incidents demonstrate well his total devotion to this *mitzva* of *davening* with a *minyon*.

Papa was sick with a temperature of 103 degrees. The doctor's explicit instructions were for him to remain in bed until his temperature returned to normal.

It was late afternoon when Papa suddenly threw off his blankets and started to get dressed. "Where are you going?" Mama asked anxiously, knowing in advance the answer she would receive.

"It is almost *mincha* time. I must hurry or I will miss *davening* with a *minyon*," Papa said simply.

"Yankev Yosef," Mama pleaded, "the doctor gave orders for you not to leave your bed, let alone go out in the street." Her coaxing was to no avail. Papa hurried out of the house.

daven: pray

He returned several hours later flushed and tired, after *davening mincha* and *mairiv* and also teaching his daily *shiur* in Talmud to the men who came to *daven* in the *shul*.

"Papa," I queried, "do you want me also to follow your example and disobey the doctor when I'm ill?"

"Oh no!" Papa exclaimed. "Ruchoma, you must do exactly what the doctor orders. However, I know my own physical strength and how much I can tax it."

Papa recovered from his illness none the worse for having gone to *shul*.

Papa arranged to have a daily *minyon* for *mincha* in his fur store, as there was no synagogue in the immediate vicinity. Many shopkeepers and workers were encouraged by Papa to join this *minyon*. His shop was closed whenever the services were taking place.

My nephew, Moshe Aaron, told me about an unusual occurrence concerning Papa. Each day, around noontime, Papa closed his store to say special prayers, *tikun chatzos* (for the coming of the Messiah).

One day a very old man who lived near Papa's fur shop came to Papa and excitedly repeated a disturbing dream he had had the night before. "I dreamt that I was ordered to go to you with a message: you should discontinue your special prayers for the Messiah. The time is not yet ripe."

Papa stopped saying these special prayers, just as the message in the dream had specified.

Papa noticed a *talmid* of his daydreaming during prayers. As soon as the young man spied Papa, he gave his attention to his prayers. When the *talmid* finished, Papa said to him, "You are *davening* to me and not to Hashem. During your prayers you can speak to the Boss. What a pity that you are throwing away such a golden opportunity."

Mr. Silverman, a close friend of ours who lived in Hazelton, Pennsylvania, visited us whenever he came to New York. He had a seltzer route for many years. Each day he rode out with his horse and wagon to deliver seltzer to all parts of the city. When he retired, he sold his horse to a non-Jew. A few days later, the buyer, puzzled, came to our friend and asked him, "What's wrong with your horse? Each day in the late afternoon, he suddenly stops for about a quarter of an hour. Though I whip him, he refuses to budge. Then he starts off on his own accord."

Mr Silverman understood immediately and explained to the buyer, "It is a law that a Jew must pray each day at sunset. My horse became accustomed to stopping along my route until I finished my prayers. I will gladly return the money to you that you paid for my horse."

Our friend took back the horse and cared for it until its death.

When Papa heard the story, he remarked that when an observant Jew prays daily, even his horse has the merit to be returned to its Jewish owner.

Once Papa had occasion to travel west on business. His train was scheduled to make an hour's stop in St. Louis. It was very early in the morning when the train pulled into the station.

Papa jumped off the train and hailed the first taxi he saw. "Drive me quickly to an Orthodox synagogue," Papa directed the driver. Fortunately, the cab driver knew where to go, and in a few minutes the taxi was parked outside a synagogue.

In the meantime, Papa had put on his *tallis* and *tefillin*. He told the driver to wait for him, while he hurried into the synagogue. The early morning prayers were about to begin. As Papa entered, the congregants looked in amazement at this stranger who seemed to have appeared from nowhere.

"I would like to *daven* at the *omed*," Papa requested courteously. Speechless, they nodded their heads in assent.

omed: lectern used by prayer leader

Papa's praying always inspired his listeners to the heights of spiritual elevation. In this strange synagogue, in his usual way, he stood straight as a soldier, pouring out his heart and soul to Hashem.

As soon as the prayers were over, he immediately departed from the synagogue. The taxi took him to the train, which he reached on time.

During this period, Reb Boruch Ber Leibowitz from Kaminetz and his son-in-law, Reb Reuven Grozovsky, were *orchim* at our house. They traveled through many parts of the United States in order to raise funds for their yeshiva, and on one of their trips they arrived in St. Louis.

At the home where they were staying, their host related a remarkable incident that had happened recently in their synagogue.

"A stranger entered our synagogue with early morning, dressed in *tallis* and *tefillin*. His prayers were the most inspiring we had ever heard. Immediately after the *shachris* prayers, he disappeared. He might have been Eliyohu Hanovi," the man ended his tale with awe.

When Reb Boruch Ber and Reb Reuven returned after an extensive trip, Reb Reuven said to Mama, "I always thought that there is only one Reb Yaakov Yosef in America." He then went on to describe in detail the incident that they had heard while in St. Louis.

Mama smiled knowingly, for Papa had told us when he returned from his trip how the Boss always helped him carry out the *mitzva* of *davening* with a *minyon*. "Reb Reuven, there is only one Reb Yankev Yosef. It was he who was in St. Louis."

"I should have known that it could only have been Reb Yankev Yosef," Reb Reuven agreed. Reb Boruch Ber added that Papa was the Chofetz Chaim of America.

Though Papa preferred not to leave home, there came a

Eliyohu Hanovi: the prophet Elijah

time when he had to travel to Europe on business. Papa boarded the boat, carrying his *sefer Torah* with him. Accompanying him were four of his *talmidim*, whom he had encouraged to study in Mirrer Yeshiva: Shachne Zohn, Chaim Joselit, Reuven Epstein and Binyomin Bernstein. He also gave them financial assistance towards their expenses.

Reb Shachne Zohn related to me that Papa revolutionized the ship with his actions. First, he made sure that there would be a *minyon* three times a day. Early in the morning, he was already knocking on the cabin of any Jew who was aboard. Though he traveled third class, he did not hesitate to enter first and second class to awaken the sleepy passengers for prayers. At the end of the trip Papa was dubbed, "Mr. Minyon."

Under Papa's supervision, the pool became a kosher *mikveh*. Papa ingratiated himself with the cook from the kosher kitchen. For Shabbos, there was a delicious *cholent* served to all the delighted passengers who ate in the kosher section.

When the ship docked, the captain, as well as many passengers, sighed with relief.

Papa combined his business trip with a visit to Nochum Dovid, Chaye Dube, Chaim, Bessie and their children, who were then in Mir, Poland. There he met his former *orech* Reb Lezer Yudel Finkel and his family, who were overjoyed to meet Papa. While he was in Mir, Papa also visited the *mashgiach*, Reb Yeruchem Levovitz, and was inspired by this meeting.

During this trip, Papa made it his "business" to meet with the Chofetz Chaim in Radun. Nochum Dovid, who accompanied Papa to the Chofetz Chaim, told me this about the visit:

Three kilometers before Radun, Papa alighted from the wagon and walked in the deep, muddy road to gain *sechar halicha*.

Just before they entered the house, the Chofetz Chaim asked his *rebbetzin* to prepare his Shabbos garments, which he wore, on occasion, out of respect for special guests. The Chofetz

---

rebbetzin: Rabbi's wife / *sechar halicha*: merit for walking

Papa during his visit in Mir, photographed on a horse-driven wagon, the standard means of travel in that part of the world.

Chaim's custom was to quote an appropriate passage in the Bible when an important guest arrived. When Papa walked through the door, he quoted from the Prophet Yechezkel (44:15), "But the Priests, the Levites, the sons of Zadok, that kept the charge of my Sanctuary when the children of Israel went astray from me, they shall come near to me to minister unto me. . . ."

Without advance notice of Papa's arrival, the Chofetz Chaim chose the exact passage which is a perfect portrayal of Papa, who always was close to the Boss and obeyed his commands, when others shunned the Torah precepts.

Each *erev* Shabbos of Papa's European trip, Mama and I received a telegram from Papa with the exact time for lighting the candles and his "Good Shabbos" to us and the *orchim*. When Papa returned home, he told us, "I did not miss a *minyon* though I traveled by boat, train and plane through many countries. Where there is a will, you can always find a way to do a *mitzva.*"

On his way home, after spending time in several cities in Poland, he arrived in Leipzig, Germany. From there he was scheduled to travel to London. Papa realized that if he followed his itinerary and traveled by train, he would miss *davening mairiv* with a *minyon.*

On the spur of the moment, he decided to travel by plane. In 1931, plane travel was expensive and hazardous, and few people used this new means of transportation. Papa boarded the tiny plane, which flew into the horizon with few passengers aboard. The trip was a very rough one but within a short time Papa arrived in London.

When he disembarked from the plane, the customs officer checked his passport and noticed that Papa had no visa to enter England. However, he was so impressed that Papa had arrived by plane that he allowed him to enter the country without a visa and remain for his allotted time.

It was already quite late at night when Papa knocked at the door of Rabbi Eliyohu E. Dessler, author of the famous work of *mussar, Michtav Me-Eliyohu,* who was then residing in London. Rabbi Dessler greeted Papa warmly, as he ushered him into his home. "Reb Yaakov Yosef, now I have an opportunity to repay a little of your *hachnosas orchim* to me when I was in New York. Tell me what I can do for you to make you comfortable."

"I need a *minyon* for *mairiv,*" Papa said quickly.

"It's very late, but I will see what I can do," Rabbi Dessler said graciously. He went from door to door, until he succeeded in gathering a *minyon* of his neighbors.

After *mairiv,* Papa said thankfully, "This is real *hachnosas orchim,* Reb Elya."

In connection with the above incident, I have translated from Hebrew the major part of a letter of Rabbi Dessler's in which he expresses his great esteem and admiration for Papa. He wrote this letter to his father, Rabbi Reuven Dov Dessler,

Rabbi Dessler, as he looked in London, 1932—about the time when Papa visited him.

then *mashgiach* of the renowned yeshiva of Kelm, Lithuania.

To my honorable father, my guide, Shlita:

I delayed in writing to you my weekly letter, because an unusual guest suddenly arrived last Thursday night, and I was occupied with him until yesterday.

This exceptional guest was Reb Yaakov Yosef Herman from New York, at whose house I stayed when I was in the United States. He treated me with great hospitality, so you can understand that I tried in some measure to return the consideration he had shown me, and showed him the greatest respect.

He is a businessman, brought up in America. However, he is an outstanding *y'rei shomayim,* who observes the *mitzvos* of the Torah meticulously. He influences many people and guides them to become observant Jews. Reb Yaakov Yosef is known for

....
Shlita: acronym for "May you live for many long, good years"

his strict adherence to the *mitzva* of *hachnosas orchim*. On Shabbos, there are approximately twenty *orchim* at his table.

During his travels from America through Europe these last three weeks, only twice did he fail to *daven* with a *minyon*. He took along a *sefer Torah* and other important *seforim* he would need on this trip.

He traveled to London from Leipzig by plane when he discovered that it would be impossible for him to *daven mairiv* with a *minyon* if he came any other way.

He arrived at my home at 11:30 PM, and the first thing he asked of me was to arrange a *minyon* for him.

I saw how Hashem especially watches over him. Had he traveled by train instead of by plane from Germany to England, since he had no visa he would have been refused entry, unless he paid a substantial sum. The difference in cost between traveling by train or plane was that exact amount, so that it actually cost him no more to travel by plane.

We enjoyed each other's company immensely over Shabbos. He is not a rich man in money, but he is wealthy in good deeds.

Your ever-devoted son, *Elya Eliezer*

11

The last six days of a tzidkonis

PROLOGUE

Zeidy and Bobie Andron immigrated to Eretz Yisroel in March, 1922, leaving all their children and grandchildren in the United States.

Although I was a young child when they left, I remember their departure vividly. There was a huge crowd of relatives, friends, and acquaintances who came to see them off at the port. Zeidy Andron was very well known in New York by then for his many accomplishments in the field of Jewish education, and their leaving for Eretz Yisroel was noted in the newspapers.

All my uncles, aunts and cousins milled about. Mama held my hand tightly, showing her emotions at her parents' departure by squeezing my hand every so often. When the boat set sail, Mama's tears fell silently, but she did not utter a word.

Zeidy and Bobie Andron settled in Givat Shaul, Yerusholayim, a sparsely inhabited area at that time. After building their home, they piped water in from the center of Yerusho-

....

tzidkonis: pious woman

Zeidy and Bobie Andron before boarding ship for Eretz Yisroel (this picture appeared in the newspaper).

layim, which supplied everyone in their area with running water in their homes for the first time.

Zeidy immediately organized a yeshiva — which he helped support and in which he took a personal interest — and a synagogue in Givat Shaul which bears his name.

Zeidy lived in Eretz Yisroel for eight years and passed away on the twenty-eighth of Shevat, 5690. He is buried on Har Hazeisim.

When I was sixteen years old, Bobie Andron became ill. At Bobie's request, Uncle Yankev Leib (Mama's oldest brother) traveled immediately to Eretz Yisroel, where he was at her side during the last six days of her life.

After Bobie passed away and Uncle Yankev Leib returned to the United States, all my uncles and aunts gathered at our house to listen to my uncle read the letter he had written during his stay with Bobie. I give the letter here in translation from the Yiddish:

To my dear brothers and sisters,

I am sitting *shiva* here in Yerusholayim, and you are sitting *shiva* in New York, for our dear holy mother, *zatzal*. We weep and lament together over our great loss. We had two crowns taken away from us in one year: our father, *zatzal*, and now our mother, *zatzal*. Yes, we had a father and a mother, but we never realized whom we had.

You cannot imagine the spiritual uplift I experienced by being near Mama during the last six days of her life. I see a repetition of *parshas Vayechi*. Our Patriarch Yaakov called for his children when he saw his days were numbered, and he blessed each child according to his needs. Our dear mother telegraphed me, "Come immediately," and I came at her bidding.

A remarkable scene took place an hour and a half before she passed away. I stood near her bed, and she held onto my hand. Men and women were crowded into her room. At first, she spoke in a weak voice, almost a whisper, but when she talked about Torah, the holy Shabbos, and *yiras shomayim* her voice was strong and vibrant. The walls seemed to shake from the impact—*kol Hashem bako'ach*.

Those fortunate people who were there when the holy soul left the body of our mother, *zatzal,* realized what a great *tzidkonis* she was. I consider it the greatest privilege of my life that I was present at *yetzias neshomo*.

My pen is too feeble to write and describe all that I witnessed. I wish all of you could have been here with me. Again, I thank Hashem that I could obey the last wish of our dear mother that I be with her the last six days of her life in this world. These days will remain etched in my heart forever.

And now to go back and relate to you what I saw and heard

....

zatzal: acronym for "May the remembrance of the pious be a blessing"
kol Hashem bako'ach: the voice of God is powerful
yetzias neshomo: literally, going out of the soul: death

from the moment I arrived, so that you will then be able to transmit this to your children and grandchildren so that they will know the greatness of their grandmother and fulfill her last dying wishes.

I arrived at Givat Shaul, Yerusholayim, at 10 AM, on Thursday, the eighteenth of Shevat—*parshas Yisro*. I found Mama lying in bed in a very weak condition. I kissed her, and her face shone with joy at seeing me. She called out, "*Boruch Hashem* that I lived to see your face."

She asked about each of you, your children and grandchildren, the *mechutonim* and their families. After the initial excitement, I sat down to breakfast. She requested that I eat in her bedroom. As I ate, she asked about the welfare of this relative and that friend.

When I finished breakfast, I sent for the doctor. I was told that the night prior to my arrival Mama had felt very ill. She had said *viduy*, and then called out, "*Ribono shel olom*, strengthen me so that I should live to see my son."

When the doctor arrived, he examined Mama and gave her an injection. He told me, "You mother is very ill. Her heart is weak and her kidneys are not functioning properly. What more can I tell you?" I understood that I must pray for the best and expect the worst.

After lunch, Mama told me to go to the *Kosel* to *daven mincha*. I prayed for her and for all our loved ones. When I returned, I found her happy and content. She again thanked Hashem that she could have me near her. She told me about Papa's last days. She then asked me to buy the grave adjacent to Papa's, saying, "I worked my entire life helping him to learn Torah and build yeshivos. I deserve to be near him in death also."

I arranged to meet with the *chevra kadisha* on Har Hazeisim on Friday morning. I asked them to show me Papa's

mechutonim: in-laws / *viduy*: confession
Ribono shel olom: Lord of the world
Kosel: Western Wall / *chevra kadisha*: burial society

kever and discussed with them Mama's request. You can understand, my dear brothers and sisters, my emotions as I stood near the grave of our father, *zatzal,* whose first *yahrzeit* will be on the twenty-eighth of Shevat.

My childhood years passed before me. I realized how much Papa had instilled the love of Torah in us. Though we were separated from our parents during the past nine years, nevertheless, we sought their advice on every occasion. We hoped and prayed that someday we would all be reunited, but this was not destined to be.

Now as I stood near Papa's *kever,* the tears flowed from my eyes and dampened his grave. I prayed again for Mama and for all of you.

I told the *chevra kadisha* that I wished to buy the grave right near Papa, *zatzal,* for Mama. They refused, saying, "Only very great men lie in this row: the Klausenberger Rav; the Tavriger Rav; the Alter of Slobodka and his son, Reb Moshe; Dr. Munk; the Lubaner Rav; and many more great *geonim* and *tzaddikim,* but no women."

I told them of Mama's wish; I said that she deserves to lie right near Papa and that I must carry out her wish. After much persuasion, they finally acquiesced. I signed the necessary papers.

The graves face Har Habayis. All of Yerusholayim unfolds before your eyes. It was difficult for me to tear myself away from this holy place, where these great men who have played such a decisive role in our Jewish heritage lie buried.

I returned to Mama with the news that I had bought the grave right near Papa, *zatzal.* She was elated. "You see, Yankev Leib, how important it was for you to come. I myself could never have gotten this *kever* which means so very much to me."

Late Friday afternoon, Mama asked if it was time to light the candles. I told her the siren had not yet sounded. [In

---

kever: grave

Yerusholayim a siren is sounded to announce the time to light the candles for Shabbos.]

"Give me the candles. Why do I have to wait for them to *fife* at me? It's better if I *fife* at them," she smilingly said.

Friday night Mama felt better. I made *kiddush*, and we ate in her room. She asked me to sing *zemiros*. Afterwards, a young man, Yosef, Papa's *talmid*, came and read to Mama from *ma'asey alfas* [Rabbi Ben Zion Alfas wrote in Yiddish on *parshas hashovua*, drawing from *midrashim*], as he did each Friday night.

Shabbos afternoon, Mama told me to visit Rav Isser Zalman Meltzer, the Slutsker Gaon, so I understood that she was holding her own.

Saturday night, she again felt very ill, and I hardly slept a wink. I wanted to call the doctor early Sunday morning, but she asked me not to. However, on Monday, she herself asked that I call for a consultation of doctors. The family doctor called in Dr. Wallach, the director and chief physician of Shaare Zedek Hospital, who told me, after an examination, that nothing could be done for her medically. Only prayers could help.

I was at her bedside constantly. In fact, from the time I arrived, I ate all my meals in her room and slept there also.

Monday toward dusk, Mama first *davened mincha* and then *mairiv*, all by heart. Soon after *mairiv*, I noticed that she was reciting the morning blessings. I thought her mind must be wandering. "Mama, it is now nighttime; why are you saying the morning prayers?" I asked.

"My son, I know it is night, but I wanted especially to say the blessings: 'Blessed be You, Hashem our God, King of the Universe, who girds Israel with might', and the other *brocho*, 'who gives strength to the weary.' I need His strength now."

I then said to Mama: "Papa always *davened* with a *siddur*, and even recited *kiddush* and *havdolo* with the *siddur*, and you say everything by heart."

....

fife: whistle

"Don't you know that Papa was not adept at saying these prayers?" she retorted jokingly.

"But, then, Papa, *zatzal,* was always better than I. He passed away so quickly. He just fell asleep. Hashem gave me two 'gifts': I cannot sleep, and I cannot eat."

She then raised her voice and cried out, "*Ribono shel olom,* you did not torment my dear husband; why are you tormenting me? You placed the soul into the body so quickly, but when it is time for You to take it back, You give the body so much pain and tribulation. I want to say *viduy,* but I feel so very weak. The *viduy* I said last week will have to do."

Mama then told me that she was sorely troubled because she could not remember the *pesukim* referring to her name, Fruma Rochel. "When I appear before the Angel at the Gate, he will ask me for them. The *posuk* for Fruma I do know, but the one for Rochel is so long that I cannot remember it all. I will have to tell the Angel at the Gate, 'You know very well that now it is too late for me to study these *pesukim,* so why must you bother me over such a trivial matter? Why do you not ask me for the many good things I have done in my life?' And I hope he will let me pass."

I would like to note at this point a few bits of conversation Mama had with different visitors who came to visit her during her illness, which showed her clarity of mind and her keen sense of humor even during her dying days.

An American visitor seemed to be in a great hurry, so she asked him, "Why are you in such a rush to leave; is the cloak business so busy in the United States?" [Many of the Jews worked in the clothing business during this period.]

When another friend wished her a *refua shleima* in Russian, she answered in perfect Russian.

Yosef, Papa's *talmid,* who is learning to be a *shochet,* told Mama, "I slaughtered several sheep today."

---

pesukim: verses / *refua shleima*: complete recovery

Mama answered, "*Mazel tov!* And how many of them turned out to be kosher?"

He asked her advice as to whether he should give up the learning of *shechita*, as he had been offered a different job.

"Do not give up the learning of *shechita*, because half measures are not the method of a good businessman," she advised him.

Yosef further related to Mama that someone wishes to introduce him to an American girl for the purpose of matrimony. The girl is willing to provide five hundred pounds sterling as a dowry [a small fortune in those days].

"Yosef, find out how old the girl is. I know all about these American *shidduchim* that are proposed here. One hundred pounds is given for every ten years, so I assume the girl is nearing fifty years old."

Feiga, the housemaid, was asked by Mama to bring her a *siddur.* She refused, because she felt Mama was too weak to recite any prayers. "You are an '*apikorus*,'" Mama said to her jokingly.

As Yosef was leaving, he advised Mama to drink warm milk so that she would perhaps be able to fall asleep. "Since when did you learn this new medication? Does your information stem from Sisera and Yael?" she retorted immediately.

Mama finally drifted off to sleep, but I could not sleep at all. In the middle of the night Mama awoke. Her cheeks were quite flushed. "We have a lot of work to do today. We have to decide what to do with all of Papa's *seforim*: which things you will take back with you to the States and which shall be divided among the relatives and friends here." She told me that Yosef had all the keys to the closets, and which closet the silver was in.

Tuesday dawned. Mama told me I could go to *shul* to *daven.* I felt relieved, because she seemed to look and feel better. When I returned from *davening*, she told me to eat

....
apikorus: heretic / **Sisera and Yael**: See Judges 4

breakfast. While I was eating, she said to me, "Everything must be attended to today. The day is short, and there is much work to be done. You must go to the lawyer, to the American consulate, and write letters home. When guests visit today, do not spend too much time with them, as I have much to discuss with you. You must return home, as it is nearing Purim, and I do not want to keep you. Many well-meaning people advised you not to come because the parting would be too difficult. Don't you know that I understand that you must return to your loved ones, until you and the entire family will have the *zechus* to settle in Eretz Yisroel?"

When I returned from my errands, Mama requested every detail of what had transpired at the lawyer's and at the consulate. She then said I should write home, for they would be worried. When I finished writing the letter, I asked her to sign her name, but she said to me, "Yankev Leib, I feel too weak to sign my name, but I will speak to you, and you will transmit my words to the entire family."

Toward dusk, Mama called to Feiga, the housemaid, "Wash me completely. Give me clean clothes, and change the bed linen," she ordered.

When all was done, Mama *davened,* first *mincha* and then *mairiv.* She told me that I could go *daven* also. She warned me not to delay and to return immediately after I'd finished my prayers. I hurried back, and Mama told me to eat my supper.

After supper, Mama asked me if the relatives were there. I told her that they had all come. I had notified them and many of our friends that Mama was weakening. The house was crowded with people.

Mama then called me to come close to her bedside. She turned her face to me, grasped my hand, and said:

"My son, I asked especially for you to come, because you are my oldest son. Fifty-six years ago, at about this time, I gave birth to you. You were born on the twenty-first day of Shevat in the year 5635. Papa, *zatzal,* passed away on the twenty-eighth of Shevat, on the same date as your *bris.*

"Tell all the children to be observant of the holy Shabbos; do the bidding of Hashem; be honest and upright; wear *tzitzis*, and bring up a generation of God-fearing Jews. Then you will be blessed with *hatzlocho* in all you will undertake.

"I never asked for any material things from Papa. All I wanted was to have him learn the holy Torah. I took care of him so that he would have time to learn and feel comfortable in every way. I sacrificed my entire life for Torah.

"When we arrived in the 'Golden Land' [America in the 1890s], I carried the burden together with Papa so that he could devote his time to learning Torah and teaching Torah.

"I chopped wood for the stove in the cold, early dawn so that no one would see me. One day a woman spied me chopping the wood and asked, 'You have such a fine husband. Why doesn't he make a living for you?'

"I answered her, 'My husband is busy working for the yeshiva.'

"Another neighbor once heard me sawing wood. She screamed out, 'Who lives above me — gypsies?'

"For Shabbos, I did not buy fish when everybody bought theirs, because it cost too much. I waited until *erev* Shabbos when the price was cheaper. The fish lady asked, 'You have such a noble husband, but he does not support you properly.'

"My reply was always the same, 'My husband has to learn Torah and work for the yeshiva.'

"I was satisfied with very little. I brought up a family of seven children. When I saw a woman buying beets and throwing away the greens, I asked her to give me the greens. From the beet-greens I made a meal for the children. There was a store near our house where all the day-old bread from the various grocery stores was collected. I bought the bread much cheaper that way.

"Our children were very good. They never asked for anything special, such as candy or other sweets. As long as

tzitzis: ritual fringes

there were bread, fish and beet-greens to eat, they were satisfied. We never borrowed any money. When Yisroel Isser started to work, he bought Papa a fur-lined coat with his first earnings. People said that Papa made a living from the yeshiva. We never took a penny from the yeshiva. Papa always said, 'I will find *parnoso* some other way.' I accepted what Papa said, and we never had any arguments.

When the older children began to earn a living, we bought a house. For the first time, we had enough room. I used to wash the *tallis-koton*s and hang them out on the line. The neighbors would ask in jest, 'Will your children really wear them?'

" 'Is there a different God in America?' I would answer them. *Boruch Hashem*, our children wore them. [There was little *yiddishkeit* in America at that time.]

I always worked together with Papa, encouraged him, and helped him with all his undertakings. When there were any arguments in the yeshiva, I supported him.

"I asked for no luxuries in my life—no jewelry or fancy clothes, like other women. The fact that Papa learned Torah and spread Torah was more important and dearer to me than anything else in life.

"When Papa decided that we should settle in Eretz Yisroel, I went along with his wishes. Of course, you can well understand how difficult it was for me to leave all our children and grandchildren. However, in no way did I make Papa feel that I did not wish to do his bidding.

"We came to Yerusholayim and you, my dear children, helped us very much. You sent us enough money for all our needs. Whatever we asked of you was gladly fulfilled. Yes, we could have lived very comfortably here on the money you sent us, but I could not stand by and witness the terrible poverty that surrounded us. I've been living here in Eretz Yisroel for nine years. I have not even bought myself a new garment.

---

tallis-koton: small four-cornered garment with *tzitzis*

"I did not have too much *nachas* here. Papa became blind, and I took care of him with my last strength. [Bobie even read the *gemora* aloud to him.]

"Now everything is past. Toward you, my dear children, I have no complaints. You tried to make our last years sweet. Hashem will surely bless you for the honor you granted your parents. Now I need nothing more. I am going to a better and brighter world. I am going to my dear, beloved husband.

"But before I go, I am asking once again from you, my dear children: be upright and good Jewish children. Be true *shomrey Shabbos* and observe all the laws of the Torah.

"You, my oldest son, promise me that you will influence all your brothers and sisters and their children and children's children to be Jews who will not shame our previous generations, who were all *tzaddikim, geonim,* and *rabbonim.* Do not break the golden chain that has linked us to our parents. Live together in peace. Help each other in time of need. Get together often.

"I shall not ask you for anything more. You do not have to write me any more letters. But I am asking you to put on *tefillin,* to *daven,* to wear *tzitzis* and observe the holy Shabbos and the holy Torah. Bring up your children in the way of the Torah. Then Papa and I will always pray for you in the other world that you should have great *hatzlocho* in all your endeavors, and be worthy to come to this holy land, Eretz Yisroel."

When Mama finished speaking, she blessed me and all who were in her room, each one according to his needs and by name. She blessed Yosef that he should find the right partner in life and bring up a true Jewish generation. She thanked Feiga, the housemaid, for the faithful way she had taken care of her. She blessed Reb Meyer Acker for his true friendship. She told Reb Shleima Kalman to bring his father-in-law from Vilna to Eretz Yisroel. She kissed Cousin Malka and blessed her that her

....
nachas: (spiritual) satisfaction

children should learn Torah and that she should raise them as upright Jews.

Then Mama recited *Oshamnu* by heart until the end. She told me that she had prepared her own shrouds, and she requested that they purify and cleanse her on the same table that they had used to do Papa's *tahara*, the table from the yeshiva. "I have a share in their learning."

A remarkable scene then took place that I and all who were crowded into her room will never forget. Mama suddenly called out in a strong, ringing voice, "My dear Mama, my dear uncles, Reb Itzele Rabbaver [she wanted to say something about him, but held back], Reb Gimpel [Reb Mortchi Gimpel, the Rodzenauer Rav, one of the greatest *geonim* of his generation] and my dearly beloved husband are all coming to greet me."

She turned her face, looking upward and stretched out her legs. Her face began to radiate such light that all in the room remained transfixed. And then she called out, *"Shema Yisroel Hashem Hu HoElokim!"* Her lips moved and, with a sweet smile on her face, her holy *neshomo* left her body.

It was exactly 10 PM on Tuesday night, the twenty-fourth day of Shevat, 5691.

Everyone in the room broke out in great wailing and cried out, "Such a *tzidkonis*." What can I write? . . . All I can say is that whoever did not witness this scene will not believe that it really happened.

I immediately tore *kri'ah* and said the blessing *dayan hoemes*. They took our dear holy mother, placed her on the floor, and surrounded her with lit candles.

Several of the relatives remained in her room the entire night to say *tehillim*.

In the morning, all the neighbors gathered. "What a very great *tzidkonis* she was," one said.

....

Oshamnu: first word of the *viduy* (confession) / **tahara**: purification
Shema Yisroel Hashem Hu HoElokim: Hear, O Israel, Hashem is God
kri'ah: mourner's rent / **dayan ho-emes**: true Judge

"What a big *ba'alas tzedoko*—how will I get along without her help?" another asked. "To whom will I turn for a *gemilas chesed*? She always gave readily when needed." Each of the women had something else to say of Mama, *zatzal*, of her greatness and goodness.

In the very early morning, Reb Meyer Acker went to notify the *chevra kadisha* and the *roshei yeshivos*. He hired someone to call out in the streets of Yerusholayim the time and place of Mama's funeral.

By eight o'clock in the morning, forty students from the Diskin Orphan Home had come to say *tehillim*. Fifty of the best *talmidim* were sent from Etz Chaim Yeshiva. From another Sephardi yeshiva another large group of yeshiva boys came.

In every corner of the house *tehillim* was being recited in lamenting tones that touched everyone's heart. The added cries from all the relatives, friends and neighbors seemed to rend the heavens above.

By 11:30 AM the *tahara* was done. I was called into her room. I put some earth on dear Mama's face, which still radiated a special light. I then said the *posuk*, "And Joseph placed his hand over his eyes."

The house was packed with people, and the outside courtyard as well. Therefore, the eulogies were delivered in the courtyard adjoining the house. I gave the first *hesped*. Then the *gaon* Reb Michel Tukechinsky from Etz Chaim Yeshiva, Rav Daniel Zaks, Rav Adler, and the city *maggid*, Reb Ben Zion Yadler, all gave moving eulogies.

The funeral procession then began. At the head walked all the *roshei yeshivos, rabbonim,* and *talmidim* from the various yeshivos. Then came the relatives, friends, neighbors, and other people who came to pay tribute to our dear mother, *zatzal*. There was great wailing and crying as they said, "*Tzedek lefonov yehalech*" [Justice will proceed before him—the verse

----

baalas tzedoko: possessor of the quality of charity
gemilas chesed: free loan / *hesped*: eulogy / *maggid*: preacher

recited when a righteous person's body is carried to the grave].
Maamodos and Psalm 91 were said at each *shul* and institution
as the procession passed by, and at each stop I said *kaddish*.

When the funeral procession passed the home of the *gaon*
Rabbi Kook, he came out to the street and delivered a eulogy.
That is how it continued until we came to Har Hazeisim. It is
several miles from Mama's house to Har Hazeisim. The entire
way she was carried and the throng walked. There was light
rain when we left the house and then again on Har Hazeisim.

At 3:30 PM Mama was placed in her grave. There I said the
mourner's *kaddish*. Then we all departed, leaving our beloved
mother on Har Hazeisim opposite the Har Habayis, near her
dearly beloved husband, our holy father—two graves we leave
in Yerusholayim. Our parents went to their final resting place,
and we are left to mourn our great loss.

We have become orphans in one year; our dearest treasures
in life, Papa and Mama, are not separated any more. I want to
remark here that Papa and Mama were never apart for more
than a year in their lives. When Papa went to America, he saw
to it that Mama would follow within the year. Papa passed
away on the twenty-eighth day of Shevat, and now Mama has
passed away on the twenty-fourth of Shevat, less than a year
later.

I returned to our parents' home. The entire house was
surrounded in mourning, as I sat down to *shiva*. There was a
large *minyon* three times a day. *Mishnayos* were also learned
daily.

Hundreds of people came to be *menachem ovel*, among
them the greatest *gedolim* from Yerusholayim and Eretz
Yisroel: Rabbi Isser Z. Meltzer, Rabbi Kook, the old Lubliner
Gaon, Rabbi Klatzkin, the Yansheker Rav and many, many
others.

I started this letter when I sat down to *shiva*, but could not

....
Har Hazeisim: Mount of Olives / **Har Habayis**: Temple Mount
menachem ovel: comfort the mourner

finish it until now, after *shiva*. I asked Yosef to write down each word that Mama spoke to me during her last days, so none of her precious words would ever be forgotten.

When I come home, I shall read this letter to you, which is the last will and testament of our dear mother, *zatzal*. Her wishes must be very dear to us. We must obey all that she asked of us in the last minutes of her life.

Papa's and Mama's lives must be a shining example to us on how to conduct ourselves. Mama, *zatzal,* said to me in her last words that she and Papa, *zatzal*, in heaven will pray for us to have *hatzlocho* when we follow in their footsteps. We should feel confident that they can do much for us, as it is written: "The righteous in their death can accomplish by prayer even more than in their lives."

Your oldest brother, writing with a broken heart and hoping for Hashem's help. May He comfort us among all the mourners of Tzion and Yerusholayim.

Yankev Leib

EPILOGUE

Two exceptional occurrences prompt me to add this epilogue.

Chaim and Bessie were living in Mir, Poland, where Chaim was studying in the Mirrer Yeshiva. Bessie was five months pregnant with her first baby, when she had a dream about Bobie Fruma Rochel.

Bobie came to her in the dream and said, "You will give birth to a girl. I want you to name her after me." Bessie awoke very disturbed. As far as she knew, Bobie was alive and living in Yerusholayim.

She immediately wrote to Papa and Mama asking about the welfare of Bobie Fruma Rochel. In due time, Bessie received a reassuring letter confirming that Bobie was all right. However, Zeidy Shmuel Yitzchok, *zatzal,* who had passed away several months earlier, was greatly missed by her.

Bessie kept the dream to herself, afraid to voice it even to Chaim.

Four months later, Bessie gave birth to a girl. Chaim sent a telegram to Papa and Mama announcing the good tidings and asking them to telegraph the name they wished for their granddaughter.

The answer came promptly: "*Mazel tov!* — name — Fruma Rochel."

Of course, Chaim and Bessie named their first daughter after Bobie, *zatzal.* It was then that Bessie wrote to Papa and Mama telling them about the extraordinary dream she had had when Bobie Fruma Rochel was still alive.

Forty-five years later the second remarkable occurrence took place.

Reb Chaim and Bessie live in the same building in Yerusholayim as Moshe and I. One evening, Bessie came into our home very excited. "Racoma, I found a very moving letter that Uncle Yankev Leib wrote to Mama, her brothers, and sister forty-five years ago when he sat *shiva* after Bobie Fruma Rochel Andron, *zatzal.*" She unfolded a large sheaf of pages, yellowed with age.

"Where did you get this letter, Bessie?" I queried very curiously.

"When Chaim and I were preparing to leave for Eretz Yisroel nine years ago, Uncle Yankev Leib's [second] wife brought me an envelope and told me it belonged to Uncle Yankev Leib, *zatzal.*

"I filed it among my other documents and did not look at it, because I was so busy getting ready to leave for Eretz Yisroel. Eventually, I forgot that I had it in my possession.

"Today, while searching in my file cabinet for an important document, I came across the envelope that Tante Yetta had given me and started to read the letter it contained.

"It has been in my possession for nine years, and I had no idea of the great treasure it held. It took me hours to read it because it is so discolored, but it held me spellbound until the very end."

Of course, Bessie read the letter to Moshe and me. It brought back the memory of my adolescence when I had heard it originally, but this time it left a tremendous impact upon me, as I realized the greatness of Bobie Fruma Rochel, *zatzal.*

When Bessie left our house late that night, I said to Moshe, "I want very much to go to Bobie's *kever* on Har Hazeisim tomorrow. Bobie promised that she and Zeidy will pray for her children if we go in the way of the Torah."

Moshe dissuaded me. "It's difficult to get there. In three weeks, it will be your mother's *yahrzeit,* when we go with a *minyon* to her *kever.* [Mama, *zatzal,* is buried right near Zeidy and Bobie Andron.] You will be near your Bobie's *kever* also and can say prayers at that time." I accepted his advice. That entire night I felt a close communion with Bobie Fruma Rochel.

The following morning, my close friend and neighbor Mollie Isbee (who later married Rabbi Leib Gurwicz, *zatzal,* Rosh Yeshiva of Gateshead Yeshiva in England) called me. "Racoma, I want a very special favor from you. You know Mimi, who is staying with me, is leaving for the States in two days. Her great-grandparents are buried on Har Hazeisim. Her mother wrote her, telling her to visit their graves, which are very near the graves of your mother and grandparents. She wants very much to go to Har Hazeisim today, but has no idea where they are buried. Would you take the time to go with her? She's willing to hire a taxi, which will wait to take us home again. I, too, want to come along."

For a moment I was thunderstruck. It seemed that Bobie Fruma Rochel had descended from Heaven to arrange for me to visit her *kever* that day so very conveniently.

"Mollie," I said, "don't say another word. Whenever Mimi and you are ready, just give me a call."

At three PM the taxi was waiting in front of our building. On the way to Har Hazeisim, I related to Mollie and Mimi the very moving experience of listening the night before to Uncle

Yankev Leib's letter about Bobie Fruma Rochel, and my very great desire to visit her *kever* today. They were amazed by this turn of events.

As we neared Har Hazeisim, I said to Mimi, "I know you were going with a fine young man. Now, that you are leaving, did you break off?"

Mimi told me that the situation was still pending. I then said to her, "Mimi, I formally adopt you as part of my family. Now you can also pray at my Bobie's *kever*."

Mimi did not leave two days later as planned. The young man she was seeing called her and asked her to postpone her trip.

Six weeks later she was a *kalla*.

12

Papa's power of persuasion

Just before my high school graduation, my official teacher, Miss Skolsky, asked me to which college I was applying. "I don't think my father will allow me to attend college," I replied frankly.

"Racoma, college is for you," Miss Skolsky said with conviction.

She wrote a note to Papa and asked me to deliver it to him. Papa read the note carefully and then commented, "Ruchoma, I am preparing you for college." I gazed at him in wonder. Whenever the subject had come up for discussion, Papa was adamant: "No daughter of mine will attend college to study strange ideas." Now, Papa's smile and his added words, "The college of marriage" clarified his surprising remark.

"What will I tell Miss Skolsky? I'll be so ashamed," my voice quavered.

"Aidel, go to school with Ruchoma and explain our view to her teacher," Papa advised.

Mama accompanied me to school the next day. On being informed of Papa's unusual plans for me, Miss Skolsky was aghast. "You mean you are contemplating marriage for Racoma at her age? She is a mere child."

After my graduation, I approached an employment agency that dealt specifically with Sabbath observers. I informed them that I was looking for a secretarial position. They sent me to the Standard Dry Goods Company, a large importing firm in lower Manhattan.

The owner expressed surprise when I handed him the slip from the agency. "How old are you?" he asked condescendingly.

I straightened — all five feet, one inch of me — and replied with dignity, "I am almost sixteen years old." With my low-heeled oxfords, double-breasted navy-blue coat, and beret on my head, I most probably appeared to him like a fourteen-year-old.

"I do need a secretary, but I didn't expect to hire a child worker. I will give you a two-week trial period to see if you prove satisfactory. You will work only half days for the trial period. The salary will be five dollars a week. Come in at 8:30 AM tomorrow morning." I realized he was taking advantage of me because of my age and appearance, but I didn't argue.

When I returned home with the news, Papa and Mama congratulated me on my first position, though they were skeptical about my meager salary. To Mama, I confided my hurt pride. "Everyone thinks I'm a child."

Mama comforted me. "Someday, you'll appreciate that you look younger than your age." However, she advised me to wear my Shabbos coat and black pumps with heels and to comb my bangs away from my forehead.

When I entered the office promptly at 8:30 the next morning, my employer looked twice at me to make sure I was the "child worker" he had hired the afternoon before.

Within half a year, I was earning $12.50 a week, but I was still grossly underpaid for the full day of work and effort I put into my job. Each week I brought home my paycheck in the sealed envelope and dutifully handed it to Papa. He then gave me fifty cents for my carfare for the week. Mama quietly added a few extra coins for spending money.

Papa was a most generous person, but this was his method of teaching me the value of money. He saw no necessity of giving me extra money when I received all my needs at home. And in fact, whenever Mama shopped for clothes or other items for me, Papa always advised her to buy the best.

Once Mama asked Papa to buy Esther a briefcase for school. "Buy a strong one," she suggested. Papa lost no time and soon came home bearing the largest, most expensive, genuine cowhide leather briefcase the store had to sell.

"How much does it cost?" Mama asked as she examined the shiny tan leather case.

"Twelve dollars, but it is well worth it," Papa assured her.

"Twelve dollars!" Mama exclaimed. "You could have bought five briefcases for that amount of money."

"You will see, Aidel, this briefcase will outlast five others," Papa soothed Mama. His prophecy was realized. When I inherited it after Esther, Frieda and Bessie used it, the briefcase still showed little wear and tear. In fact, after my school years, I used it to pack lunches for picnics and outings.

Papa secured a better position with a higher salary for me in a fur shop not very far from his fur store. I had been working at my first place for over a year. When I informed my employer of my intention to leave, he offered to raise my salary to the level that I would be receiving at my new position, but I proudly refused.

One evening, as I was leaving work, a salesman, who often came to the fur shop, asked me cordially if he could escort me to the subway station. I nodded in the affirmative. It was gratifying to have a young man pay special attention to me.

We walked several blocks, engrossed in our conversation, when I saw Papa walking towards us. "Ruchoma, who is this young man?" Papa's tone showed his annoyance.

"He is a salesman who comes to the fur shop," I explained, blushing from embarrassment.

Papa turned to the flustered young man. "I do not approve of my daughter walking with a strange man in the street. Ruchoma, go home; I will soon be there."

I ran toward the subway, tears of shame staining my pink blouse. "Mama," I cried, as I burst into the house, "Papa embarrassed me. I will never be able to face the young man again." She listened intently as I poured out the episode between choking sobs.

"Papa understands what is best for you, Ruchoma. He will get you a fine young man with whom you will be proud to walk in the street. Go wash your face. I have a hot cup of cocoa and a chocolate bun ready for you." Mama patted me soothingly.

From that time on, that salesman made sure to skirt my office whenever he visited the fur shop.

This incident led Papa to think seriously about marriage for me. I was the only daughter at home now. Lipman and Esther, and Philip and Frieda, with their families, lived fairly close to our house. Nochum Dovid and Chaye Dube and Chaim and Bessie were in Mir, Poland, where Davie and Chaim were studying in the Mirrer Yeshiva.

One late evening Papa had a serious talk with me. "Ruchoma, you are seventeen years old; it is time to get married."

"Papa, I'm too young. I don't feel that I am ready for marriage. None of my friends are even considering marriage for the next few years. I'm working and bringing home my salary, which helps towards the expenses. I want to wait at least for another year, until I am eighteen." Papa listened patiently to all my arguments, but I realized they did not move him at all.

A few days later, Reb Shimon Shain visited our home. His son, Noach, was studying in the Mirrer Yeshiva. He came to inquire about shipping certain items to him.

I had just returned from work. Papa always insisted that we make *brochos* aloud over our food. I made a *brocho* aloud over a fruit, and this impressed Reb Shimon.

He hurried home to tell his wife, Gneshe, that he had found

the girl suitable for their son Moshe who, at twenty-two, was the oldest of ten children—seven sons and three daughters.

Mrs. Shain visited us shortly after. She struck up a conversation with me. My Yiddish was not the best nor her English, but we managed to understand each other. "I have a fine son," she mentioned to me.

"That's very nice," I answered courteously, though her words did not make any impression.

A few weeks later, Papa cornered me again. "Ruchoma, I have several outstanding young men who would like to meet you." Fearing I might become conceited, he added quickly, "They are interested in being members of our family." Papa placed a list of names on the table. I recognized most of the names, as they were Papa's *talmidim*. Moshe Shain's name topped the list.

"I think you should meet the Shain boy first," Papa advised. He used his most persuasive powers.

"This young man has exceptionally good qualities. He is studying for the rabbinate at Yeshivas Rabbi Yitzchok Elchonon. At night, he attends City College."

Papa waited for his words to sink in. He knew my "weak point"—that secular education meant a great deal to me.

Papa had investigated the Shain family thoroughly after Reb Shimon approached him about his son Moshe. Papa was very impressed with the family and with Moshe in particular.

Reb Shimon Shain had emigrated from Mohilev, Russia, in 1905, to avoid serving in the Russian Army.

At about the same time, Gneshe Ganelas also arrived from a small village near Mohilev. Gneshe's older brother, Reb Shmuel Ber Ganelas, already married and living in the United States, had advised her to come to America, with the intention of finding a suitable young man for her to marry.

Gneshe had felt impelled to take Molly, her deaf sister, with her. However, she was warned that the Department of Immigration in America would not permit Molly entry to the United States because of her defect.

Gneshe was undaunted. With a great deal of effort she trained Molly to pronounce her name. When they arrived, Gneshe explained to the immigration officer that her sister was brought up in a small village and had never gone to school. When the officer queried Molly for her name, Gneshe used the prepared signal and stepped firmly on her foot. Molly uttered a guttural "Moooooolie," and much to Gneshe's relief, she was given permission to enter the United States. Though Gneshe was a young girl, she took care of Molly and, in time, found a young man who was also deaf. Molly married him, and they brought up a large family of healthy children.

When Shmuel Ber Ganelas became acquainted with Shimon Shain, he knew at once that he had found his future brother-in-law. Not very long after their arrival in America, Reb Shimon and Gneshe were married.

They settled in a small apartment on East 40th Street in Manhattan, near the slaughterhouse where Reb Shimon worked as a *shochet*. As the family grew, the Shains moved from place to place to make sure that they would live in the vicinity of a yeshiva. "Go play near the yeshiva," Mrs. Shain wisely told her little boys. In this way, she hoped they would glean the Torah spirit emanating from there.

Now, their oldest son, Moshe, was ready for marriage. Reb Shimon and Gneshe Shain decided that the Herman family and I suited them perfectly. They looked forward to their son's meeting me.

Papa had not given up his verbal attacks. Mama was torn: Although she did not want to "lose" me as yet, she didn't intrude; she agreed with Papa that their children should marry at a young age to ensure that they would not stray from the path set for them.

Papa wore me down. Two weeks later, Reb Shimon and his son Moshe, who lived just a few blocks away from our house, were invited for Shabbos afternoon. Some of our *orchim* were

shochet: ritual slaughterer

still drinking tea when they arrived. I served hot tea and cake to our guests. Moshe was a handsome young man, well-dressed and personable. However, I did not have the opportunity to speak personally with him that Shabbos.

After Shabbos, Papa asked my opinion. "Well, I would consider going out with him, but that does not mean I am marrying him already," I said determinedly. Papa was not eager for me to go out in the street with any young man until I was engaged. He preferred that all the meetings be in our home. However, he surrendered to my plea when I complained, "Papa, how can I possibly talk with him in our house? The door opens every minute. There is no privacy at all."

Ten days later, Moshe Shain arrived promptly at eight PM. Mama hurried into my bedroom, where I was putting the finishing touches to my hair. "Ruchoma," she said excitedly, "he's wearing spats." These were little, suede, buttoned coverings over the shoes, the last word in men's style. I had often mentioned to Mama that a gentleman should wear them.

Moshe escorted me to the pier where a large steamship was leaving for Europe. We went on the ship, exploring all its nooks and crannies. He was acquainted with many subjects and kept my interest.

Returning home on the subway, Moshe yawned several times. I looked at him queerly. Was he bored? Finally, he excused himself and explained, "As you know, my father is a *shochet* and must be up very early to get to the slaughterhouse on time. In our house, at nine-thirty in the evening, lights are out." I glanced at my wristwatch. It was almost eleven PM. I felt relieved and added, "In my home, at nine-thirty the evening is just beginning, with the *orchim* coming and going, this one to eat and that one to sleep. I rarely get to bed before midnight."

Papa and Mama awaited me anxiously when I returned. "*Nu?*" they asked.

"He's a nice boy, but how can I know him from talking to him for such a short time?" I answered. Papa arranged another date.

This time Moshe took me to the courthouse and explained the various functions enacted there. The third date, on a Sunday afternoon, we spent walking and discussing various topics of mutual interest.

Papa was getting impatient. After each meeting, the *"Nu"* brought the same reply. "He is a fine young man, but I really do not know him well." After my fourth date with Moshe, when Papa still received my noncommittal reply, he acted!

That Shabbos morning the *orchim* were already seated at the table when Papa and Mama came home from *shul* later than usual. "Good Shabbos, Ruchoma." Their tone had an undercurrent of excitement.

"Tell her, Aidel," Papa prompted Mama.

"You tell her. It was all your idea," Mama retorted.

"Tell me 'what'?" I asked curiously.

"We just visited the Shains. Next Saturday night, God willing, you are becoming engaged to Moshe Shain," Papa said boldly.

"What!" I exploded.

Papa did not let me get any further. "The *orchim* are hungry. Get busy." This statement of Papa's always halted any argument.

Mama was busy serving the fish, pretending not to see me. "Mama, how could you do this to me? I told Papa and you that I do not know him well enough," I accused her.

Papa walked into the kitchen, overhearing my remark. "Look Ruchoma, *I* know him. That is enough. You are fortunate to get such an outstanding, educated young man from an excellent *yiddishe* family." I was in a turmoil. I knew arguing with Papa would be to no avail. It was a *fait accompli*.

When Moshe and I next met, I confided to him Papa's role in hurrying our engagement. Moshe, in turn, told me, "My parents also applied their special kind of tactics to convince me that it's not wise to wait."

We became engaged in February. One concession Papa granted me: I could choose the date of our wedding. Though my in-laws wanted the wedding much earlier, Papa kept his word to me. The wedding was scheduled for Tuesday, September 13, 1932—the twelfth of Elul—at the Hennington Hall on East Second Street in Manhattan. By that time, I fully agreed with Papa that Moshe was the perfect mate for me.

Added note:

Rabbi Moshe Mortchi Epstein, Rosh Yeshiva of the Slobodka Yeshiva in Chevron, was one of our *orchim* at the time of our engagement. He was filling out the *tnoiyim* and Papa noticed that he wrote "Ruchoma bas *Harav* Yaakov Yosef Herman."

Papa quickly said to him, "Rebbe, I am not a *rav*; I have no *smicha*."

Rabbi Epstein responded, "Reb Yaakov Yosef, I am giving you *smicha* right now, so you are a *rav*."

The title remained as Rabbi Epstein had written it.

During my engagement period, I became very attached to Moshe's parents and to his brothers and sisters. I was accepted as one of the family. I was often invited to their home for Shabbos dinner, and basked in the royal treatment I received as the first daughter-in-law.

The loving atmosphere that was prevalent in their home was a source of deep satisfaction to me. Reb Shimon sat at the head of the table with his wife, Gneshe, at his side. The children were seated around the table in graduated size and age. The boys, Boruch Mordechai, Dov Ber, Shmuel, Raphael, and Eliyohu sat on one side, while the girls, Bashe, Dvoshe and Elka sat on the other side. (Noach was in Mir, Poland.)

When my father-in-law made his comments on *parshas hashovua,* even the young children listened attentively. However, it was a normal, lively household with sibling rivalry, as was to be expected in such a large family.

tnoiyim: engagement document

My parents-in-law leading Moshe's younger brother Eliyohu to the chupa. At the left is my mother-in-law's deaf sister Molly.

I marveled at the extreme patience of my mother-in-law. She rarely raised her voice at the children, though there was great provocation. During the week, she awakened at dawn to prepare breakfast for my father-in-law and get the boys ready for yeshiva and the girls for school. Since she had very little time to iron the younger boys' shirts, she put the shirts on them a bit damp, and then straightened the collars. She bought all the food in bulk, explaining to the storekeepers that she had a family restaurant.

My mother-in-law gave birth to her children at home, as was customary in those days. After each birth, Moshe awakened in the morning, surprised to be greeted by a new brother or sister. My father-in-law would then take a ten-day leave from the slaughterhouse to care for her and the other children. He would then do all the cooking and even bake *challos* for Shabbos.

My mother-in-law and the children spent the summer months in the mountains. My father-in-law joined them for most weekends. Whenever he could not come up to the mountains, Papa and Mama invited him to spend Shabbos with us. He brought his own little pot of chicken and soup *erev* Shabbos, as he never ate any chicken or meat that he himself did not slaughter.

Added note:

My nephew, Reb Moshe Aaron Stern, told me that his father, Reb Yom Tov Lipman, once said to him on a Shabbos afternoon, "Moshe Aaron, come, I want to show you what a pious Jew from a previous generation must have looked like."

My sister, Esther, and her family lived on South Ninth Street, Brooklyn, in the building next to my in-laws. Moshe Aaron went to the window and looked down into the neighboring back yard. My father-in-law, Reb Shimon, sat in an armchair, his large *tallis koton* covering his outer shirt, swaying back and forth, as he learned *mishnayos* in a lyrical voice that echoed throughout the yard.

It was an exciting, happy time for me, except for one major problem that marred my joy. Papa insisted that Moshe and I follow Davie and Chaye Dube and Chaim and Bessie to Mir, Poland.

Moshe was amenable, but he did not want to influence me when he saw that I was very adamant about not going. Papa, of course, did not hesitate to apply pressure, as he usually did, when a religious principle was involved.

This time I gave Papa a rough time. Night after night, Papa did his utmost to convince me. "Ruchoma, you will take away a golden opportunity from Moshe if you do not go with him to Mir. He is young. His mind is clear. He can absorb much Torah."

"Papa, he has *smicha* already. He can continue to study Torah in New York. Why must we travel so far away from you and Mama?" I countered. I knew Mama did not really want us to leave, but she never took any stand against Papa when it came to religious issues.

Papa did not let up. I racked my brain for sound arguments. Late one night I protested, "There is no need for you to support us, Papa. Moshe has a B.A. and can get an excellent position as a public school teacher, which pays a high salary." I was fully aware that the financial situation in Papa's fur business was precarious.

Papa was not influenced or impressed. "Ruchoma, Moshe's learning Torah stands above everything else. It will be my greatest satisfaction to support Moshe and you as long as he is learning Torah."

One night, when I was half asleep, Papa sat down at the edge of my bed and delivered his clinching argument. "Ruchoma, you always wanted to travel abroad, visit different countries, see the world, and broaden your horizons. Here is your opportunity. Many young couples go abroad for a honeymoon after their wedding. I will buy you return tickets. Any day you decide you want to return, you will have your tickets available."

I had no fight left in me. Sleepily, I gave in. "All right, Papa, but just for a short time."

Papa gave me a broad smile, "Sleep well, Ruchoma."

The wedding date was drawing nearer. One hot day towards the end of July, Mama said to me, "Let's go to Clinton Street to buy you a wedding gown."

As we were preparing to go, Papa suggested, "Aidel, wash out my *tallis*; it will be a *segulo* for Ruchoma to buy a very beautiful wedding dress."

Mama did not hesitate. She soaked the large *tallis* in the bathtub and scrubbed it. She rinsed it several times and hung it on our outside line to dry. "Have *hatzlocho*," Papa called out to us as we walked out of the door.

....
segulo: good omen

We walked along Clinton Street, peering into the windows of the dress shops. Mama stopped in front of one store that displayed wedding gowns. "Let's go in here."

The store was dark and cool after the bright, sunlit street. The shop owner stood up and greeted us pleasantly. "What can I do for you?"

"I would like to buy a wedding gown for my daughter," Mama said.

"We have a large selection of exclusive wedding gowns; however, it is always advisable to have the bride try it on," the shop owner suggested.

Mama and I stared at her bewildered. Then it dawned on us that she did not realize that I was the bride. Dressed in a blouse and skirt, with flat-heeled sandals, and my hair cut short in a wind-blown style, I hardly looked like a potential bride. (In those days most girls got married in their mid-twenties.)

Mama smiled at the owner, "The bride is with me."

"Oh no, not this child!" she exclaimed, eyeing me from head to toe.

"I'm not as young as I look. I'm seventeen and a half," I said proudly. She still gawked at me, trying to regain her composure.

"I have just the gown for a 'child bride.' " She went into the back room and returned with a lovely, white, lace-trimmed wedding gown with a vest to match.

"Try it on." She escorted me to the dressing room. It fit perfectly. Mama was very pleased, as I stood gazing at myself in the long mirror.

"She will also need a special headdress to wear, as her hair must be covered after the ceremony," Mama explained. (In those days, wigs were not worn by young women. In fact, not very many young women covered their hair after marriage. Wigs, worn only by elderly women, had no real hair style and were all alike.)

The owner had never heard of such a demand before but

was too overawed to question Mama. "I will make one up especially for the bride to match the wedding gown." She took a tape measure and encircled my head with it. She wrote down the measurements on her little pad. "I will also match a veil to the headdress," she offered. "It will be ready in two weeks' time. The price is eighteen dollars." Mama didn't bargain and gave her a deposit. "Lots of luck to you," the woman said, shaking Mama's hand and giving me a peck of a kiss on my cheek.

Papa looked up from his *sefer* when we entered the house. "Papa," I gushed, "I got the most elegant wedding dress with matching headdress and veil. I'm sure it's because Mama washed out your *tallis*."

When we returned two weeks later to pick up the gown, veil and headdress, the owner asked Mama timidly, "Mrs. Herman, may I possibly attend the ceremony? I am anxious to see this 'child bride' at her wedding." Of course, Mama graciously invited her and gave her the date and place of the wedding.

Moshe and I had to obtain a marriage license. Since I was under eighteen years of age, Papa and Mama were required to give their approval. We took the subway to City Hall, where the license bureau issued the necessary papers. When we entered the vast hall, there was a waiting line. We were asked to be seated until our turn came.

A large table and chairs stood in the middle of the room. Papa and Mama sat at each end of the table, while Moshe and I seated ourselves near each other.

I noticed our seating arrangement, which was spontaneous, and quipped to Papa and Mama, "You see, Moshe and I are being married, and we are close to each other, while both of you, who are married for such a long time, are far from each other."

Papa spoke up, "Ruchoma, let me explain something to you. Moshe and you are just starting out in your married life. Your marriage foundation is not firm as yet. You need the physical closeness to assure each other of your devotion.

However, Mama and I, who have lived together for many years, understand each other. We can be on different sides of the table or, for that matter, in different parts of the world, and our marriage remains strong and secure."

Mama was listening intently to Papa's every word. Her face shone. I noticed a fleeting look between them that spoke volumes. For the first time, I realized the great devotion and affection that Papa and Mama had for each other. I had always taken it for granted. It was part of my life and our home. It was an unforgettable and poignant moment for me. Then and there, I prayed in my heart that Moshe and I would also be blessed with the *sholom bayis* that characterized Papa's and Mama's life together and made their marriage meaningful and sweet.

The summer flew by as if on wings. Papa made active preparations for my wedding. The invitations were mailed at the beginning of August. They included, of course, the printed statement, "Women are requested to please come dressed according to the Jewish law."

Papa's doctrine of *tznius* at our weddings was firmly established in the minds of all our relatives and friends, my wedding being the fifth in the Herman family. Papa, therefore, did not have too much opposition to cope with.

The wedding day dawned cool and clear. Papa and Mama hovered over me, as I was fasting. Mama seemed pensive. There would be no more children in the home, since I was the youngest. She already felt a sense of lonesomeness.

Aunt Molly, Papa's sister, came early to help me get dressed. However, by the time she arrived, I was all ready. I did not especially enjoy all the fuss. Moshe and his parents arrived a little after five PM. He looked pale but very handsome in his tailored cut-away suit. His smile of assurance soothed me.

We had made arrangements with a photographer to have pictures taken of us as bride and groom. (In those days the

---

sholom bayis: marital harmony

Rabbi Avrohom Kalmanovitz, the noted head of the Mirrer Yeshiva in the difficult war years, was our mesader kiddushin.

Our engagement picture (1932).

photographer did not take the photographs at the wedding reception, and we had to go to his studio.)

The large car hooted its horn as Mama and I, Moshe and his parents were driven down the street, with all our neighbors waving us on. Papa had left for the hall earlier to make sure everything was to his satisfaction.

When we arrived at the wedding hall after leaving the

studio, most of the guests were already there. The *mazel tovs* rang in our ears, as I was hugged and kissed by all our women friends and relatives.

Rabbi Avrohom Kalmanovitz, who was then an *orech* at our house, performed the wedding ceremony and recited all the blessings. (At that time, it was customary for one rabbi to have all the honors.)

The wedding was a lively one. The men and women danced separately, enjoying the uniqueness of a Herman wedding. The meal was catered to perfection; however, an innovation was introduced by Papa. At each table, there was a printed card which read: "In remembrance of the destruction of our Holy Temple, the pudding and special dessert will not be served." Papa paid for the full meal, including these delicacies.

After the *sheva brochos,* the preparations for our trip to Mir began. There was a great deal of shopping and packing; we had passports to apply for, and we visited relatives and friends to say good-bye. I was in a whirlwind of activity that did not permit too much introspection about my leaving the United States and going so far away from home.

For the short period of time until our departure, Papa rented a furnished room for us not very far from my parents' house. We ate our meals at Papa and Mama's and occasionally at my in-laws.

Originally, Papa had booked passage for us on the *Queen Elizabeth*, one of the largest ships sailing the Atlantic Ocean. However, I had a series of disturbing dreams three nights in succession: The first night I dreamt that I lost my diamond ring; the second night that one of our *orchim* passed away; on the third night I dreamt that a fire broke out aboard the ship Moshe and I were on.

Mama insisted that Papa cancel the tickets for the *Queen Elizabeth* and purchase others on a different steamship. Papa quoted to Mama: "In the merit of going to learn Torah, Moshe and Ruchoma will surely be protected from all harm." This time, however, Mama could not be swayed.

Papa exchanged our tickets and booked passage for us on the *Manhattan*, a ship making her maiden voyage and leaving two days later, December 1, 1932. (While we were sailing on the *Manhattan*, the news came through that a fire had broken out on the *Queen Elizabeth*, but it was fortunately brought under control.)

Papa handed me the return tickets that were valid for a two-year period. I tucked them safely into my pocketbook.

My mother-in-law thoughtfully bought me a rabbit-fur-lined coat. "The Russian winters are very long and cold. You will need a very warm coat, Ruchoma." She well remembered her years in Russia. Though Mir was in Poland, it was very close to the Russian border.

My father-in-law brought us the largest tongue he could buy from his slaughterhouse and smoked it. As an after-thought, my mother-in-law bought a five-pound farmer cheese to make sure that we would have enough food for the trip, though there was a supervised kosher kitchen aboard.

Mrs. Schroit prepared a ten-pound tin can of honeyed prunes and almonds for her sons Yankel and Yosel, who were studying in the Mirrer Yeshiva through Papa's prodding. We packed the can in with our hand luggage.

The parting was an emotional, tearful one—for all except Papa. Though I knew how much Papa would miss Moshe and me, he stood like a soldier controlling his emotions. Everyone from our immediate family was there. All Moshe's brothers and sisters, besides many relatives, close friends of the family and my girlfriends were on hand to see us off. They stood in small groups chatting with each other.

I overheard Mama say to Aunt Molly, "When Yankev Yosef sent Nochum Dovid to learn in far-away yeshivos, first to New Haven, then to Chevron in Eretz Yisroel, I was thankful that I had daughters as well. But now he even sends our daughters away."

The ship's gong bellowed: "All visitors, please leave the boat." There was a last minute parting—hugs, kisses and good wishes. My father-in-law, teary-eyed, blessed us. My mother-in-law, crying softly, added, "*Kinder, zait gezunt un shtark un est gut.*"

Papa whispered to me, "Take care of Moshe; he is a prince of a young man." He clasped Moshe's hands in his and shook them warmly, "Have *hatzlocho* in your Torah learning."

Mama, sobbing, held me close to her. I tasted her salty tears. "Take good care of Ruchoma; she is so young," she said tearfully to Moshe.

Then the last wave of good-byes. Tears blurred my eyes. I had an intense desire to run down the gangplank to be held once more in Mama's arms, but the ship slowly sailed off—belching its black-gray smoke from the large chimney stacks.

We were on our way!

Kinder, zait gezunt un shtark un est gut: children, be healthy and strong and eat well

2

New Horizons: Mir

13

"Honeymoon"

Before we left the United States, Papa and Mama asked me to write them as often as possible. Since my original letters were lost through the years, I have re-created them from memory, with the facts intact.

Dearest Papa and Mama,

Our cabin was a small one, three floors below the main deck. Its furnishings consisted of bunk beds, a small clothing closet, a little night table, two chairs and a sink. The bathroom facilities and showers were situated in the long corridor and had to be shared with the other passengers.

Ten of our twelve valises were stored in the baggage room, but even the two we kept, plus our hand baggage, dwarfed our cabin, so that we had very little space in which to move about. Moshe graciously offered to sleep on the top bunk.

We unpacked some of our clothes and stacked the gift boxes of chocolate on our night table. Though my mother-in-law had given me explicit instructions to make sure to have the food they gave us refrigerated to prevent spoilage, I temporarily stuffed the smoked tongue, the farmer cheese, and Mrs.

Schroit's tin of jelly into the bottom of our clothing closet. I thought that the next morning would be soon enough to search for the kitchen, as I was too overwrought and tired that first night.

The next morning we awoke to a pitching boat. Moshe could hardly climb down from the bunk bed to put on his *tallis* and *tefillin*. We both could not stomach the thought of food, so we remained in our cabin.

The following two days passed in a daze of nausea. The chocolate was our only diet, which came up as soon as it went down. The boat was tossed about like a toy on the high seas.

The third day out, I called up to Moshe, "We'll die of starvation, and no one will know." There was no response from above. "Moshe," I screamed louder in panic. A faint grunt — he was alive.

The room reeked with a foul odor. With trembling hands and feet, I crept off my bed to investigate. The smoked tongue was covered with a fine mold of gray. The five-pound farmer cheese was shaded a lovely moss of green. Mrs. Schroit's ten-pound tin had sprung a leak. The honeyed prunes and almonds covered our cabin floor with a sticky golden brown.

Our "HONEYmoon" had started in earnest!

Moshe carried the leaky tin of jam, while I took the tongue and cheese in either hand. With superhuman effort, we wended our way to the upper deck. Bobbing and weaving like drunken sailors, we managed to reach the railing. The towering waves were angrily dashing against the side of the ship, and the salty spray of the foaming breakers drenched us from head to foot.

First, Moshe heaved the ten-pound tin overboard. For a moment I saw Mrs. Schroit's accusing face and finger mirrored in the large round tin can. Then it disappeared. Poor Yankel and Yosel — no honeyed prunes and almonds. I was sure that their mother had devoted many hours in its preparation, and it had cost so much.

Then went the five-pound farmer cheese, which blended with the green-blue ocean. The smoked tongue was last. As it rode the waves with glee, it stuck its tongue out to us in defiance, relieved to be freed from being imprisoned in the tiny closet. Our eyes were glued to it until it was swallowed up by a giant wave.

"Moshe," I asked, as we tremblingly left the flooded deck, "do you think fish enjoy eating cheese, tongue, and honeyed prunes and almonds?" I could visualize the schools of fish at the bottom of the ocean hungrily devouring our precious gifts to them. It salved my guilty conscience a bit.

Love, *Moshe and Ruchoma*

Dearest Papa and Mama,

The next morning, the ocean miraculously calmed. It was a shimmering carpet of different hues of green and blue, with bits of white foam.

For the first time since we boarded the ship, we entered the dining room and reached the kosher section. The passengers were eating heartily. Though Moshe and I felt less seasick, the food still did not whet our appetite. We were both pale and wan. Our clothes hung loosely on us. We forced some food down. Lo and behold! It stayed down. During the remaining days of our trip, we tried our utmost to recoup our lost strength.

Moshe and I celebrated my eighteenth birthday on December 6th, aboard the *Manhattan*. Without my knowledge, Moshe discreetly told the waiter about my birthday. The waiter ordered the cook to bake a special birthday cake for me. All the passengers at our table sang, "Happy birthday." It lifted my spirits a bit.

Love, *Moshe and Ruchoma*

Dearest Papa and Mama,

The stormy weather at the outset of our trip caused a two-day delay, so that the boat docked at the port of Hamburg, Germany, on Shabbos afternoon, ten days after we had boarded. The captain granted us permission to remain aboard until Saturday night. All the other passengers disembarked, and we felt a sudden sense of lonesomeness.

Saturday night, right after Moshe made *havdolo*, we hurried off the ship with a porter assisting us with our baggage. We hired a taxi and, fortunately, Moshe was able to converse with the driver in German, as that was one of the languages which he had studied in college. He asked that we be driven to a hotel that would not be too far from the railroad station, where we were scheduled to board the train for Poland the next afternoon. We checked our cumbersome valises at the hotel desk.

Carrying our hand luggage and Moshe's briefcase with his *tallis* and *tefillin*, we were directed to our room. We were hungry, but too exhausted to search for a grocery store that sold kosher items. I thought longingly of the cheese and tongue. . . .

The next morning we found a small grocery. We bought kosher rolls, butter, and a container of milk, which we finished to the last crumb and drop.

We then went to the post office to send telegrams — one to you, which I hope you received, and the other to Nochum Dovid in Mir, which read, "Arriving Tuesday, December 12th — seven PM Horodzei — God willing."

Our train was scheduled to leave Hamburg for Poland at four PM. We left the hotel in ample time and hired a taxi to drive us to the station. After being driven around for a half-hour, we realized that the driver was taking us "for a ride" to hike up his fee.

We reached the train station just minutes before our train's departure.

Love, Moshe and Ruchoma

Dearest Papa and Mama,

The journey by train lasted almost two days, but we had prepared enough food for the long, drawn-out trip. We dozed fitfully in our seats during the nights.

When we finally arrived at the Polish border, we were

ordered off the train for passport control and to have our baggage checked. The customs officers ransacked our valises until they were convinced that we carried no contraband.

We were on the last leg of our trip. Though we were both exhausted, our excitement mounted as we looked forward to greet our loved ones, and, at last, our new home—Mir.

The train stopped with a shrill shriek at Horodzei. Though it was two-and-a-half hours from Mir, it was the nearest station.

We alighted with our twelve valises and all our hand baggage surprisingly still intact. The station was dark and deserted.

For a moment we thought it was completely vacant. Suddenly, two figures emerged out of the shadows. There was a cry of recognition. It was Nochum Dovid and Moshe's brother, Noach.

I introduced Moshe to Davie, who kissed him and gave me one of your "Papa pinches" on my cheek. Moshe then introduced me to Noach, who was delighted to have his "big" brother near him.

Two *fuhrs* (wagons with saddled horses) awaited us outside the station. One was for all of us to travel in, and one was for our luggage.

Chaim, Bessie, Chaye Dube, and their children were awaiting us in Mir.

We climbed onto the wagon. Large, heavy, moldy-smelling blankets were thrown over our feet. The horses trotted gaily along the rock-strewn road, with the driver "giddiyapping" them along. The wagon rolled and rocked, swaying from side to side, so that we had to hold on tightly to prevent being thrown off. The sky was starry, with the moon lighting the dark-shadowed road.

Love, *Moshe and Ruchoma*

14

Initiation

Dearest Papa and Mama,

During most of the trip to Mir, Davie and Noach plied us with questions about our loved ones. Moshe supplied the details; I could hardly speak coherently. My teeth rattled from cold. Every bone in my body ached from the constant heaving motion of the wagon.

I thought of both of you and home. What would you be doing now? A tremendous wave of lonesomeness enveloped me. I welcomed the darkness, as I did not want Davie and Noach to notice my tears, which fell silently on the moldy coverings. I was already married, and acting like a baby.

A short distance from Mir, we heard shouts. Chaye Dube and Bessie ran toward our moving wagon. The driver brought the galloping horses to a halt. Chaye Dube and Bessie climbed aboard the wagon, kissing and holding me tightly to them. It felt good to have them near me. I introduced them to their new brother-in-law.

We entered the tiny town of Mir, with the clippety-clop of the horses' hoofs on the cobblestones loudly proclaiming our arrival. We stopped in front of a small wooden house. I was helped down from the wagon, my toes icy and feeling wobbly. I leaned on Bessie for support.

Chaim greeted us from the doorway with a warm, "*Sholom aleichem.*" Yankel and Yosel Schroit were also there and helped carry in the valises.

We marched into Davie's small apartment. It consisted of a dining room and a bedroom, and a kitchen which they shared with their *balebuste*, Dverke. The dining room was lit with one tiny bulb, which cast eerie shadows on the walls.

Some of your *talmidim* were seated around the table, and I recognized Shachne Zohn, Shmuel Shechter, Moshe Gordon, Reuven Epstein, and Binyomin Bernstein. There were a few other young men whom I did not know.

"Turn on another light, so I can see better," I suggested. There was complete silence for a moment, then a loud chuckle from the young men. Davie was dismayed. He had made a special effort to borrow a "large" twenty-watt bulb from the yeshiva especially for our arrival. Normally, they only used a fifteen-watt bulb.

We were served cookies and hot drinks that warmed me a little. Though our family and everyone present were hardly able to contain their curiosity and wanted to hear regards from home, they wisely did not ask too many questions when they realized how very exhausted Moshe and I were.

Love, *Moshe and Ruchoma*

Dearest Papa and Mama,

For our first night in Mir, Davie magnanimously made arrangements for us to stay at the only "hotel" in the city. We left our baggage in Davie's house and took only our nightclothes.

Davie, Chaye Dube, Chaim and Bessie walked us to the hotel and introduced us to the owner. They left, after reassuring us, "We will see you first thing tomorrow morning. Rest well."

....

Sholom aleichem: Peace unto you / *balebuste*: landlady

We were shown to our room, which was lit by a kerosene lamp. Two small iron cots stood on either side of the room. A wooden closet with several hooks in it occupied one wall. An old, shaky wooden table and a rickety chair completed the furnishings.

I glanced through the window, and only the darkness of night and a deep silence greeted me. It was very cold in our room, and I shivered inwardly.

I hoped morning would bring a lighter and happier note.

Love, *Moshe and Ruchoma*

Dearest Papa and Mama,

That first night in Mir I got into my bathrobe and told Moshe I'd be back in a few minutes. I went looking for the hotel owner, who sat all alone near a table, knitting a woolen garment.

In my best Yiddish I explained to her that I needed a ladies' room. She stared at me for a moment and then requested, *"Tut zich on"* (get dressed). I looked at her in bewilderment and ran back to our room.

"Moshe, the woman is not normal. I asked her for a ladies' room, and she told me to get dressed. I'm sure I understood her."

"Humor her," Moshe advised me with psychological wisdom.

I hurriedly got into my blue woolen suit again. The woman was waiting outside our door. *"Tut on aiyer mantel"* (put on your coat), she said. I asked no questions but ran into the room once again and came out wearing my fur-trimmed winter coat. This time she eyed me from head to toe. *"Tut on de volokes,"* and she handed me a pair of long black woolen boots, which I pulled over my high-heeled pumps. They reached well over my knees.

I wondered what ritual she was preparing for me. I followed her out of the hotel. The swaying kerosene lamp she held created bizarre designs on the cobbled alleyway. I felt I was being led to the gallows.

She stopped in front of a tiny, wooden shack, opened the creaky door and shoved me in. Through the slats of the door, the kerosene lamp barely lit the dark interior, from which emanated a damp, offensive odor. It was a primitive outhouse, which nauseated me.

When we re-entered the hotel, the lady showed me a pail of water that was placed on a tall stool. She handed me a large cup with which to wash my hands. The water was ice cold.

Moshe was anxiously waiting for me. "What happened?" he asked.

For a moment I was speechless. "Moshe, you go next. You'll find out." He immediately put on his warm overcoat and hat without being instructed. When he returned much the wiser, I cried to him, "Moshe, we cannot possibly live in a place where there are no plumbing facilities."

"Maybe in the house that was rented for us there will be better accommodations," Moshe tried his best to comfort me. I discovered all too soon that this type of "ladies' room" is used exclusively here.

Papa, I know you will think me a coward, but we intend to use our return tickets shortly. Right now they bolster my courage.

Hoping to see you soon.

Love, Moshe and Ruchoma

Dearest Papa and Mama,

Very early the next morning, Chaye Dube and Bessie came to the hotel. They listened with compassion as I described the catastrophic events of the night before.

"Why didn't you ever write about this?" I demanded. Their silence was the answer. I understand, Papa, that you wisely advised them not to mention this "delicate" subject in their letters; otherwise, I do not think Moshe and I would be here now.

They are both trying their best to comfort me, telling me that in time I will adjust. I did not confide in them that as soon as we recuperate from our trip, we are seriously contemplating returning to the States. I should add that Moshe is willing to stick it out, but I am not so brave.

You surely want to hear all about your darling grandchildren. Nochum Dovid's Shmuel Yitzchok, who is two-and-a-half years old, resembles him. He is a smart little boy, who speaks Yiddish so quickly and fluently that I can scarcely understand him. Their daughter, Baile Golde, is ten months old and stands up already. She is a very cute *maidele*.

Bessie's Fruma Rochel is a twenty-month, blonde version of Chaim, who adores her. She sits on his lap while he is learning. He is such a *masmid* that I rarely see him without a *sefer*.

The children were delighted and excited with the many toys I brought for them. It keeps them busy for hours. The new outfits you sent for them fit them perfectly. Chaye Dube and Bessie will have photographs taken of the children in their new clothes and send them to you.

Papa, I took care of all the letters and personal regards you sent to your *talmidim*. They are all gaining in their Torah studies, and *yiras shomayim*—which they say is "All thanks to you." I also gave Mr. Marcus's son Bobby the letter from his parents, and he was most appreciative. I asked Yankel and Yosel Schroit not to reveal to their mother what happened to the jelly she sent them, as it would only upset her.

Love, *Moshe and Ruchoma*

Dearest Papa and Mama,

By now you have surely received my previous letters describing our trip, our arrival to Mir, and our first night in the hotel. I can see you, Papa, smiling broadly when you read about our "initiation." However, it was a harrowing experience and a

---

maidele: young girl / *masmid*: diligent student

major problem, especially now in the winter months, when it is freezingly cold.

I still toy with the thought of using our return tickets, but I do not want to be dubbed a "baby."

We are sleeping temporarily in Bessie's house until our furniture and bedding, which Chaye Dube ordered for us, arrive from Baranowitz. There is a couch in her dining room, and for the night we open a folding cot bed. We eat our meals alternately at Chaye Dube's and Bessie's homes; they live across the street from each other and close to the yeshiva.

They are not only devoted wives and mothers, but also excellent *balebustes* who cook, bake, and shop like pros. You can be proud of them. I hope someday to attain their status. Right now it seems like reaching up to the twinkling stars.

Moshe is settled in the yeshiva. Nochum Dovid arranged for very suitable *chavrusos* and he is very pleased.

The first day Moshe went to the yeshiva, he returned with gratifying news. The yeshiva has plumbing facilities! A wealthy man donated the money for it. I never experienced such keen jealousy. For the first time in my life, I wished I were a man—as you originally hoped I would be—and could change roles with Moshe. Learning in the yeshiva and having a real men's room nearby seemed like a dream come true.

My jealousy was short-lived. The next day Moshe returned from the yeshiva chagrined. The plumbing breaks down regularly. Then it is even worse—if that is possible—than the incredible outhouse. So, we are in equal misery once more.

As you know, we have a rented apartment a few blocks from where Chaye Dube and Bessie live. It is opposite the large city *shul* and is one of the very few brick houses in Mir. The rent is fifty dollars a year, which certainly is reasonable enough. I am sure the twenty-five dollars monthly post-dated checks you gave us for the first year will be sufficient for all our expenses.

Love, *Moshe and Ruchoma*

....

chavrusos: learning partners

Dearest Papa and Mama,

What an exciting day! Our furniture and bedding finally arrived from Baranowitz. Half the town was on hand when the two wagons stopped in front of our house.

I will now describe our apartment and furnishings.

Our main room, the dining room, has four large windows, from which we can see much of the town. During the winter months, double windows are installed and sealed, with only a *fortichke* (a tiny window, which is installed in the upper corner of one of the large windows) for fresh air.

The dining-room table is dark mahogany wood, with five matching chairs. The *canope* (couch) has a raised headrest and is covered with a heavy cotton material of paisley design. The wardrobe closet will have to suffice for all our clothes and linens. We ordered an open bookcase from the carpenter for Moshe's *seforim*.

Our small bedroom has one window. The two dark-brown metal beds fit into it. I converted our trunk, which arrived here earlier, into a night table and placed it between the beds. Our kerosene lamp stands on it, as we have no electricity in our bedroom. The spring mattresses are a novelty here and are not too comfortable. [We did not realize until much later that we were actually sleeping on box springs without mattresses.] I guess it is better than the *shenicks* (straw mattresses) most people use here.

Now on to our kitchen, which has a decided advantage over Chaye Dube's and Bessie's, as I do not have to share it with my *balebuste*. There is a small, white wooden table, on which my primus stands, and a high stool where the pail of water is placed. About the primus and the "water-drawing" process, I will write in future letters.

Right off the kitchen is a very small room, which we are converting into sleeping quarters for Noach, as soon as we buy a cot bed.

Our feather pillows are the largest I have ever seen. They

occupy half of our beds. The *perrennes* (down quilts) keep us comfortably warm.

Love, *Moshe and Ruchoma*

Dearest Papa and Mama,

Our apartment is heated by means of a *kachal* stove made of white tiles, which extends from the floor to the ceiling, allowing the smoke to escape through the chimney. It is of rectangular shape, with two sides exposed to our dining room, one side to our bedroom, and the opening side to our kitchen. One side of our *balebuste*'s stove also reaches into our bedroom.

During the winter, it is also used for cooking, with a special little compartment (*kachale*) to keep the food warm after it's cooked.

To heat the stove and cook in it is a complicated procedure, which I still have not mastered. Wood is bought in the market place and stored in the barn outside our house. The wood is then chopped into small logs to be able to fit into the stove. About eight to ten pieces of wood are placed into the dark interior. The *shpendlech* (slivers of wood that fall from the logs during the chopping process) are placed on pieces of newspaper and lit. This, in turn, is supposed to kindle the larger logs. But only if the wood is exceptionally dry does it catch the first time. After the logs become small burning embers, they are shoved to one side to make room for the pots of food to be cooked.

To get the pot of food in and out of the stove a *vilke* (a wooden handle about forty inches long, with a half-moon shaped piece of iron attached to it) is used. The piece of iron is shaped to hold the pot in place. Since I have small pots, my *vilke* is a special size to fit them. The pots themselves are made of black iron outside and white enamel inside.

Once the pot is held by the *vilke*, the next precarious step is to place it safely near the embers at the exact spot where the food will neither burn nor remain raw.

I still have not tested my expertise in cooking in the stove, as we still eat our main meal and Shabbos meals either with Chaye Dube or Bessie.

Love, *Moshe and Ruchoma*

P.S. Please tell my mother-in-law that the rabbit-fur-lined coat she bought for me is a "life-saver" and keeps me warm in the freezing weather. I shall write my in-laws a separate letter very soon.

Dearest Papa and Mama,

I was always proud that I was the forward on my basketball team in high school and that I scored many points getting the ball into the basket. Now I am all thumbs when it comes to placing the pot of food at the right spot in my *kachal* stove.

My pot either turns over when it is halfway into the stove, or my food is burnt or undercooked. Whichever way, it is a disaster. When the pot overturns, the raw chicken, carrots, and water choke the burning embers. A black pall of smoke covers my kitchen and even infiltrates my *balebuste*'s dining room. Each time I "goof," she comes running into my house with a look of disapproval in her eyes.

One day, I successfully placed the pot safely into the stove. However, I must have shoved it too far from the cooking area. When Moshe returned from the yeshiva several hours later for his dinner, the food had not even come to a boil. I lit my primus as a last alternative. The food takes on an odor of kerosene, especially if it needs cooking on the primus for any length of time. The fumes choke me. It took me all of eight hours to prepare one meal, but we had a cooked meal for *supper.*

The primus is a weird contraption that is used for minor cooking, like a boiled or fried egg, cereal, or boiling water for tea. It has a round copper-colored container with a little pump attached to it, where the kerosene is stored. Halfway up the primus is a small round plate, which you fill with "spirit" (purplish alcohol). You kindle the spirit, pump and pray. It should light up with a uniform flame, but it does not always follow instructions.

The entire primus exploded several times. My *balebuste* (I will write about her and her family in another letter) "tactfully" told me that it is fortunate her house is a brick one; otherwise I would already have burned it down.

I try not to use this "fire hazard" too often, so Moshe and I are eating a lot of cheese and cream for breakfast and supper. Bessie's *balebuste*'s sister, Rochel, prepares these herself and sells them.

Continued:

From the fire into the water: the water is drawn from a well that is about a half block from our house. A heavy cord is rolled on a wheel with a handle, to which a large pail is attached. By turning the handle, the pail is lowered into the deep well and then raised again: hopefully, it's filled to the brim with water.

It looked simple. I tried it. I lowered the pail until I heard a splash. With great effort, huffing and puffing, I turned the handle to bring up the pail of water. To my utter consternation, there was just "a drop in the bucket."

I watched the *shikses* draw water and bring up a full pail without any strain. They usually bring up two full pails of water, which they carry on a heavy stick extending on both sides of their shoulders.

I am convinced that I could never be a farmer's wife. It is fortunate I married a *ben Torah*. However, I am trying to face the challenge and hope someday to win the battle of "fire and water."

Until I do, I needed someone to chop wood, draw water from the well and discard the accumulated dirty water and garbage. My *balebuste* recommended Luba, a *shikse*, whose fee is eight zlotys (one dollar) a month. She arrives each morning

---

shikses: gentile girls

The picture of me near the kachal *stove, in our apartment in Mir (1933).*

and tends to these chores. She also washes our dark-brown wooden floors several times a week.

Luba also takes care of our soiled laundry, for which I pay her separately. She takes it home with her and delivers the washed and ironed laundry in a week or so. The clothes do not come back sparklingly clean like the laundry in the States, but rather, already have telltale gray on them.

Love, Moshe and Ruchoma

P.S. After I painstakingly described our *kachal* stove in a previous letter, one of the American yeshiva boys photographed me near it. I am enclosing the photo. The only place to reap the full benefit of its warmth is where I'm standing.

Dearest Papa and Mama,

Papa, in your letter, you ask why Moshe's name is signed on all of my letters with nary a line from him. There is a valid reason. You taught me that a husband and wife should be "one." Since Moshe and I are sharing each other's experiences, it is fitting for his name to be signed on my letters.

However, he did take your words to mind, and he is preparing a "piece" of Torah, which I hope to include in my next letter. I am sure this will make amends for any lack of writing on his part.

Moshe is most patient and understanding of my hardships in the process of becoming a genuine *balebuste*. Fortunately, he is not fussy about his food. I guess this results from his being part of a large family, where his mother had no time to fuss with meals.

Esther and Frieda certainly had it easy when they married and set up house. The gas ovens, running water, plumbing facilities, steam heat, and other comforts so taken for granted in the States would be heaven to me here. However, I will have to come down to "earth" and master the complex tasks.

Papa, I am sure you will be pleased to hear that we decided for the time being not to use our return tickets. Moshe is learning very well, which is of prime importance and the real purpose of our coming to Mir.

Love, *Moshe and Ruchoma*

P.S. Please tell Frieda that I still did not receive the subscription to the *Sunday News* she gave me as a going-away gift. It takes weeks to receive mail from the States. Ask her to keep writing, as her letters lift my spirits—not the primus kind.

15

Getting acquainted

Dearest Papa and Mama,

Moshe and I took a long walk to acquaint ourselves with Mir. Though you visited Mir about two years ago, Papa, I am sure you did not have the time to see the town as it really is. You, Mama, have never been here, so I will picture it for both of you.

There are five main streets. The yeshiva is situated on Wysoka Gass (street), where the Rosh Yeshiva, Rabbi Finkel, the Rav of Mir, Rabbi Kamai, and their families live. Nochum Dovid and Bessie also live on that street.

Vilna Gass, the longest in the town, extends for a few blocks. There are several small shops on that street: dry goods, hardware, a store that sells coffee, tea, and other dry foods, a liquor store, a barber shop, and the post office. There is also a small kiosk where the *goyim* come on market day to eat and drink.

Miranka Gass is the street where the *mashgiach* lives. He usually passes our house on his way to the yeshiva. We live in a corner house, on Cierkiewna Gass, bordering Wysoka, so that we have a clear view almost to the yeshiva.

The street of the *mark* (market place) has a row of stores selling all kinds and types of material. Since ready-made clothes, such as coats, suits and dresses, are unavailable here, everything is sewn by tailors or dressmakers.

The entire town is no larger than an area of five or six city blocks on the East Side of New York, with a population of five hundred Jewish families (approximately two thousand people). The *goyim* live in the outskirts of the town, in little villages.

Just outside the town, there is a small river, spanned by a bridge. The river is used by the people to bathe in during the warm weather. Clothes are also washed by the river edge in the spring and summer months. About a kilometer from the town the *Giminy* (local town council) is housed, and the small schoolhouse is close by.

The townspeople engage in horse and oxen trading. There are a few *sofrim*, tailors, and shoemakers. However, most of the people earn their livelihood by providing the yeshiva boys with food and sleeping quarters.

This is Mir—a tiny town in its physical aspect, but gigantic in Torah and ethics—where five hundred young men from all over the world are studying in the Mirrer Yeshiva.

Love, *Moshe and Ruchoma*

Dearest Papa and Mama,

The snows came. There is a thick layer of snow covering all the streets in Mir. I understand that it remains until the warm spring sun thaws it. The only means of travel now is by a horse-drawn sleigh.

One evening during Chanuka, Davie, Chaye Dube, Chaim, Bessie, Moshe and I went sleigh riding outside the town. Although I had a sled when I was a child, I've never before gone in a horse-drawn sled. It was very exhilarating.

From the distance, we were able to see the imposing castle

....

sofrim: scribes

Chaim (the middle one of the 3 in front) with other talmidim, *with the castle in the background.*

overlooking the town. The *knasz* (prince) and his serfs live in this castle.

For several centuries before the nineteenth, Mir was the property of the Radziwill princes. Now it is an autonomous estate, not under the jurisdiction of the Polish government.

As I gazed at the castle, it brought back all the fairy tales I'd read about kings and princes when I was a very young child. I realize now that it was not all "fairy tales."

I am enclosing a photograph of Chaim with some *talmidim* of the Mirrer Yeshiva posing in front of the castle.

Though I mentioned my *balebuste* to you in previous letters, I did not really "introduce" her to you. Her name is Esther Mirel Kaplinsky. Her husband, Reb Avrohom, is a *ben Torah*, who learns in the yeshiva. They have three children: Yehuda Leib, Zalman Yoel, and Yehudiske, who range in age from two-and-a-half to seven. The children are very shy, but I hope in time they will become more friendly.

Her brick house, which she inherited from her parents, is a source of pride to her. Part of her livelihood consists of the income she receives from our apartment, and from the rental of a bedroom to yeshiva boys. In her home she also sells linens, which remained from her parents' store.

More about my *balebuste* in my next letter.

Love, *Moshe and Ruchoma*

Dearest Papa and Mama,

Our apartment is separated from my *balebuste*'s by a flimsy door, adjoining her dining room. It is fortunate that Moshe and I speak English, as every word can be heard clearly from both sides of the door.

We share the cellar in her kitchen, which, interestingly enough, doubles as a unit to keep vegetables from freezing during the cold winter and as cold storage to protect the food from spoilage in the hot months.

We also share the large cooking stove in her kitchen, which is used during the summer, when we do not heat our *kachal* stove. The barn and outhouses in the yard are also shared.

Esther Mirel is doing her utmost to transform me into a real *balebuste* and has taken me in tow. We have a language barrier because her Yiddish is liberally interspersed with Polish words, while mine is with English. I have made progress and can communicate with her intelligently; however, sometimes her strange expressions defy interpretation.

For instance, when I asked her for simple instructions in cooking, "How much salt is required?" her terse answer was "A *chuch*," for my question on the amount of sugar, "A *hoifen*," and for liquid, "A *shpritz*."

I finally got up enough courage, when Esther Mirel was not at home, to ask her husband, Reb Avrohom, who is a very understanding person, to demonstrate what these "foreign terms" mean.

He patiently showed me: *chuch*—a pinch of salt; *hoifen*—a handful of sugar; *shpritz*—a few drops of any liquid. I am still experimenting with these measurements, but my food does not always taste the way it should.

Mama, I regret never having interested myself in learning the art of cooking. I did not think it was of major importance, but I realize now the mistake I made.

I am learning the hard way!

Love, *Moshe and Ruchoma*

Dearest Papa and Mama,

The first Shabbos we were in Mir, Nochum Dovid, Chaye Dube, Chaim, and Bessie accompanied us to the Rosh Yeshiva, Rabbi Lezer Yudel Finkel. He lives with his family in the yeshiva courtyard. He has four sons and one daughter.

Of course, Reb Lezer Yudel looks much older since I last saw him when I was a child. He asked many questions about your welfare and sends his blessings and personal regards.

He remembered my teaching him English, when he was our *orech*. I used to teach him numbers—say "One," and he said, "Von." It made me recall vivid memories of my childhood. My visit brought home to me the greatness of the many *roshei yeshiva, rabbonim*, and learned men who were just *orchim* to me.

Here, Rabbi Finkel, whose name reverberates throughout the Torah world, is the Rosh Yeshiva of the renowned Mirrer Yeshiva. He and his Rebbetzin Malka treated us royally. She is a friendly, motherly person, to whom I was immediately drawn.

Rebbetzin Finkel is the sister of Rabbi Avrohom Tzvi Kamai. He is considered one of the greatest *poskim*.

Rabbi Finkel's only daughter, Miriam, is married to Rabbi Chaim Shmulevitz, who is known as one of the outstanding *lomdim* of the Mirrer Yeshiva. Their little girl, Ettel, is the same age as Bessie's Fruma Rochel, and they play together.

poskim: halachic authorities / *lomdim*: scholars

Reb Lezer Yudel Finkel   Rabbi Avrohom Tzvi Kamai

We visited Rabbi Kamai and his family as well, as they, also, live in the yeshiva courtyard. They have three daughters, two of whom are married. Here, too, we were greeted very warmly.

On most Shabbosim, Chaye Dube and Bessie visit their homes, so there is a close relationship, which I also wish to cultivate.

Love, *Moshe and Ruchoma*

Dearest Papa and Mama,

Our second Shabbos in Mir, we visited the *mashgiach* and his family. They live a few blocks from our house. As you know, Rabbi Yeruchem Levovitz is one of the greatest *mashgichim* of this generation. He is a disciple of the famous Yeshiva of Kelm, where the *mussar* movement of Rabbi Yisroel Salanter developed. He has been *mashgiach* in Mirrer Yeshiva for over twenty years, and all revere him.

His oldest daughter, Chasal, is married to Rabbi Yisroel

Reb Yeruchem Levovitz, the mashgiach *in the Mirrer Yeshiva. In the pictures below, his son Moshe Leib is behind him.*

On datche *(vacation), reading a letter.*

*Rabbi Yechezkel
(Chatzkel) Levenstein*

Chaim Kaplan, and his oldest son, Reb Yisroel, is married to
Rabbi Kosovsky's daughter, Chava. Both his son-in-law and his
son are great *talmidei chachomim*. Chava's father is the well-
known Rabbi of Johannesburg, South Africa, and a brother-in-
law of Rabbi Chaim Ozer of Vilna. The *mashgiach* also has
three younger sons, who are not married.

The *mashgiach* and his *rebbetzin* made us feel very much
at ease. The *rebbetzin* invited me to come to her house often. It
is uplifting to visit these Torah giants and their families.

Rabbi Yechezkel (Chatzkel) Levenstein is a very great
talmid chochom and *tzaddik*. Reb Chatzkel studied in the
Yeshiva of Kelm, where the *mashgiach* also learned.

Though he has no official capacity in the yeshiva, his
presence is inspiring to all the *talmidim*. He gives *shmuessen* in
his house to small groups of yeshiva men, but not on a regular
basis.

He lives with his *rebbetzin* and two daughters, Zlotka and
Yecheved, who are in my age group, just up the street from us. I
have become very friendly with them and visit their home
often. They all treat me like one of their family.

....
shmuessen: talks

I set my clock by watching Reb Chatzkel walk from his home to the yeshiva twice a day. He never varies by a minute, even in the heaviest snowstorm. Moshe told me that one of the practices in Kelm is the strict observance of punctuality.

Love, *Moshe and Ruchoma*

Dearest Papa and Mama,

I became acquainted with Liba Gulevsky, who is just my age. Her father, Rabbi Elchonon Tzvi Gulevsky, is Rosh Yeshiva in Harav Sorotzkin's yeshiva in Lutsk, where he is well-known as a *marbitz Torah*. Since Lutsk is quite a distance from Mir, he returns home only twice a year, for Pesach and Sukkos.

Papa, when I think of our close relationship, I feel sorry for his children who have so little communication with their father.

Liba's two older sisters, Chana and Leah, are studying in the Bais Yaakov founded by Frau Schenirer in Krakow. Liba also has two younger brothers. Her mother, Nechama, has a *stanze*, which means that several yeshiva boys eat all their meals in her house. This helps toward the support of her family, as Rabbi Gulevsky's salary does not suffice.

Both Liba and her mother make me feel very comfortable in their home. In fact, Liba's mother asked me to call her by her first name, "Nechama" and not "Rebbetzin."

There is a young woman with whom I have also become friendly. Though she is older than I am, Bat Sheva Leshinsky treats me like a younger sister of hers. Her *stanze*, which is considered one of the best in Mir, caters mostly to the American or foreign yeshiva boys. There is always a waiting line to get into her *stanze*. Her husband, Reb Dovid, learns in the yeshiva. She has three young children, Rochel, Rivka, and Yankel.

I am impressed with the custom of wives supporting their families to permit their husbands to devote all their time to Torah learning. In the States it is unheard of. You, Papa,

....
marbitz Torah: disseminator of Torah / *stanze*: lodging

Yecheved and myself on the staircase, Liba and Zlotka below.

introduced the concept of married couples emigrating to a place of Torah, where the husband can learn without the worry of earning a livelihood. However, you undertook the burden of support.

Love, *Moshe and Ruchoma*

P.S. I am enclosing a photograph of my girlfriends and me on the steps of our house. Yecheved stands right near me. Below her is Liba, and Zlotka is below me.

Dearest Papa and Mama,

Moshe and I were pleased to hear that you received a letter from the Rosh Yeshiva, Reb Lezer Yudel, with a special mention about us. I am sure you had a lot of *nachas* from the fact that Moshe is learning diligently and progressing very well in his Torah studies.

I wrote in detail about my problems in acclimating to life in Mir, but I have been neglectful in writing how smoothly Moshe adjusted to yeshiva life.

His schedule is as follows: The morning prayers start at 7 AM. It takes willpower to arise in the cold of dawn to get to the

The Yeshiva in Mir

yeshiva on time. Moshe returns about an hour later for his breakfast.

At 9 AM the first *seder* starts: it lasts until 1:30 PM. Then there is a half hour allotted for each person to learn *mussar* individually. The *mincha* prayers follow.

Moshe returns for his dinner and rest at about 2:30 PM. This is the only time during the day that I can spend with him discussing a variety of subjects.

The second *seder* starts at 4:30 PM, and is a very long one. It ends at 9:30 PM and once again time is set aside for the learning of *mussar*, followed by *mairiv* at 10 PM. Moshe is so exhausted when he returns that he eats his supper hurriedly and falls into bed.

seder: learning session

The Rosh Yeshiva gives *shiurim* twice a week, Monday and Thursday, and Rabbi Kamai, once a week on Tuesday. The *mashgiach* gives *shmuessen* on Mondays and Wednesdays in the yeshiva, and in his house to smaller groups on Friday nights after *kabbolas Shabbos* and on Saturday nights before *mairiv*.

During Elul, the *shmuessen* are increased to three times weekly in the yeshiva, and sometimes even daily.

Moshe told me that the first time he entered the yeshiva and heard the resounding voices of almost five hundred young men learning, it affected him so profoundly that all problems paled and he reached new inspirational heights.

I can understand why the daily morning blessing for men, "I was not created a woman," should be said with emphasis.

Love, *Moshe and Ruchoma*

16

Action and reaction

Dearest Papa and Mama,

I am called the *"yunge Amerikanka."* Though Chaye Dube and Bessie were also about my age when they arrived here, it seems that my slight build and shortness make me appear younger.

My every action evokes much gossip. The other day, as I walked down the street, a group of little girls were chanting, *"De Amerikanka ken nit kochin"* (the American cannot cook). Of course, they overheard this enlightening piece of news from their mothers. I was caught "red-handed," as I burned my hand using the primus. Don't worry, it is healing.

The children also taunt me, *"De Amerikanka laift"* (the American runs). You know my habit of walking briskly. Here the people saunter along at a very slow pace. Life in Mir does not have the hustle and bustle of a large metropolis like New York City. I am trying to slow down my walking, but it is difficult to break a habit.

One morning, very early, Moshe and I decided to take a walk. We finished breakfast quickly, and Moshe had some time before the *seder* began. Though it was extremely cold, the sun shone brightly, and the soft, clean snow, which had fallen the night before, looked inviting.

As we walked along the empty streets, my wristwatch fell off my hand into the snow. When I picked it up, I saw the latch was broken.

Later in the day, I visited Chaye Dube, and she asked me anxiously, "What happened to your wristwatch?"

I was amazed. "How did you know?" I asked her curiously.

"Oh, one of the neighbors came running into my house this morning to tell me that she had heard that your wristwatch dropped into the snow." Unknowingly, I was being "watched."

There is an expression that really is borne out here, "If you sneeze in the privacy of your home at night, the next morning your neighbors will wish you 'Good health.' " I am very much on display, but I am sure they mean well. I suppose in due time we shall adjust to each other.

Moshe also has his share of "display problems." Since most of the yeshiva boys marry at a late age, because they wish to continue in Torah learning as long as possible, Moshe, who is younger, is conspicuous when he wears his *tallis* during the morning prayers.

Love, *Moshe and Ruchoma*

Dearest Papa and Mama,

Mama, you advised me to take along a carton of Ivory soap. Lately, I've noticed that I have only a few cakes left. I could not by any stretch of the imagination figure out how we could have used so many cakes of soap.

When Zlotka visited me, I mentioned this fact to her. She immediately said, "Most probably your *shikse*, Luba, is stealing them. You need four eyes to watch some of these *shikses*." When I expressed surprise, Zlotka retorted, "Ruchoma, you are so naïve."

Isn't it peculiar that I, born in the immense city of New York, am considered naïve? In essence, it is true. All my life you impressed upon me the inherent goodness of people. It never entered my mind that Luba would stoop to stealing my soap. Now that I am aware of the fact, I've hidden the few remaining precious bars of soap, and I watch Luba carefully. Though she attends to her chores well, I would like to replace her with a *shikse* who has a streak of honesty in her.

Luba had the effrontery to steal one of my robes. I cannot imagine how she was able to sneak it out of my house. However, she is pregnant, and must have stuffed it into her clothes without it being too noticeable. When I realized my robe was missing, I did not mince words with her. With the few Polish words at my command, and with my best sign language, I made her understand that she had better return my robe, or I would alert the *commandant* (mayor of Mir). The next morning, it was once again hanging in my closet. She has absolutely no qualms about taking my possessions and showed no shame when I confronted her.

When I witness such actions, I realize how fortunate I am to have been raised in a home where Torah concepts are taught and practiced. Moshe told me that even the minute action of taking someone's time unnecessarily or occupying too much walking space in the street can be construed as stealing. Of course, this is an ethical approach on a very high level.

Luba did not come to work for three days. On the fourth day when she appeared, I was very surprised to see that she was not expecting anymore. It seems that her mother-in-law, with whom she lives, forced her out of bed to return to work. As far as I know, a woman must stay in bed for at least a week or more after giving birth. I was worried about any consequences as a result of her working. It served as a good excuse for me to tell Luba that I did not require her services any longer.

Love, *Moshe and Ruchoma*

Dearest Papa and Mama,

My *balebuste* was very kind and allowed her *shikse* to help me with the heavy work—heating our stove and bringing in the pails of water—until I could find another *shikse* to replace Luba.

I finally hired Vara, who is seventeen years old and will live in our house. Her mother has been working for a reputable family in Mir since Vara was born. She was a war baby; her father was a soldier.

The greatest advantage for me is that I can communicate with her, because she speaks Yiddish perfectly. Since she was brought up in a Jewish home, she even knows our customs, including the different blessings on food. She generally dislikes *goyim*.

She has been working for different families for a number of years, but has not been taught elementary hygiene. When she arrived at our house, she wore a kerchief which covered her short-cropped hair. Her previous *balebuste* had had her hair clipped to solve the problem of keeping her head clean.

I bought a large basin especially for Vara, in which she could wash herself. I actually had to teach her the basic methods of cleanliness. I hope that in due time her hair will grow back and that she will look like a normal teenager.

She is exceptionally thin, and I doubted if she could carry two pails of water from the well at one time. Much to my surprise, she does the heavy chores without any visible effort.

She is bedded down on the kitchen floor, which I padded with a mattress. I gave her a pillow and a quilt to keep her warm. She has the warmest spot in our house, right near our stove.

Her appetite is enormous. She can eat half a loaf of our large bread at one meal. I wonder where the food goes to. The bread must be highly nutritious, because she is certainly a healthy specimen.

Vara is a big help. Our stove is kept hot most of the day, and we always have a supply of water on hand. At least, I do not think she will steal as Luba did, because she lives with us. However, I do keep a sharp eye on her.

I am paying her five zlotys a month (less than Luba), as she boards with us. I feel like a millionaire having a maid living-in. She costs less than a dollar a month.

Love, *Moshe and Ruchoma*

Dearest Papa and Mama,

My *balebuste* is exposed to all the idiosyncrasies of the foreigners who rent apartments and rooms from her.

One of her boarders is a young yeshiva boy who recently arrived from Germany. He became quite ill, and Dr. Shlepak was called.

He does not have much of a reputation as a qualified doctor, as only a very mediocre one would take up a practice in such a small town as Mir. One of the yeshiva boys told us the following illuminating incident about him. Dr. Shlepak was attending a critically ill yeshiva boy. One night, the boy's friends, who were sitting at his bedside, realized that the end was near. One of the boys hurried to the doctor's house, even though it was well after midnight. He awoke the doctor and said urgently, "You better hurry, or it will be too late."

Dr. Shlepak refused to go, giving this strange excuse, "If the patient passes away, I will be blamed; if he recovers, Hashem will be thanked. Either way I am the loser." Of course, he was pressured to come to the sick boy, who subsequently recovered, *boruch Hashem*!

Now to return to Esther Mirel's yeshiva boy, whose illness was diagnosed as pneumonia. This is very prevalent here, as the houses are very cold and the temperature outside is below freezing. The doctor prescribed fever powders, which he gives for every kind of illness. He suggested that sweating it out would relieve the boy's congestion a bit. Esther Mirel gave the sick lad hot tea and an additional quilt.

A few hours later, she excitedly called Moshe and me to witness an extraordinary scene. We went into the sick boy's room and found several valises piled on his feet. Though the temperature in the street is much below zero, the *fortichke* was wide open, with the icy air blowing straight at him.

Since Moshe speaks German, he asked him, "Why are the valises on your feet and the window open?" The boy's explanation was astounding. He recalled that when he carried his heavy valises from the train to the wagon, and, then again, from the wagon to his *stanze*, he perspired profusely. Therefore, he hoped it would achieve the same results. As to the open *fortichke*—"One must have *luft*" (air). Miraculously, he is well again. However, my *balebuste*'s reaction is still one of shock.

Love, *Moshe and Ruchoma*

Dearest Papa and Mama,

Bessie and I went to the movies. Papa, I am sure you will approve of our going after reading the following:

Once in a long while, a movie is shown in the schoolhouse, right near the *Giminy*. It is about a mile's walking distance.

It was a very cold night when we went, but Bessie and I dressed warmly and wore our heavy *volokes,* braving the inclement weather.

When we arrived, the schoolhouse was crowded to capacity, mostly with Polish peasants. The benches were hard and narrow. Bessie and I found two small spaces into which we squeezed.

A man played screechy "music" with his fiddle. It was so raspy that it grated on our nerves. Finally, the technician arrived with the film. He tacked a white sheet to a flimsy stand.

The excitement and enthusiasm of the peasants were unbelievable. As soon as the first scene was flashed on the shaky screen—which had only Polish titles—the unruly audience went into hysteria. Their frenzy brought down the entire screen in a heap. Their frantic outbursts were repeated each time a picture was shown.

Well, Bessie and I did not see much of a movie, but the actions of the peasants were the best show I have ever witnessed. However, this experience cured me of ever wanting to attend another movie in Mir.

Moshe enjoyed my hilarious description of the movie.

Tell Frieda that the *Sunday News* finally arrived, two months late. One of the Americans discovered it lying in the post office and graciously brought it to me. I hope it will now come regularly.

Between the *sedorim* there is a steady stream of Americans who come to read the newspaper. I really do not mind, as I understand what it means to them. For me, it is a piece of home.

We received word that Moshe's brother, Shmuel, will be arriving shortly. Mama, could you send some bars of Ivory soap with him, as the soap here is very rough. Thank you.

Love, *Moshe and Ruchoma*

---

sedorim: learning sessions

17

Highlights

Dearest Papa and Mama,

Monday is *Mark* Day, the highlight of the week. The *goyim* from the neighboring villages converge onto the market place to sell their wares and also to stock up with the necessary groceries that can be bought only in a town. From early morning, the wagons roll through Mir.

My *balebuste* suggested that it was high time I learn to shop in the market. When we got there, we were greeted by a chorus of neighing, mooooing, baaaaaing, and squawking from the horses, cows, sheep, and chickens.

It is a most interesting place to shop. During the summer season, there is a variety of fruit and vegetables; however, now, in the cold of the winter, only chickens and eggs are readily available. Since I needed chickens, Esther Mirel went from stall to stall, with me following close by.

At each stall, she pinched the bottom of the chicken to see if it had much fat. The chicken squawked in protest, but that did not deter her. The fat of the chicken is melted to make shmaltz, which is used for smearing on bread and is included in most of the meat meals.

Finally, she was satisfied. After a babble of bargaining, I gave her the zlotys to pay for two chickens. Without advance notice, she shoved one of the live chickens into my hands. I froze from sheer fright, as the chicken flapped its wings wildly in my face. It then flew out of my hands and darted away.

"Quick, chase her or you will lose your chicken," Esther Mirel commanded me. I felt like running in the other direction, but she held onto me. The chicken gave us a merry chase all through the market place. Each time Esther Mirel swooped down to catch her, she teasingly eluded her. She was finally cornered. This time my *balebuste* held on tightly to both chickens.

As we proceeded home, she muttered over and over again, *"A farhairite frau hot mayre far a kleine hun"* (a married woman is afraid of a little chicken).

The repercussions were not long in coming. My escapade is common gossip for the townspeople. I am now branded a coward!

Love, *Moshe and Ruchoma*

Dearest Papa and Mama,

Buying the chickens is just one small part of the ordeal. They then must be taken to the *shochet* for slaughtering. Chaye Dube tied the chickens' feet and placed them into a deep basket, so I was brave enough to carry them.

After the slaughtering, the *flicking* (plucking the feathers) began. It is a most tedious task that took me hours, though Chaye Dube helped me. She also taught me how to open the chickens and remove the insides. By the time the chickens were *kashered* by soaking and salting them, I lost all appetite to cook or eat them. I think I will buy meat more often because it requires only one process — *kashering*.

Bessie introduced me to the butcher store. It is a small store but has a good supply of meat and is very reasonable.

Guess what? When I bought my first order, I was given a liberal portion of calf's liver and lungs free of charge. Though the people are poor, they buy fat breast meat, which costs most, not realizing the high nutritional value of liver. The liver is given free with each order. In the States, calf's liver is very expensive, and we had it as a treat. Here I serve chopped liver as an entree daily. It is a messy task to broil it on the primus, but it is worth all the effort of cleaning up afterwards.

When I visited Liba's mother and saw the small portions of meat she serves her yeshiva boys, I felt guilty at the large portions Moshe and I eat.

I understand that each yeshiva boy receives an allowance (in the form of a note) from the yeshiva of two pounds of meat a week, which include the fat and bones, and twelve pounds of bread. The yeshiva also gives *chaluka* (a small amount of money for general expenses) to the boys.

Each *balebuste* exchanges the notes at the butcher store and the bakery and receives the supply for her yeshiva boys. She has a difficult job trying to stretch the portions of meat, as she has so little to divide. However, bread is consumed in great quantities at every meal.

With approximately five hundred *talmidim,* the Rosh Yeshiva certainly has a great burden on his shoulders to raise enough money for the tremendous expenses. I still remember Reb Lezer Yudel's sigh of relief when he returned to our house after being away for some time on a fund-raising campaign.

Love, Moshe and Ruchoma

Dearest Papa and Mama,

The poverty in Mir is extreme. I have made friends with a very fine woman. Her name is Fradel. I visited her tiny hut, where she lives with her husband and ten children. I do not know where the children can find room to sleep. She had just given birth to a baby boy, and I brought her a little gift.

When I gave her the gift, she cried. "Imagine," she said to me, "I am given charity when my baby is born." I was amazed. I explained to her that in the States the richer the mother, the more expensive the gifts she receives after the birth of an infant. This appeased her.

I noticed several large round loaves of bread stacked on a high shelf. When she saw me gazing at them, she said matter of factly, "I keep them up there so that the children will not get to them. The more stale the loaves get, the less the children will eat. The bread lasts longer. . . ."

I would like to offer her financial help, but she is too proud to accept it. I shall have to search for tactful ways and means.

Remember, Mama, how I loved to *nosh* halvah? Here it's not used as a luxury but smeared on bread instead of butter. I tried it, and it tastes delicious.

Sometimes, I crave a piece of chocolate, and they have delicious chocolate in the grocery store. However, I hesitate to buy it when other shoppers are present, as I do not want to be conspicuous as the "wealthy Amerikanka."

Living here we've noticed a very interesting relationship between one man and his son. Wherever the father goes, he takes his son along, holding tightly to his hand. I enjoy watching them as they walk down the street.

When there is a wedding or a *bris* and the father is served his portion of food, he immediately asks that his "*yingaleh*" be given an adequate portion also.

What is very unusual about this father-son relationship is the fact that the father is in his mid-nineties, and the son in his mid-seventies. Both are great-grandfathers. May they continue to have long, healthy years.

Love, *Moshe and Ruchoma*

Dearest Papa and Mama,

My shoemaker tries his best to eke out a living from his trade. It certainly is not easy. The people wear their shoes until they are completely worn out and cannot be repaired.

Last week, I went over to his house to have a pair of Moshe's shoes resoled. The shoemaker was nowhere to be found. His wife was in a terrible mood. "Where is your husband?" I asked her. "I have a pair of shoes to be fixed."

She answered bitterly, "That good-for-nothing, lazy man is on vacation."

"Vacation!" I exclaimed. I had no idea that word even existed in the Mirrer vocabulary.

She went on to explain, "You see, it happened like this. Shmerel did not clean our front walk properly. Zabusky [the tough Polish gendarme] imposed a fine of ten zlotys, which Shmerel refuses to pay. He was sent to prison."

"You told me he is on vacation," I said to her in confusion.

"He sits on the *Giminy* porch most of the day. He does nothing but eat and sleep. I am left not only with all my housework, but I must also bring him three meals a day. I offered to exchange places with him, but, of course, he refuses.

"I guess he will be home in a few days, as the *commandant* wants to be rid of him. Leave the shoes here. I will tell him that work is waiting for him; maybe that will encourage him to come home." She sighed deeply, ending her tale on a note of despair.

This is prison, Mir style. At least in Mir there are no bona fide criminals. I never lock my door.

Of course, the experience I had with Luba, my former *shikse*, was only a case of petty pilfering. Vara seems honest and is working out well.

Love, *Moshe and Ruchoma*

Dearest Papa and Mama,

I think I wrote you in a previous letter that each apartment has one fifteen-watt electric bulb in the dining room. In the other rooms, we are obliged to use kerosene lamps.

The electricity is controlled by the town electrician, who switches on the lights before nightfall and extinguishes them at midnight.

I had noticed that on most evenings our bulb flashes on and off. To my surprise, I was informed that the electrician uses this as a signal to alert his wife that he will be coming home shortly for his evening meal.

When Bessie arrived, she brought with her a small electric travel iron. She told me that the first time she connected it, the entire town was plunged into total darkness. It seems the voltage of her tiny iron was too powerful for our town's electricity.

The iron used here is very cumbersome. It has a small vent where burning embers are inserted, which, in turn, heats the iron. I tried to use it, but it's so heavy that I could hardly lift it up. Fortunately, I send my laundry out.

In spite of the meager electricity, I am being exposed to many situations in Mir which are very "enlightening."

Love, *Moshe and Ruchoma*

Dearest Papa and Mama,

Some of my neighbors have asked me to write letters in English to their relatives in America asking for assistance.

One woman, in particular, depicted her situation as critical. She told me to write her very rich cousins that "The ship is sinking."

You know I have a vivid imagination. In my letter to them, I wrote an eloquent description of abject poverty.

Her relatives decided to surprise her and visit during one of their trips to Europe. They discovered that she owns her little house, a cow, and some chickens. The ship is far from sinking. In fact, it is laden with provisions and riding high on the financial waves. Her relatives accused her of taking their hard-earned money under false pretenses.

In a way, I feel sorry for her, as they parted on a note of anger. Most probably, the cousins will cut off all support and connections with her.

I lost one of my steady writing customers.

People here have a wrong concept of life in America. They truly believe that most people are very wealthy. If they met some of our poor *orchim*, they would change their minds quickly.

How is the *"orchim* business" doing? Has it hit the over-thirty mark lately?

Love, *Moshe and Ruchoma*

Dearest Papa and Mama,

We have a new *commandant*. He is stirring up a great deal of trouble for the townspeople. First he issued an order for every house owner to paint the top of his chimney black. So my poor *balebus*, Reb Avrohom, climbed up to the rooftop and painted it black. A few days later, he came up with a new order. "Paint the chimney white." Then he commanded that the fences of each house be painted first orange and then green.

Finally, in desperation, the townspeople presented him with a substantial "gift" of money, which stopped these absurd orders.

When the *commandant* walks down the street, the people usually make room for him by walking onto the road as a sign of respect — or is it fear??? The cows, however, not burdened by any feelings, often walk on the sidewalk, so the *commandant* has their company.

Zabusky, the policeman, also delights in tormenting any available victim. At dawn, he bangs on our bedroom window with his club, mistakenly thinking it is our *balebuste*'s, to order her to clean her sidewalk.

Moshe and I wake up with a shudder. I pleaded with him not to bang on our window, or, at least, not so early in the morning, but he smirks and continues as before.

He did, however, get his just deserts. On the day Zabusky inspected our backyard, our cesspool overflowed. Unsuspectingly, he stepped right into the muck. His shrieks were heard far and wide.

My *balebuste* received a heavy fine, which she paid with glee for the first time.

In a few days, the cesspools from all the outhouses in the

city will be emptied. This filthy job is done twice a year. We close all our windows and remain indoors until this ordeal is over.

I still think longingly of the plumbing facilities we have in the States.

Love, *Moshe and Ruchoma*

Dearest Papa and Mama,

Something terrible has happened here. A member of the Polish Senate condemned the slaughter of animals in the kosher, Jewish way. She claims the humanitarian way is to shoot them. The Polish Senate just passed a law forbidding slaughtering, except in very small quantities.

The entire town is very upset. Meat is one of our most important foods. Of course, slaughtering continues behind barred doors, in the stealth of the night. Prices have soared, and I cannot always buy the full amount that I require.

I am most disturbed to come face to face with anti-Semitism. I was never confronted with this problem in New York, though I attended public school with the gentiles.

Papa, I recall that after our Pesach *seder*, the policeman on our beat used to come up to turn off all our electricity. He was so friendly, as were all our *goyishe* neighbors.

Vara, our *shikse*, tells me, when she returns from Sunday services, that the *galach* (priest) stirs up much animosity against the Jews. She ridicules him saying, "*Ehr vaist nit vos ehr ret*" (he does not know what he is talking about). But it does promote hatred.

I asked Vara why she attends these services each week if she disagrees with his views. She answered that for her it is a social event, where she hopes to meet a suitable young man who will be interested in marrying her. She does make a respectable appearance now that her hair has grown back and she dresses decently.

My *balebuste*'s *shikse* is engaged. She is an elderly girl, close to thirty-five years old. She brought her intended husband — a six-foot *goy* — for Esther Mirel's approval. Esther Mirel tried to impress upon him to treat his wife well. His appalling answer was, "I will beat her only if she disobeys me."

When my *balebuste* told me this revealing bit of information, I thought of the tremendous contrast with Jewish couples, who are taught the beauty and sanctity of marriage, according to our Torah.

Love, *Moshe and Ruchoma*

18

Blossoming forth

Dearest Papa and Mama,

Pesach not only commemorates the liberation of the Jews from slavery in Egypt, but its coming also heralds the end of the winter season in Mir.

The high mounds of snow that covered our streets during the entire winter are slowly melting. There is mud all over. It sticks to our boots, creeps into our shoes, and dirties our stockings. It is tracked all over the floors. It is not worthwhile to continue scrubbing the floors while the mud is still enjoying its last capers. After Pesach, it finally disintegrates.

Moshe often discusses with me the *mashgiach's shmuessen*, from which I gain better *hashkofos*.

The *mashgiach* said that a *ben Torah* cannot realize the immense reward he will receive just for the discomfort he suffers from the accumulated mud on his rubbers, as he walks from his *stanze* to the yeshiva. Papa, many times I have heard these wise words from you also, "Any sacrifice one does for Torah pays off great dividends." Since Moshe assures me that I am receiving 100% dividends from his studying Torah, I hope that I, too, will be rewarded for having to contend with the deep, black mud that invades Mir.

I greeted our first Pesach in Mir with mixed emotions. On the one hand, it was gratifying to be with Moshe at the *sedorim*, but, on the other hand, I missed you very much and also all the *orchim*.

Though I've improved in my cooking ability, I still did not have the full confidence to prepare *pesachdikke* meals in my *kachal* stove, and Nochum Dovid and Chaye Dube graciously invited us. For the *sedorim*, Chaim, Bessie, and Fruma Rochel joined us. We certainly ate the matzo with "relish," as it is baked only once a year for Pesach.

Most of the yeshiva men hurry through their *seder* in order to listen to the *mashgiach*'s comments on the *haggada*. After the second *seder*, when Moshe went to the *mashgiach*'s house, it was so crowded that he could hardly find an available spot. He came home deeply inspired by the "pearls of wisdom" he heard from the *mashgiach*.

Love, *Moshe and Ruchoma*

Dearest Papa and Mama,

During Pesach, we were served not only delicious food which Chaye Dube prepared but also food for thought which Nochum Dovid provided.

He told us the following inspirational thoughts from the *mashgiach* and Reb Chatzkel:

The *mashgiach* was delivering a *shmuess* on a very lofty *mussar* topic one Friday night in his house. Suddenly, he stopped in the midst of his talk and left the room. This was unusual.

Some of his close *talmidim* — Reb Yona Minsker, Reb Leibel Malin, and Reb Zedel Tiktiner — went over to the door of the room in which he had closed himself and heard him say, "Yeruchem, Yeruchem, you know that you have not reached this high level. Whom are you trying to fool?"

When Moshe and I heard this, we realized more than ever before the *mashgiach*'s gigantic spiritual stature.

Reb Chatzkel gave a *shmuess* in his house, and Nochum Dovid was among the listeners. Reb Chatzkel related the following incident: He saved a sum of money to help towards the marriage of his two daughters. He gave his entire savings to a man who had a business. The business failed, and Reb Chatzkel's money was lost.

Since then, Reb Chatzkel has had to borrow quite often to cover his expenses. He said, "If I had my savings, I would rely on that. However, since I have no money, I must rely fully on Hashem. I have seen great *hashgocho*. Sometimes just fifteen minutes before I must repay my debt, Hashem sends me a source from where I can obtain the money. See what *chesed* Hashem did for me that I lost all my savings: now my entire faith is only in Him."

Papa, this is your kind of talk, and it is most uplifting.

Love, *Moshe and Ruchoma*

Dearest Papa and Mama,

Spring is here. The days are sunny and mild, the nights cool and moonlit. The icy wall near our dining-room window is almost completely dry. The mildew that painted the wall a moss green is slowly disappearing. The townspeople have emerged from their hibernation and stroll in the streets once again.

But best of all—the market has an array of mouth-watering fruits, of which I am taking full advantage. The season for each of the fruits is a short one, lasting only a few weeks.

The *truskavkes* (strawberries) are a much smaller variety than in the States, but luscious when served with sour cream. I prepared the *brushnitzes* (cranberries) into a jellied sauce, and I used the *shvartze yagodes* (blueberries) as filling for my pie.

I understand that plums, pears, and apples are expected to make their appearance very soon.

Since I did not taste any fresh fruit the entire winter, I have learned to appreciate the many blessings I took for granted in New York.

Bessie's *balebuste,* Merke, planted *kokorooza* (sweet corn) for her cow. When I told her that I enjoy eating corn, she looked at me quizzically, "Who eats animal food?"

I finally impressed upon her that when the corn sprouts, I would like to have some.

By now, most of the people are becoming accustomed to my strange "Amerikanka habits."

Love, *Moshe and Ruchoma*

Dearest Papa and Mama,

Merke's corn sprouted. Bessie and I cooked and ate them in front of an audience of goggle-eyed neighbors, who were called in to witness the peculiar Americans who eat fodder.

The corn does not taste as sweet as that in the States, but it is edible.

My *balebuste* planted tomatoes. It is still a relatively unknown vegetable, especially among the *goyim*, and they hesitate to eat it.

When I sliced a tomato and was about to bite into it, Vara shouted, *"Balebuste, es iz som* (it is poison)." I demonstrated to her that I was still very much alive after having consumed several red-ripe tomatoes. She is not convinced and refuses to eat them.

Moshe and I are looking forward to *bein hazemanim.* Outside the town, the grass is green, the trees are in full blossom, and the air is pure and sweet. It is a real *datche* (summer resort) where we can hike and picnic.

Some of the Americans are already preparing bats and balls in anticipation of their vacation. They have included Moshe in their baseball team. He is an excellent ball player and

....
bein hazemanim: literally, between times: vacation

was a top athlete in college. It will be interesting to see if he is still in shape. He certainly needs physical exercise after months of sitting in one place.

Shepsul Broyde told me that his parents temporarily moved into the ground-floor apartment in your building until theirs on Henry Street is renovated. Please give our special regards and good wishes to Mr. and Mrs. Broyde. Tell them that their sons, Shepsul and Yudel, are learning very well. They visit us often, and Moshe keeps a brotherly eye on them.

Love, *Moshe and Ruchoma*

Dearest Papa and Mama,

Davie, Chaye Dube, and the children are preparing to leave shortly. Pangs of lonesomeness already overwhelm me at the thought of their departure. They are very devoted to us, and they helped us over some difficult hurdles during our first months in Mir.

I understand that Chaye Dube's parents asked them to return as they long to see them and meet their grandchildren. It was a great sacrifice on their part that they were willing to allow Chaye Dube, an only child, to leave them. They spent almost four years in Mir, a long period of time.

I am sure you will be very proud of them. Nochum Dovid progressed in his Torah studies. He is very popular among all the yeshiva boys and is known to assist anyone who needs a helping hand. Chaye Dube is beloved by all the yeshiva wives and townspeople. She is like one of them.

Since she was born in Poland and lived here for the first nine years of her life, I think she adjusted much easier and quicker than I. Maybe, it is only rationalization on my part, but for me it is a slow process adapting to life here and overcoming the many inconveniences. However, I have made great strides.

You will enjoy their two blooming offspring, Shmuel Yitzchok and Baile Golde, who are real little foreigners.

Davie's friends prepared a moving going-away party for them. There were *grammen* (verses) describing their life here, which made us all laugh. Then there were the speeches that made us all cry.

The day arrived. There were last minute good-byes, quick kisses for Chaye Dube, and hugs for the children. My tears refused to stop, as they boarded the wagon with their luggage. There was a large turnout of yeshiva boys, friends, and townspeople.

The wagon rolled down the cobbled streets. I hurried after it, waving to them until I could not see them any more. They are going home, and part of me is going along with them.

I am relieved that Chaim, Bessie, and Fruma Rochel are still here. It will make my loneliness easier to bear. As you know, Bessie's confinement is imminent. She expects to give birth in Mir, using the services of the Polish midwife, who delivers most of the babies here. Of course, I shall be on hand to help out.

Love, *Moshe and Ruchoma*

Dearest Papa and Mama,
                    Mazel Tov! Mazel Tov!
The telegram bringing you the glad tidings that Bessie gave birth to her second daughter must have brought you much joy. What you do not know is that I am now an assistant midwife. Let me describe how it happened.

As soon as Bessie started to feel the first labor pains, Chaim called for me. I ran over to their house. The midwife was on hand. Fruma Rochel was sent to Rebbetzin Shmulevitz. Bessie's *balebuste* Merke, too squeamish to remain, ran to the barn, where she spent the night.

Bessie started to give birth actively after midnight, and the only electric bulb in the house had gone off. The bedroom was lit by a kerosene lamp. The midwife explained to me that she would require my assistance. Though she spoke rapidly in Polish, I understood that she expected me to hold the kerosene lamp to give her light.

The birth began. I did my utmost not to shake the kerosene lamp, but it swung like a pendulum. The midwife was irate. She screamed at me to hold it steady, but my trembling hands refused to obey her.

Despite the flickering light moving in all directions, the baby was born, a roly-poly girl, as rosy as could be. It was the first day of Rosh Chodesh Elul.

Birth is truly a miracle to behold. Anyone who remotely believes in evolution is out of his mind. Only Hashem can create such wonders to bring new life into the world.

Mother and baby, Rivky, are doing fine. I am taking care of Bessie. One of the neighbors comes to help out in taking care of Rivky. Bessie is nursing the baby, and she seems to be thriving nicely.

Fruma Rochel is adjusting to her new baby sister, though she shows the normal pattern of jealousy. Someday, she will appreciate having a sister close in age, as I do with Bessie.

Love, *Moshe and Ruchoma*

P.S. Please write me all the details of Davie, Chaye Dube, and the children's homecoming. Send them our love.

Dearest Papa and Mama,

On the day that Bessie gave birth to her baby girl, new adults also arrived, adding to our American population. They are Mrs. Bender and her son, David, and Avrohom Pincus. David and Avrohom are Torah Vodaas boys. Mrs. Bender accompanied her son, an only child, because her husband, Rabbi Bender, is away a good part of the year raising money for a yeshiva.

It is pleasant to have an older American woman to whom I can talk in my own language. She is warm and motherly.

Mrs. Bender is going through her own process of initiation. She cannot fathom why she is not understood by the townspeople when she speaks "perfect" Yiddish.

Her Yiddish is mostly English, as in *"Vu iz de* kitchen? *Gib mir a* broom and dirt pail. *Ich darf* chicken and meat. *Nem mir tzum* butcher store."

I share her frustration, as not too long ago, I also spoke very little Yiddish. Now I converse in a Yiddish-Polish dialect, much to my satisfaction.

Mrs. Bender and David rented the apartment vacated by Nochum Dovid and Chaye Dube. I am trying as much as possible to help her get acclimated to her new environment.

I am sure you will be gratified to learn that in a very small measure I am beginning to fulfill the *mitzva* of *hachnosas orchim.*

Some of the families here undertake to feed boys from the *yeshiva ketana.* It is called *essen teg.* One day of the week the yeshiva boy eats all his meals with that family.

I offered to accept one of these boys every Monday. A fifteen-year-old was sent to me, the hungriest boy I have ever encountered. I serve him huge amounts of food, which he finishes to the last morsel.

At least, I have gained confidence that my meals are appetizing.

Love, Moshe and Ruchoma

Dearest Papa and Mama,

We had an interesting visitor, Chava Weinberg, the daughter of Reb Yitzchok Matisyohu Weinberg, a friend of yours. She spent some time with us, which was most enjoyable and revealing.

Chava is presently studying in the Sara Schenirer Bais Yaakov in Krakow. Her father shares your views on *chinuch* for girls.

Imagine, he sent Chava, a teenager, all the way from the States to study in Poland, as he wanted her to be under the

....

yeshiva ketana: preparatory school / *essen teg*: eating days
chinuch: education

influence and guidance of teachers with a true Torah outlook. Unfortunately, this education is not available for girls in the States.

Papa, you did not allow your daughters to attend a Talmud Torah, whose teachers did not meet your standards of *yiddishkeit*. You even hired special teachers for us at a much higher cost than the tuition in the regular Talmud Torah.

I was fortunate to have a strong home environment that enabled me to withstand the alien street and public-school influences. It is mainly your teachings, Papa, that remain uppermost in my mind. Some of my girl friends were not so fortunate. It was your talking to them, and the special interest you took in them when they visited each Shabbos, that kept them from drifting away.

Of course, Mama, your delicious coffee cake and other goodies were an added attraction that encouraged their coming.

Why are there no religious schools for girls in the States, on the same level as yeshivos for boys?

There definitely is a vital need for such Bais Yaakovs, where girls can blossom into true Jewish daughters.

Love, *Moshe and Ruchoma*

It should be noted that Chava became a teacher in the first Bais Yaakov Seminary in America and subsequently married Rabbi Avrohom Pincus, former principal of the elementary department of Yeshiva Torah Vodaas in Brooklyn, and presently principal of the Kaminetzer Yeshiva Ketana in Yerusholayim.

Mrs. Hilda Weinberg, Chava's mother, founded the first Bais Yaakov elementary school, on Manhattan's Lower East Side, in 1944, which eventually developed into the Esther Schonfeld High School and Seminary.

19

Reaching up

Dearest Papa and Mama,

The entire Jewish nation has lost her leader. The greatest *tzaddik* of our generation, the Chofetz Chaim, *zatzal,* was *niftar* on the twenty-fourth of Elul (5693-1933). He was ninety-four years old.

He passed away *erev* Shabbos, and Reb Chaim Ozer of Vilna decreed, out of respect for the Chofetz Chaim, that the funeral should be postponed until Sunday. Tens of thousands were present at his funeral.

Moshe and I feel deprived that we did not meet the Chofetz Chaim during his lifetime. I wish that I had followed your wise advice, Papa — "When an occasion arises to do a *mitzva*, hurry to do it, or the *mitzva* might escape."

In the back of our minds, we expected to visit the Chofetz Chaim at our first opportunity, but we delayed. Now it is too late.

You, Papa, had the *zechus* to meet with the Chofetz Chaim during your trip to Europe a few years ago. I remember when

niftar: passed away

you returned, how inspired you were by your visit with him.

Nochum Dovid and Chaye Dube, Chaim and Bessie were also fortunate to have visited the Chofetz Chaim and receive his blessings.

Both Chaye Dube and Bessie were expecting their first child when they came to his house. In fact, Bessie told me that she did not feel so well from the ride in the wagon, and the *rebbetzin* understandingly served her a glass of tea and some crackers with jelly.

The Chofetz Chaim's words were prophetic when he blessed Nochum Dovid and Chaye Dube to have a son who would be a *ben Torah*, and Chaim and Bessie to have good children. Chaye Dube gave birth to her son, Shmuel Yitzchok, and Bessie to her daughter, Fruma Rochel.

It is a few days before the New Year. Moshe and I look forward to our first Rosh Hashona in Mir. The wives of the yeshiva men are granted the special privilege of *davening* in the *mashgiach*'s room, overlooking the entire *beis medrash*. Of course, I shall miss your *davening*, Papa, which always brought all the congregants to tears. Your ringing voice calling out to the Boss reached the heavens.

May you both be inscribed in the Book of Life for a happy, healthy and peaceful New Year with *nachas* from your children and grandchildren.

Love, *Moshe and Ruchoma*

Dearest Papa and Mama,

From the first thunderous *Amen* on Rosh Hashona night, I was transported into a spiritual world. The prayers in the yeshiva during Rosh Hashona and Yom Kippur are so fervent and solemn that they penetrated every fiber of my body and soul.

The sounding of the *shofar* evoked in me not only a sense of awe for this Day of Judgment, but also the hope and expec-

beis medrash: study hall

tation of the coming of *Moshiach* in the near future.

Here each *shmoneh esrei* lasts over an hour. There is time for deep concentration on every word. The *davening* on Rosh Hashona ended about four PM.

Rabbi Kamai, Rabbi Finkel, the *mashgiach*, Reb Yeruchem, and Reb Chatzkel stood *shmoneh esrei* during most of the day. In fact, on Yom Kippur they stood on their feet almost the entire day.

As I watched them from the little window, I realized that they are almost transformed into angels, and they therefore did not feel a sense of physical strain.

Moshe discussed the Rosh Hashona and Yom Kippur prayers with me and amplified them, so that they take on new meaning.

The *aseres yemei teshuva* were days of introspection.

As a young girl, my interest in going to *shul* was centered on wearing my new dress. This year in Mir, my "spiritual" clothes took precedence. When the *shofar* blew after the Yom Kippur fast, I felt cleansed.

I hope that Hashem will answer my prayers and grant Moshe and me a fruitful year that will guide us towards deeper understanding in our Torah life.

Now I am busily preparing for Sukkos, which I will describe in my following letter.

I will miss decorating your *sukka* this year. Who is taking my place?

Love, Moshe and Ruchoma

Dearest Papa and Mama,

Sukkos is a combination of both the physical and the spiritual. Joy pervades every house in Mir. There is dancing and singing in the yeshiva each night of *simchas beis hasho'eva.*

....

shmoneh esrei: literally, eighteen: the main prayer
aseres yemei teshuva: ten days of repentance
simchas beis hasho'eva: celebration commemorating the water-drawing ceremony in the Holy Temple on Sukkos

The *sukka*, which we share with our *balebuste* and her family, has an advantage over yours. It is a ready-made one, adjoining her kitchen. All that has to be done is to lift the roof and replace it with *sechach*. I helped with the decorations.

I prepared holiday meals and was proud to serve them. I have come a long way in my cooking abilities. Moshe and Reb Avrohom get along very well and were busy discussing their learning most of Sukkos. Esther Mirel and I are close. She feels she has a share in my becoming a full-fledged *balebuste*. Their children livened up each meal with their constant chattering.

The culmination of the Yomim Tovim is Simchas Torah. To witness five hundred yeshiva men dancing together with such enthusiasm that the walls of the yeshiva are bathed in sweat is awe-inspiring.

The *mashgiach* stands in the center of the dancing circle, which was prepared by moving all the benches of the *beis medrash* to one side. After each *hakofo*, which can last up to one hour, he raises his hand to indicate the end of that *hakofo* and the exuberant dancing halts immediately.

Some of the yeshiva men were very drunk. However, this kind of drunkenness is uplifting to behold. One young man carried a *sefer Torah*, tears streaming down his cheeks as he kissed the Torah over and over again with deep emotion. Another tipsy young man, who is known for his genius in learning, spouted such excellent Torah comments that Moshe would have jotted them down had it not been Yom Tov. Our *shikurim* make a *kiddush Hashem* during their bout of drinking. How different it is from the drunkards I used to see in New York on their New Year's Eve.

Love, *Moshe and Ruchoma*

Dearest Papa and Mama,

We had an enjoyable *orech* during Sukkos. Chava Gordon, who was in Europe for a convention, came to Mir to visit her

---

shikurim: drunks / *kiddush Hashem*: glorification of God's name

brothers, Moshe and Yudel. She slept on our couch during the entire Yom Tov.

She mentioned that her father, Reb Yitzchok Dov Gordon, is still involved in your *Agudas Baale-Batim*. Papa, it was you who encouraged her father to send her brother Moshe first to New Haven and then to Mir. Yudel followed him, and now Chava told me that her younger brother, Shleima, is scheduled to arrive as well. You have a share in so many young men learning and advancing in Torah. The Boss will surely repay you with children and grandchildren who will be *bnei Torah*.

Now that the Yomim Tovim are over, there is feverish activity preparing vegetables for the winter season. I have already bought large sacks of potatoes, carrots, onions, and cabbage. They are stored in my cellar, which I share with my *balebuste*. It looks as if there is enough for an army, but as I wrote you in a previous letter, I cannot get these vegetables during the winter months. I also prepared jars of plum and blueberry jam, which my *balebuste* helped me to make.

I hope this winter will be easier than our first in Mir. I dread the short, gray days, and long, cold nights. I will not be able to leave the house for days at a time because of the heavy snow and ice. However, I do have friends, and I have "weathered" many obstacles.

Love, Moshe and Ruchoma

It might be noted that Chava Gordon married Papa's talmid Rabbi Shmuel Shechter.

Dearest Papa and Mama,

I don't think that I've ever written you about our Shabbos *cholent*. Since there is an *eiruv* for the entire town of Mir, I take my pot of raw *cholent* to the bakery each Friday before lighting the candles. His special baker's stove not only cooks the *cholent*, but also keeps it piping hot until I pick it up Shabbos

....
eiruv: partition which makes it permissible to carry objects

morning when Moshe returns from *davening*. There is no charge for this service.

It is pleasant to watch the many women, with their different-sized pots of *cholent,* hurrying to the nearest bakery. Mine is about two blocks from our house.

For me it has a great advantage. My food does not always come out perfectly cooked in the *kachal* stove. For Shabbos, I am assured of a well-cooked meal. Here the *cholent* is prepared with beans, *perel groipen* (barley), and potatoes. I place the breast meat on top of this preparation.

Since we now have another boy from the *yeshiva ketana* who eats with us on Shabbosim, I prepare a very large pot of *cholent*. He, too, eats as if he's never had a decent meal. Vara, our *shikse*, loves the *cholent*, so it is usually finished to the last drop.

Of course, Mama, my very large *cholent* pot is very small in comparison to your gigantic one.

Love, *Moshe and Ruchoma*

20

Birth and rebirth

Dearest Papa and Mama,

During the last few months, I dreamt two extraordinary dreams. In the first dream, a very large bus was scheduled to ride to a yeshiva. (I do not know which yeshiva.) As soon as I saw it, I jumped on the bus and asked the driver to provide me with a comfortable seat. I paid him $10.

Aboard the bus, there were many young men surrounding a short man with a long, white beard. There was a great tumult. Someone said to me that this old man is the "Alter of Kelm" (Reb Simcha Zisel Ziv, the *rebbe* of the Mirrer *mashgiach*).

Suddenly, large pieces of gefilte fish formed in the palm of my hand. I placed them on every available spot. More kept coming and I could not find place for them. I then awoke.

When I told Moshe my dream, he immediately quoted from *Bereishis* (48:16): "And let them grow into a multitude in the midst of the earth." Rashi explains that the word *v'yidgu* is derived from the root *dag* (fish), a symbol of multiplying.

Bereishis: Genesis

Moshe, therefore, interpreted my dream as an indication that our family will increase.

His interpretation was correct. A few weeks later, I discovered that I am expecting.

In the second dream, which I dreamt after I already knew I was pregnant, I once again saw a short man with a white beard. When I asked, "Who is this man?" a voice answered, "He is the *kohen godol* (High Priest). Call him Yisroel Meir."

When Moshe told the *mashgiach* and Reb Chatzkel the dreams, they both agreed that if I give birth to a son, we should name him after the Chofetz Chaim. I had no idea that the Chofetz Chaim's name was Reb Yisroel Meir, because almost everyone called him "Chofetz Chaim."

Ever since the Chofetz Chaim was *niftar*, I was troubled that I did not have the merit to meet him in his lifetime. Now I am pacified. At least, I had the *zechus* to see him in my dream.

I know this news will give you both much joy. I hope it will be a son, and my dream will be realized.

I am enclosing our return tickets for you to cash in before they expire. Now that I am expecting, there is no thought of our returning in the near future.

Love, Moshe and Ruchoma

Dearest Papa and Mama,

Moshe and I discussed my giving birth. We have two alternatives. One choice is the hospital in the city of Slonim with maternity facilities, which, I understand, are not very adequate. Bessie gave birth to Fruma Rochel there and was not pleased. The second choice is to remain in Mir and hire the Polish midwife who delivered Bessie's Rivky. She has wide experience, as most of the women use her.

After due consideration, we decided to remain at home because the expected date of delivery would be, God willing, when the *zeman* (winter session) is in full swing. I went to the midwife's house and engaged her for the birth.

Everyone encourages me to "eat for two." I am doing my

best to follow the instructions and have gained much weight. None of my dresses fit me. I am wearing some of Bessie's dresses, which are two sizes larger than mine. There is no such phenomenon as maternity clothes here.

Esther and Frieda wrote me that they have excellent baby clothing from their children. I went to the *Giminy* to ask for a permit to receive used baby clothes. The *commandant* flatly refused. "Packages are for the poor. You are a 'rich' American. You can buy clothes here," he answered curtly. My friend, Yecheved, offered to shop for the material and sew some baby shirts and nightgowns.

Mama, I am sure you will be proud to hear that I have advanced into a grade A *balebuste* — well, maybe B-plus, as I am far from perfect.

Erev, Yom Kippur I *shlogged kaporos* (the rite that atones for one's misdeeds) with an egg, a rooster, and a hen, which is the custom here: The egg denotes the fertilized egg within the pregnant woman; the rooster is in case it is a boy; the hen, for myself and in case it is a girl. The live chickens do not faze me in the least.

I chuckle when I recall my intense fear the first time my *balebuste* plopped a live chicken into my hands. Now I am a pro. In fact, the chickens were most respectful as I whirled them above my head and recited the prayer three times.

I remember that you used live fish with which to *shlog kaporos*. Papa, you held it above my head because I would not touch the wiggly fish.

Love, Moshe and Ruchoma

Dearest Papa and Mama,

The women are wagering among themselves whether I will have twins. Are there twins in our family? I've gained a tremendous amount of weight, which I hope to lose after the birth.

Winter has set in. Thick, slippery layers of snow cover the streets. Last week, I felt a sense of loneliness and decided to risk going to Bessie. Moshe was in the yeshiva, and the long night stretched ahead.

I walked only one block, when wham — I slipped on the icy snow. I tried my utmost to get up, but without having anything to grasp, I found it impossible. I lay on the icy snow for what seemed an interminable time, praying for help to come soon. It did. Fortunately, one of the townspeople came by. He was astounded when he saw me sprawled on the snow. But he soon understood my predicament. He helped me up and escorted me home. Luckily, my rabbit-fur-lined coat padded my fall, so that no part of me was injured except for my pride. I will not attempt such "bravery" again.

You know, Mama, here the mothers do not diaper their newborn infants as in the States. They *vickel* them (roll them up). First they pad the baby on the diaper area. Then, on top of a nighty, they roll the baby in a heavy cotton bandage which is five to six inches wide and extends from the shoulders down to the toes. I saw the babies here. They look like little mummies. Many of the children have rickets. I guess they feel that this method will alleviate the problem.

I wrote to the Department of Health in the States asking them to mail all kinds of booklets on "bringing up baby." I hope I receive them in time, as the mail takes weeks to get here.

Chaim and Bessie are making arrangements to leave for the States in March. Since Chaim was born in Poland, he will lose his American citizenship if he remains here more than five years consecutively.

I am relieved that Bessie will be with me during the birth and a bit after. I will miss them terribly.

Love, Moshe and Ruchoma

P.S. Mazel Tov! Zlotka, Reb Chatzkel's older daughter, is engaged to one of the outstanding Mirrer Yeshiva *talmidim*. They met several times in our house, as they needed privacy. His name is Reb Mordchi Ginzburg. However he is known as Reb Mordchi "Lipnishke." The European yeshiva boys are usually called by the name of the city from which they originate.

Dearest Papa and Mama,
MAZEL TOV!

By now you know from our telegram that it is a boy — only one — a ten-pounder. Though the midwife has no scale, she estimates the weight of the baby and is known to be quite accurate.

Yesterday was the *bris*. We named him after the Chofetz Chaim, Yisroel Meir, as was indicated months ago in my dream. First let me describe the *bris*: Rabbi Kamai was *sandik*. The other honors were shared by the Rosh Yeshiva, the *mashgiach* and Reb Chatzkel. Yisroel Meir had an array of the greatest *tzaddikim* at his *bris*.

The American yeshiva boys were all present, as were many others from the yeshiva. With friends and neighbors adding to the guest list, our house was bursting at the seams. There was a special table set up for poor people, as is customary here.

Now to go back to the birth, which was a most difficult ordeal. On Sunday of last week, the signs of birth began. Bessie summoned the midwife. Even though it was a little early, according to my reckoning, she said that the birth was imminent — certainly an understatement.

It was a long, drawn-out birth. By the third day, the midwife was frantic. She confided to Moshe, Bessie, Esther Mirel, and our other good friends, sitting it out in the dining room, that she surmised the baby was no longer alive.

Finally, Wednesday before dawn, our son was born. Through a daze, I was able to see the midwife holding the baby, but no sound came from him. The midwife had prepared a pail of ice-cold water from the well in anticipation of such a complication. Splash! She poured the icy water over his little body. He shuddered and uttered a low cry. Our son was alive.

....
sandik: the one who holds the child on his lap during the *bris*

Moshe and I are very thankful to Hashem for this special gift to us. May he grow to be a great *ben Torah* and a pride to our family.

I'm nursing him. I make sure to drink great quantities of milk. I am also drinking beer, which is supposed to increase the flow of milk. All I feel is woozy.

I wrote in a previous letter that the babies are *vickelt* here. Yisroel Meir shows signs of resistance. Every time he is bandaged, he manages to get one little hand and foot free from his tight "bondage." I hope he will always fight for his principles and follow in your footsteps, Papa.

> Love, *"Papa Moshe" and "Mama Ruchoma"*

Dearest Papa and Mama,

It is over five months since I last wrote to you. It seems like a lifetime. Today, for the first time, I was carried into our dining room. I am sitting at our table, my legs propped up on a chair, and my left hand in a sling.

I know that you received a detailed report of the start of my grave illness, when Chaim and Bessie returned to the States. Moshe has been writing you little notes from time to time to keep you informed. However, I want to share my harrowing experience with you, for I feel that you are both with me.

A few days after the *bris,* I awoke with a great pain in my thigh. I was shocked to see that the color of my entire leg was deep purple. Moshe called Bessie, who, in turn, brought the midwife. She was very perturbed and suggested that Dr. Shlepak be summoned immediately. All he prescribed were some fever powders to lower the high temperature which was hovering at over 104 degrees. He knew very little about diagnosing my illness. Of course, my condition became worse. A few days later, my other leg turned purple. By then, I was delirious from fever and pain.

A doctor from Stolpce, a city about twenty kilometers from Mir, was ordered, but a raging snowstorm hindered his coming right away. When Doctor Greenberg arrived a week later, after the storm had abated, my left hand had joined my legs to become the same purplish hue.

The doctor told our anxious loved ones that I had a serious case of blood poisoning. It was traveling through my body and at all costs must be prevented from reaching the heart or kidneys, as that would be fatal. He prescribed injections and strong medication against the poisoning, and the most powerful pain killers possible. As he left, he advised, "Prayers might help."

No one needed that advice as everyone in the yeshiva was already praying. In fact, the neighboring yeshivos, Baranowitz and Kaminetz, were also alerted. Of course, in Mir, all our dear ones prayed constantly.

I am very tired and will continue in my next letter.

Love, *Moshe and Ruchoma*

Dearest Papa and Mama,

I have no memory of Yisroel Meir's *pidyon ha-ben*. I was told that just the *kohen* and ten people were invited. A little meal was prepared. I do remember, through a haze, Chaim, Bessie, and the children saying good-bye to me.

One night, through my delirium, I saw some of our *orchim* walking back and forth in front of my bed, and, Papa, I heard you repeat over and over again, "Ruchoma, in the merit of Torah and *hachnosas orchim* you will surely recover."

Papa, I decided to follow your method of speaking to the Boss directly: "Hashem, you know that Moshe and I came to Mir in order for him to study Torah. I did not go to the Slonim hospital for the birth so that Moshe should not interrupt his learning. If anything happens to me, other young couples will fear coming to Mir."

The Boss heard my fervent prayers and all the many prayers being said on my behalf. The raging fever subsided and

....
pidyon ha-ben: ceremony of redeeming the first-born son

the pain lessened. However, both legs and my left hand were still paralyzed, and it was already four months after the birth.

During all this time, Yisroel Meir was being cared for by a host of our good friends. Rebbetzin Miriam Shmulevitz, Rabbi Finkel's daughter, came each day to prepare food for him. Most mothers nurse their babies, so formula is unheard of. She concocted her own preparation, by cooking *gritz* (a kind of cereal), straining it, and mixing the liquid with milk. They do not have regular baby bottles, and half-pint whiskey bottles were substituted. They do have nipples, but overly-large ones. Bat Sheva Leshinsky still comes daily to bathe Yisroel Meir. A woman was hired to take care of the cooking, and Vara does the heavy chores.

Moshe's brother, Shmuel, and some of our American friends took turns to remain the entire night to give Yisroel Meir the attention he needs. This gave Moshe a chance to rest. Our friends showed intense devotion.

Reb Chatzkel came up to visit me. His encouraging words were a comfort: "You are far too young to go through such an ordeal. Most probably, your suffering is also for *klal Yisroel*."

Love, *Moshe and Ruchoma*

Dearest Papa and Mama,

I realize you are anxiously awaiting my letters, but I find that each letter is a stress and strain physically and emotionally, as I relive the last tragic months.

I am becoming acquainted with my son. He is a very cute little boy, the image of Moshe. I can hardly believe he is mine. He gives me a toothless smile to show that he forgives me for neglecting him these first precious months of his life.

He outgrew his "bandages" and is dressed in his nighties and diapered as a baby should be. He is receiving the formula, but more milk is added. It obviously agrees with him as he is developing normally.

There is a serious problem that confronts Moshe and me. I need highly professional medical advice, which is not available in Mir. Our friends advise us to seek help from a very reputable orthopedic doctor in Vilna. However, I do not see how Moshe and I can get there in my condition. Perhaps, in a few weeks, when I will grow stronger, we can then attempt this trip. Keep up your prayers!

Now for some happy news: Do you remember that I wrote you before Yisroel Meir's birth that Zlotka was engaged? She was married last week. Of course, I was disappointed that I could not attend her wedding. However, she came to visit me before the wedding ceremony to show me how she looks. She was a lovely bride. Mama, you were so right to advise me to take along my wedding dress. It fitted Zlotka perfectly.

It is very interesting how a wedding is performed here. The ceremony is usually held *erev* Shabbos, about two hours before sunset. The entire city is present at the ceremony, which takes place in the courtyard of the main *shul*. After Friday night prayers, the close relatives and friends are invited to the wedding supper. Many other guests come after the meal to join in the *sheva brochos*.

Reb Mordchi and Zlotka rented an apartment near our house. May they have much joy in their married life.

Love, Moshe and Ruchoma

P.S. Please thank everyone in the family for their encouraging letters which mean so much to me.

Dearest Papa and Mama,

Moshe and I are now in Chichichineck, a natural spa near the German border. Now to fill you in on all the details:

With me on crutches, and Moshe carrying me on and off the train, we reached Vilna. We immediately contacted Dr. Zarcyn, the orthopedic doctor recommended to us. He gave us an appointment for the same day. Fortunately, he speaks English. I was able to give him a detailed case history of my illness, which he recorded carefully.

After concentrating on his notes for a few minutes, he looked up and said, "You must be a wicked young lady." Moshe and I were astounded. Then he added, "According to your case history, with the medication and care you received, you should have been up in heaven. I guess they did not want you up there and threw you back to earth." He winked at us, enjoying his own little joke.

He advised that we go to this spa and I take a series of natural salt and mud baths that might help me regain some of my circulation. He gave us no assurance that these baths would make me all well. But that is not in his hands, but in the hands of Hashem.

The trip was most exhausting for Moshe and me. Chichichineck is at the other end of Poland, and it took us a full day to get here. Many kind people assisted us along the way when they realized how helpless we were.

We are staying at a hotel that is very close to the building housing all the various types of baths. We have a sunny room, and the meals are appetizing. The guests are very friendly and helpful. In fact, one old lady has adopted us. She makes sure we receive our morning fruit and afternoon tea and cake.

Moshe registered me for a series of twenty salt baths and twenty mud baths taken alternately. I've already taken one salt bath. Moshe wheels me to the bathhouse, and then the women attendants take over. The salt bath is powerful and carefully timed with a sand-timer. I am allowed twenty minutes for each bath. Afterward, I must rest for an hour. Tomorrow I am scheduled for the first mud bath. I wonder what kind of mud they use.

Love, Moshe and Ruchoma

Dearest Papa and Mama,

I have already taken seven salt and seven mud baths. The mud is heavy, black, hot mud which covers half of the body. It would be a good idea if Mir would donate some of the mud that plagues us during the spring thaw.

The mud baths bring to mind what Moshe told me the *mashgiach* said regarding the reward a *ben Torah* receives even for the mud that sticks to his rubbers on the way to the yeshiva. I pray that I, too, will reap reward for the distress I have from the mud in Mir, and that I will regain the use of my legs and hand through the mud baths in Chichichineck.

I am doing my utmost to move my legs a bit, but they refuse to obey me. I have not lost faith. My left arm does show improvement.

A few days ago, I had an upsetting experience. Moshe was wheeling me toward the bathhouse. A woman walking near us said to her partner, loud enough for Moshe and me to hear, "What a pity! a young man with a crippled wife."

Moshe's comment was heartwarming, "Racoma, I have no doubt that you will get all well and walk again." He also added, "Some people are crippled in mind, which is far worse than being crippled in body." His response was a potent prescription to calm me.

We received a letter from Shmuel, who, as you know, has been taking care of Yisroel Meir, with our other friends helping him. He writes that the baby is doing very well. I look forward to giving Yisroel Meir some maternal attention when I return.

Shmuel also writes that Reb Chatzkel, his *rebbetzin* and Yecheved are shortly leaving for Eretz Yisroel. He has been offered a position as *mashgiach* in the yeshiva in Petach Tikva. Moshe and I will miss them very much. We gained considerably from Reb Chatzkel's *hashpoeh* (spiritual influence). Rebbetzin Levenstein treated me like a daughter, and Yecheved was a most devoted friend.

Reb Mordchi and Zlotka are remaining in Mir.

Love, *Moshe and Ruchoma*

Dearest Papa and Mama,

Boruch Hashem, I finally stood on my feet for a few moments without support. This gives me renewed encouragement. I felt like an infant who makes his first attempt at standing, swaying from side to side. My legs swelled up when I lowered them to the floor, but this is to be expected because of my circulatory problem.

Moshe wheels me daily to the beautiful flower gardens. There we breathe the pure fragrance of the red roses and other bright colorful flowers that adorn the garden. Hashem created a world and embellished it with growing and blossoming seeds that sprout from the dark, damp earth. If the soft, brown earth can give birth to new buds each spring, why cannot my inactive veins and arteries be rejuvenated with vibrant blood racing through them?

Continued a week later:

I walked! I really walked a few steps!

Moshe patiently illustrated to me over and over again how to place one foot forward followed by the other. Finally, I mastered the rudimentary principles of walking.

The tremendous effort of walking just a few steps left me exhausted for hours. For the first time since my illness, I am beginning to see a silver lining behind the dark clouds.

I have already taken eighteen baths. As you know, the numeral eighteen, *chai,* has a deep connotation in our Hebrew alphabet. *Chai* means life. There was a rebirth of my paralyzed legs following the eighteenth bath. Thank Hashem for His *chesed.*

I am scheduled for two more baths. We hope to leave Chichichineck within a week's time. I look forward to writing you more glad tidings.

Love, Moshe and Ruchoma

P.S. Moshe and I were happy to hear that Bessie gave birth to a third *maidele.* I am sure they will be blessed with sons also. Give them our *mazel tov* and heartfelt good wishes.

Dearest Papa and Mama,

We returned to Mir. We parted from the many new friends in Chichichineck, who promised to keep in touch with us.

Riding home to Mir was a far cry, or I should say a "near

smile," from our riding to Chichichineck. Moshe did not have to carry me on and off the train. With the aid of my crutches, I was able to manage on my own.

You cannot imagine the excitement when we arrived in Mir. All our friends and neighbors turned out *en masse* to greet us. I demonstrated my walking ability so many times that my legs began to look like balloons. Mrs. Bender insisted that I dance with her. I was not graceful by any means, but I did take one or two light steps, and I was also able to embrace her with my left arm.

I am able to walk the length of my dining room with no support. Each day I practice walking. I hope to be able someday to walk once more with the bouncing steps which the children mocked when I first arrived, "*De Amerikanka laift.*"

Papa and Mama, your prayers, and the prayers of the many great men and of our loved ones, reached the Boss.

It is almost Rosh Hashona. There is much preparation, both physical and spiritual. In the spiritual arena, I am greeting the New Year with thankfulness to Hashem for the miracles He wrought. We are blessed with a darling son, and I am on the road to recovery. It was a difficult year, but the dividends are paying off.

During the period we were away, Yisroel Meir grew into a chubby little boy with two front teeth. He refuses to go to my outstretched hands from his Uncle Shmuel. I must be patient and woo him slowly until he realizes I am his Mama, who loves him.

I was sitting on our little porch with Yisroel Meir in his carriage, when the *mashgiach* walked by on his way to the yeshiva. He stopped and came up to the porch to ask me how I was feeling. He then looked into the carriage at the sleeping Yisroel Meir and blessed him. The greater the person, the more humble he is.

Love, *Moshe and Ruchoma*

21

Strides ahead

Dearest Papa and Mama,

Lately, I have made great strides in my walking. My legs do not swell up so much. I can walk almost an entire block, although very slowly. Most people take their physical motions for granted. For me, the miracle of walking and the wonder of using my left hand will always remain a living reality.

I was able to be in the yeshiva for part of the Rosh Hashona and Yom Kippur prayers. Wheeling Yisroel Meir in his carriage, it took me almost an hour to walk the three blocks. I had to rest after every few steps.

Not only was I anxious to be there for the *davening*, but I also wanted Yisroel Meir to see *gedolim* and hear hundreds of yeshiva men raising their voices in prayer.

He was well-behaved and did not cause any disturbance at all. I guess he too felt the awe of the High Holy Day prayers. Though he is only a baby, I hope he absorbed this inspiring experience.

As you know, Berelia and Miriam Gordon arrived for the Elul *zeman*. Having another young American couple lifts my spirits. It was good to talk to Miriam and hear, first hand, all the news from home.

Miriam told me that you, Papa, introduced her to Berelia, a *talmid* of yours, and that they acceded to your suggestion to come to Mir. I am sure Mr. Sheinerman must be very grateful that he listened to your sage advice to leave Washington, D.C. and settle in New York City—especially now that Miriam, their oldest daughter, married such a learned *ben Torah*.

I am trying to ease her adjustment period in every way possible. However, Miriam finds it easier than I because she is not a novice at cooking and the people in Mir are becoming accustomed to American women, both young and old.

Speaking about the Sheinermans, their son Chunie is making good headway. Though he was only fifteen years old when he arrived last year, he adjusted very well.

Papa, it seems that the American boys coming to Mir are becoming younger and younger. Chaim's youngest brother, Shmuel, who is only thirteen-and-a-half years old, arrived in time for Rosh Hashona. He told us that his mother initiated his going to study in Mir, and you, Papa, with your intervention and encouragement, convinced his father to give his tacit approval. In fact, you even went with Shmuel to obtain his photographs and passport.

I remember when you "kidnapped" Chaim to send him to the New Haven Yeshiva. How irate his father was! Now Mr. Scheinberg has joined you. I am sure Shmuel will make excellent progress, as he is quite mature for his age. Tell the Scheinbergs we shall keep a friendly eye on him.

Love, *Moshe and Ruchoma*

P.S. Tell Frieda that Yisroel Meir was delighted with the toys she sent him with Miriam Gordon. Thank her also for the sailor suit, which will fit him once he grows a little. I will have him photographed when he wears it for the first time.

Dearest Papa and Mama,

The days have turned cold and the nights are long. Vara heats our *kachal* stove regularly. We must stand right near it to gain from its warmth. Our bedroom benefits very little from the heat of our stove. Though I keep Yisroel Meir covered with layers of heavy blankets, his little hands are frigid when he wakes up in the morning. He stretches his hands out to me in expectation of the daily brisk rub to warm them up.

When the Mirrer babies are ready to stand, they are kept in a *stoike* — a prison-like contraption that, I would imagine, stunts their growth. It has a small, round wooden frame, which stands on a high tripod. It has just enough space to encase the larger part of the baby's body. Sometimes the baby stands for an hour or more in one position, unable to move his legs.

Moshe and I decided, therefore, to have a playpen built, similar to the ones in the States. I went to the carpenter to place an order for it. He had no idea what I meant. Though I never excelled in art, I drew a picture of how a playpen looks. He told me it would be ready in two weeks.

The playpen finally arrived. It could hardly get through our front door. It looks like an antique, square, with large, dark heavy wooden slats with very little space separating them. It is a double-decker to protect Yisroel Meir from the cold floor. Since it is made from unpolished wood, I padded its floor to prevent Yisroel Meir from getting splinters in his feet.

As I write this letter, he is struggling to get up on his little chubby legs. It brings back a clear picture of myself trying to stand up for the first time after my prolonged illness.

Much to my satisfaction, he is now standing on the "top deck" of the playpen, peering through the slight opening of the slats. He seems wary of this strange innovation. I hope he will adjust to his new surroundings and take his first steps soon.

Our friends and neighbors came to view the playpen. The word is spreading throughout the city that the Amerikanka keeps her son in a *shteig* (chicken coop).

Love, *Moshe and Ruchoma*

Dearest Papa and Mama,

I do not recall too much of last year's Pesach, when I was still in the throes of delirium and excruciating pain following Yisroel Meir's birth. This Pesach, however, I wanted to do all I could to make our Yom Tov a joyous one. I invited eight American boys and one Belgian, with whom we are very friendly, to our *sedorim*, so that we could have a *minyon*.

My *balebuste* promised to teach me how to prepare the gefilte fish and the *kneidlach* for the soup. While Bessie was here, she provided us with the gefilte fish each Shabbos. Since she left, I don't bother with it, but, instead, cook plain boiled fish.

A few days before Pesach, Zalman Yoel, my *balebuste*'s son, contracted the dread disease scarlet fever, which is considered a near-fatal sickness here. (I remember when I had it as a child and you, Papa, sat up with me night after night so I would not scratch my face.) In order to protect Yisroel Meir from catching it, we bolted our kitchen door to make sure there would be no contact with our *balebuste*'s house.

Of course, Esther Mirel could no longer assist me with my cooking. I was in a dilemma. However, an unexpected source of help came my way. Shleima, the Belgian, who happened to visit us, graciously offered to show me how to prepare the gefilte fish when I frankly mentioned my problem to him. "Nothing to it," he said confidently. "I've watched my mother make it many times. Just have plenty of eggs and matzo meal."

I painstakingly cleaned the large four-pound carp. When Shleima arrived *erev* Pesach, the fish and onions were already ground. "Eggs make the gefilte fish fluffy," he advised. After adding a dozen eggs, Shleima told me to pour in enough matzo meal to make the mixture very stiff. I poured and poured the dark brown *shmura* matzo meal until the fish mixture looked

---

kneidlach: matzo-balls / *shmura*: stringently supervised

like tar. I added the salt and pepper. It was ready to be cooked. Half the morning was gone.

I placed the large pot of fish on my primus, which I had *kashered* for Pesach. The longer the fish cooked, the harder the balls became. I couldn't even stick a fork into them. After three hours, I removed the pot from the primus. More in the next letter.

Love, *Moshe and Ruchoma*

Dearest Papa and Mama,

I will continue with the "saga of mishaps" of my first attempt to prepare a Pesach *seder*.

I decided to use my own discretion in the preparation of the *pesachdikke kneidlach*. I used fewer eggs and a very small amount of matzo meal. I placed the pasty *kneidlach* mixture very gently into my boiling chicken soup. They completely disintegrated into a dark brown kasha.

When we reached the *shulchon orech* stage of the *seder* I served our starving guests the gefilte fish. It was pure cement. All attempts to bite into it failed. I tried to apologize but found no words to placate my company.

Shleima was busily enjoying his piece of plain cooked fish, which I had prepared separately for him. He follows the custom of not eating *gebroks*. The soup did nothing to raise the spirits of the boys. The *kneidlach* had melted into a brown gruel. Again, only Shleima enjoyed his clear chicken broth, which I had put aside especially for him. My over-cooked chicken was portioned out in slivers. Everyone certainly observed the mitzva of eating the *afikomen* with hearty appetites.

For our second *seder*, only Shleima and three hardy souls showed up. The others were able to find a place of refuge.

My *balebuste*'s little boy is on the road to recovery. As soon

---

shulchan orech: literally, set table: i.e. eating
gebroks: matzo soaked in water

as I unbolt the door, I will ask her to teach me to cook gefilte fish and *kneidlach*. I have some matzo meal left over.

Love, *Moshe and Ruchoma*

Rabbi Shleima Rottenberg is today a well-known educator, author and historian.

Dearest Papa and Mama,

I have just a few minutes' time, so I am writing you a short letter.

Civilization is making itself felt in Mir. We now have motor bus service from Mir to Horodzei, the train station. The bus is an old, dilapidated one that shakes the town with its vibrating. The horses jump from fright. They can hardly be controlled by the *balegola* (driver) from breaking loose from their wagons.

I still have not hazarded a ride in it. I heard that the passengers who did were obliged to get off the bus every so often to help pull it out of the muddy holes. Nevertheless, it does have four wheels and it goes. The service is available only in the spring, after the snow has melted.

Love, *Moshe and Ruchoma*

Dearest Papa and Mama,

The entire Mirrer yeshiva and *bnei Torah* the world over are now in mourning. The great Mirrer *mashgiach*, Reb Yeruchem Levovitz, *zatzal,* was *niftar* on the eighteenth of Sivan, 5697 (June 8, 1936).

For days, everyone in the yeshiva, and even the townspeople, prayed day and night for his recovery. However, he surely was needed in the *yeshiva shel maala*, for Hashem did not heed our prayers.

We are all terribly saddened and distraught. Rebbetzin Levovitz expressed herself to her children and the loved ones

yeshiva shel maala: heavenly yeshiva

The funeral of Reb Yeruchem Levovitz, the mashgiach *of the Yeshiva. In the picture at the right, the figure in the oval is Moshe.*

gathered in her house at the time of the *mashgiach's petira*. "He was an angel"—and he was just that.

Thousands of *bnei Torah* assembled for his funeral. The greatest *roshei yeshivos* and *rabbonim* were among the mourners. Many of them delivered moving *hespedim*. His *talmidim* cried like babies. Not only had he instilled in them the love for Torah and the deep understanding of what it means to be a *ben Torah*, but he was also a father to each and every one of his *talmidim* and he worried about them all.

As I wrote you when we first arrived in Mir, Reb Yeruchem, *zatzal*, was an outstanding *talmid* of the *mussar* movement, whose founder was the renowned Reb Yisroel Salanter. He studied in the famous *mussar* yeshiva in Kelm, Lithuania. For a time he was *mashgiach* in the yeshiva of Radun, the home of the Chofetz Chaim.

....

petira: passing away

When the former Mirrer *rosh yeshiva,* Reb Elya Boruch Kamai (whose son is the present rabbi of Mir, and whose son-in-law is the present *rosh yeshiva* of Mir), decided that it was of fundamental importance to institute a *mussar* program in the yeshiva, Reb Yeruchem, *zatzal,* was called upon to become the first *mashgiach.* For twenty-six years he served as *mashgiach.* During this period of time, his thousands of *talmidim* spread his teachings of Torah, combined with the teachings of profound ethics, throughout the yeshiva world.

There is talk that Reb Chatzkel, who is now in Eretz

Yisroel, will be recalled to become *mashgiach* in Mir. I hope so. In order to fill the immense void left by the *mashgiach*'s passing away, the yeshiva needs a person of Reb Chatzkel's caliber to inspire the *talmidim* to take higher spiritual strides on the path of *mussar.*

Moshe and I look forward to being close once more to Reb Chatzkel and his family.

Love, *Moshe and Ruchoma*

P.S. I am enclosing a photo taken at the funeral. I've encircled Moshe's face: as you can see, he was standing close to the *oron.*

Dearest Papa and Mama,

Yisroel Meir is progressing steadily. When he sees Moshe learning, he too must be given a *sefer.* He points his little finger at the words, and mimicking Moshe, chants, *"omar Abaye, omar Rova."* Of course, he looks up every now and then to make sure that I'm paying attention.

Vara takes an active role in training him. She makes sure that he recites a *brocho* before eating any food. She keeps his *yarmulke* from slipping off his head. When he is naughty, she admonishes him, *"Du vilst zein a yeshiva bochur, darfst du folgen"* (if you want to be a *yeshiva bochur*, you must obey).

On Tisha B'Av, she excused herself for not greeting me with the normal "Good morning." She said that it is not proper on such a sad day for Jews. When a *goy* comes to my door asking for charity, she advises me, *"Nasent em nit—er iz en orel"* (do not give him any money; he is a *goy*). It is difficult to believe that she, herself, is a *goya.*

Happy announcements:

David Bender married Basya Epstein from Otvosk. She studied at the Sara Shenirer Bais Yaakov, and is an outstanding girl from a well-known family. Rabbi Bender arrived to

....
oron: casket

attend the wedding. It took place in her home city, Otvosk, near Warsaw, so it was too far for us to travel. Mrs. Bender is delighted with her new daughter-in-law. David and Basya are living with her.

Boruch Kaplan is engaged to Vichne Eisen. As she is an orphan, her uncle, Reb Yisroel Yaakov Lubchansky, the *mashgiach* of Baranowitz Yeshiva, brought her up. She is one of the best *talmidos* of the Sara Shenirer Bais Yaakov. Though Boruch is presently learning in Kaminetz Yeshiva, he comes to Mir for Elul and the High Holy Days. When he visited us, he asked about you, Papa, his *rebbe*. He expressed his deep gratitude to you, saying that whatever he attains is due only to your teachings and devotion. He is leaving shortly for the States and will make arrangements for his *kalla,* Vichne, to follow.

It seems, Papa, that you sent your *talmidim* to Poland not only to grow in Torah learning but also to find their true partners in life.

Love, Moshe and Ruchoma

....

talmidos: female students

22

Towards a healthier policy

Dearest Papa and Mama,

Moshe became ill with *angina* (strep throat). His temperature was high, and he felt very sick. I was worried and called Doctor Shlepak. He prescribed the same medication he gives every patient of his—fever powders—and advised that I give Moshe lots of fluids. His throat is so sore and painful that he cannot drink or eat anything. I cooked *hirshene* (yellow kasha), which I felt would not irritate his raspy throat, but he could not swallow even one spoonful. Without nourishment, he was becoming weaker.

In desperation, I ran to Reb Chatzkel, who had returned to Mir not long before. I told him about Moshe's condition and that he wasn't eating or drinking. He asked no questions. He put on his coat and hurried to our house. He asked me to reheat the cereal. Then he, himself, fed it to him. Of course, Moshe finished the entire portion despite his sore throat. Since then, he is eating and drinking much better. I guess he fears that the next time I might go to Reb Lezer Yudel and tattle on him.

So your dear son-in-law was spoon-fed by Reb Chatzkel,

the present *mashgiach*. It was a great *chesed* not only for Moshe, but for me as well.

I wanted to stimulate Moshe's appetite. Since I heard that there are oranges imported from Spain, I went to the grocery to buy some. The grocery lady asked me, "Who is sick?" One must be an invalid to eat an orange. I bought a few small, blood-red oranges, which are very expensive. I dole it out to Moshe in tiny pieces, and he sucks out the juice.

A few days later, I braved another visit to the grocery. This time I asked for grapes, which are also a rarity here. The grocery lady eyed me with pity, "Your husband must be very ill." I bought a small bunch of green grapes. I give them to Moshe one at a time.

Boruch Hashem, Moshe is on the road to recovery. Color has returned to his pale cheeks, but he will remain home a few more days. He is impatient to return to the yeshiva, as he does not want to miss vital learning.

Rebbetzin Chave Levovitz, the daughter-in-law of Reb Yeruchem, *zatzal,* visited me. She was most considerate to bring me a small, ripe banana for Yisroel Meir. She received some bananas from a visiting relative. I have not seen any since I came to Mir. I have learned that every fruit is precious.

Love, *Moshe and Ruchoma*

Dearest Papa and Mama,

Do you remember my writing you that I contacted the Department of Health in the States requesting booklets on baby and child care? After many months, I received them. I am reading them carefully and have learned important information on how best to feed a child nutritiously. The book advises that in order for the bones to develop properly, adequate doses of vitamins A and D must be added to the diet. Cod liver oil is recommended as having high quantities of these vitamins.

I went to our one and only drugstore. After a lengthy explanation on my part, the druggist said it is called *fishtron*. I asked him to order it for me as soon as possible. I waited impatiently for it to arrive, worrying that Yisroel Meir might in the meantime develop rickets.

Last week, the druggist notified me of its arrival. The *fishtron* came in the most evil-smelling, black, oily barrel. With a ladle, he filled up a pint bottle of the oil. I hope it is real cod liver oil. The book says that a normal dosage is two tablespoons daily.

I was sure that Yisroel Meir would turn up his little nose and refuse to take it. To my utter astonishment, he not only swallowed the *fishtron* but also licked off the spoon. I read that a child will accept nourishment readily if it is lacking in his body. I suppose that Yisroel Meir might be deficient in vitamin D, as he gets very little sun during the winter. I am giving him large portions of raw carrots, which I strain, to provide him with more vitamin A.

The druggist spread the word that the Amerikanka ordered *fishtron* for her son. There was a run on it, and the barrel of oil was sold out in a few days. Every baby and child now smells of cod liver oil, and his clothes show telltale signs of the brown thick oil.

I made a horrible mistake the other day. I grabbed the bottle of cod liver oil, which looks identical to my cooking oil, and I fried fish in it. Our apartment reeked with the smell for days. It even found its way to our *balebuste*'s house. We both had to open our sealed double windows to clear the air. I asked Vara to dump the fish outside the city, otherwise the entire neighborhood would be exposed to the foul odor.

Love, *Moshe and Ruchoma*

P.S. I should mention that I also had to *kasher* my frying pan, which still contained the "fragrance" from the cod liver oil.

Dearest Papa and Mama,

Ever since we received the pamphlets from the Department of Health, Moshe and I are faced with a problem — although, in essence, it is humorous. Yisroel Meir is known as the "book baby." Lately, we have a steady stream of mothers coming to our door asking for medical information. They ask us to look up in the "American book" for a cure for every conceivable ailment from which their babies might suffer.

One night, when the electricity had already been extinguished in the entire city, which means it was after midnight, a hysterical woman banged on our door. We were startled out of a deep sleep. She did not ask for any information from the "American book" but for the "American doctor"— meaning Moshe, of course.

She blurted out that her baby was burning up with fever and shaking violently. I gathered from this that her baby had convulsions. I practically forced her out of our house. I told her to call Dr. Shlepak immediately and advised her to sponge the baby with alcohol while she waited for the doctor.

Now Moshe has acquired another degree—"Doctor of Medicine."

I had another experience with one of my neighbors' children. Her little son was ill. She asked me to read the thermometer, which she had borrowed from the drugstore, as most people do not possess one of their own.

I was shocked to see the temperature was all the way up to the top—which was hovering over the forty-two mark, centigrade. I did not wish to alarm her, so I did not divulge the very high reading. I suggested that I go with her to see her son.

I was relieved to see Berele sitting up in bed, playing with some large buttons. Certainly, he did not appear very ill. I could not understand the enigma.

I decided to take the child's temperature myself. It was just over thirty-eight degrees, which is not considered high fever for a sick child. After prodding the mother, I discovered that she warmed up the thermometer in the *kachala* fearing it was too cold to use.

All's well that ends well. . . . I, too, have joined the medical profession.

Love, *Moshe and Ruchoma*

Dearest Papa and Mama,

Yisroel Meir came down with *kochlush* (whooping cough). Most probably he caught it from one of the neighbors' children. Now that he is a "big" boy, he awakens very early in the morning, often before we are up. He climbs out of his crib and marches out of the house. I find him eating breakfast in the homes of different neighbors. They pamper him.

Not only does Yisroel Meir whoop, but Moshe caught it from him. Our house resounds with a chorus of whoops in various tones. My neighbors suggest different *babske refuahs.* "Walk Yisroel Meir over the Mirrer bridge back and forth for three consecutive times." "Keep him outdoors day and night." "Keep him indoors with a steaming kettle near him." "Change the climate."

The only advice that makes sense to me is to ride to Nowojelnia, a *datche* (resort) which has a forest of pine trees. It's about a two-hour ride by *droshke* (horse and carriage) from Mir. Next week the official summer vacation begins in the yeshiva. We hope to go then.

Continued:

We arrived in Nowojelnia a few days ago. Our sleeping accommodations also provide a primus so that I can prepare breakfasts and suppers on my own. For dinner, we go to a nearby restaurant and order two portions of a chicken meal, which we divide with Yisroel Meir. The exhilarating air is already having its beneficial effect on both of my patients. Moshe's cough has eased considerably, and Yisroel Meir can now hold down his food.

There are *gamocken* (hammocks) hanging from most of the pine trees. The sap oozes down from the trees, filling the air with its potent aroma. I find it very relaxing to swing back and forth in my hammock.

There are interesting vacationers who have joined us. Reb

---

babske refuahs: old wives' cures

Chaim Shmulevitz, his wife, Miriam, and their daughter, Ettele, are also here. Each morning after breakfast, Reb Chaim, Reb Shmuel Brudna, also a Mirrer, and a few more yeshiva men get together for Torah discussions. So even here, Moshe is gaining in his Torah learning.

A *meshuloch* found a novel way of collecting charity, while on vacation. He is raising money for the Baranowitz Yeshiva. He brought along with him a phonograph with records of prominent cantors. Each time we want to hear a record, we must deposit some money in his charity box. One gets one's money's worth: we have the *mitzva* of *tzedoko* while listening to the *chazonim*.

Love, *Moshe and Ruchoma*

Dearest Papa and Mama,

The time in Nowojelnia is passing very quickly. Moshe and Yisroel Meir are almost completely cured from their whooping cough bout. I shall be sorry to leave, as it is very enjoyable to be here.

We have an interesting vacationer, Reb Elya, a Mirrer Yeshiva boy, who is very friendly with us. He was recently rejected from serving in the Polish Army. He starved himself almost to the point of resembling a human skeleton in order not to be drafted.

Serving in the Polish Army means that it is almost impossible to observe Shabbos and the laws of *kashrus*. Most of the yeshiva boys go on a starvation diet, so that the army has no recourse but to reject them. The fortunate ones among them receive a permanent rejection, while others, not so fortunate, have to experience this grueling ordeal several times. Some of the boys contract tuberculosis as a result.

Reb Elya lies in his hammock almost immobile. He is very intent upon regaining his lost weight as quickly as possible. He consumes large quantities of sweet cream and beer, which are supposed to add many calories to his diet and consequently increase his weight.

It is hilarious to watch him drink this mixture, his protruding Adam's apple working furiously as he gulps it down. After each swallow, he touches the bottom of his bony chin and asks Moshe, "Reb Moshe, *es iz kontig?*" (is it noticeable?) He has gained back some of his lost weight, so that he doesn't look quite like a scarecrow anymore.

I've become quite friendly with a young woman who is here with her husband. Her father is a rabbi in a little city not very far from here. She noticed that I keep my hair covered and expressed surprise. "Imagine, you were born in the great America and still are extremely religious." Though the young women here observe many of the *mitzvos*, surprisingly, when it comes to keeping their hair covered, they are lax.

I explained to her that one of the important *mitzvos* of a married woman is to keep her hair covered. I gave her a pretty kerchief as a gift.

A few days later she came to my room with the kerchief prettily draped over her head. Papa, I have one recruit to my credit.

Love, *Moshe and Ruchoma*

Rabbi Elya Yurkansky is a rosh yeshiva *in the Mirrer Yeshiva of Brooklyn.*

Dearest Papa and Mama,

The tailors here are experts. They can take any old garment, turn it inside-out and transform it into a completely different piece of clothing.

The rabbit-lined winter coat my mother-in-law bought for me before I left for Mir is worn out and does not fit me properly any more. I took it to one of the tailors and asked him to remake it into a winter coat with a matching hat for Yisroel Meir. He did an excellent job. The coat is too long. However, the tailor insisted that if he makes it any shorter, Yisroel Meir will outgrow it too quickly.

The first Shabbos he wore his "new" outfit, I took him to

Yisroel Meir in his
fur-lined coat,
dressed up to travel.

the Rosh Yeshiva and his *rebbetzin*. I usually visit them on Shabbos afternoon. I look forward to seeing them, and Yisroel Meir enjoys the attention they shower on him. They are very devoted to us. I guess this is in appreciation of your *hachnosas orchim* to Reb Lezer Yudel when he was in our house.

As Yisroel Meir walked down the street with his *futter* (fur-lined coat) everyone stopped to admire him. He looks like a little prince in it. I am enclosing a photo of him wearing his fur-lined coat and hat.

I had an interesting but frightening experience with Yisroel Meir during our visit. The *rebbetzin* served tea and cake. Usually, Yisroel Meir is satisfied with the cookies and candies she prepares for him. This time, he asked for a glass of tea. I imagine he wanted to prove that he is a "big boy."

Their glasses are very thin and decorative. Yisroel Meir is used to drinking from a heavy mug. As he sipped his tea, he bit into the glass, which cracked on top, and a small piece of glass remained on his tongue. Of course, he immediately spit out the piece of glass, which fortunately did not split into slivers. However, Rabbi Finkel and his wife went into a panic. They were very concerned that a slight sliver of glass might have remained on his tongue.

Over and over again, Reb Lezer Yudel insisted: "Yisroel Meir, *shteck ois dain tzung*" (stick out your tongue). Reb Lezer Yudel and the *rebbetzin* examined it closely. As I watched Reb Lezer Yudel hover over Yisroel Meir with his tongue sticking all the way out, I thought this must be the first time anyone dared to stick out his tongue at the Rosh Yeshiva. There is no sign of any ill effects from the accident.

I am certain that next Shabbos when we visit, the *rebbetzin* will prepare a much thicker glass for Yisroel Meir's tea.

Love, *Moshe and Ruchoma*

Dearest Papa and Mama,

MAZEL TOV!

As you recall, I introduced your *talmid*, Shachne Zohn, to my girl friend, Liba Gulevsky, and they got engaged several months ago. This past Sunday night was the joyous occasion of their wedding. Moshe and I felt like part of the family. In fact, I've known Shachne since he was a young boy, and Liba has grown very close to me these past five years. Yisroel Meir wore his new little sailor suit and was very excited with all the happy goings on.

We were invited to the *sheva brochos*, so that we spent a very pleasurable week. Reb Shachne and Liba are going to live in Kaminetz, where he will be learning in the yeshiva.

I am enclosing photographs taken at Liba's wedding. Yisroel Meir did not come out too clearly, as he moved when the picture was snapped. In the other photograph Liba and Shachne are seated at the table after the *chupa*. Liba's mother, Nechama, and her older sister, Leah, are seated on one side of the table. On the other side, her little brother, Aaron Lezer, and her father, Reb Elchonon Tzvi, are seated.

*Pictures from the wedding
of Reb Shachne Zohn
and Liba Gulevsky.*

I am peeking from the doorway. By the way, Liba's father
has a striking resemblance to you, Papa, and whenever he
comes home from Lutsk, I get a wave of lonesomeness for you.

Papa, I was overjoyed to read your description of Reb
Boruch Kaplan's marriage to Vichne. I can understand that a
talmid is like a son, and I realize how dear he is to you.

Your further correspondence that Reb Boruch and Vichne
started the first Bais Yaakov Seminary in the States was
rewarding news to Moshe and me. Though it is a modest
beginning, with just a few *talmidos,* I am sure that in a short
period of time, it will grow by leaps and bounds. At least, our

daughters, when Hashem will bless us with them, will have a Bais Yaakov where they will be able to study and gain a valuable Torah education under the guidance of teachers with proper *hashkofos*.

This first Bais Yaakov Seminary in America originates with you, Papa, because you were instrumental in helping Reb Boruch become what he is today. All the spiritual blossoms that will eventually grow from the tiny seed that is being planted will be to your credit. Your policies are paying off.

I am busy with my *erev* Pesach chores. Several American boys will be with us at the *sedorim* and during the entire Yom Tov. They do not need any urging to come to us, as I now have a reputation as a good cook.

Now that spring is here, Yisroel Meir sits on our large window sill watching with fascination all the *goyim* with their horses, cows, and sheep heading for the market place. He claps his hands in glee and calls out *"zrepchikel"* whenever a pony passes by. He speaks an excellent Polish-Yiddish.

Love, Moshe and Ruchoma

Dearest Papa and Mama,

From time to time Rabbi Yisroel Yaakov Lubchansky, the *mashgiach* of the Yeshiva of Baranowitz, is invited to deliver a *shmuess* in the Mirrer Yeshiva.

Moshe told me the gist of one of his talks, and it has been of immense help to me. His *shmuess* centered on the topic of concentrating on *shmoneh esrei*. I usually find it very difficult to keep my complete thoughts on the prayers, and my mind wanders, much to my chagrin.

Reb Yisroel Yaakov gave practical advice. First of all, he said, do not expect perfect concentration from start to finish, but try to concentrate on one blessing at a time. Also, if one realizes during the prayers that he has been faulty in his concentration, he should not be discouraged, but should start from whichever blessing he is praying.

I followed his advice and find that I am making headway and my concentration has improved.

Moshe told me another interesting *shmuess* from the Mirrer *mashgiach*. Before Pesach, the boys from each *stanze* bake matzo. Reb Yeruchem became aware that one boy did not show up to pitch in with the baking of the matzo. The other boys in the *stanze* felt that he did not have a valid reason for not helping—but he just wanted the others to do his work for him. They decided not to bake any matzo for him and allow him to fend for himself.

The *mashgiach* berated the boys, explaining that one must not judge a person harshly, even though the boy was not correct in shirking his duty.

I remember, Papa, that on many occasions you said one must act *"Lifnim mishuras hadin."*

Love, *Moshe and Ruchoma*

Dearest Papa and Mama,

Our sixth Pesach in Mir was most gratifying. The *sedorim* were inspiring and my meals tasty. Yisroel Meir asked the "four *kashes*" with a little prompting from Moshe.

I had a "comedy of errors" with one of my *pesachdikke* cakes. I prepared a potato-starch sponge cake. I placed the pan with the raw cake into my *kachal* stove. In about fifteen minutes, I heard strange crackling sounds emanating from my stove. I opened the door gingerly and, with a candle lighting the dark interior, I peered inside. The cake had risen to an enormous height. Most of it was pasted to the roof of the stove. The cake was pitch black.

Vara, who was looking over my shoulder, saw the grotesque shapeless mass, and screeched out: "A *gilgul*," and fled the house in panic.

When I removed the cake from the stove and tasted it cautiously, it was bitter like gall. I couldn't understand what

---

lifnim mishuras hadin: beyond the letter of the law
gilgul: transmogrified spirit

had gone wrong. After some detective work, I discovered that Vara had mistakenly bought bicarbonate of soda instead of potato starch. I had mixed an entire glass of the soda into the cake. As you know, Mama, only a level teaspoon is used to make a cake rise.

I dumped this cake into the garbage. My other cakes were delicious.

During one of our Yom Tov meals, Moshe told me an interesting thought, which brought home to me, Papa, your similar thoughts on this subject. When a person is a *ben Torah* and dedicates his life to the study of Torah, then he will reap full reward even for the time he is eating his meals or relaxing. He is doing these necessary activities in order to provide himself with strength to continue his Torah life. So he will receive excellent dividends for twenty-four hours a day.

You expressed it in a different manner: When a person is *mezakeh es harabbim* it is the best insurance policy. "It works while you sleep." He receives a share of all the *mitzvos* that are being done by the people through his intervention.

Torah thoughts are potent. When you spoke to me on so many occasions during my adolescence, I absorbed your many religious concepts without realizing that they were finding a niche in my mind.

Love, *Moshe and Ruchoma*

23

Homecoming

Dearest Papa and Mama,

Your express letter advising us, "It is time to come home" caught us unawares. We are so much a part and parcel of life in Mir that the thought of going home has not entered our minds for a long time. Of course, we shall immediately start making arrangements for our departure.

According to the date of the tickets you purchased for us, we have two months. It should be ample time for us to sell most of our furniture and pack our valises with the clothing and other items we intend to take home with us. Moshe bought many *seforim* while living here. He will pack them separately in cartons and send them through the post office.

He hopes to receive *smicha* from Rabbi Kamai and the Rosh Yeshiva. Moshe also wants to visit Kaminetz and meet with Rabbi Boruch Ber, from whom he would like a *smicha*. We shall therefore stop off in Kaminetz on our way home.

We anxiously await the moment when we will see you both and all our many loved ones whom we have not seen for five-and-a-half years. There are new nephews and nieces from both sides of our family. On Moshe's side, there are two new brothers-in-law and one sister-in-law to meet. There is much news to catch up on.

Papa, I remember so clearly when you were trying to influence me to go to Mir. You said to me at that time, "Ruchoma, you always wanted to broaden your horizons." It had an entirely different connotation then from what it means to me now.

Yes, we have broadened our horizons. Moshe made much progress in his Torah studies. The many *shiurim* of the Rosh Yeshiva and the *shmuessen* he heard from the great Reb Yeruchem, *zatzal,* and from the great *tzaddik*, Reb Chatzkel, *yibodel l'chaim*, have changed his outlook, and mine. We suffered much, but gained even more. Because Moshe and I went through so much together, our marriage is secure and satisfying. We have a strong foundation that makes life rewarding.

And, as our additional precious "dividend," we take back with us our son, Yisroel Meir, a Mirrer—a sturdy little boy, who we pray and hope will follow in the footsteps of his *zeidies.*

Please give our love to everyone back home. Tell them how much we are looking forward to greeting them. I have not received a letter from Frieda for some time. She must be busy with her *kinderlach.*

Love, *Moshe and Ruchoma*

Dearest Papa and Mama,

We are making the rounds saying good-bye to our many friends. We visited Rabbi Kamai and his family and Rabbi Lezer Yudel and his family. Reb Lezer Yudel asked us to take along with us his personal regards and good wishes to you.

When Moshe and I went to Reb Chatzkel to inform him of the news of our leaving, the message he gave us left a deep impact. This is part of what he said: "You have absorbed much

....

yibodel l'chaim: may he be separated (from the previously mentioned person) for life / *zeidies*: grandfathers / *kinderlach*: children

Torah in the time you spent in Mir. How can you be assured that it will remain steadfast with you when you will be living in the great America? You must look for *hashgocho* (Divine Providence) in every phase of your lives and in every step you take. This will keep your Torah and *emuna* strong." He blessed us, and also blessed Yisroel Meir to become a great *ben Torah.*

It was an immense *zechus* for me to have been so close to Reb Chatzkel and his family during my years in Mir. One of the many impressive actions that I noticed while in his home was the gracious manner in which he gave charity. The family was always in difficult financial circumstances, so that Reb Chatzkel could only give small amounts to the many poor people who knocked at his door. However, he always made the poor person feel welcome in his home. He engaged him in conversation, inquiring after his welfare, and showing concern for him.

Rebbetzin Levenstein, Zlotka, and Yecheved are very sad at our leaving. I will miss them all.

My *balebuste* went into a crying spell ever since she heard the news, and she looks at me through teary eyes. Reb Avrohom and the children are also very disturbed at our going away. We have been like one family.

Vara, our *shikse,* still does not accept our decision that she cannot come with us. She swears she will serve us hand and foot. If she ever came to New York, the people would think she is a *rebbetzin,* as she knows so many of our customs and speaks perfect Yiddish.

We are trying to make Yisroel Meir understand that he is leaving Mir and will be going to a far-away land. He will meet his Zeidies and Bobies, aunts and uncles, and many cousins. I do not think he grasps it fully. But he was very excited when I told him that he will be traveling in a great, big boat and showed him a picture of one.

Love, *Moshe and Ruchoma*

....

emuna: faith

Avrohom and Esther Mirel Kaplinsky (my balebuste*) with Moshe and me. At the right are their 3 children, with our Yisroel Meir in front (1937).*

P.S. We took pictures with my *balebuste* and her family. I am enclosing them in this letter. They dressed in their Shabbos clothes for the occasion. Yisroel Meir was in the midst of play and had no time to change.

Dearest Papa and Mama,

We received your registered letter with the enclosed ship tickets for the *Acquitania*, which leaves Cherbourg, France on June 28th and arrives in New York on July 4th. Now I *really* believe we are going home.

The last few weeks have been hectic ones. We sold some of our furniture. We gave our dining-room table and chairs to Esther Mirel. To Bat Sheva Leshinsky, we are leaving Yisroel Meir's playpen, crib, and highchair, as she recently gave birth to her son, Yeruchem.

The yeshiva boys gave a farewell party for us that tugged at our hearts. The *grammen* were very creative and filled with both pathos and humor. The many speeches brought tears to all who were present.

My friends and neighbors also made a special party for me. I received very lovely hand-made tablecloths, knitted pillow covers and art work. Moshe was given a *megilla* written by a *sofer* who is a friend of ours.

As the townspeople discover that we are leaving soon, we have such odd requests. One woman asked if I can visit her relatives and bring them a gift. When I asked for the address, she showed me a letter from them. They live in San Francisco! I tried to explain to her that I could not possibly visit them as they live on the other side of America. She was amazed that I could not ride over to them. Another woman came with a more bizarre request. "I have a friend who lives very near to where the boat docks," she said simply. She had no address, only a name in Yiddish. These people, who have never ventured outside of Mir, have no concept of the scope of America.

We have just a few more days before our departure. I walk along the streets of Mir looking into every nook and cranny. I shall never forget it. Though it is a tiny town measured by physical breadth, it is immense in spiritual stature, as I wrote to you in a previous letter.

I wonder if Yisroel Meir will remember his birthplace. He is so young. Everyone is doing his utmost to spoil him. He's away from the house most of the day. I go searching from neighbor to neighbor to discover where he is.

In my next letter, I shall write you the details of our departure.

Love, *Moshe and Ruchoma*

Dearest Papa and Mama,

I am writing this letter from Reb Shachne and Liba Zohn's home in Kaminetz. We arrived last night and will remain here for two days.

Let me go back to our poignant parting from all our dear friends and from Mir, our home for almost six years.

The day of our departure was an emotional one. We were scheduled to leave Mir at 3:30 PM on the one and only bus that

megilla: scroll (of Esther)

connects to the train in Horodzei. From early morning on, our friends and neighbors were with us. They were all helpful, even preparing our meals for us. Vara did not let Yisroel Meir out of her sight.

At 3 PM we started for the market place where the bus is parked. A large procession followed us. When we arrived at the bus stop, many yeshiva boys and townspeople were waiting for us.

Yisroel Meir was hugged and kissed so much that his little round cheeks were rosy, red apples. Moshe received his share of kissing from the yeshiva boys, who encircled him, dancing and singing. My close friends and Esther Mirel and her children let out such heart-rending cries that for a moment I wondered how I could part from them.

The bus hooted, howled, screeched, and shrieked—the motor tuning up. These noises blended with the cries of hysteria from all our friends. Through the haze of smoke and tears, the bus drove off slowly, black gasoline pouring from its exhaust pipes.

I saw hands waving and heard a shout that pierced the heavens—*"Fort gezunterheit—Zeit matzliach—Fargest unz nisht!"* (Travel in good health. Have success. Do not forget us.)

Then the little houses with their white-painted chimneys disappeared. The tall steeple of the castle faded into the horizon. I could not see Mir any more, but its poignant memories came along with me.

Would I ever see Mir again, or the many loved ones who had been part of my life these memorable last years?

Love, *Moshe and Ruchoma*

I never saw Mir again, nor many of my beloved friends. The Germans captured Mir on June 27, 1941. Within a few months, most of the townspeople were executed by the Nazis. Very few escaped.

Rabbi Kamai remained with his people as they were led to

their death, bolstering their courage to the last moment. His rebbetzin *and two of his daughters and their husbands were among the victims. A third daughter and her husband had immigrated, fortunately, to Eretz Yisroel several years before the war.*

Esther Mirel and her three children were also among the victims. Reb Avrohom escaped to the forest and joined a group of partisans, only to be captured and murdered at a later date.

Liba (Gulevsky) Zohn's parents and her younger brother were killed. Miraculously, the remainder of the family were able to make their way to America by different routes.

The mashgiach's *oldest son, Reb Yisroel Levovitz, his wife, Chave, and their three children were lost in the Holocaust.*

The rest of the mashgiach's *family, along with Reb Lezer Yudel and his family, Reb Chatzkel and his family, Reb Dovid and Bat Sheva with their family, and most of the Mirrer Yeshiva boys escaped to Shanghai.*

After the war, Rabbi Finkel and his family settled in Yerusholayim, where the Mirrer Yeshiva was transferred. He remained Rosh Yeshiva until he was niftar *on the nineteenth of Tammuz, 5725 (July 19, 1965).*

Reb Chatzkel and his family and some of the yeshiva boys went to New York in 1947. The Mirrer Yeshiva Central Institute, under the leadership of Rabbi Abraham Kalmanovitz, was inaugurated in Brooklyn, New York.

Reb Chatzkel served as mashgiach *for two years in the yeshiva in Brooklyn. In 1949, he decided to leave the United States for Eretz Yisroel with his wife and daughter, Yecheved, and her husband, Reb Reuven Ginzburg, a brother of Reb Mordchi.*

Reb Chatzkel served as mashgiach *of the Mirrer Yeshiva in Yerusholayim until 1954, when he was called to Ponievezh Yeshiva in Bnei Brak to become its* mashgiach. *He remained there until he was* niftar *on the eighteenth of Adar, 5734 (March 12, 1974).*

Reb Mordchi and Zlotka stayed in New York, where he was

This picture was taken before we left Kaminetz. From left to right: Reb Reuven Grozovsky (partially out of the camera's range), Moshe, Reb Naftoli Leibowitz (the mashgiach*) and Yeshaya Kotler, holding his baby.*

Rosh Yeshiva in the Mirrer Yeshiva Central Institute until he was niftar.

Reb Dovid and Bat Sheva Leshinsky and their family settled in New York, where she passed away in middle age.

The departed will always live on in my memory.

Dearest Papa and Mama,

The last two days in Kaminetz have been memorable. The Rosh Yeshiva, Reb Boruch Ber Leibowitz, greeted us very warmly when we came to his home. Over and over again, he repeated, "Now, through his children, I can repay Reb Yaakov Yosef for just a small part of his *hachnosas orchim* to me."

Rebbetzin Leibowitz prepared an elaborate dinner for us. Yisroel Meir sat right next to Reb Boruch Ber, who made sure that he finished his meal. Reb Boruch Ber spent a great deal of time with Moshe discussing Torah. The very special *smicha* that he wrote for Moshe will be a source of pride to you.

Before we left for America. From right to left: Reb Boruch Ber's wife, their daughter Rebbetzin Nechama Bernstein, then myself with Yisroel Meir. Further left: my friend Liba Zohn, Rebbetzin Sara Grozovsky, and 2 of Reb Boruch Ber's granddaughters.

Reb Reuven Grozovsky and his *rebbetzin*, Reb Boruch Ber's son-in-law and daughter, insisted that we also eat a dinner with them. They live in the same building — one floor up. Reb Reuven also mentioned to us during our stay with them his great appreciation to you for the time he spent in your house.

Reb Shachne and Liba have gone out of their way to make us feel comfortable. They are a very compatible couple. Moshe and I are proud that we introduced them to each other. He is learning well and making excellent progress.

Reb Yeshaya Kotler and his wife, Rivka, are building their lives along the path of Torah. They have a little son, Yossie. Rivka told me that you, Papa, brought them together and encouraged their coming to Europe.

Your *talmid*, Reb Binyomin Bernstein, has gained greatly in his Torah studies. He is preparing to return to the States to meet a girl whom Rivka Kotler recommended. I understand that you've already met her to make sure that she is suitable for

Binyomin and that she will be willing to go to Kaminetz if the *shidduch* is successful.

Papa, I am sure you will derive great joy that your impressive influence has taken deep root and is being spread in Europe as well as in the States.

We are leaving Kaminctz tomorrow morning. We shall catch the train in the late afternoon, which will take us from Poland through Germany and finally to Cherbourg, France, where we shall board the *Acquitania* on our last *leg* home. I should say: "With two healthy *legs* I am coming home, *boruch Hashem.*"

Love, *Moshe and Ruchoma*

Dearest Papa and Mama,

Our touching send-off from Kaminetz will long be remembered by us. Rebbetzin Leibowitz, her daughter, Rebbetzin Grozovsky, their children, Reb Shachne, Liba, Reb Yeshaya, Rivka, their little son, Yossie, Reb Binyomin, and some of the yeshiva men came to the bus to see us off.

Reb Boruch Ber and Reb Reuven asked us to convey their warm greetings and personal regards to you. Rebbetzin Leibowitz also sends her special regards to her brother, Rabbi Zimmerman, and his family.

This is the last letter that I shall be writing to you before our arrival, God willing.

My excitement is mounting! Each minute seems an hour!

I am ending this letter with a little poem that expresses my feelings:

Our Homecoming

The stately ship enters port;
It blasts farewell to the mighty oceans.
Its proud white mast is gently lowered,
To dry the deck's salty tears.

Two heavenly stars, bright and twinkling,
Guided the ship on its long voyage.
New vistas appeared on the glowing horizon,
Where the sky dips low to greet the earth.

The ship never veered from its steady course,
Though buffeted by high winds and waves.
The darkness of night was slowly dispelled,
By the dawn's birth to the brightness of day.

One sigh, one cry, one burst of joy,
As yearning hearts find their haven.
Secure in your loving arms,
Our ship is anchored safe ashore.

Love, *Moshe and Ruchoma*

BACK HOME AGAIN

The train's wheels and the ship's motor hummed one tune for me throughout the rest of our trip. "Soon, soon, we shall be home again."

The ship sailed along on the calm, diamond-studded sea. The summer weather made it a delight to be on board. Yisroel Meir was enchanted with the special children's toy room. I had to coax him to come out for meals and naps. The kosher kitchen served excellent meals. This journey bore no resemblance to our seasick trip five-and-a-half years ago.

On our first morning out, when we entered the dining hall and seated ourselves at the kosher table, we noticed an old man with a long, gray beard, who was seated in the non-kosher section. We were sure that he was Jewish, so Moshe approached him. He was traveling from Soviet Russia. When Moshe informed him that kosher meals were available, he expressed astonishment, asking in disbelief, "Is there still kosher food to be had?" Of course, we immediately made space for him at our table and kept an eye on him throughout our trip. He told us that the Russian Jews, especially in the big cities like Moscow, are very far from *yiddishkeit*. It is a catastrophe that so many of our brothers and sisters are lost to the Jewish nation.

The last night before landing, I could not sleep. In my mind's eye, I saw our loved ones waving and greeting us with excited cries.

The ship emitted its last roar before dropping anchor. It was 2 PM July 4th, 1938. There were hundreds of people crowded on the pier. Then the ship opened its doors. Moshe and I, each holding on tightly to Yisroel Meir's hand, hurried down the gangplank.

I heard a shout, "There they are!" Papa and Mama, my in-laws, Lipman and Esther, Nochum Dovid and Chaye Dube, Chaim and Bessie, some of their children, Moshe's brothers and sisters, aunts, uncles, cousins, and many friends surrounded us. I was dazed for a moment. Everyone spoke at once. Yisroel

Meir was kissed and hugged by one relative after the other. He was a trooper by now and accepted it without a word of complaint.

Papa's beard had turned gray-white. Soldier that he was, he stood straight and tall, his piercing eyes gazing at us with deep affection. Mama had changed drastically: she had aged considerably, and her face was pale and wan. I held her hand, clutching it tightly. She scarcely spoke.

Then it dawned on me that Frieda and Philip were not there. "Where are Frieda and Philip?" I asked. Mama let go of my hand abruptly and moved away. Papa went to her side. All our loved ones stood at a distance. Only Esther remained near me.

"Esther, where is Frieda?" I asked again.

"She's not well," Esther said quietly.

"What's wrong with her? Let's go to her house. I want to see her," I demanded.

"She doesn't live in New York anymore," Esther added.

"Where does she live?" My questions were becoming more urgent.

"She lives very far away," Esther's voice was almost a whisper.

"Can I speak to her on the phone?" My heart pounded violently.

"She won't hear you," Esther answered slowly. I was afraid to ask any more questions for fear of what I might hear, but I was impelled.

"Esther, what happened to Frieda? Tell me! Tell me!" My voice rose to a crescendo.

Esther's eyes clouded with unshed tears. "Frieda passed away three days before Purim. It was sudden. The doctors do not know it if was a heart attack or something else that caused her death. Racoma, Papa did not want to spoil your dreams and anticipation of your long-awaited homecoming. He wanted you to hold on to them as long as you could. He made us all promise not to write you."

For a moment I could not truly grasp the significance of what Esther had told me. Then it came to me—my darling, sweet, beloved sister, Frieda, was dead. I uttered a piercing cry. Papa ran over to me.

"Ruchoma, be strong. Have pity on Mama."

Mama was bent over, sobbing. I threw myself into her arms. "Mama, Mama . . ."

All our loved ones encircled us—each one giving vent to his pent-up emotions. A heart-rending cry echoed throughout the pier.

Yisroel Meir tugged at my dress. *"Far vos vainin alemen?"* (Why is everyone crying?) I could not find adequate words to explain to my three-and-a-half-year-old son that his dear Aunt Frieda was not alive.

Our homecoming was transformed from a joyous one into one of deep grief. We rode home. No one said a word.

I sat *shiva* for an hour. (Since it was past the thirty-day mourning period, I did not have to sit *shiva* the full seven days.)

When I got up from *shiva*, Papa came over to me. "Ruchoma, come with me. I want to talk to you." I followed him down the two flights of stairs. I was still in a state of semi-shock. I had not allowed myself the luxury of tears because of Mama.

The day was hot, the air stuffy. Children were blowing red, white and blue horns. As if in a far-off dream, I remembered that today was July 4th, American Independence Day.

Papa held my hand tightly as we walked along the dusty pavements, lost in our own thoughts. "Papa, you wanted us to come home because of Frieda," I said softly.

"Mama and I need you," Papa answered quietly.

"Papa, Frieda was so young, only thirty-one years old. She was brilliant, kind, a true Jewish mother. She had so much to offer to this world. She left seven young orphans." My pent-up tears found release as they coursed down my cheeks.

"We are not here to ask questions. We are soldiers of the Boss to do His bidding," Papa's voice was firm.

"Where are Frieda's children?" I questioned.

"I sent Avremal [he was the oldest—eleven years old] to Eretz Yisroel with Rabbi Shmuel Greineman. He is staying with a niece of Rabbi Greineman's, Rebbetzin Shulamit Alfa, who lives in Haifa. Chaim and Bessie accepted Rivky as their own daughter. Yitzchok Meir and Minna are unofficially adopted by Yankel and Gussie Halpern. [They had no children. Gussie is the daughter of our old and dear friend and neighbor, Mrs. Waldman.] Shmuel Yerachmeil and Fruma Rochel are boarding in temporary homes. Yosef Yechezkel, the youngest, is living with Nochum Dovid and Chaye Dube. Philip is staying with his parents."

Papa gave me a complete picture of a family torn asunder by the loss of a loving mother.

"Ruchoma, I want to tell you about some dreams that Frieda and I dreamt several years ago. They were premonitions of what occurred to Frieda and you.

"One morning, very early, Frieda came up to the house. She was very upset about a dream she had had the night before. In her dream, she saw you dressed up as a bride in a white wedding gown. However, you wore black stockings. Frieda said to you, 'Racoma, you cannot go to your wedding wearing black stockings.' After she insisted, you changed into white stockings. I told Frieda that it is a very good dream, and we shall hear good tidings from you.

"Esther, Frieda, Bessie and you were in different stages of pregnancy at the time of our dreams.

"I dreamt two dreams. In the first dream, I saw a tremendous branched candelabra that stood on the floor, reaching halfway up to the ceiling. It leaned against the wall. Two of its branches were firmly attached, and two were shaky. A voice said to me, 'Throw a sheet over the candelabra. It will protect it from an *ayin hora*' (evil eye).

"In the second dream, I stood near a cage with four bright-feathered birds in it flying gaily around and around. Suddenly, there was a great gust of wind. The door of the cage flew open, and two of the birds escaped through the open window. I quickly stretched my hands out as far as possible. With much exertion, I caught one bird by the edge of its little foot. The other flew away.

"I was very disturbed by these dreams. I prayed constantly to the Boss for all of you to have normal deliveries with healthy babies. When word came that you were critically ill after Yisroel Meir's birth, the dreams haunted me. However, my prayers for you were answered. Not only were you saved, but you recovered the use of your feet and left hand.

"It was only after Frieda passed away so suddenly that I fully understood the awesome meanings of these dreams.

"It seems that both you and Frieda were destined to be lost to us. Most probably, you were given years because of the extra *zechus* (merit) of Torah. You and Moshe sacrificed a great deal to go to Mir to study Torah. I didn't even tell Mama the dream of the birds; I feared it would alarm her. But I want you and Moshe to know about the dreams."

Papa finished talking and gazed at me lovingly. I was overwhelmed by what Papa had confided in me. The sharp pain I felt at the loss of Frieda became less intense. Papa and I walked home slowly.

Yisroel Meir was keeping Mama company. I could see that his presence was a calming influence on her. "Ruchoma," Mama smiled, "though I speak Yiddish very well, I cannot understand Yisroel Meir's Yiddish. I offered to give him supper, but I do not know what he wants to eat."

"*Vos vilst du essen,* Yisroel Meir?" I asked him.

"*Ich vill a spotka smetena mit truskavkes,*" he answered promptly.

"Mama, he wants a saucer of strawberries and sour cream, his favorite summer dish," I translated.

Mama added, "He asked for something else in his Polish-Yiddish that was strange to me."

"Yisroel Meir, *vos hosdu gefregt Bobie?*" (What did you ask Bobie?)

"*Vu iz di pamunitze? Di podloge iz brudne,*" he said. (Where is the dirt pail? The floor is dirty.) Mama smiled broadly at my explanation.

"You will get used to his Polish-Yiddish vocabulary very quickly, Mama. All too soon, he will forget his Yiddish with all of us speaking English in the house and in the street," I predicted.

24

Transition

The three months following our arrival were a most difficult period of adjustment for us.

Papa rented a room for us from his neighbor Reb Yosef Kalinkowitz, *zatzal*, who was a *talmid* of Papa's and became very attached to him. Even though he could afford a steam-heated, more convenient apartment, he wanted to be near Papa, so when an apartment became vacant in Papa's building, he immediately rented it. As a favor to Papa, he rented us one of his bedrooms even though it meant overcrowding his own family.

Our room was a small one. With three cot beds needed, there was little space for any other furniture. We ate our meals with Papa and Mama. I spent most of my time with Mama, trying to give her comfort. She controlled her emotions, but her far-away look told me that her thoughts were very much with Frieda, of blessed memory.

Moshe joined the *kollel* which Rabbi Yitzchok Shneider, the son-in-law of Rabbi Faivelson, established. It was one of the first *kollel*s in America. A group of about ten married men studied in this *kollel*, located in the Adas Yisroel Synagogue on

East Broadway. The meager remuneration he received did not cover our expenses, and the burden of our support fell on Papa's shoulders.

Yisroel Meir attended a nursery school in the neighborhood, since there was no available *cheder* for children his age. He returned home each day with new English words added to his vocabulary and excited with the many activities the nursery offered. The teacher took a special interest in our little "foreigner." Though they did not have complete verbal communication, teacher and pupil spoke a common language all their own.

Yisroel Meir's secular progress was more than balanced by the influence Papa exerted over him. At the Shabbos table, he sat between Papa and Moshe, not only digesting the Shabbos food but also the spirit of Shabbos with the *orchim*. He tried to keep up with the *zemiros*, humming along. He revered his Zeidy and most nights waited up for his return. Papa took an interest in every detail of his activities, and Yisroel Meir basked in his favor.

Our relatives and friends made an effort to visit us as often as possible. However, they were all preoccupied with their own lives.

My in-laws had moved from the East Side to their own two-family house on South Ninth Street, in the Williamsburgh section of Brooklyn. My sisters-in-law, Bashe and Dvoshe, were married and lived together with my in-laws.

Lipman, Esther and their family lived in Brooklyn and were neighbors of my in-laws. Nochum Dovid, Chaye Dube, their two children, and Frieda's Yosef Yechezkel resided in a different section of Brooklyn. Nochum Dovid was the Rabbi of the Gates Avenue Shul. Chaim, Bessie, their three daughters, including Rivky, Frieda's daughter, lived on Suffolk Street, not very far from us. Chaim was *mashgiach* in the Chofetz Chaim Yeshiva in Brooklyn.

....

cheder: elementary school

My girlfriends, most of whom were not married as yet, visited us each Shabbos afternoon. They encouraged Yisroel Meir to talk his "foreign Yiddish," which delighted them. He enjoyed expanding on his traveling experiences. *"Ich bin geforen oif a tramvay, a bahn, un oif a groise shif, de Acquitainerel."* (I rode on a trolley car, a train, and a big ship, the *Acquitania*.)

Fortunately, Yisroel Meir acclimated to his new environment very quickly. He was a source of joy, who lifted our spirits during those trying days.

Papa's financial situation was serious, as he was forced to give up his fur business. He had a route selling *cholov yisroel*, which he had originated many years before. His earnings were small, and most of it was used for Shabbos and the *"orchim* business," which was still thriving.

Moshe and I realized that we could not be supported by Papa indefinitely. Moshe therefore actively began to search for a suitable position. With his rabbinic ordinations and his secular education, I was sure he could obtain a well-paying one. He canvassed all the yeshivos, but there were no openings available at that time.

One of our relatives came with the good news of an excellent, high-paying position that would be perfect for Moshe. However, it was not in New York City, but upstate.

Papa rejected it immediately. "You cannot consider this position, whatever the salary be. Yisroel Meir will soon be ready for yeshiva and needs suitable friends to play with. The environment outside of New York City could endanger his *yiddishkeit*." Moshe and I fully agreed with Papa.

Moshe finally was engaged as a teacher in a small Talmud Torah in upper Manhattan. The salary was much less than what had been offered him outside of New York City. But he had no alternative and accepted this position, as we could not afford to wait any longer. He continued his Torah studies in the *kollel* during the morning hours and taught in the Talmud Torah in the afternoon.

We rented a small three-room apartment on Monroe Street, not very far from Papa and Mama. Because of our limited funds, we furnished our home with second-hand furniture, which we bought in a warehouse. Our pots, pans, dishes and linens were graciously given to us by Mama and my mother-in-law.

Though the apartment had few conveniences, we were able to stretch a bit after the cramped quarters of the single room we had occupied for our first three months back home. It had its own lavatory, which was still a luxury for us. However, there was no separate room for the bathtub, so it occupied part of our kitchen. Each time we had to bathe, I had to clear off the entire enamel baseboard that covered the bathtub and served as my working table.

The icebox had to be filled with ice every other day. The water dripping from the melting ice into the pan underneath had to be emptied twice a day; otherwise it would flood the kitchen.

Despite all the drawbacks, with the "hand-me-down" bedspreads on our beds, and the "hang me-up" curtains on our windows, I was very proud of our new home.

We were corresponding with our friends in Mir, who were very interested in the details of our resettling in the United States. Their letters were already tinged with the worry of Hitler and the Nazis. However, the thought of leaving Mir did not enter their minds. They hoped that the happenings in Germany were merely a phase which would pass and not affect their lives.

As the Nazi crackdown on Jews in Germany became more prevalent and more intense at the end of 1938, many Jews who saw the "handwriting on the wall" tried to leave and escape to America.

Papa went daily to HIAS (Hebrew Immigrant Aid Society) in downtown Manhattan to see if any newly arrived refugees needed help. On January 1, 1939, such a family arrived at the HIAS office.

Yosef Dovid and Mirel Leah Hess came from Vienna with their three little ones; the oldest was two and a half. Mr. Hess, imprisoned in Germany on a trumped-up charge, managed to escape by a miracle. He wrote to the Agudas Yisroel in New York requesting an affidavit to enter the United States. A Mr. Hausman, a complete stranger to the Hesses, underwrote the affidavit, and in due time it was issued. They immediately set sail and arrived at the HIAS building on a very cold, wintry day.

As they sat alone and bewildered in the hall, an angel, as they tell it, suddenly put in his appearance. Papa went over to them. "Do you speak Yiddish?" he asked in a friendly manner. When they nodded their heads in the affirmative, Papa engaged them in conversation. He soon discovered that they were refugees from Vienna and did not know a soul in America.

This was no problem for Papa, and he rectified the situation immediately. With their few belongings, he brought them to his house, where they stayed for a few days. A vacant apartment, fortunately, became available in the building on Monroe Street where Moshe and I lived. Papa rented the apartment, paying three months' rent in advance. With the help of good friends, whom Papa recruited, their small home was soon furnished. Papa's help and devotion during the first few months of their stay in America gave the Hesses the emotional and physical security they so urgently required.

Living in the same building with the Hesses brought Moshe and me into close contact with them. The friendship that developed became a permanent one.

Added note:
The Hess family today is one of the prominent Torah families in America, whose influence on Torah and *yiddishkeit* is spread far and wide.

Two of the Hesses' sons have become our nephews through marriage.

25

Farewell once more

Since our arrival the previous year, I had become very close to Papa. His talks elevated me. Through his every action I was able to discern that he was a true soldier of the Boss, who followed His every command.

Moshe, Yisroel Meir and I also became Shabbos *orchim*. We looked forward to spending each Shabbos with Papa and Mama and the *orchim*.

One day Papa visited us. "I am worried about Avremal," he said. "I received a letter from Rabbi Greineman notifying me that his niece is finding it difficult to cope with him."

"Papa, he must be very lonesome. Not only was it a great shock for Avremal to lose his mother at such an early age, but being away from all his loved ones surely adds to his emotional insecurity." I finished talking and a sudden pang of lonesomeness for Frieda overwhelmed me. Papa did not answer, but I realized he was sorely troubled.

A short time later on a hot, humid morning late in June, Papa phoned me. Moshe had already left for the *kollel*. I had just returned from taking Yisroel Meir to the yeshiva kindergarten. "Ruchoma, come over tonight with Moshe. I have something to tell you. I am phoning the other children as well to tell them to be here."

I replaced the receiver wondering what Papa had to tell us. I was not unduly concerned. Papa often called us children together to discuss various problems: our role in spreading *yiddishkeit* among our friends and neighbors; the *chinuch* of our children; and a host of other subjects he felt were important to bring to our attention.

With supper over, and having tucked Yisroel Meir in for the night, I called my neighbor to babysit. Moshe and I sauntered over to Papa and Mama's house, a five-minute walk away. We climbed the two flights of stairs. Everyone was there already except for Papa. He was still in the Beis Medrash Hagodol on Norfolk Street, where he taught a *shiur* nightly.

It was good to see our loved ones. We greeted each other and sat chatting and catching up on all the news. Mama's delicious home-baked coffee cake and her special iced lemonade were on the table.

I went to look for Mama. She was busy in the kitchen. "Mama, what does Papa want to discuss with us tonight?" I asked her curiously.

"Let him tell you himself." Her voice sounded strained. I looked at her questioningly, but she did not elaborate. How tired she looks, I thought.

When Papa walked into the dining room, we all stood up. He sat down in his large leather armchair at the head of the table and wiped his sweaty brow. He was pale after fasting the entire day.

Mama had already prepared Papa's frugal meal, which he ate after his daily fast: canned Portuguese sardines, pumpernickel bread, and a large yellow-green pear. After Papa drank his second cup of steaming coffee, he cleared his throat.

"Children, you know that I came to this country when I was eight years old. Fifty years have passed since. For more than thirty years, I endeavored to spread Torah and *yiddishkeit*, with Mama's help, of course." We all turned to Mama, who sat next to Papa. She usually had a quip to add, but this time she said nothing.

Papa continued, "You, children, are all married and have families of your own, *boruch Hashem*. You are staunch Jews who will continue to spread Torah and *yiddishkeit*, not only to your own children but also to others. Now it is time for Mama and me to leave America. We are going to settle in Eretz Yisroel."

It was a bombshell! In electrified silence, we all tried to digest this incredible news. Papa and Mama leaving us — how could that be? Papa, our bulwark, our guide, our solution to every problem. We depended on him so completely. And Mama, sweet, kind, gentle Mama, who not only taught us to be good wives and mothers with her sage advice, but also stood by our side through every hardship. I always piled in on Mama with my family, for Shabbos and for Yomim Tovim, and on other occasions when I needed her help. She was always there to receive us, with her open, loving arms.

What about the *orchim*? There were almost thirty *orchim* who were eating their Shabbos meals at their house. We all started to speak at once, asking questions. Papa silenced us with his raised hand.

"I understand that this news is very difficult for you to accept. I have thought about it very carefully for some time. My mind is made up. We are leaving, *b'ezras Hashem*, on Rosh Chodesh Elul, by boat. We hope to be in Yerusholayim for Rosh Hashona," Papa ended firmly.

"About the *orchim*: I already spoke to Mrs. Schroit [our close friend who came each Thursday to help Mama peel the potatoes for the *cholent* and the carrots for the *tzimmes*], and she has undertaken this great *mitzva* of *hachnosas orchim*. Of course, I shall expect our daughters to pitch in to help her with anything she needs. As for my *shiurim*, I expect each of our sons to take over one *shiur*."

---

b'ezras Hashem: with God's help

Now all eyes focused on Mama, who had not yet spoken. "Children, I do not want to leave you, but Papa wants very much to go to Eretz Yisroel. My place is at his side, as it has been all through our married life. Also, Avremal needs us, as he is very lonesome." Mama ended the last words with a sob. I was too stunned to cry. The tears came later.

Among Papa's most ardent *"chasidim"* was Reb Yaakov Safsel, known as the Visker Iluy. From the moment he reached the shores of America, he latched on to Papa. He depended upon him for every religious issue that came up in his life.

He studied the entire day in the Anshei Maimod *shul* on Henry Street and was known for his vast knowledge of Torah learning. He walked the streets of the East Side, both summer and winter, with his *tallis koton* over his clothes.

He had reached his late forties without having married, so Papa introduced him to a suitable woman, a friend of our family. Much to Papa's satisfaction, Reb Yaakov finally married, and his wife bore him a son.

Moshe and I were visiting Papa and Mama when Reb Yaakov burst through the door. He had just found out that Papa was leaving for Eretz Yisroel. His agitation was great, and his words came out in a jumble. "Reb Ya-a-kov Yosef, I heard you are going away. I will starve from hunger. You know I do not eat anything without first getting your *haskoma*" (approval).

Papa forced him to sit down and said soothingly. "Do not worry, Reb Yaakov. I will leave you in good hands. I have someone who will fill my place." Papa turned to Moshe. "My son-in-law, Reb Moshe, can answer all your questions on *kashrus*. You can follow whatever he tells you."

Papa's solution seemed to placate and satisfy Reb Yaakov. "Reb Moshe," he warned, "whenever I need you, I will come over to your house."

....
chasidim: followers

When Reb Yaakov left, Papa said to Moshe, "It is a great *chesed* for you to help Reb Yaakov with his many religious problems. Though, of course, he is a great *talmid chochom* and can surely find the answers to his many questions himself, he is fearful."

So Papa bequeathed Reb Yaakov Safsel to Moshe, and he came at every opportunity to question Moshe about different foods and other religious problems that confronted him. "Reb Moshe, can I definitely eat this cheese?" A nod of Moshe's head sent him away completely reassured. We also took over Papa's role in supplying him with the Pesach *charoses,* which we prepared ourselves.

He wrote a great deal of *chiddushei Torah* in his lifetime, which his only son, Reb Yosef Shleima, published after Reb Yaakov was *niftar.*

The next two months passed in a daze of physical and emotional effort for me. Every afternoon, I came to help Papa and Mama pack their belongings.

Papa's large package of old cancelled checks revealed the tremendous amount of charity he had given through the many years. Each one told a different story. There were checks made out to every yeshiva, in America and other parts of the world. Every worthy cause that needed assistance through the last thirty years was represented. Hundreds of checks were also made out to private individuals who needed help or loans.

There was the cancelled check for $1000, the first donation that helped found Yeshiva Tiferes Yerusholayim. Another $1000 check was made out to the Lomza Yeshiva, dated 1929.

It was at that time that Papa had lost most of his money in the crash. He had just a little over a thousand dollars in his bank account. Papa decided then that since his fortune had deteriorated, he would at least give *tzedoko* with his remaining funds. He withdrew a thousand dollars to be given to a yeshiva.

Rabbi Yechiel Mordechai Gordon, Rosh Yeshiva of the

....

chiddushei Torah: Talmudic novellae

Lomza Yeshiva in Poland, later told my nephew, Reb Moshe Aaron Stern, the following incident:

"In 1929, the Lomza Yeshiva was completely destitute. There was no money left to feed our few hundred *talmidim*. I was afraid that the yeshiva would be forced to close down. I did not know where to turn and could not rest day or night.

"One morning, I received a notice from the post office telling me to pick up a registered letter from America. I hurried to the post office and was handed a letter that came from a Reb Yaakov Yosef Herman from New York City. In the letter was enclosed a check for one thousand dollars from a man whom I had never met. The yeshiva existed an entire month on this money. After that, I received other help, so Reb Yaakov Yosef was instrumental in keeping the Lomza Yeshiva open and allowing hundreds of *talmidim* to continue to learn Torah."

To this day, I have not discovered how Papa came to choose the Lomza Yeshiva as the place to send his one thousand dollar donation.

As the house was slowly being emptied, memories of my childhood crowded in. Mama gave me a bundle of all my old report cards, and my public school and high school diplomas. I noticed that Papa carefully packed into one of his valises a folder of the compositions and poetry that I had written during my adolescence, and another package of my letters from Mir.

On another occasion, Mama forced me to accept the crystal fruit bowl and some of her other precious objects that had been her wedding presents. I went home laden with her loving remembrances, but with a heavy heart.

Papa and Mama tried to keep up my spirits instead of vice versa. For almost six years I had been separated from them. Now I had had Papa and Mama for only a little over a year, and they were leaving. Each moment with them was precious. Each word they spoke was seared deeply into my heart and memory.

The time for their departure was nearing. All their worldly possessions, including Papa's priceless *seforim*, were packed into sixteen large wooden crates. They also had ten large valises, one of which contained Papa's *sefer Torah*, which he kept near him at all times.

Rosh Chodesh Elul dawned bright and clear. I steeled myself for the ordeal of the farewell. Moshe, Yisroel Meir and I rode in the taxi with Papa and Mama. I held Mama's hand. Papa clutched Yisroel Meir's hand. We were enveloped by a silence that spoke volumes.

When we arrived at the pier, we found a very large crowd of relatives, friends and *talmidim* who had come to wish Papa and Mama *tzeisschem l'sholom*. The children and grandchildren were crowded into their stateroom. There was a babble of voices.

Suddenly, the loudspeaker blared the message I feared. "Visitors, please clear the ship."

I threw myself into Mama's arms. I could not let go.

"Ruchoma, Ruchoma," she repeated over and over again. Mama's tears mingled with mine. The other children crowded around her, each one wanting to hold on to a little piece of her love.

Then Papa's voice rang loud and clear. "Children, *chazak, chazak* — be strong — be strong. We shall meet *b'ezras Hashem* in Yerusholayim." I ran over to him. His steel-gray eyes softened as he tenderly pressed my cheek with his pinch. I touched my cheek to make sure his pinch was there.

Then, somehow, I was being pushed and led along with the crowd. I held on to Yisroel Meir's hand tightly, saying over and over to him, "Do not forget Zeidy and Bobie Herman. Yisroel Meir, you must always remember them." I looked down at my little son and thought sadly: you are so young and have witnessed so little of their greatness.

I looked up to see Papa and Mama standing together at the railing of the ship. Papa, the staunch soldier, and Mama, bravely controlling her sobs, waved good-bye to all of us, as the boat slowly set sail.

....

tzeisschem l'sholom: farewell in peace

3

Higher Aspirations

26

On holy soil

It was on August 16, 1939, that Papa and Mama began their voyage to Eretz Yisroel. They were scheduled to dock at Haifa port on Wednesday, August 30. Arrangements were made for Papa and Mama to stay in Haifa for a few days at the home of Rabbi and Mrs. Alfa, where Avremal was boarding.

In mid-route, the captain received orders to sail in a circuitous route in case the waters of the Mediterranean Sea had been mined because of the impending war. Instead of arriving on Wednesday as scheduled, the boat docked on Friday, September 1, one hour before sunset. A few hours before that, World War II had erupted with the German invasion of Poland.

There were loudspeakers ordering the passengers to debark immediately. All the baggage from the hold of the ship would be unloaded onto the pier, and the passengers would be responsible to have it removed as quickly as possible.

Pandemonium reigned!

Papa and Mama were terribly upset. It would soon be Shabbos. How could they take care of their baggage when they

*The identification photo of Papa and Mama,
taken after their arrival.*

had to leave the port immediately in order to get to Rabbi Alfa's
house in time for Shabbos?

Papa grabbed the valise that contained his *sefer Torah* and
his *tallis* and *tefillin,* and Mama took only her pocketbook.
They edged their way through the pier and asked to be shown to
the head customs officer.

A tall English officer listened as Papa explained to him, "I
have never desecrated the Sabbath in my life. To arrive in the
Holy Land and desecrate it here is impossible." Tears rolled
down Papa's cheeks.

The officer answered curtly, "Rabbi this is *war;* you must
make allowances."

"Just stamp our passports and let us through. We shall
pick up our baggage after the Sabbath," Papa pleaded.

"That would be impossible. We are removing all the baggage from the ship and leaving it on the pier. Once the boat
clears port, everything must be cleared off it also."

"I do not care about our baggage. Just stamp our passports
so we can leave."

The officer looked at Papa quizzically, "How much
baggage have you?"

"Sixteen crates in the hold and nine suitcases in our
cabin."

"Do you realize that once you leave here, your baggage will be on the pier with no one responsible for it? By tomorrow night you will not find a shred of your belongings. The Arabs will have stolen them all," the officer said emphatically.

"I have no alternative. It's almost time for the Sabbath. We must get to the city in time. Please, please, just clear our passports and let us go," Papa's voice rose in desperation.

The officer, incredulous, called another English officer, "Stamp their passports and let them through. This rabbi is willing to lose all his belongings in order to get into the city in time for their Sabbath." The second officer stared at Papa in amazement, as he stamped their passports and cleared their papers.

Papa, clutching the valise with his *sefer Torah*, and Mama, holding on to her pocketbook, grabbed a taxi and arrived at Rabbi Alfa's house just in time for Mama to light the candles.

That entire Shabbos, Papa was spiritually elated. Over and over again he repeated to Mama, "The Boss does everything for me. What could I ever do for Him? Now at last I have the *zechus* to give all for the Boss for His *mitzva* of Shabbos and to be *mekaddesh Hashem.*"

For Mama it was difficult to share his elation fully. She was physically exhausted and bereft emotionally. The lonesomeness for her children weighed heavily on her mind and heart. The additional loss of all her worldly possessions was not an easy pill to swallow. But Mama did not complain.

Saturday night, after Papa had waited seventy-two minutes after sunset to *daven mairiv* and then make *havdolo*, Rabbi Alfa suggested to him, "Let us go to the port. Maybe some of your crates are still there." Papa and Mama did not share his optimism, but they went along with him.

It was pitch dark at the port. However, they spied a little light at the far end. As they neared the lighted area, a clipped English voice rang out, "Who goes there?"

Papa called out, "Some passengers from the boat that docked late yesterday afternoon."

The English guard approached them. "What is your name?" he asked tersely.

"Jacob J. Herman," Papa answered.

"Well, well, Rabbi, it's about time you put in your appearance. I was assured that you would be here the minute the sun set. You are a few hours late. I have been responsible for your baggage for more than twenty-four hours. My commanding officer said he would have my head if any of your baggage is missing. Kindly check to see that all is in order and sign these papers. Please remove it all as quickly as possible ... I am totally exhausted."

Papa and Mama, together with Avremal, settled in Yerusholayim. Papa bought an apartment for *shlissel gelt* in the Zichron Moshe section. (With such a keymoney arrangement, the apartment belongs to the original owner, with the tenant paying a nominal rent. However, the tenant has the right to reside in it as long as he wishes.)

Mama mothered Avremal, and Papa trained him. He needed both. Papa's unyielding approach led Avremal to rebel against his demands. Mama tried to ease the tension, but there came a day when Avremal confronted Papa.

My nephew, Shmuel Yitzchok Stern, told me an incident which Avremal had related to him:

Avremal faced Papa with bravado. "Zeidy, I cannot take it any longer. You know I am an orphan. You are too strict with me, so I am leaving." Avremal waited for his words to take effect. Papa was not intimidated. Mama was very upset, but a glance from Papa told her not to interfere.

Avremal picked up a basket with some of his belongings and strode out the door. He walked down the two flights of stairs very slowly, looking up to see if Papa would regret his leaving and ask him to return.

When he reached the bottom landing, he heard Papa call to him, "Avremal, wait." He stood expectantly waiting for Papa to show his remorse and plead with him to return.

"Avremal, when Avrohom Ovinu sent Yishmoel away because he feared that Yitzchok would be influenced by Yishmoel's bad qualities, he nevertheless gave him food to take along."

Papa handed Avremal the bag of food that Mama had quickly prepared and some silver coins he took out from his pocket.

Avremal hesitated for just one minute. Then he bounded up the stairs straight into Mama's arms.

Avremal lived with Papa and Mama until his marriage.

After Papa settled in Yerusholayim, he decided that he would not sleep overnight outside the holy city. One evening he found it necessary to be in Tel Aviv. He was delayed and missed the last bus. There were no long-distance taxis available.

Papa started his long trek by foot from Tel Aviv to Yerusholayim — approximately 45 miles. The night was dark and damp. Not a person or a car was to be seen on the dusty road. Papa marched briskly along for fifteen minutes, when the lights of a car pierced the darkness. It passed him by. Suddenly, he heard the car screech to an abrupt halt.

The driver approached Papa, looked closely at him and exclaimed, "*Rebbe*, is it you?" He was a businessman who had recently become one of Papa's *talmidim*. "What are you doing so late at night all alone on this forsaken road?" he asked in wonder.

"I am walking to Yerusholayim. I do not sleep outside of the holy city, and I could not find any means of transportation," Papa explained.

"*Rebbe*, get into my car. I will drive you home."

The *talmid* turned his car towards the direction of Yerusholayim, and off they sped. As they rode along, the *talmid* questioned Papa. "*Rebbe*, how could you possibly undertake to walk such a great distance? Even if you had walked all night long, you would not have reached your destination."

"If you want to do a *mitzva*, you have to jump in and start.

Hashem takes care of the rest. You see," Papa added smilingly, "the Boss sent you to help me accomplish this *mitzva*." The *talmid* nodded his head in complete agreement.

27

Papa quickly set up his "Business of *Mitzvos*." Before long he was at the hub of religious life in Yerusholayim.

There was no dearth of customers for his *hachnosas orchim*, as refugees were pouring onto the shores of Eretz Yisroel. His Shabbos table was soon filled with *orchim* from different parts of the world. The yeshiva boys from the Novarodok Yeshiva were also eating in Papa's house. The Rosh Yeshiva, Rabbi Ben Zion Brook, asked Papa to allow them to eat there, as he had no place to feed them.

As Papa's reputation grew, he was asked to give nightly *shiurim* in the Zichron Moshe *shul*. A large group of men came to hear his *blatt gemora*, *Ein Yaakov* and *mishnayos*. Every Shabbos during *sholosh seudos* he gave a *dvar Torah* at the Amerikaner *shul* on Reishis Chochma Street. From there, he proceeded to the Yeshuas Yaakov *shul* in Meah She'arim, where he spoke about the *parshas hashovua*.

Each *erev* Rosh Chodesh he led the congregants in the prayers of Yom Kippur Koton in the Zichron Moshe *shul*. His praying had a quality that brought many Jews to the *shul*, who otherwise would not have come. During the "Three Weeks" Papa said *tikun chatzos* daily before a packed *shul*.

His army of *talmidim* grew. They came from all walks of life: doctors, lawyers, bankers, businessmen, grocers, and others who felt the need for encouragement and inspiration. Papa's house was soon a replica of the one he had left in New York. Mama was kept busy day and night. Not only were there Shabbos *orchim*, but also during the week many a poor person came for a warm meal and a cheery word. Mama worked very hard, but the work helped to alleviate some of the longing for her children and grandchildren.

In addition to Avremal, Boruch Reisner, a fifteen-year-old, came to live with Papa and Mama. One of Papa's *talmidim* brought him to the house. Boruch had escaped the Holocaust and was alone and destitute. He knew almost nothing about *yiddishkeit*, and Papa spent a great deal of time teaching him.

Among Papa's *orchim* was a very old man. Though he had children living in Yerusholayim, he sorrowfully confided in Papa, "I cannot eat or stay with my children."

One morning he came to Papa carrying a small parcel. With trembling fingers he opened the wrappings, which revealed a torn, stained *tefillin* bag with a pair of *tefillin* inside.

"Reb Yaakov Yosef, I feel my end is drawing near. I *davened* with these *tefillin* for many years. I want you to have them. I have another pair that I can use."

Papa patted the old man on his back. "May you have many more long and healthy years." He placed the torn *tefillin* bag with the *tefillin* into his *oron kodesh*. Soon after this meeting, the old *orech* passed away.

Several weeks later, a stranger knocked at Papa's door. "Are you Reb Yaakov Yosef of New York?" he asked anxiously. Papa nodded and invited him into the house.

....
oron kodesh: holy ark

"I am Shmuel the son of Reb Nesanel, the *sofer*. I understand that many years ago you ordered a pair of *tefillin* from my father, *zatzal*. You sent $25 with your order, but never received the *tefillin*." Papa nodded again.

The man continued: "Lately, I had a very disturbing dream in which my father commanded me to search his records and repay anybody to whom he owes a debt. After searching through many old papers, I found your letter ordering *tefillin* from my father and specifying that you enclosed the full price of the *tefillin*—$25.

"My father became ill and could not complete your *tefillin* before he passed away. I have a large family and do not have the means at this time to repay my father's debt," he said tearfully.

Papa assured the visitor that he completely forgave his father, and he need have no further worries about the debt. The man grasped Papa's hand gratefully, "Thank you, thank you with all my heart. Now my father, *zatzal*, will have peace."

Papa clearly recalled ordering Reb Nesanel's *tefillin*. He had heard that there was an exceptional *sofer* in Yerusholayim whose *tefillin* were the most *mehuder* (perfect) in the entire world. Reb Nesanel wrote the *parshios* of the *tefillin* with such religious fervor that he immersed himself in the *mikveh* each time before he wrote the name of Hashem.

A pair of *tefillin*, including the *batim* and *retzuos*, was prepared so meticulously by him that it took him a year or more to complete one pair of *tefillin*.

It was soon after Papa's marriage that he mailed a registered letter with the payment of $25 enclosed (a huge sum of money in the year 1903) to Reb Nesanel in Yerusholayim. Papa received a letter from Reb Nesanel acknowledging his order and the enclosed payment. He waited anxiously for the day he would possess this precious pair of *tefillin*.

When a year went by and Papa heard nothing further, he wrote several letters to Reb Nesanel without receiving any

....

parshios: small parchment scrolls / *batim*: boxes / *retzuos*: straps

reply. He then heard that the *sofer* had passed away. His hope of ever having a pair of these special *tefillin* faded.

Boruch Reisner had no *tefillin* when he was brought to Papa. Papa went to his *oron kodesh* and took out the *tefillin* the old *orech* had bequeathed to him. "Boruch, take these *tefillin* to my *sofer* and ask him to check them carefully to see if they are kosher." Papa wrote the address of his *sofer* on a piece of scrap paper and handed it to Boruch, together with the *tefillin*.

A short while later, a panting Boruch came hurrying up the steps, with the *sofer* following breathlessly behind him.

"Reb Yaakov Yosef," the *sofer* asked excitedly, "where did you get these *tefillin*?"

Papa stared at him in amazement. "An old *orech* of mine gave them to me before he passed away. I never had them checked."

"Do you know who wrote the *parshios* and made the *batim* and *retzuos* of these *tefillin*?" the *sofer* asked tremulously. "These are Reb Nesanel's *tefillin*. There are just a few pairs of these most precious *tefillin* in the entire world. They are worth a fortune." The *sofer* handed the *tefillin* to Papa reverently.

"*Boruch Hashem*," Papa cried out, "the debt has been repaid after all."

While Papa and Mama were in the midst of religious activities in Yerusholayim, Moshe and I were confronted with the aspects of irreligious life in New York.

In Mir, we had become accustomed to the serenity of Shabbos, and the *tznius* of the girls and women. In New York, *chillul Shabbos* faced us on every street. There was no way to protect Yisroel Meir from it. If Yisroel Meir ever saw a horse and wagon being driven on Shabbos in Mir, he knew the driver was a *goy*. In New York, as he watched the many cars speed by our window on Shabbos, he was heard to remark, "So many *goyim*."

Moshe was also dissatisfied with his teaching in the

Talmud Torah. When an opening presented itself in Yeshiva Rabbi Jacob Joseph, though it was in the elementary department, he accepted it gladly.

When Yisroel Meir was almost eight years old, we were blessed with glad tidings. Despite the verdict of the doctors I had consulted several years earlier, who did not think it possible for me to bear any more children, the Doctor above all doctors decreed otherwise. I gave birth first to our daughter, Masha Dvora, named after our old neighbor and friend, Mrs. Waldman, and thirteen months later to our son, Yitzchok Isaac, named after Zeidy Herman, Papa's father.

Papa and Mama were elated when I telegraphed them the news of each birth. For me it was a vindication. Though none of my relatives ever said anything to me openly, intuitively I sensed their pity for the fact that I had only one son. Now I had joined the clan. Yisroel Meir was delighted to be released from the burden of being an only child. He promptly took the role of big brother.

With the hot summer approaching and two active youngsters aged two-and-a-half and a year-and-a-half, besides Yisroel Meir, we were faced with the problem of where to spend our vacation. We could not remain on the East Side, in our cramped apartment, and with no playground facilities for the children.

We started to search in earnest for a *shomer Shabbos* bungalow colony, almost non-existent in the summer of 1945. Fortunately, a friend of ours recommended us to the Leisers. I contacted them by phone. They informed me that they had a bungalow colony in White Lake, in the Catskill Mountains. They had a single bungalow still available. After we spoke to them in person, they were convinced that we would fit into their *shomer Shabbos* bungalow colony.

Now we encountered a second problem. We hired a hack to transport us, our bedding, our clothing, our kitchen utensils,

....

shomer Shabbos: Sabbath observant

and Yitzchok's crib, carriage and high chair to the mountains. The driver of the hack told us that traveling time would be at least four hours, especially with the car loaded to capacity. We had to pass through every town, village and small city on our way up, as there was no thruway at that time.

How could we control Yitzchok, a bundle of activity, for such a length of time? Mashi could be kept busy with picture books and crayons, but not Yitzchok. I noticed that on the few occasions that Moshe *davened* at home with *tallis* and *tefillin*, Yitzchok watched him with rapt attention, not uttering a sound. It occurred to me to get a pair of *posul* (non-kosher) *tefillin* and put them on Yitzchok himself. My father-in-law came to the rescue with a pair of old empty *batim* and worn-out *retzuos*. Moshe prepared Yitzchok for the long trip, wrapping him up in an old *tallis* and placing the *batim* on his head and hand and tying the *retzuos* around his little arm.

My novel idea served the purpose. He sat like a little *tzaddik* most of the way to the mountains.

When we arrived, Moshe alighted from the car carrying Yitzchok in his arms, still wrapped in *tallis* and *tefillin*. We did not realize the impact this spectacle made on the Leisers and other families who had preceded us.

After I unpacked, I went outside to find Yitzchok happily absorbed in play with Yumi, a little boy his age. I engaged the mother in conversation, inquiring about shopping and laundry facilities. After a few mintues, she said to me hesitantly, "I hope you will not be offended if I ask you a question. Why was your little son wearing *tallis* and *tefillin*? We have never heard of nor seen such a custom."

I exploded in laughter, explaining to her what prompted us to take this unusual action. Then she confided to me that everyone thought we had descended from a "strange planet." With the air cleared, we soon became a harmonious group.

Mashi, able to spread her wings, ran around on the wide expanse of grass chanting, "This is my country."

And indeed it was!

For the first time since we had departed Mir, we saw no *chillul Shabbos*, because our bungalow was quite a distance from the main road. All the women dressed properly. With a *minyon* for prayers three times daily, the Leiser Bungalow Colony was truly a haven for us.

Moshe taught Yisroel Meir for a two-hour session each morning. In a short time, all the boys of the colony joined the learning, much to the satisfaction of their parents.

From this modest beginning, *shomer Shabbos* bungalow colonies mushroomed all over the Catskill Mountains. In a few years, it became the hub of summer yeshivos, and a stronghold of *rebbeyim* and *chasidim*.

During the ten wonderful summers we spent at the Leiser Bungalow colony, the Sigeter Rebbe (now the Satmar Rebbe) and his family occupied one of the bungalows. Rabbis Aaron and Shmuel Teitelbaum, sons of the Chenchkivitzer Rebbe, and their families spent many summers at the Leisers'. Rabbi Aaron Teitelbaum, the older son, became the *rebbe* after his father, *zatzal*, was *niftar*.

The Bobover Rebbe and his *chasidim* rented an entire bungalow colony just down the road from us.

The *misnagdim* and the *chasidim* blended into a homogeneous group. To this day, we remain close friends with the Leisers and most of the families who were summer tenants in their colony.

---

rebbeyim: hasidic leaders / **misnagdim**: opponents of hasidism

28

A queen departs

Mama was ill. In each letter, Papa wrote us in detail about her illness. From a case of neglected diabetes, she developed uremia (a serious toxic condition). Doctors were summoned, but Mama continued to fail.

I longed to be at Mama's side, but with two little ones who needed constant care, I could not possibly leave.

Before Chanuka, I came down with an acute attack of the flu. During the entire week, I was bed-ridden. I wondered a bit that none of the family visited me, but I assumed they were busy with the Chanuka festival.

After Chanuka, Esther and Bessie came to my home. As soon as they entered, I said to them anxiously, "I am terribly worried about Mama. Papa has not written to me the last few weeks. Have your received any word from Papa?" Their silence was my answer.

Mama was gone. She had passed away *erev* Chanuka. They had just gotten up from *shiva*. Because of my illness, they had decided not to inform me of the tragic news.

I sat *shiva* alone. It came to my mind that the lights of the Jewish nation all over the world were dimmed with Mama's passing on. It needed the miracle of Chanuka to rekindle them.

I relived her dearness, her gentleness, her goodness, her kindness, and her wise ways. I was lost and frightened. Though I had lived far from Mama in physical miles when I was in Mir, and now again, when Mama was in Yerusholayim, she was always close to me emotionally.

I thought of Papa. How much he would miss her. She was so much a part of him. Papa's letter, in which he wrote simply, "I have no complaints to the Boss. He gave me a queen for forty-three years" depicts in a few eloquent words his life with Mama.

He described her funeral in detail. Mama was carried the entire way to Har Hazeisim by Avremal and Papa's *talmidim*. She was buried alongside her father and mother, Zeidy and Bobie Andron, *zatzal.*

The only consolation I could give Papa was a poem I wrote about Mama. Papa always encouraged my writing when I was a youngster. In fact, he kept some of my poems in his pocket and recited them to his patient customers when they came to his fur shop.

MAMA

There came a knock at midnight;
I hurried to open the door.
Mama was an angel, dressed in white,
More beautiful than ever before.

I rushed into her open arms;
She pressed me to her heart.
I was afraid to let her go,
For fear she would depart.

"Mama, Mama, where have you been?"
Scalding tears filled my eyes.
She gazed at me with deep concern,
As she answered my anguished cries.

"I am 'Home' where I can rest,
For my work is already done.
I am given my just reward,
In my place above the sun.

"I have been crowned a queen";
A halo enveloped her head.
I listened as her soothing voice
Brought me comfort as she said,

"My life on earth, you know, my child,
Was one of hardship and much toil.
But through all the many years,
To our Father, I was ever loyal.

"I obeyed His laws and statutes;
And now I am repaid.
I walk among the greatest,
In my 'Home' that I have made.

"Wherever I turn, I am never alone,
So you see, I am really not dead.
They come to me from all corners of the sky,
All the poor people whom I have fed.

"I sit on a throne of gold,
With the *Shechina* surrounding me.
My ministering angels play their harps,
As I live in Heaven's ecstacy."

Her calming words healed my wound.
Mama is truly blessed.
But the fear that she would leave me
Stirred a feeling of deep unrest.

....

Shechina: Divine Presence

Once more she embraced me lovingly;
I heard her whisper, "Have no fear.
I walk by your side and guide your steps;
Ruchoma, my daughter, I am always near."

Times were difficult for Papa. He missed Mama. He also
needed help for his *hachnosas orchim*. Though Avremal's wife
tried to assist as much as possible, she could not contribute too
much because she was expecting her first child. Papa learned to
cook. He shopped and prepared the meals for the *orchim*.

Several months after Mama's death, Moshe and I received
a letter from Papa asking us to come live with him in Eretz
Yisroel. We deliberated for days until I answered Papa. Our
response read as follows: "With financial circumstances what
they are, Mashi and Yitzchok so very young, and tensions high
in Eretz Yisroel, we cannot settle in Yerusholayim at this
time." I also added: "I had a discussion with the other children.
We are sure no one can take Mama's place. However, if you
know of a woman who could understand your needs, perhaps it
would ease your burden if you married." After penning the
letter, I walked around for days with a heavy heart, feeling a
sense of betrayal to Papa and Mama.

Before Pesach, we children decided to phone Papa and
cheer him up. It was no simple matter and entailed involved
preparations in 1946. Papa had no phone, but we were informed
that a *gemach* on his landing did have one. We contacted the
long-distance operator to arrange our call. She, in turn, reached
the operator in Jerusalem. Finally, we received word from the
operator that our call would be processed at nine o'clock the
following morning.

We gathered nervously and expectantly in Bessie's house.
It was decided that Nochum Dovid, as the only son, should
speak first, then Esther, Bessie and I according to our place in
the family.

....

gemach: free loan fund

My heart beat rapidly as nine o'clock drew near. Then the ring of the phone — Nochum Dovid picked up the receiver. The operator instructed him to hold on. His party would soon be connected. Papa had been alerted to wait for our call in the office of the *gemach*.

I watched Nochum Dovid's expression as he listened to Papa. "Yes, yes," he said, "I hear and hope to come." Then Esther's and Bessie's turns came.

The sweat poured down my face, as my trembling hand grasped the receiver. "Ruchoma, my *tochter*," for a fleeting second I detected a break in Papa's voice. I could not speak. Then his voice grew firm.

"Ruchoma, how much does it cost to speak to me per minute?"

"About $8 a minute, Papa," I answered quickly.

"If it costs you $8 a minute to speak over three continents, how much should you pay when you talk to the Boss three times a day over continents too numerous to count?"

His words both inspired and soothed me. Papa is Papa. He had not changed despite the loss of Mama.

After I placed the receiver back on its cradle, we compared notes about each word Papa had spoken. He had asked Nochum Dovid to try to visit him, and Nochum Dovid had agreed. Esther told Papa that her son, Moshe Aaron, was making arrangements to go to Eretz Yisroel to study. Papa was overjoyed with the news. On many occasions, he wrote us, "Send me your 'living baggage.'" Bessie asked his advice regarding surgery for a gall-bladder condition. He advised her to go ahead with it.

The call cost $50. I paid my share feeling that I had received the greatest bargain of my life.

29

Papa talks to the Boss

From the time Papa arrived in Yerusholayim, he made it a habit to walk to the *Kosel* each day—"to talk to the Boss and get everything off my chest."

Reb Avrohom Tzvi, who lives in Yerusholayim, met me recently and said, "I heard you are writing a book about your father, *zatzal.* I would like to tell you this story.

"When I was fourteen years old, I came with my family to Eretz Yisroel. We were among the fortunate ones who escaped the Holocaust. I was a short, skinny lad, looking much younger than my age.

"One day, I decided to go to the *Kosel.* When I got there, I realized that I was alone. Suddenly, a band of Arab youths surrounded me. They beat me mercilessly. My cries echoed through the stillness. Would I meet my death here, after being saved from the Nazis?

"From nowhere, an elderly man with a gray beard appeared. He ran over to where the group of Arab bullies had dragged me. In a tone of fierce anger, he scolded me, 'Why must you always be fighting? I am taking you home. You will receive your punishment.'

"The Arab hoodlums, taken aback when they heard the old man berating me so loudly, let go of me abruptly. He grabbed my hand, pushed me forward and shielded me with his body.

"When we were a distance from the *Kosel*, the old man took me into his arms and comforted me, as he quieted the sobs that still shook my body. 'I did not mean to scream at you. But I knew of no other way to save you from their clutches. Had I defended you, they would, no doubt, have attacked me also.'

"He held my hand tightly and took me home. From that day on, I became attached to your father, Rav Herman. I attended his lectures very often and stayed in contact with him.

"It was almost twenty years later that, in a small measure, I was able to repay the debt I owed your father for saving my life.

"On a Friday, well past midnight, when most of Yerusholayim was fast asleep, I was walking on a lonely side street. I, too, am usually in bed at that time, but that Friday night I had to visit someone.

"From afar, I saw an old man shuffling along. I ran over to him and was very surprised to recognize Rav Herman. 'What are you doing here all alone so late at night?' I asked him.

" 'I went for a walk. I am very tired,' he said to me slowly. I understood that he must have lost his way and did not know how to get back to Reb Nochum Dovid's house. [In his latter years, Papa lived with my brother.]

"I held his hand tightly and took him home. When we got to the house, we saw Reb Nochum Dovid, who was very upset. He was just about to go out to search for him. He had not heard your father get dressed and quietly leave the house.

"*Boruch Hashem*, I had the great *zechus* to help Rav Herman."

When Avremal was eighteen years old, I received a letter from Papa with the news that Avremal was becoming a *choson*. Papa wrote further, "The *kalla* is a true *yiddishe tochter*, who is just right for him. However, her family is poor and financial help is needed to marry and settle Avremal and Chaya."

As I was reading the letter, Bessie came into my house after shopping for a hat. She showed me the stylish, beige hat she had bought. I admired her good taste, as she tried it on.

I read Papa's letter to her, remarking, "I cannot understand why Papa is in such a hurry to have Avremal marry. He just turned eighteen, and the girl is so very poor." Bessie agreed with me.

No sooner had Bessie left, when the hot oil from the pancakes I was frying spattered over my hand, scalding me. As I was applying medication, the phone rang. It was Bessie. Her voice quavered. "Racoma, on my way home, my new hat slipped out of the bag and fell under a truck. It is covered with mud."

"Bessie, I, too had an accident. I burned my hand." I added quickly, "I see it is not wise to start up with Papa. I am writing him immediately that we shall help in every way possible."

Avremal married Chaya, and they were settled in an apartment that had one room besides the kitchen.

Moshe Aaron, Esther's oldest son, arrived in Eretz Yisroel in May, 1946, and lived with Papa. There was another relative who also stayed there. Papa was having a very hard time of it, still trying to keep house himself. However, Moshe Aaron's arrival raised Papa's morale greatly.

A year later Moshe Aaron became a *choson*. By that time, Papa had married Tante Mirel. Her younger sister was Mama's first cousin through marriage. Mirel used to visit the house quite often when Mama was living. She had been a widow for many years and had lost two young children in the Holocaust. She had two married children living in Eretz Yisroel. Mirel took over the care of the house and the *orchim* conscientiously.

Nochum Dovid and Esther came for Moshe Aaron's wedding. At Papa's suggestion they brought along Yosef

Yechezkel, Frieda's youngest child, aged twelve, to live with Papa and Tante Mirel.

The Jews in Eretz Yisroel found life very taxing. There was strife between the British—who were granted the mandate over Palestine—Jewish defensive units, and the Arabs. A curfew was often imposed by the British. Vital food products such as flour and sugar were rationed.

Esther prepared the wedding meal with the help of Tante Mirel. It was a meager one by American standards, but considered almost extravagant in Yerusholayim. Large portions of fish, different kinds of salads and dessert were to be served.

The invitations to Moshe Aaron's wedding were printed with the added notation: "If there is a curfew in force, the ceremony will be held at 1 PM, otherwise it will take place at 4 PM."

The Shabbos before the wedding, Esther also prepared a lavish *kiddush* after *davening* for all the guests and congregants in the *shul*. At great expense she ordered the customary *Yerushalmi kugel*. When it was taken down from Papa's house to the courtyard on Shabbos morning to be brought to the *shul*, Papa discovered that one of the three *eiruvim* around Yerusholayim was broken. Though there were still two remaining, Papa refused to allow the puddings to be carried to the *shul*. He invited the young boys from a nearby yeshiva "to come and get it." The hungry lads swooped down on their prey and finished it to the last morsel.

When the day of the wedding arrived, everyone was relieved that the curfew was not in effect. However, just before the ceremony was about to begin, word was received that a curfew had been imposed suddenly because fighting had broken out between the English soldiers and one of the Jewish defense units.

This meant that by seven PM no one was allowed to be in the streets. After the ceremony, most of the guests did not stay

---

Yerushalmi kugel: hot noodle pudding

to partake of the wedding supper. The few close relatives who did remain hurried through the meal.

After the *sheva brochos*, they, too, ran from the wedding reception to reach home before the curfew. Even the *choson* and *kalla*, still in their wedding clothes, flew through the streets of Yerusholayim to get to their new apartment in time.

Esther was in a dilemma. Much of the food remained on the table. She commandeered a taxi, paying the driver a large sum to take her with the trays of food to Papa's house.

In addition to the many tribulations Esther encountered, Moshe Aaron developed hepatitis immediately after the wedding. She delayed her departure to nurse him back to health.

Nochum Dovid was spending every available minute with Papa, accomplishing his mission — the *mitzva* of *kibbud av*. He was thus fulfilling the promise he had made when he spoke to Papa on the telephone after Mama passed away.

The tentative reservations Nochum Dovid and Esther had made for the return trip on the *Marine Carp*, the ship they came on, were already taken. They were forced to book passage on a plane in order to reach home before Rosh Hashana. A one-way ticket to the United States cost $675, which was a fortune then.

The redeeming feature of their trip to Eretz Yisroel was Papa's great *bitochen*, which kept up everyone's spirit. He showed no anxiety about the tense situation, both political and economic. In fact, he repeated quite often, "I wish all my children and grandchildren would settle in Eretz Yisroel."

When it came time to bid farewell to their loved ones, Nochum Dovid and Esther could not attain Papa's high level of faith. They left with heavy hearts and a feeling of trepidation.

My nephew Reb Moshe Aaron Stern, told me the remarkable manner in which Papa chose mates for Avremal and him.

kibbud av: honoring father / *bitochen*: faith

Papa's first step was to visit the home of Chaya, who had been recommended for Avremal. He arrived at her house without prior notice. When Papa saw that she was suited for Avremal, he allowed them to meet.

Then Papa went to the *Kosel* to ask the Boss to give His blessing to the match. As Papa stood near the *Kosel*, a page from the Hebrew Bible fell from a crevice in the Wall. The page included the verse: מה' יצא הדבר "The thing came forth from Hashem" (*Bereishis*, Genesis 24:50). Papa was uplifted that the Boss had given him a clear answer that Chaya was Avremal's true *zivug*.

When Papa arrived unannounced *erev* Shabbos at the home of Rochel, the girl suggested for Moshe Aaron, he found her busily washing the floors.

Papa said to her, "My grandson intends to remain in the field of Torah his entire life."

Her wise answer impressed him, "Torah is the best *sechora* [merchandise]."

Moshe Aaron and Rochel met.

Once again Papa sought the blessing of the Boss at the *Kosel*. A fragment from a *siddur* blew towards him. He picked it up and read וארשתיך לי לעולם "I will be betrothed to you forever." Each day when a man puts on the *tefillin* and *retzuos*, he recites this verse from the Prophet Hosea (2:21).

This, too, was a definite indication of the will of Hashem.

30

In the merit of
helping the many

Moshe Aaron lived with Papa for a year before his marriage. Later, during the siege of Yerusholayim, he once again stayed at Papa's house, this time with his wife.

These are incidents, which he witnessed or of which Papa told him.

Papa continued his daily walks to the *Kosel,* despite some danger involved. As the expiration of the British Mandate drew near, and the partitioning of Palestine became more of a reality, the Arabs grew more hostile. They burned many of the Jewish shops in the Old City and were constantly on the rampage.

One day in early May, 1948, Papa set out as usual for the *Kosel.* When he came to the Old City, he noticed that the streets were unusually quiet. There was not one other Jew visible.

Papa decided not to walk through the Arab market place—the short-cut he always took to the *Kosel*—but chose, instead the longer way, a circuitous route.

As he strode ahead, Arabs, with knives protruding from

their garments and daggers of hatred from their eyes, lined the road on either side. It was too late to turn back. Papa marched—eyes straight ahead, praying to the Boss to watch over him.

Only when he arrived safely at the *Kosel* did Papa realize the great miracle the Boss had performed for him. As a matter of routine, two British soldiers were on duty daily in a booth near the *Kosel*. Several times a day there was a change of guard. Without Papa being aware of them, two armed British soldiers had been following him the entire way to the *Kosel*, since it was their turn to relieve the guards on duty. Evidently, the Arabs, seeing Papa escorted by two armed English soldiers, hesitated to attack him. Papa had a few minutes to say a psalm of *tehillim* at the *Kosel* to thank the Boss for protecting him from harm, before the two English guards going off duty marched him safely back to the new section of Yerusholayim.

Papa was probably the last Jew to visit the *Kosel*, as the War of Independence broke out a few day later. For nineteen years the *Kosel* was barred to Jews. In June, 1967, after the Six Day War, the Jews were able once again to lift up their voices in prayer at the Wailing Wall.

As the War of Independence intensified, and the siege of Yerusholayim tightened, most of the Jews were confined to their shelters. Their situation was desperate, as food was scarce.

Papa refused to stay or sleep in the shelter. The civil guards allowed Papa free rein in the streets of Yerusholayim, and he became a "one man army."

There was a bakery called Avi Chayil, on Pri Chodosh Street. Each morning Papa bought as many loaves of bread as he could carry in a sack over his shoulders. He went from shelter to shelter distributing the bread. Gas and kerosene were also in short supply. Papa painstakingly gathered firewood, kindled a fire on his porch, and cooked a tremendous pot of lentils daily. The people in the shelters perked up when Papa brought them plates of hot food.

Many Jews had no place to sleep. They slept on the hard benches in the Zichron Moshe *shul*. With a great deal of effort, Papa provided them with mattresses to make their lot easier.

Papa wrote letters to us asking for help for his *orchim*. We sent him many "CARE" packages and cartons of canned *glatt* kosher meat. Of course, he could only serve his *orchim* small portions of meat, but with the large *cholent* which he himself prepared, at least they were not hungry.

The dangerous situation then prevailing did not deter Papa from his dedication to prayer. He made sure to pray with a *minyon* three times a day.

Only once during the entire war did Papa consent to go into the shelter. It was a day of heavy shooting and bombing. Tante Mirel insisted that Papa join her there, and in the late afternoon he yielded to her wishes. No sooner had he entered the shelter, than a bomb struck their top floor apartment. The head of the bomb pierced the thick, outer stone wall, shattered the large metal bookcase, destroyed many of the *seforim*, then pushed its way into the neighboring apartment, damaged a large clothes closet and finally lodged itself among the clothes. Under normal circumstances, Papa was usually in the room in which the bomb had created such havoc.

With the war's end, a steady stream of people in need of different kinds of assistance came to Papa. His *hachnosas orchim* business thrived, and he renewed his *shiurim*. In his letter, Papa wrote, "I am like a fish in water in Yerusholayim."

There was one major problem that troubled Papa. Yosef Yechezkel, Frieda's youngest son had been living with him throughout the war. Though Papa gave him special attention, and Tante Mirel took care of his physical needs, Yosef was

....

glatt: stringently supervised

unhappy and lonesome for his family in the United States.

Papa was at his wit's end. He decided to seek the advice of the Chazon Ish (Rabbi Avrohom Yeshaya Karelitz, perhaps the greatest Talmudic sage of our time). Since Papa's marriage to Tante Mirel, he had become very friendly with him, because her son-in-law, Rabbi Shleima Karelitz, a *dayon* in Bnei Brak, is a nephew of the Chazon Ish.

The Chazon Ish listened carefully as Papa detailed the problems with his grandson. He advised Papa to send Yosef Yechezkel back to the United States, declaring, "His future is there."

For Papa, it was difficult to part with Yosef, but he followed the Chazon Ish's advice.

In time, Yosef married a very fine girl, and he is raising a true *yiddishe* family. He is on the staff of Yeshiva Chasan Sofer in Brooklyn. The advice of the Chazon Ish that his future lay in America proved true.

My nephew, Yitzchok Meyer Kaufman, told me that one day he traveled in a taxi from Ashdod to Yerusholayim with Rabbi Hager, one of the *dayonim* of Ashdod. When Rabbi Hager heard that Yitzchok Meyer was a grandson of Reb Yaakov Yosef Herman, he said, "I would like to tell you an incident about your grandfather that I witnessed many years ago when I was a young man. I have never forgotten it.

"Your uncle, Reb Nochum Dovid, bought your *Zeidy* an expensive, well-tailored *kapota*. He wore it for the first time on Shabbos.

"Your grandfather used to portion out the *cholent*, and he himself served it to the *orchim*. One of the *orchim* was emotionally unstable. When your grandfather placed the plate of hot *cholent* on the table in front of him, he took the large soup plate, dumped the contents all over your grandfather's new *kapota*, and shouted, 'I don't like this.'

....

dayonim: judges

Papa on his 70th birthday (in 1950), which he celebrated, thanking the Boss that he had lived the full 70 years that He allots a person (Psalms 90:10).

"All the *orchim* gasped out loud. Your uncle, who was also seated at the table, was aghast at what had occurred.

"The *orech*, frightened at what he had done, jumped from his chair and ran out of the house. Without even wiping off the hot, greasy *cholent* from the front of his *kapota*, your grandfather gave chase.

"In a few minutes he returned with the *orech*, holding his hand and soothing him, 'I will give you another plate of *cholent* that you will like,' your grandfather said kindly.

"When your grandfather had wiped his *kapota* as much as is permissible, your uncle said to him, 'Papa, you need so much *savlonus* [patience].' Your grandfather answered, 'If you have *rachmonus* [pity], you need no *savlonus*.'"

In another incident, there was an *orech* who ate sloppily, spilling his food all over the tablecloth. One Shabbos, when Papa returned from *shul*, he found the *orech* seated alone at a little table in the far corner of the room. The other *orchim* had managed to find him a place where he would not disturb them.

When Papa washed his hands to eat, instead of seating himself at the head of the table as he always did, he took his armchair, carried it over to the little table and joined the *orech*.

The *orchim* were very perturbed. "Reb Yaakov Yosef, why are you not sitting at the head of the table?" they asked.

"I do not think Reb Meyer likes sitting all alone," Papa answered quietly.

It was only after much coaxing on the part of the *orchim* that Papa consented to return to his regular place—with Reb Meyer seated next to him.

31

With Papa in Yerusholayim

"Fasten your seat belts—arriving Tel Aviv."

I awoke from my deep reverie. It took me a few minutes to return to the present from the magic carpet of my past, where the forty-hour plane flight had whisked me.

Papa!!! After fifteen years of separation, I would soon see him, touch him, talk to him. My heart beat a fast tattoo. A giant lump settled in my throat.

The plane touched down at Lod Airport. Still wobbly from the long flight, I hurried off the plane and cleared customs.

I saw Papa from afar. He stood tall and straight. His beard was snow-white and glistened like silver in the rays of the sun.

Then Papa saw me. Suddenly, the crowds of people bustling about became immoblized as Papa's loud *brocho* of *shehecheyonu* shook the rafters of the airport.

I ran on winged feet towards Papa. For one brief moment we both stood transfixed. My heart pounded in my ears. The lump in my throat rendered me speechless.

Papa's piercing blue-gray eyes glistened with unshed tears.

shehecheyonu: thanksgiving

Papa on the porch of his apartment in the Zichron Moshe section of the city.

He touched my cheek, caressing it gently. I waited expectantly.

"Ruchoma," his voice broke, "Ruchoma, my dear, dear *tochter*, you are too good to pinch—just too good to pinch!"

Papa held my hand tightly during the entire trip to Yerusholayim. My voice sounded strange and strained to me as I answered his questions about Moshe, my children and the family.

We arrived at his house in the Zichron Moshe section of Yerusholayim. I met Tante Mirel, who greeted me warmly. My nephews—Avremal, Moshe Aaron, and his young brother, Yosef—who accompanied Papa to Lod Airport, had kept their distance during the poignant meeting. Now they plied me with many questions about all our loved ones back home.

I had not seen Avremal since he was a six-year-old child. In front of me now stood a husky, mature man with a long beard, the father of several children. But when he said with a slight quiver in his voice, "You are still the same Aunt Racoma," I was once again holding his little hand as I walked with him to his house.

My niece Minnie, Frieda's youngest daughter, who did not come to the airport, was overjoyed when we met. She had married Reb Rafael Waldshan, the son of Rabbi Chaim Shmulevitz's sister.

Papa arranged for me to sleep at the home of Boruch Reisner, who had lived with Papa until his marriage to Minna, another young survivor of the Holocaust. Their wedding had taken place in Papa's house, and he treated them as his own.

Boruch and Minna graciously gave me their children's bedroom. "You are our 'Doda' Ruchoma and part of our family. Our home is your home." And that is exactly how I felt during my entire stay.

Reb Moshe and Ahuva Kurzweil lived in the apartment below Papa's. As soon as Ahuva heard that I had arrived, she came up to visit me. "Your father speaks so much about his *muzhinik*, Ruchoma, that I feel I know you. Oh, how anxiously he awaited you!"

When the Kurzweils moved into their apartment, Papa and Mama had been living in theirs about a year. Within a short time, Papa and Mama became very friendly with the young couple. Their son, Zev, was born a year later, and Papa kept a grandfatherly eye on him.

I, too, became friendly with them during my stay and our friendship continued after I settled in Yerusholayim.

I gleaned the following from my visits with them.

Ahuva related, "Your mother was a great *tzidkonis* and tried to help everyone as much as possible, though she was having a difficult time herself. She kept up our spirits with her words of encouragement and her sense of humor.

"During the war, my husband and I were very poor, as were most Jews in Yerusholayim. For each Shabbos, though, I

....

muzhinik: youngest child

bought a small piece of chicken. But I did not have the money to buy ice to store it in.

"Your mother used to call down to me as soon as ice was delivered to her, 'Ahuva, bring up your *ganz*. I've made plenty of room in my ice box for it.'

"There was a *shomer*, a six-foot Sephardi, who on Shabbos guarded the *gemilas chesed* located on Papa's landing. He used to sit on the steps, and your mother would carry out the entire Shabbos meal to him. The many blessings he gave your mother resounded throughout our building.

"My mother, who was a widow, lived with us for a time. She enjoyed spending time with your mother. She offered to help her with *hachnosas orchim*, but your mother politely refused, saying, 'I don't want to give away my *mitzva*.' However, she added graciously, 'I will give you a small part of the *mitzva*,' and she allowed my mother to help *kasher* the chickens.

"I was at your mother's bedside during much of her illness. She never complained, even though she was in pain. She longed for her children and grandchildren, and her thoughts were constantly with them. Though it is almost nine years since she passed away, I think of her and miss her very much."

Reb Moshe Kurzweil told me that he had never met a person like Papa. His devotion to the *orchim* was superhuman. Every poor, bedraggled, and even disturbed person was welcomed by Papa and treated royally. Judging by their appearance, these people would not have been permitted into a restaurant even if they had wished to pay for a meal. He also helped them financially.

"Whenever he bought food in the market and there were special fruits or other scarce food, he remarked, 'I will save this for my *orchim*.'

"Your father never took advantage of his *orchim*. He always recited the blessings after the Friday night and Shabbos

ganz: goose / *shomer*: watchman

meals with a *minyon*. Many of the *orchim* hurried through their meal and left before your father was ready for the blessings. He never detained them. When he did not have a *minyon*, he ran in the streets looking for people who were pleased to come up, eat dessert, and be part of his *minyon*.

"*Erev* Shabbos, he had a *minyon* in his house for *mincha, kabbolas Shabbos* and *mairiv*. Here again, he could have asked the *orchim* to come earlier and *daven* in his house, but he never bothered them. Many a time, I used to see Reb Yaakov Yosef hurrying down the steps to search for a ninth and tenth person to make up his *minyon*. I always deemed it an honor to be part of his *minyon*.

"For a *mitzva*, he spared no effort. I think he would have given even his life. There were poor couples who had no money for a wedding. He shopped, cooked and arranged the wedding in his house. In fact, out of respect for your father, the *gaon* Rav Yosef Tzvi Dushinsky would come especially to officiate.

"In the Zichron Moshe *shul* courtyard there was a 'loiterers' bench,' where some of the men used to spend time between *mincha* and *mairiv*. With your father's tact and understanding, the bench soon emptied, and a large group gathered to listen to his teaching of *Ein Yaakov*.

"I do not know where he found them, but many irreligious Jews became *baalei teshuva* through his soft-spoken words and his show of interest in them.

"He gathered the boys, who were playing in the street and persuaded them with goodies to come up to his house, where he taught them varied religious subjects. After a time, they needed no enticement and came up on their own. Everyone loved him and wanted to be near him.

"On Purim and Simchas Torah, you could not get into Reb Yaakov Yosef's house. People stood on the porch and on the steps. Everyone wanted to hear your father read the *megilla* on

----

kabbolas Shabbos: prayer for welcoming the Sabbath
baalei teshuva: repenters / *Simchas Torah*: final day of Sukkos

Pictures from the wedding of my nephew Yosef Stern in the summer of 1954. Yosef became a regular shtreimel-*wearer, but Papa (his grandfather) and his father, Yom Tov Lipman Stern (who came*

Purim. He pronounced each word so loudly and clearly that it re-echoed throughout the courtyard.

"People came especially on Simchas Torah to watch your father's ecstatic joy when he danced with the *sefer Torah.* Of course, the tables were laden with all kinds of good food, which he had prepared."

Ahuva joined in again, "I must tell you that during the war, when the bombs were flying overhead and we were all huddled in our shelter, Reb Yaakov Yosef was upstairs busily tinkering with a broken kerosene stove. He wanted to cook food for his *orchim* or for anyone else who was hungry.

"We used to call up to him, 'Reb Yaakov Yosef, it is very dangerous, please come down.'

"He answered, 'Do not worry, I am being protected up here.' And surely Hashem watched over him. Your Tante Mirel was very disturbed, but he did not listen to her. In fact, I noticed many times when she served him a better or larger

specially for the wedding), put on their shtreimels *only for the occasion. Above (clockwise): myself, my sister Esther, Papa, Yom Tov Lipman, his son Moshe Aaron, and the* choson *and* kalla.

portion on Shabbos, he handed it over to one of the *orchim*."

Reb Moshe added, "Reb Yaakov Yosef was on such a high spiritual level that he seemed to belong not to our present, lowly generation, but to a generation of long, long ago."

Ahuva finished off with, "And your mother stood by his side."

Papa had a little store in Meah She'arim where he sold *sifrei Torah, tefillin,* and *mezuzos.* There were few customers to disturb us. In the quiet, dimly lit store, I sat for hours each day sharing thoughts with Papa.

I discussed problems that needed his sage advice. I listened to his wise words of Torah. I filled him in about all his loved ones in the United States. I told him about my experiences, and they brought laughter or sometimes a shade of sadness to his face.

And Papa unburdened his heart to me. He relived Mama's

passing away and his years of loneliness and revealed his high aspirations, and his constant closeness to the Boss.

I went everywhere with Papa. When he shopped for the *orchim*, I accompanied him to the grocery store. He ordered sacks of beans, barley, flour, and smaller bags of sugar. After Papa handed the grocer his payment, the man removed his apron, came from behind the counter and said, "Now , Rebbe, tell me a *dvar Torah*." He was one of Papa's *talmidim*.

Papa kneaded the dough for the Shabbos *challos*, and Tante Mirel baked them. My childhood returned vividly when I went with Papa *erev* Shabbos to several *shuls* to bring *challos* for *sholosh seudos*. Ever since Papa had come to Eretz Yisroel, he continued this *mitzva* that he had begun in the United States many years before.

Papa prepared the large pot of *cholent* himself. He hovered over it, tasting it from time to time to see if he had seasoned it properly. Papa was very proud when he handed me a full plate of hot *cholent* on Shabbos and I complimented him on it.

Papa and I were walking uphill on Yechezkel Street. As I was huffing and puffing trying to keep up with Papa's long strides, he said to me, "Ruchoma, I will show you how to ease the strain of climbing a hill."

He zigzagged from one side of the street to the other, thus cutting the incline by half.

It did not faze him one bit that people stared at his strange manner of walking, with me following close on his heels.

The first Saturday night after I arrived, I noticed Papa preparing to leave the house. It was after 10 PM. "Where are you going, Papa?" I asked curiously.

"I borrowed an enema bag for one of the *orchim* and promised to return it to the *ezras cholim* tonight."

"Papa, I will go. Just tell me the address."

At first, Papa was hesitant, "Ruchoma, you will not know the way." However, when I insisted, he wrote the address on a piece of scrap paper and gave me a few directions.

"Papa, don't worry. I will find the place, and from there I will go to the Reisners. *Gut voch*," I said to Papa and Tante Mirel. "I will be at your house early tomorrow morning."

I followed Papa's directions as best as I could. After walking for about twenty minutes, I was lost in a maze of streets and alleyways. There was no one in the deserted street to whom I could turn. I had just decided to knock on some strange door to ask for help, when I heard welcome footsteps. It was a bearded man walking quickly towards me.

As he approached, he cried out in great surprise, "Aunt Racoma, what are you doing here all alone so late at night?"

"Avremal, surely Hashem sent you to me." I poured out my frustration at trying to locate the *ezras cholim*.

Avremal walked me to the *ezras cholim* and then to my sleeping quarters at the Reisners. "Aunt Racoma," he said to me as we walked together, "a peculiar thing happened tonight. I was preparing for bed, when I remembered that I owed a man some money. I decided not to wait until tomorrow morning, but rather attend to this debt tonight. I was in deep thought about a problem, and by mistake I walked down the side street where I met you."

When I told Papa the next morning about my experience, he said matter-of-factly, "Ruchoma, it's simple — like adding one plus one. When you want to do a *mitzva*, you jump right into it, and leave the rest to the Boss."

In my effort to fulfill the *mitzva* of *kibbud av*, I was able to see confirmation of Papa's religious principle.

---

ezras cholim: society for helping the sick / *Gut voch*: (have a) good week

Sunday morning Avremal came to visit me at Papa's house. "Aunt Racoma, what can I do for you? You took care of me when I was a little boy, and now I would like to repay you," he said graciously.

I expressed a desire to see where Bobie Aidel was buried. (In 1954 Har Hazeisim was occupied by Jordan and Jews had no access.) Avremal went with me to one of the tallest buildings in Yerusholayim, and we climbed to the roof.

"Look, over there, Aunt Racoma." He pointed to a far-away area. With the benefit of binoculars, I strained to see the spot, but all I could see was a stony piece of land, and I could not discern Mama's grave.

I walked down the stairs very disappointed, not realizing that thirteen years later I would be standing right near her *kever*.

As soon as I had rested from my trip, I told Papa that at the earliest opportunity I would like to visit Reb Lezer Yudel Finkel and Reb Chatzkel Levenstein and their families.

From Papa's store in Meah She'arim, it was only a short walk to the Mirrer Yeshiva and the adjoining house where Reb Lezer Yudel lived.

Reb Lezer Yudel greeted me with a broad smile and a loud "*Brucho haboah*." Though his face was lined and his beard white, he had not changed very much. His daughter, Miriam (Rebbetzin Shmulevitz), was delighted to see me. She was already a grandmother. Ettel, her oldest daughter, whom I had left in Mir as a child, was married to a brilliant *talmid chochom*, Reb Nochum Pertsovitz, and had a family.

Miriam's first question was about Yisroel Meir, to whom she had been very devoted when he was an infant. "He is a *choson bochur*," I smilingly answered.

Rebbetzin Malka Finkel was very ill and almost blind.

....

Brucho haboah: literally, Blessed is she who comes: i.e. welcome
choson bochur: eligible for marriage

Reb Chatzkel Levenstein, sitting next to Rav Yosef Kahaneman (head of the Ponievezh Yeshiva), on a bus trip.

Miriam tiptoed into her mother's bedroom to see if she was awake. "Mama," she said, "a special guest is here to visit you."

My heart ached, as I said softly, "*Sholom aleichem*, Rebbetzin." Then to everyone's amazement, she asked hesitantly, "Ruchoma? Is it Ruchoma?" Though sixteen years had elapsed, she recognized my voice.

I hurried to her bedside and clasped her thin, wasted hand. Fortunately, she could not see the hot tears coursing down my cheeks. She was anxious to hear about Moshe and Yisroel Meir. I vividly described them to her, and she listened intently. When it was time for me to leave, I was reluctant to say good-bye.

The next day I went to visit Reb Chatzkel and his family. Although I had seen them five years earlier, when they immigrated to Eretz Yisroel, my excitement mounted as I neared their home.

Reb Chatzkel's daughter Yecheved, her husband, Reb Reuven Ginzburg, and their children lived with her parents. Yecheved flew out to greet me. We kissed and hugged each other. Rebbetzin Levenstein kissed me soundly on each cheek and would not let go of my hand for quite a while. I gave them personal regards from their daughter, Zlotka, Reb Mottel, her husband, and from each grandchild, with whom I was in close contact. (Reb Reuven is now a *mashgiach* in the Ponievezh Yeshiva in Bnei Brak.)

Yecheved knocked on Reb Chatzkel's door. "Ruchoma is here," she said with feeling. Reb Chatzkel greeted me very warmly. He questioned me closely about my family and our life in the United States.

I asked his advice. "My father very much wants Moshe and me to settle in Eretz Yisroel with our children. We have very little savings. Moshe is quite satisfied in the yeshiva, where he is a *rebbe* in the *mesivta*. Our children are progressing well in their studies."

Reb Chatzkel answered immediately, "If you have the *bitochen* of your father, I would advise you to settle here."

During my stay in Yerusholayim, I visited Reb Chatzkel and his family several times to renew the friendship that had left such a deep impact on me throughout the years.

I had promised Dov Lederman, Yisroel Meir's friend, that I would bring personal regards from him to his mother, who had a bakery shop in Tel Aviv.

Papa took me there. We walked in the crowded streets of Tel Aviv, and as we neared a main intersection, Papa suddenly tugged at my hand. I stopped in my tracks. "Look, Ruchoma, just look." His hand pointed to the multitude of people as they crossed the street from every direction. "They are ours — all ours!" he exclaimed. His eyes shone with pure love and adoration. His arms seemed to embrace each Jew.

But Papa could also be very harsh. We were absorbed in conversation, as we strolled down Yaffo Street in Yerusholayim. Papa looked up just in time to see two young ladies coming towards us wearing off-the-shoulder dresses. Papa's eyes blazed.

"Are the streets of Yerusholayim a bathhouse that you dress so improperly?" he cried out. The ladies gasped at the sudden onslaught. They answered something in Hebrew under their breath. Papa continued berating them loudly.

A huge crowd of people gathered. A policeman was summoned. He tried to calm the young ladies — who were shouting madly by this time — and the many others who defended them. The policeman urged Papa to leave the scene. I stood nervously on the side lines calling, "Papa, Papa, please, please come."

After what seemed an interminable time, Papa extricated himself from the crowd. His face was flushed, his eyes bright.

"Ruchoma," Papa said emphatically, "when I am asked 'Upstairs,' 'Herman, what did you do when you saw a lack of *tznius* in the streets of Yerusholayim?' I will answer, 'Bring the recording and hear my protest.' You must never be ashamed to voice your objection when you witness anything opposed to *yiddishkeit*."

This religious principle, which I often saw Papa put into action, had a deep effect on me.

After high school, I had wanted very much to register for college. Papa would not hear of it.

When I was a mature woman, I decided to enter the teaching field. I was advised that I required a college education in order to be hired.

I registered for two courses in the evening session, Sociology and Language in Thought and Action.

The first session of my sociology course dealt with human culture during the Stone Age, which includes the Eolithic, Paleolithic and Neolithic periods, and which, as the instructor explained, dates back several hundred thousand years.

I could not accept this false doctrine of evolution. I raised my hand, and the teacher nodded. "I understand that sociology is a science. If so, it should be exact." The teacher agreed with me. I pursued my reasoning. "If it is an exact science, would you please give the date of the different periods down to the year, month and day?" The students snickered.

The instructor's first reaction was surprise, then anger, but he controlled himself. "I do not have the time to go into such details at present. See me after class," he answered curtly. After class, the teacher said to me, "Mrs. Shain, do not start up

The United States penny (one cent), with the words that declare where America puts its trust.

with me, and I will not start up with you." He kept his word, as he minimized discussion of the first chapters, which dealt with this topic.

My language course was challenging. The book we used gave an adequate illustration of the role of language in human life.

"With words, we sugar-coat our nastiest motives and worst behavior, but with words we also formulate our highest ideals and aspirations."

It brought Papa into sharp focus because he used "words" to teach, encourage and inspire thousands to Torah and *yiddishkeit* and to strive for higher aspirations.

In the discussion of "inference," i.e. a statement about the unknown made on the basis of the known, the teacher gave the Jewish Bible as an example. He said that there is no actual proof other than what is written there.

I recalled that in one of Papa's lectures, he mentioned that America exists because of a penny. On each American cent the words, "In God we Trust" are imprinted.

My hand flew into the air, and my teacher acknowledged me.

I questioned, "On each penny the words, 'In God we trust' are engraved; moreover, how can you refute the Bible and describe it as inference, when it was handed down by God to Moses during the revelation on Mount Sinai and witnessed by 600,000 men, and many more women and children?"

There was an uproar in class. Some agreed—others disagreed. The teacher stopped the heated discussion without giving an adequate response.

After my college experiences, I realized how wise Papa had been in preventing me from attending college.

Papa enjoyed listening to every incident about my life in the United States, even though I might have mentioned them before in some of my letters to him.

"Papa, a short while after you left for Eretz Yisroel, I entered my grocery store one morning. The wife of the great *gaon* Rabbi Moshe Feinstein was also shopping there. As I greeted her, I noticed she was purchasing cheese. 'Rebbetzin,' I said, 'I am pleased to see that your *rav* permits eating this cheese. I will also buy it.'

"She smiled broadly and said, 'When we arrived in New York, my *rav* was advised to consult Reb Yaakov Yosef Herman on matters of *kashrus*. It was your father who approved this cheese.'

"Well, Papa, all the customers and Willie, the owner of the grocery, had a good laugh."

Papa chuckled loudly when I finished relating this experience.

Papa had asked us to take over his Pesach business when he settled in Yerusholayim. Moshe and I found it very taxing, but we did not want to give it up because we knew how much it meant to Papa.

Several months before Pesach, we ordered prunes — kosher for Pesach — from Oregon. They were specially supervised by a *mashgiach*, whom we paid a large sum of money. One Pesach, our crates of prunes were exchanged en route to New York. We received, instead, prunes that did not have *hashgocho*.

Of course, we could not sell our prunes for Pesach. We lost a great deal of money, as we were forced to sell them for less than cost price after Pesach.

"Papa, Moshe and I are not cut out to do business. After this episode, we decided to give up your Pesach business. But now many observant people have gone into the business of providing strictly kosher Pesach products. It is not an emergency as it was when you first started it," I explained.

"Your other 'businesses' are still going strong. Moshe is continuing to give a *shiur* to a large group of young men at Hapoel Hamizrachi, and they are very pleased.

"I try to help Mrs. Schroit with the *hachnosas orchim*. However, it is not 'full house' as it was when you, Papa, took care of it.

"I am continuing to deliver the *challos* to the three *shuls* for *sholosh seudos*."

Papa beamed his approval.

There was steady traffic in Papa's house. He headed a loan society and a charity fund. He was president of Kollel America Tiferes Yerusholayim. And people came to him with all sorts of requests and seeking advice.

The grandchildren did not do anything without first consulting him. If their children excelled, Papa was first to hear about their *chochmos*. If they misbehaved, Papa was asked how to handle them. If they needed financial aid, it was to Papa they came.

And Papa interested himself in everyone. His patience was infinite.

There was the old, wizened Jew from Yemen, a Shabbos *orech* who claimed he was one hundred and three years old. Each Saturday night, he slowly climbed the two long flights of iron steps to Papa's house, where Papa was waiting to serve him the left-over *cholent* that had remained on the stove the entire day.

As I watched him clean his plate to the last drop, I thought, "No wonder he has longevity." If he could digest that *cholent* he must have an iron-clad constitution. I served him several glasses of hot tea, hoping they would help dilute the *cholent*.

There was also a lawyer from London who had settled in

Yerusholayim a few years before. He popped in a few times a week just to say hello to Papa.

One day, he explained to me why he tried to visit Papa at every opportunity. "I see it this way. Your father is a very great *tzaddik*. With the world so topsy-turvy, *Moshiach* must surely be on his way. When he does come, I am sure your father will be in the front line. I would like to get into the picture a bit. If I am near Reb Yaakov Yosef, I might stand a chance."

One early morning, I was seated with Papa at the table in his dining room.

"Look, Ruchoma," Papa pointed to the sun's bright rays streaming through his open window. "I am fortunate to have a combination of Florida and California in my apartment. From my southern exposure, the sun brightens the dining room in the morning, and from my western exposure, the sun warms my bedroom in the afternoon. Deduct sixty to seventy rainy, cold days throughout the year. During the remaining three hundred days the weather is pleasant.

"The Boss gave us a precious gift, Eretz Yisroel, which is truly a blessed land. I wish all our children could live here and enjoy these many blessings."

For Tante Mirel, life was not easy. We got along well, and she found in me a willing ear to listen to her problems.

She tried her utmost to feed Papa well and help as much as she could with the *orchim*, but Papa took over much of the responsibility and work. She went out of her way to prepare meals for me.

Each morning I was greeted by her, "Sholom, Ruchoma, I have a *salatkele* ready for you." Vegetables were very cheap and in great abundance at that time. Most of the population existed on vegetables, as fish, chicken and meat were expensive. The grocery shelves were sparsely filled with a few cans of green peas

....
salatkele: little salad

and carrots, and small cans of sardines. I ate more raw vegetables in my four-week stay in Papa's house than I did in half a year in the United States.

One day, Tante Mirel aired her views to me. "Your mother is very fortunate. She did not have any pleasure from this world, as she worked very hard helping your father with the *hachnosas orchim*. She did this without ever uttering a word of complaint. I am sure she is sitting in a fine seat in *gan eden* and is enjoying the other world.

"Your father lives in a higher world where material possessions have no meaning. Many times I object to my situation. Not only am I deprived of physical comforts in this world, but because I complain, and your father is such a big *tzaddik*, I am afraid I will lose the other world also." It was difficult for me to placate her.

Papa was very devoted to Tante Mirel's children. They came often to visit and seek his advice. Tante Mirel's son, Reb Avrohom Weiner, his wife, Sarah, and their daughter resided in Ramat Gan. Tante Mirel's daughter, Dvora, with her husband, Reb Shleima Karelitz, and her family lived in Bnei Brak. I visited both families and received a warm and gracious welcome. A close relationship developed that gave Papa and Tante Mirel great satisfaction.

When I entered Papa's house one Friday morning, Papa's face was aglow. "Ruchoma, do you realize that a *sefer Torah* is alive?" he asked me animatedly.

"I rarely have a problem falling asleep when my bedtime comes. If I do, I examine my actions of the day to see if I was amiss in anything I did. If I find that some action needs correction, I try to right it as soon as possible.

"This past Wednesday night, I could not fall asleep. After making sure that my actions were in order, I decided to review the *parshas hashovua* in my *sefer Torah*.

"As I read the Torah, I noticed that one of the letters was

posul. This meant that on Shabbos I would not have been able to read further in my *sefer Torah.*

"Thursday morning I brought the *sefer Torah* to my *sofer* and asked him to make sure to correct it before Shabbos. When I went back this morning to pick it up, the *sofer* asked me if I had any idea when my *sefer Torah* was written. I did not know. He then told me that he had found a small notation that it had been written many years ago, in the year 5640 (1880).

"Ruchoma," Papa said elatedly, "that was the year I was born. I bought this *sefer Torah* when I was a young man in the States. Since then, I've always read the *parshas hashovua* from it each Shabbos.

"My *sefer Torah* disturbed my sleep on Wednesday night to make sure that I would correct it in time for me to read from it on Shabbos, as is my weekly custom."

Papa finished telling me of his experience with the quote from *Mishle* (Proverbs 3:18): "Torah is a living tree."

On another occasion when sleep did not come and Papa found all his deeds correct that day, he turned and twisted in bed seeking an explanation for his insomnia.

A close relative was living with Papa. He finally woke him. "What happened in the house today?" Papa questioned the half-asleep relative.

"Nothing, nothing at all," he answered.

"Who visited?" Papa questioned further.

"Your grandson, Avremal, came this afternoon."

"Did he want anything?" Papa asked.

"No, he stayed a few minutes and left."

Papa did not let up. Finally, the relative admitted that he had had a slight argument with Avremal and "in jest" told him not to come to the house any more.

"Get dressed. We are going to Avremal's house. He is an

....

posul: halachically unfit

orphan and might have been offended. We must ask his forgiveness," Papa said firmly.

The relative remonstrated. "It is the middle of the night. Avremal is surely fast asleep. He knew I did not mean it seriously. We will go first thing in the morning."

"When a wrong is done, you cannot wait. It must be corrected without delay," Papa said sternly. Knowing Papa, the relative did not argue further but got dressed.

Off they went through the quiet streets of Yerusholayim. When they came to Avremal's house, Papa saw that a small light was lit in his dining room. They climbed the two flights of stairs. Papa knocked gently on Avremal's door.

Avremal unlocked his door and asked in alarm, "Zeidy, what is the matter? Why are you up in the middle of the night?"

Papa did not answer his questions, but asked Avremal, "Why are *you* up so late at night?"

"I could not sleep since something was troubling me," Avremal answered.

Papa then called to the relative, who was waiting in the hallway. He rushed in and blurted, "Avremal, you surely did not take me seriously when I told you not to come to your Zeidy's house any more? If you did, I beg your forgiveness." Avremal forgave him.

"Zeidy," Avremal said with deep emotion, "you lifted a heavy weight from my heart by coming now. I could not imagine that I would not be welcome in your house where I grew up."

Papa went home and fell asleep immediately.

Papa was persistent and consistent in concerning himself with every breach of religious education.

He became aware that a tuition-free *cheder* for Sephardi children in Givat Shaul had been closed down. Papa was appalled by the indifference of the parents in not decrying the closing of the *cheder*.

He organized and headed a "Committee of *Baalei Batim* of Givat Shaul" and printed a leaflet which he distributed to the parents:

"Your fathers educated you as Jews. They told you that our forefathers taught us Torah, by which we know the Creator of the world, and we are His chosen nation. Hashem commanded us to teach our children His ways."

Papa berated the parents for the lack of interest and neglect of their children's religious training. He pleaded with them to find a suitable place to reopen the *cheder* and pledged his financial support to keep it functioning.

Papa concluded his words with the blessing, "May you see your children strengthened by Torah for your honor and the honor of our nation."

Papa's call bore fruit, and many Sephardi children were encouraged to continue their Torah learning.

Papa's desk drawer contained letters he had received from many different people and organizations. Among them were several letters from Reb Boruch Ber Leibowitz from Kaminetz, one letter from his son-in-law, Reb Reuven Grozovsky, one letter from Rabbi Kamai, the *rav* of Mir, and a few from Reb Lezer Yudel Finkel. These letters were written to Papa many years ago when he was living in the United States.

The salutations of these letters bear witness to the high esteem in which these great *tzaddikim* and *roshei yeshiva* held Papa. Since they were written in Hebrew I have translated these salutations:

Rabbi Kamai:

To the honorable *rav*, the *gaon*, the *tzaddik*, a foundation of the world, a treasure of Torah, who fears Hashem, reveres and honors *talmidei chachomim*, and helps the many, his star will last forever . . .

Rabbi Finkel:

To my esteemed friend, who is crowned with outstanding

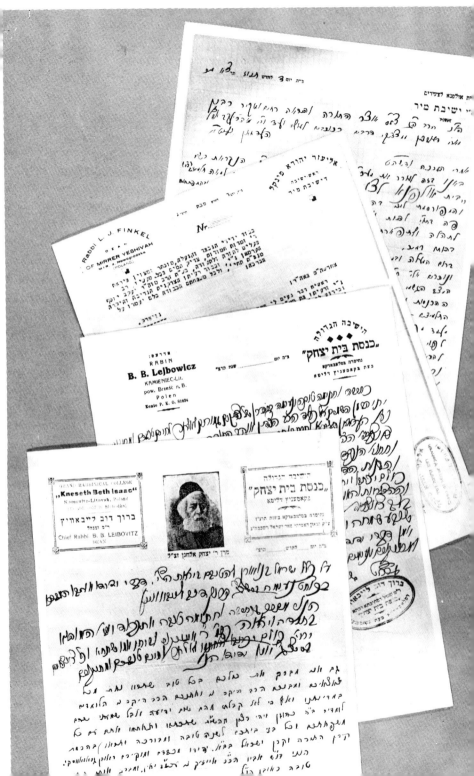

fear of Hashem, with a sterling character, a total *tzaddik* in all his actions, who is occupied with Torah . . .

Rabbi Leibowitz:

My dear friend, the *rav*, the *tzaddik*, lovable person, a man with many actions on behalf of Torah, who is happy to do justice, and stands as a bulwark to protect those in distress . . .

Rabbi Grozovsky:

To my respected, dear friend, the *rav*, distinguished in Torah, whose fear of Hashem is pure, the well-known *tzaddik* . . .

"HIGHER LIGHTS"

I came into Papa's house very early one morning. He was closeted in his Torah room (so called because he kept several *sifrei Torah* and his *seforim* in that room), and I heard him crying. I waited anxiously for him to make his appearance. He finally emerged red-eyed.

"Papa, why were you crying?" I asked in concern.

"Well, *tochter*, I will tell you. Do you have any idea how many of our Jewish brothers are lost in Russia without any source of *yiddishkeit*? Surely, there must be about two or three million. I prepared a special prayer that I say each morning after *shachris* to plead with the Boss to save them from total spiritual destruction. They need great *rachamim*."

One day, I saw Papa busily writing some figures in a ledger with a red pencil. I peered over his shoulder. "Are these your business accounts?" I asked curiously.

"Oh, no," Papa answered, "this is my *maiser* book."

"So what are these figures in red?" I asked further.

"I am over-drawn on my *maiser*. The Boss owes me this amount." He pointed to a large sum on the credit side of the ledger, but hurried to add, "I never have to wait too long before

....
rachamim: (heavenly) mercy / *maiser*: tithe

ne of the letters that Papa received from gedolim.

the Boss pays His debt. One of these days I will sell a *sefer Torah*, and the debt will be wiped off. Once again I will be on the debit side."

Papa was rarely downcast. He showed righteous anger at a wrongdoing, but otherwise his countenance was cheerful.

"Papa, don't you worry about anything?" I asked, as I sat with him in his store.

"Worry? Me? What have I got to worry about? The Boss provides me with all my needs. Does an infant sucking at his mother's breast worry from where he will receive his milk? No, he opens his mouth, and the milk flows in. That is how I feel with the Boss."

Papa then quoted *Tehillim* (Psalm 131): "Surely, I have pacified and stilled my soul, like the suckling at its mother's breast."

However, one morning when I walked into Papa's store, I noticed he looked dejected.

"Papa, why are you so sad today?" I asked in concern.

"I am troubled because I am not sure the Boss likes me," he answered worriedly.

I stared at him in amazement. "Papa," I said with conviction, "whom else would the Boss like if not you? You are one of His most devoted sons and a dedicated soldier who obeys His every command."

My words penetrated. Papa perked up and once more became his cheery self.

One day, as I sat with Papa in his store, I said to him, "I am very disturbed whenever I think of the Holocaust. I wish I could blot out this terrible, tragic happening from my thoughts. Six million Jews were slaughtered by the Nazis, among them many of my close friends from Mir. There are many questions that pound at my heart and in my mind."

Papa spoke slowly. "Listen, Ruchoma, the Boss does only

what is good for *klal Yisroel*. At the rate our Jews are sliding downhill spiritually during the last decades, there might be a danger of our nation being lost through assimilation and conversion.

"A certain number of Jews must depart from this world before *Moshiach* can come. By taking six million Jewish souls from us in such a short period, the Boss will bring *moshiach* a few hundred years sooner."

Moshe Aaron, absorbed in his thoughts, met Papa in the street. "What are you thinking about?" Papa asked him.

"Nothing very special," Moshe Aaron answered.

"You must *think* where you are heading for and what *nachas* the Boss will have from your going there," Papa advised him.

Moshe Aaron's little son, Michel, was very ill. His temperature was high, and the medications the doctor prescribed had no effect.

Papa came to see how Michel was feeling. He found Moshe Aaron and Rochel looking haggard. They had not slept for several nights.

Moshe Aaron poured out his anxiety to Papa.

"Moshe Aaron, did you look over your *mezuzos* lately?" Papa questioned.

"I don't remember when I last did," answered Moshe Aaron.

"Take down your *mezuzos*. I want to check them."

Moshe Aaron immediately took down the *mezuzo* from the children's room where Michel lay so sick. Papa examined it closely. "Moshe Aaron, this *mezuzo* is *posul*. Look at this letter." Papa pointed to one of the letters: a part of it was missing.

"How do you expect Michel to get well when you have no

---

klal: community

shmira in your house?" Papa asked. "Come with me, and I will give you a kosher *mezuzo*."

The next morning when Papa came again to visit Michel, he looked sprightly and was jumping up and down in his crib.

"Zeidy," Moshe Aaron exclaimed, "it worked! A few hours after I put the kosher *mezuzo* back on the doorpost, Michel's fever started to drop. Now it is almost normal, *boruch Hashem*."

Papa told me the following words of Torah and *mussar*:

"If you *sacrifice* for Torah and *yiddishkeit* in your generation, it is an insurance policy that the next generation will remain steadfast and observant Jews."

"Ruchoma, your making a *brocho* out loud helped you to get Moshe, your true *zivug*. See that your children make *brochos* out loud."

"A *refua* does not have to come only through a doctor, but can come through a person without a medical title." Papa then quoted the source of this statement: a passage in the Talmud, Avoda Zora 55a.

"Always say *krias shema* very slowly and exactly. It is the foundation of serving Hashem."

"When we say the daily blessing: רוקע הארץ על המים ... 'Hashem spreads out the earth over the waters,' we can have in mind the luxurious ocean liners that are now floating palaces."

"The Boss's 'signature' is *emes*. You find the letters of אמת in the first words of the *chumosh*: בראשית ברא אלקים."

And to Nochum Dovid Papa said:

"Torah is synonymous with *emes*, אמת.

"In the Ten Commandments the first word is אנכי.

"In the beginning of *mishnayos*, *Maseches Brochos*, the first word is מאימתי.

"In the beginning of Gemora, *Maseches Brochos,* the first word is תנא."

There were only a few more days until my departure. Every tick of the clock brought it closer. Each minute spent with Papa was precious.

The day dawned. I resolved that I would not cry or break down. Papa, Tante Mirel, Avremal and Moshe Aaron were to escort me to the airport.

The night before I was scheduled to leave I dreamt that Mama, *zatzal,* came to me in a dream.

"Ruchoma," she said softly, "I am with you."

I awoke with a deep feeling of comfort and realized how much I had missed her loving presence during my visit.

As the taxi arrived to take us to the airport, Avremal's seven-year-old daughter, Aidel, was tagging after her father, crying hysterically. She insisted that she, too, accompany Tante Ruchoma.

Though there was no room for her in the taxi, the kind-hearted driver suggested that perhaps she could sit on my lap. Aidel cuddled up to me.

As we drove along, I suddenly said to Papa, "Last night I dreamt that Mama is with me. The dream has come true, as Aidel is the first child named after Mama." Papa agreed.

Tante Mirel was the only one who kept up a lively chatter. Papa hardly spoke. He held my hand in a tight clasp. The loudspeaker ordered all the passengers to congregate in a room right off the airfield.

Tante Mirel kissed me and whispered into my ear, "I will miss you." Avremal and Moshe Aaron wished me *tzeisschem l'sholom* and sent their love to their families.

"Ruchoma," Papa said, "your *mitzva* of *kibbud av* is great. Tell Moshe and your children I expect to see them here very soon."

"Papa, take care of yourself. I will miss you very much." I

feared to say more because I would not be able to fulfill my resolution.

I gave one backward glance and a last wave to Papa and my loved ones, as I was jostled along with the crowd of passengers into the room set aside for us.

Then I broke down. My sobs filled the room, and the passengers stared at me pityingly.

We were ordered to proceed to the plane, which was parked nearby. As I walked slowly towards the plane, sobs still racking my body, I heard Papa call, "Ruchoma, Ruchoma." I turned in the direction of his voice. Papa was standing on the airfield. He had asked for special permission from the authorities to be there.

I ran towards him and threw myself into his arms. My defenses crumbled. "Papa, Papa," I cried. "I cannot leave you."

He held me tightly. "Ruchoma, you will come back to me. Now Moshe and your children need you. You must go home to them." A stewardess had to be sent from the plane to free me from Papa's arms.

As the plane taxied off the runway, I saw Papa from afar; earth and sky blended together and framed him in their midst.

I arrived at Idlewild Airport (now Kennedy Airport) into the loving embrace of my family. Mashi clutched one hand and Yitzchok held on tightly to the other. The look Moshe and Yisroel Meir gave me portrayed how lonesome they had been.

"Moshe, children," I said excitedly, "Eretz Yisroel is the place for us. We must settle there as soon as possible."

"Racoma," Moshe answered gently, "won't you first come home to drink a cup of coffee before we board the next plane for Eretz Yisroel?"

It was fourteen years after I drank that cup of coffee that Moshe and I settled in Eretz Yisroel.

By that time Papa had passed away, and our children were married and could not accompany us.

32

I visit Papa again

As Papa predicted, I visited him again, in 1960, 1963 and 1967. When I made arrangements to visit Papa in the summer of 1963, I looked forward to staying with Nochum Dovid and Chaye Dube, who had settled in Yerusholayim the summer before.

Jet travel had come of age, and flying time was considerably shortened. With Yisroel Meir and Mashi already married, and with Yitzchok studying in an out-of-town yeshiva, it was easier for me to get away.

Two weeks before my departure, my telephone rang. It was my travel agent. "Mrs. Shain, I am very sorry, but the tour scheduled to leave for Israel on Sunday, August 4th, has just been cancelled."

"Have you any other tour leaving the week after Tisha b'Av?" I asked. Since I was teaching, I had to be in class by early September and could not delay my trip.

"I checked that possibility before I called you but find no available space on any other airline for the next few weeks. I have 103 scheduled tours, and this is the only one that had been cancelled. I still don't know the reason for it.

"I do have one seat available on a tour leaving a week earlier, Sunday, July 28th, but you should be aware that it is leaving the night before Tisha b'Av. However, it's scheduled to land in Lod a few hours before the onset of the fast," the agent assured me.

"I am not interested in that tour, Mr. Shneider," I said quickly.

"Well, in that case, I am returning your hundred-dollar deposit. You will receive it in the mail. I hope to serve you some other time."

When I hung up, I attempted to straighten my confused thoughts. I was anxious to visit Papa once again, and now my hopes were shattered. Fortunately, I had written Nochum Dovid not to tell Papa of my intended visit, as I wanted to surprise him.

The agent's voice kept ringing in my ears, "I do have a seat available on a tour leaving the night before Tisha b'Av."

All through my childhood, Papa had impressed upon me the danger of traveling in the Nine Days. "It is not a time of merit for the Jewish nation," Papa always said.

I remembered in the early 1950s an El Al plane flying during the Nine Days had been downed when it strayed into Bulgarian air space. It had crashed with a great loss of life. Some of our closest friends had met their tragic death on that ill-fated plane.

When Moshe came home from the yeshiva, I poured out my woes. He thought for several minutes and then said, "Racoma, I cannot tell you what to do, but you are traveling to observe the great *mitzva* of *kibbud av*. It says in the Talmud, *Pesochim* 8b, *'shluchei mitzva einon nizokin'*—When one goes to do a *mitzva* he is protected from Above."

I recalled a conversation with Papa during a previous trip. "Papa, what does one do when the *soton* tries to get the better of you?" I asked him.

---

soton: Satan

"Ruchoma, you have to understand that the *soton* is a messenger of Hashem. However, once you decide to do a *mitzva*, be firm. Do not allow anyone or anything to stand in your way of fulfilling it. When the *soton* will be sure that he cannot get to first base with you, he will peddle his wares in greener pastures," Papa advised me.

I tossed and turned that entire night. My great desire to see Papa on the one hand, and my ingrained fear of traveling in the Nine Days on the other, kept me in conflict.

Early the next morning, I called my agent. "Mr. Shneider, if you still have that seat available leaving July 28th, I'm interested."

"Hold on for one second, while I check." I held on tightly to the phone.

"Mrs. Shain, you are fortunate. The seat is still open, and I will reschedule you for that flight. In fact, I have not put your deposit in the mail as yet," my agent said cheerily.

I placed the telephone on its cradle and said to the *soton*, "Go peddle your wares in greener pastures."

At the daily *minyon* in our house, Moshe informed Rabbi Shmuel Ehrenfeld, the Mattersdorfer Rav, that I would be leaving very shortly for Eretz Yisroel. He asked Moshe if I could go to visit his nephew, Rabbi Simcha Bunim Klein, who resides in Yerusholayim, and bring personal regards from him. He also asked if I could visit the site that was being planned for a housing unit in Yerusholayim, to be called "Kiryat Mattersdorf." Rabbi Klein would be pleased to show it to me.

Rabbi and Rebbetzin Ehrenfeld and their family lived in our co-op apartment house, two flights below us, and we were close friends.

When I had written Papa that we were moving into a new apartment on the East River Drive, he promptly wrote in return, "Before you consider buying any new furniture, you should first purchase a *sefer Torah* for your new home."

A few months after we moved in, our *sefer Torah* arrived

from Eretz Yisroel. Our made-to-order bookcase with a special *oron* awaited it.

One Monday morning, a terrible snowstorm prevented everyone from going to *shul*. Since it was known that we had a *sefer Torah*, some of our neighbors congregated in our house, including Rabbi Shmuel Ehrenfeld. From that day on we maintained a daily *minyon* for morning prayers, which was greatly appreciated by many of our neighbors, who found it difficult to go to *shul* for fear they might be late for work.

We had the honor of having the Mattersdorfer Rav as one of our steady *mispallelim*. Rabbi Moshe Feinstein, who lived across the street, also honored us by coming to our *minyon* several times during inclement weather.

We were fortunate to have as our next-door neighbors, Rabbi Shmuel Leib and Rebbetzin Malka Svei. Rabbi Svei was a well-known *talmid chochom*. He was a *meshuloch*; however, whenever he was home, he attended our daily *minyon*. (His son, Reb Elya Svei, together with Reb Shmuel Kaminetsky, son of Reb Yaakov Kaminetsky, founded the well-known yeshiva of Philadelphia, where they are *roshei yeshiva*.)

When we followed Papa's advice to buy a *sefer Torah*, we made an excellent investment.

My preparations for the trip were hectic, as I was leaving a week earlier than anticipated. Moshe and our children came to see me off. The good-byes were short, as I was tense.

I boarded the plane and found my seat. I could not wait for the flight to be over. My agent had ordered kosher meals, but neglected to specify dairy ones, which I ate exclusively during the Nine Days. I was served meat meals, which I returned without bothering to open them. In any case, I had little appetite for food.

I had hoped to arrive in Yerusholayim before the fast, but

....
oron: ark / **mispallelim**: members of a minyon

that was not to be. The plane was delayed in London, and then again in Paris, so that by the time we landed in Lod Airport, the stars were twinkling in the deep blue sky.

There was no one to greet me at Lod Airport, as I had not written to Nochum Dovid of my changed schedule. I was hungry, tired, and depressed. Tisha b'Av cast a pall of sadness over me.

I climbed into a taxi going to Yerusholayim and gave the driver Nochum Dovid's address. It was after 10 PM when the taxi parked in front of his house. The driver piled my baggage on the sidewalk and sped off. The street was deserted.

I climbed the flight of stairs and knocked softly at Nochum Dovid's door. He opened the door warily, wondering who could be coming to his home on this night.

He cried out, "Chaye Dube, Racoma is here!" Chaye Dube, who had already gone to bed, rushed out to greet me. Nochum Dovid called out, "No greeting, no kissing—it is Tisha b'Av." Chaye Dube and I jumped apart.

Nochum Dovid brought up my luggage. I sat on a low stool relating to them all the events that led up to my arrival a week earlier than expected. I mentioned to Nochum Dovid that I had fasted practically the entire day. "If you feel very weak tomorrow afternoon, then you can eat something," he said.

I weathered the two-day fast. Being in Yerusholayim, where the destruction of the Holy Temple had occurred, made me forget my hunger pangs. We decided not to tell Papa of my arrival until after the fast. Right after we broke the fast, we hurried to Papa's house. Gone was my depression, and, instead, a feeling of joyous anticipation enveloped me.

Nochum Dovid and Chaye Dube walked into Papa's dining room, where he was drinking a cup of coffee. I waited impatiently on the porch, peering through the window.

"Papa, you have a special guest," Nochum Dovid said with deep emotion. I could not wait any longer. I rushed through the door and stopped just for a moment, as Papa caught sight of me. His eyes lit up. He grasped both my hands, "Ruchoma, is it really you?" Over and over again he repeated the question, not letting go of me. Tante Mirel's welcome was also a happy, warm one.

Papa had not changed physically since I had last seen him three years earlier. His face was unlined, his eyes bright, but I noticed that his memory was poor. "Tell me about Moshe, your children and grandchildren," he asked. I told him about each and every one. A short while later he repeated the same request having forgotten that he had already asked me.

My joy at seeing Papa once more was boundless. We stayed with him late into the night, until he started to doze in his armchair. I gently freed my hand from his, and we tiptoed out of his house.

The first Shabbos after my arrival was "Shabbos *Nachamu.*" As I listened to *parshas Vo'eschanon,* in which the Ten Commandments were read, I was elated when the Fifth Commandment was read: "Honor thy father and thy mother, as the Lord thy God commanded thee; that thy days may be prolonged, and that it may go well with thee in the *land* which the Lord thy God giveth thee."

I related my experience to Papa, and how my visit to him had almost been postponed. "Ruchoma, for your *mitzva* of *kibbud av* the Boss wants you to receive the blessing that you will have long years living in Eretz Yisroel. That is why your scheduled trip was cancelled. Had you arrived one week later, you would have come for *parshas Eikev.* No wonder the *soton* was doing his utmost to prevent your coming. *Boruch Hashem* that you came."

At my first opportunity, I contacted Rabbi Klein, as Rabbi Ehrenfeld had requested. He was pleased with the personal regards I brought him from the entire family. I then said, "The *rav* wants me to see the place where you intend to build your new *kirya.*" Rabbi Klein made an appointment for the following week.

He came in a taxi, and my nephew, Avremal, accompanied us. We rode towards the outskirts of the city, and parked on a slope overlooking a stony, dusty incline. The driver explained that his taxi could go no further.

We climbed down over the stones and rubble until we came to a cleared area. Rabbi Klein stopped and pointed, "This is where Kiryat Mattersdorf will be built," he said optimistically. I was skeptical. It did not seem possible for any building, let alone a complete village, to be erected on this mountainous area.

"When do you intend to commence building?" I asked him.

"As soon as our architect finishes drawing up the plans and we get enough people interested in purchasing apartments," he answered.

"What is that over there?" I pointed to some dwellings far-off on the horizon.

"Oh, that is the city of Ramallah, an Arab city belonging to Jordan." He noticed my shocked look, and hurried to explain, "There is absolutely no danger from the Arabs. We are separated from them by an area of at least eight kilometers of no-man's-land."

On the spur of the moment I blurted out, "Rabbi Klein, when you are ready to accept applications, register us first for an apartment."

Rabbi Klein wrote down the pertinent information and asked, "What kind of an apartment do you prefer? How many rooms?"

"A three-room apartment—sunny, not too high, not too low—in the first building," I answered, thinking of it only as a dream.

I then asked Avremal to snap my picture, and I snapped a picture of Rabbi Klein and Avremal to bring back to the Mattersdorfer Rav.

When I told Papa about the apartment "I practically bought," he smiled broadly. "You see, Ruchoma, the *brocho* is already in the making."

When the photos were processed, I wrote on the reverse

Pictures taken when Rabbi Klein took Avremal and me to the site of the Mattersdorf Village—when the whole thing was only a dream. Today it is a well-populated religious neighborhood in Yerusholayim.

side, "Mattersdorf Village, entrance to our home, August, 1963."

It should be noted that several months after I returned from my visit to Papa, I received a call from Rabbi Akiva Ehrenfeld, the Mattersdorfer Rav's oldest son. "Rebbetzin Shain, I have good news for you. I just received word from Rabbi Klein that applications are being accepted, and you are the first on the list to purchase an apartment."

"Rabbi Ehrenfeld, when I asked Rabbi Klein to register me for an apartment, I did it on impulse. However, I will discuss it with my husband and call you back," I said.

"We are very interested in having people like you and Rabbi Shain living in our *kirya*. I will give you very easy terms," Rabbi Ehrenfeld said.

I waited impatiently for Moshe to return from the *yeshiva*. "Moshe, Rabbi Akiva Ehrenfeld called; applications are being accepted; we are first on the list for an apartment; he will give us easy terms; let's buy an apartment even if you feel we cannot settle now or leave the children; it pays to have an apartment in Yerusholayim," I ended breathlessly.

Moshe caught my exuberance and said, "Racoma, go ahead . . ."

I did not wait for him to finish his sentence. I rushed to the phone. "Rabbi Ehrenfeld," I exclaimed, "we are interested in purchasing an apartment. I would like to hear all the details as soon as possible."

"I will be up to see you shortly." He sounded very pleased.

I dialed Esther and Bessie and told them about our decision to buy an apartment. They both agreed that if we bought one, they would also.

Reb Chaim Scheinberg was a little dismayed when he heard that Bessie wanted to buy an apartment in Yerusholayim. He was Rosh Yeshiva of Yeshiva Torah Ore which he had established in Bensonhurst, Brooklyn, and he had many *talmidim* to whom he felt a deep commitment. He was afraid that Bessie would be carried away by my impetus and enthusiasm about wanting to live in Yerusholayim.

With our encouragement, and with Rabbi Ehrenfeld helping to finance part of his fare, he flew to Eretz Yisroel to "scrutinize the land." When he returned, he was convinced that Yerusholayim was the place for his family and the *yeshiva.*

On May 9, 1965, as soon as the first apartments of Kiryat Mattersdorf were ready for occupancy, Reb Chaim and Bessie, their son-in-law and daughter—Reb Chaim Dov and Fruma Rochel Altusky—and their family, their son and daughter-in-law—Reb Simcha, Rochel and their family—with five other families and over twenty *talmidim*, arrived in Yerusholayim.

Reb Chaim re-established his *yeshiva,* Yeshiva Torah Ore, in Kiryat Mattersdorf, where it has developed into a well-known *yeshiva* with almost two hundred *talmidim* and a large *kollel.*

Rabbi Chaim Scheinberg is also the *dayon* of Kiryat Mattersdorf.

Though we were the first to purchase an apartment in

*My brother-in-law,
Rabbi Chaim Pinchas
Scheinberg*

Kiryat Mattersdorf, it was not until July, 1968, that Moshe and I settled in our three-room apartment, in the first building. (My sister Esther settled in Yerusholayim at the same time we did.)

The *brocho* that I received when I visited Papa in 1963 was finally fulfilled.

Shmuel Yitzchok Stern, Esther's son, increased the number of grandchildren who settled in Yerusholayim when he arrived on Lag b'Omer, 1958. He lived with Papa until he married, and was greatly influenced by his teachings. He told me the following incidents:

"Zeidy noticed that I was very fussy about my food. One day, he said to me, 'Shmuel Yitzchok, I want to tell you a story that happened to me when I was about seven years old, still living in Slutsk, Russia.

" 'My father came home one afternoon very excited with the news that the Slutsker Rav, the Ridbaz, would visit us. He asked my mother to prepare special *kibbud* for such an important and respected guest.

" 'My mother sent me to the grocery store and told me to buy several pieces of lump sugar. We were poor, and until that day I had not seen or tasted sugar.

" 'When our honored guest arrived, my mother served a large bowl of fruit and a glass of hot tea. After the *rav* finished drinking his tea, my mother placed the lump sugar in a plate, and served it as an added delicacy.' "

"Zeidy ended his story with the words, 'I never had a choice of food and ate everything my mother placed on my plate. This is what gave me strength to this very day.' "

"Zeidy once said to me, 'I owe my long life and whatever I did for *klal Yisroel* to the *brocho* the Slutsker Rav gave me when I was a young boy.

" 'When he was leaving Slutsk to settle in Eretz Yisroel, my parents went to his house to say good-bye and took me with them.

" 'My father asked the *rav* to give me a *brocho*. He blessed me with long years and added that I would accomplish much for *klal Yisroel.*' "

Shmuel Yitzchok befriended Asa Wittow, a young man from Denver, Colorado. He had come to Israel in September 1960, and studied in Chevron Yeshiva in Yerusholayim.

Shmuel Yitzchok, who had recently married, invited Asa to eat his daily dinners in his home. He also advised Asa to have Papa check his *tefillin*.

Asa found his way to Papa's Meah She'arim store, where he was greeted with a friendly, "*Sholom aleichem.*"

"What language do you speak?" Papa asked him.

In answer to Asa's "I speak English," Papa said to him, "Good, I speak your language. Come to me for Shabbos."

Asa was surprised to find that several of the beggars who came daily to Chevron Yeshiva for donations were Papa's *orchim*. But what amazed him was that Papa treated all those seated around the large table equally: *rabbonim*, *yeshiva bochurim*, Ashkenazim, Sephardim, young and old.

The meal was sparse by the standard Asa was used to, but the warmth that emanated from the Shabbos table made up for any lack of food.

Asa discovered during Shabbos that Papa not only spoke his language but also the language of every Jew.

Papa's foot was red and painful. Dr. Cohen was summoned. "Reb Yaakov Yosef, you have a *roiz* (erysipelas, an acute infection of the skin). Under no circumstances are you allowed to get off the bed." Knowing Papa well, Dr. Cohen stressed this order sternly. He prescribed a sulfa drug.

As he left, the doctor called me aside. "Your father's bones are brittle. He must be careful, because there is danger of fracturing his leg."

Before *mincha*, Nochum Dovid and Chaye Dube came to visit Papa. "I am worried that Papa will want to go to *shul*," I told them anxiously.

"Hide his shoes," they advised me.

A short time later, there was roar from the bedroom. "Where are my shoes?" Papa's tone of voice left no doubt in my mind as to his intentions. I hurried into the room.

"Papa, the doctor warned me that you will be taking a great risk of breaking your leg if you move from the bed. Please, listen to his advice," I begged.

"Ruchoma, give me my shoes this minute." Papa's fierce look did not brook any interference. I retrieved his shoes from their hiding place, put them on him and laced them. Papa stood up shakily. I helped him with his *kapote*.

I walked him to the Zichron Moshe *shul* and sat in the courtyard waiting until Papa finished his *mincha* and *mairiv* prayers.

We walked home slowly, with Papa leaning on my arm. "I know Ruchoma, that you worry about me," Papa said gently, "but I have my *cheshbonos* and the Boss helps me."

The next morning when I entered Papa's house, Tante Mirel complained, "Your father went to *shul*. I cannot do anything with him. He does not listen."

Dr. Cohen hurried in and walked straight into the bedroom. He was surprised not to find Papa in bed and looked at me questioningly. "Dr. Cohen," I said hesitantly, "my father went to *shul.*"

He bristled, threw up his hands, and burst out the door. Papa recovered, though it took several weeks.

I pleaded with Papa to be examined by the doctor before I left. Papa pooh-poohed the idea. Finally, I delivered the clincher. "Papa, I left Moshe in the States in order to be with you. All I ask from you is to do me the favor of going to the doctor." Papa acquiesced.

We went to Dr. Cohen. I was sure he would be cross with Papa for not following his instructions, but he greeted him with a smile.

"How do you feel, Reb Yaakov Yosef?" he asked courteously.

"Like a Jew in Yerusholayim," Papa answered staunchly.

"Dr. Cohen," I tattled, "my father does not rest enough, never spares himself, keeps running all the time. He forgets that he is not a young man anymore.

"*Tochter*," he said, "as long as your father keeps running, you have nothing to worry about. When he stops running, then your worries will start."

We left the doctor's office with a smug look on Papa's face. As we neared the house, Papa ran up the two flights of stairs to his porch and started to chin on a horizontal bar. I was aghast as I hurried after him. "Papa, please stop this immediately. You can hurt yourself." Papa continued. "Papa, the neighbors

....
cheshbonos: considerations

will see you. I am afraid of an *ayin hora*." Papa let go. "How is that for an old man?" he asked.

Watching him then, I was vividly reminded of my visit three years earlier, when I spent Purim with him. It was my present for his eightieth birthday.

After taking care of the scores of *mishlo'ach monos*, Papa said to me, "Ruchoma, let's go, or we shall miss the Purim parade."

We ran out of the house and down the stairs. I could hardly keep up with Papa. As we came to a crossing, he grabbed my hand, and said smilingly, "Ruchoma, though you are a *bobie*, you are still my baby."

My childhood returned as we both hurried towards the parade.

We stood among the large crowd observing the variety of colorful costumes. There was a display of the usual Hamans, Mordechais, Esthers, and clowns, large and small.

Each time some unusal costume appeared, Papa jumped up and down with glee, pointing his finger at the sight.

Papa's excitement was contagious. "Look, Ruchoma, just look at that costume." A man dressed like a bear lumbered by. Papa's eye caught sight of a man dressed like George Washington.

Though Papa was chronologically eighty years old, he was young and vibrant in body and spirit. I understood why he was known as "the young old man of Yerusholayim."

When Bessie returned from her visit with Papa, she mentioned to me that she had noticed that when Papa returned from *shul* many cats followed him, waiting to be fed.

I decided to be on hand one morning early enough to witness this phenomenon.

I heard Papa's footsteps. There was a chorus of meowing

....

ayin hora: evil eye

cats of every size and description following him, with some brushing against his trousers.

He placed several saucers on the floor of the courtyard, filled them with milk, added pieces of *challa*, and made them into a mush. As the cats were busily lapping up their food, Papa climbed the steps to his house to eat his breakfast.

I came into Papa's store to find him seated in the far corner, crying. "What happened, Papa?" I called out in alarm.

"I need something from the Boss," he answered simply.

"Does the Boss always give you what you ask for?" I questioned tremulously.

"Of course," Papa said. "Who else should provide me with my needs if not the Boss?"

"Papa, if the Boss gives you all your necessities, why don't you ask Him to improve your memory?" I asked.

"Ruchoma, I only ask the Boss for things that are coming to me. At my age of eighty-three, it is normal to have a poor memory."

One early morning Nochum Dovid came into Papa's store. Papa mentioned to him that his *maiser* was much overdrawn. His credit side showed that the Boss owed him 2400 pounds. He needed money desperately to repay certain debts he had incurred in giving large amounts to charity.

"Papa," Nochum Dovid suggested, "just cry to the Boss. He always answers you."

That afternoon, while Nochum Dovid was again in Papa's store, a young man hurried in. "Are you Reb Yaakov Yosef Herman?" he asked Papa. When Papa answered in the affirmative, he said, "You were recommended as a person from whom I can purchase a kosher *sefer Torah*. I am leaving for London tonight and wish to buy one."

Nochum Dovid helped Papa carry over a few *sifrei Torah* to show the young man. He checked several and then asked Papa,

Papa outside his store in the Meah She'arim section of the city: At the right, with myself behind him. At the left, with my sister Bessie, Tante Mirel, and her son Reb Avrohom Weiner.

"How much does this one cost?" He pointed to the first one Papa had shown him.

"The price is 2400 pounds," Papa said. The young man did not bargain. He took out his wallet and counted out the exact amount.

When he left the store, Papa said, "The Boss answered me quickly. *Boruch Hashem,* I will be able to repay my debts."

A short while after Nochum Dovid settled in Yerusholayim, he hurried into Bank Leumi just before closing time. He filled out a withdrawal slip for a large amount of money, and handed it to the teller.

"Can I have your passport, please?" the teller asked him. Nochum Dovid did not have it with him. "I'm sorry, but I cannot complete this transaction without proper identification," the teller firmly stated.

"I would like to see the bank manager," Nochom Dovid told the teller. He buzzed, and a tall, stately man approached.

"May I help you?" he asked Nochum Dovid courteously.

"I must withdraw this sum of money from my account, as I need it today." He showed the manager his withdrawal slip. "However, your teller refuses, as he demands identification. By the time I go home and return with my passport, the bank will be closed."

"What is your name?" the manager asked.

"Nochum Dovid Herman," he answered.

"Are you in any way related to Jacob J. Herman?" he inquired further.

"He is my father," Nochum Dovid said.

"Come into my office. I wish to tell you of an experience I had with your father.

"Many years ago, when Britain still had the Mandate over Palestine, I was employed as a customs officer for the English government. One day, a *sefer Torah* arrived for your father. He came to claim it, and asked if there was any duty to be paid. I told him that since it was a religious object, he could avoid paying any tax.

"Mr. Herman then asked me, 'Is it a hundred percent legal?'

"I told him that if he wanted to keep precisely to the letter of the law, the duty should be paid. Your father paid the entire tax, which amounted to a very large sum."

The bank manager ended his story saying, "Being the son of Jacob J. Herman is sufficient identification for me."

He placed his signature on the withdrawal slip, allowing the teller to give Nochum Dovid the full amount shown there.

Avremal came running to Papa terribly agitated. His wife, Chaya, was giving birth and complications had set in. He asked Papa to pray for her.

Papa was kneading the *challa* for the *orchim*. "I will give Chaya the merit of this *mitzva*, so her birth should be normal," Papa said.

A few hours later, Avremal happily announced that Chaya

had given birth to a healthy son, and all had gone well.

Gershon, Avremal's son, met Papa carrying a large sack of potatoes from the Machaneh Yehuda market for the *orchim*.

"Let me carry it, Zeidy," Gershon pleaded.

"Oh no, I don't want to give away my *mitzva* of *hachnosas orchim*," Papa said, as he continued walking down the street with his heavy burden.

Gershon was close to Papa and visited him often. Once Papa said to him, "You are a young boy with no worries. You should occupy your mind with thoughts on how to give Hashem *nachas* from you.

"When I was a rich man and used to go to my fur shop, I did not think about business until I turned the corner where my store was located. Before that my mind was solely occupied with what I could do for the Boss."

While sitting in Papa's store, I discussed a letter he had written two years previously, in August, 1961. Since he wrote it in Yiddish, I have translated the pertinent part into English:

Dearest Children,

I heard the decision of the President of the United States [John F. Kennedy, during the Cuban missile crisis], and it disturbed me greatly. I realize how tense the situation is.

I cannot tell you what to do, but I have read that in the year 5750 (1989-1990) we should prepare for "Shabbos." We have twenty-eight years. In this short period of time unusual occurrences will come to pass.

Happy will be those who will be living at that time in Yerusholayim, the Holy City. We have no alternative but to pray that our Father in Heaven should grant you the privilege to come to Yerusholayim.

To explain this letter Papa said, "It is *Moshiach*'s times.

The Prophet Yoel states clearly (Joel 3:5): 'And it shall come to pass, that whosoever shall call on the name of Hashem shall be delivered; for on Mount Zion and in Jerusalem shall be deliverance as Hashem hath said, and in the remnant whom Hashem shall call.'

"Also, it states in Obadia, verse 17: 'But upon Mount Zion shall be deliverance.'"

Though Papa did not customarily wear a *shtreimel* nor use a walking cane, he bought both items in preparation so that when *Moshiach* came he would be ready to greet him in a fitting, respectful manner.

Once, after Papa had been in his Torah room for a long time, he came out looking tired and strained, and I asked him, "Papa, what were you doing in there for such a long time?"

"Ruchoma," he said, "I try with all my might to extract one *pure* tear to give to the Boss."

Each time I had to leave Papa, it became more difficult. This time Papa, Tante Mirel, Nochum Dovid and Chaye Dube accompanied me to Lod Airport.

I held on to Papa's hand, while we listened to small talk from the others. Papa hardly spoke, until it was time for me to board the plane. Then he said, "May you have the *zechus* to return with Moshe and your children and settle in Yerusholayim." To which I answered a resounding, "Amen!"

I looked back and waved to my loved ones. But the thought that clamored in my heart was: "Will I see Papa again?"

---

shtreimel: hasidic fur hat

33

At the end of May, 1967, I received a call from Eretz Yisroel. Bessie's voice sounded troubled. "Racoma, Papa is very weak. It would be advisable if you, Moshe, and Esther could come this summer."

"I will make arrangements as soon as possible," I assured her.

When I told Moshe about Bessie's call and that Papa was failing, his response was quick in coming. "I will be free from *yeshiva* at the end of June. You can make arrangements for both of us." Esther's reply was also positive. My travel agent booked us for a flight leaving June 28th.

The Six Day War broke out, and our flight was cancelled. We were very upset. My agent promised to get us other reservations on the first flight available. Finally, I received word that he had rescheduled us for July 9th.

I telegraphed Bessie the date of arrival, the airline and flight number. We arrived at Lod Airport to find no one there to greet us. We were panicky. Our hearts were heavy as we traveled to Yerusholayim.

As soon as the taxi parked in front of Bessie's building, I ran up the five flights of stairs to her apartment, leaving Moshe and Esther to pay the driver and take care of our luggage.

I knocked loudly on the door. Reb Chaim opened it with a look of surprise. I gave him no chance to speak. "How is Papa? Why was there no one at the airport, not even one of Esther's children?" My questions tumbled out.

"We had no word of your arrival," Chaim explained. (Since the Six Day War, mail was irregular, and my telegram had not been delivered.) "Papa is very weak. Bessie is with him now."

I sighed with relief. At least nothing had happened to Papa.

I phoned Nochum Dovid, and Chaye Dube answered. "*Sholom aleichem,*" I said, "Moshe, Esther, and I just arrived." I heard her gasp, and then call loudly, "Nochum Dovid, Bessie, they are here." There was a babble of excited voices.

"We are coming over right away," I did not wait to hear any more. We called a taxi, and in ten minutes we were at Papa's side.

Papa had been living with Nochum Dovid and Chaye Dube for the past three-and-a-half-years. Since Tante Mirel had become ill and could not attend him and look after the house adequately, it was decided that she would live with her daughter, Dvora, in Bnei Brak, and Papa with Nochum Dovid.

Papa was seated in an armchair with his feet raised. He had aged considerably since my last visit four years earlier. However, Nochum Dovid and Chaye Dube gave him excellent care, which was reflected in his immaculate dress. His white beard was combed and framed his face.

I recalled Dr. Cohen's remark, when Papa had visited his office at my insistence in 1963. "Yes," I thought sadly, "Papa has stopped running."

I ran over to him and grasped his thin hand. He squeezed my hand gently. "Papa, we're here. Moshe, Esther, and I came

Papa in tallis *and* tefillin, *standing with Nochum Dovid on the porch of Nochum Dovid's apartment.*

from America to visit you. Moshe has never been to Eretz Yisroel before."

His eyes brightened and I saw recognition, but he uttered no word. My tears fell silently and wet our hands.

Nochum Dovid explained, "Since Papa had the mild stroke, he does not talk. We are not sure if he cannot, or does not wish to, but he understands everything."

We stayed in an apartment in Kiryat Mattersdorf, but spent most of our time with Papa.

SIDE LIGHTS

(These are events that I learned about after my arrival in Yerusholayim in 1967:)

Papa declined to give anyone *brochos*, though he was asked countless times. However, whenever it meant helping a *talmid* of his, the picture changed.

Reb Shepsul Minsky was Papa's *talmid*. He had a partnership with Reb Itzie Meyer Lichtenstein in real estate. When business fell into dire financial difficulties, Reb Itzie Meyer went to the Gerrer Rebbe to ask for a *brocho*. The *rebbe* thought very highly of Papa and suggested that he go to Reb Yaakov Yosef Herman and ask for a *brocho*.

Since Nochum Dovid lives close to the Gerrer *beis medrash*, Reb Itzie Meyer came to Nochum Dovid and presented his request, telling him of the Gerrer Rebbe's advice.

Nochum Dovid replied, "Wait a few minutes, and I will ask my father." Papa was sitting on the porch.

"Papa, Reb Itzie Meyer the partner of your *talmid*, Shepsul Minsky, is here. Their business is failing, and he came for a *brocho*."

The word *"talmid"* galvanized Papa. When Reb Itzie Meyer came over, he blessed him and Reb Shepsul with good *parnoso*, starting that very day.

Reb Itzie Meyer left Nochum Dovid's house with renewed hope. He walked down the street and stopped in front of a store that displayed various signs about available apartments. As he stood there, a man approached Reb Itzie Meyer and asked if he knew of an apartment for sale.

That same day business picked up, as Papa had blessed him.

In the late winter of 1966, Nochum Dovid was aroused from sleep one night when he heard Papa moving about in his room. He entered Papa's bedroom and found him very agitated.

"What is troubling you? Why aren't you sleeping, Papa?" he asked anxiously.

"You will not be able to give me a haircut this morning, as I have become an *ovel*."

Nochum Dovid was very perturbed and questioned Papa, "Why are you an *ovel*?"

But Papa refused to divulge any further information. Understandably, during the remainder of the night, both Nochum Dovid and Chaye Dube could not sleep from worry over Papa's statement.

Early in the morning, Avremal knocked loudly at their

....
ovel: mourner

door with the news that Tante Mirel had passed away that night.

Though all the grandchildren and great-grandchildren were very devoted to Papa, Avremal's son, Gershon, was the one most capable of helping to take care of Papa's physical needs. He came daily to do this great *mitzva*.

Gershon told me that Papa said to him, "I once saw *chillul Shabbos* in Yerusholayim on my way to a *bris*, when a car rode by.

"I had to fast several extra days before I could return to my former spiritual level."

Papa did not recite "The Thirteen Principles of Faith" after the morning prayers. He explained: "Most people say '*ani maamin*,' which takes about five minutes, and then close the *siddur*. I think of the Boss all day."

And indeed he did. During his lifetime, Papa made a *siyum* on *shas* five times, on *mishnayos* fifteen times, and several times on *Chayei Odom* and *Ein Yaakov*.

When the Six Day War broke out, all the tenants from Nochum Dovid's building remained in the shelter. Papa could not be moved as he was very weak and needed special attention.

Nochum Dovid was very apprehensive because the Schneller military base, situated very close to his home, could be a likely target for bombing.

Papa, who was still able to talk then, said to them, "Do not worry. Your house is one of *chesed* and *tzedoko*, and no harm will befall it."

Nochum Dovid asked Papa, "If our home is so safe, should I call some of our friends to stay with us?"

"I do not know the merits of your friends, so I would not advise you to invite them," Papa answered.

---

siyum: celebration made upon completion of *shas* (Talmud)

He then fell asleep for a twenty-four-hour period. When he awoke, Papa exclaimed, *"Boruch Hashem, the war is over!"* Sure enough, the bombing and shooting had ceased.

Rabbi Nesanel Quinn, who was principal of Mesivta Torah Vodaas, came to visit his old mother in Yerusholayim. He heard that I was writing a book about Papa and volunteered the following incidents, which happened when Papa was still living in the United States.

When I asked Rabbi Quinn, "How did you know my father?" he answered, "Who did not know Reb Yaakov Yosef Herman?"

In 1937, Papa mailed letters to rabbis, *roshei yeshivos*, and *baale batim* asking them to congregate in the Tiferes Yerusholayim *shul*, to discuss a vital religious issue.

Rabbi Quinn and several others came, among them Rabbi Boruch Kaplan and Papa's old friend, Mr. Peretz Sheinerman.

Papa told them that there was supervision on the *kashrus* of meat, because *mashgichim* earn their livelihood that way. However, there was no true supervision of *tefillin, mezuzos,* and *tzitzis.*

Papa formed a committee to do something about this urgent problem.

Rabbi Quinn, who was then teaching at the Rabbi Jacob Joseph School, came to the house to write up the minutes of the meeting, and the various decisions that were adopted.

Papa excused himself for a few minutes. A short while later, Rabbi Quinn heard Papa running up the steps. He hurried in with a new notebook for writing the minutes. When Rabbi Quinn asked Papa, "Reb Yaakov Yosef, why did you not ask me to buy the notebook? I am younger than you are," Papa quoted from *Kiddushin* 41a: מצוה בו יותר מבשלוחו "It is more worthy to do a *mitzva* yourself than through a messenger." To Rabbi Quinn's second question, "Why did you have to run up the stairs?" Papa quoted *Brochos* 6b: לעולם ירוץ אדם לדבר מצוה "Always run to do a *mitzva.*"

Papa placed an ad in the *Jewish Morning Journal* inviting anyone interested in Torah courses free of charge to come to the Beis Medrash Hagodol on Norfolk Street at 8 PM.

Papa waited, expecting many people to answer his request. The advertisement brought no one at all. Papa advertised again, without any results. He did not give up, and once more placed the same ad.

This time, one teenager, wearing a lumber jacket, showed up.

Rabbi Quinn believes this young man became one of Papa's *talmidim*, and is now a *tzaddik nistar*.

In 1939, a few days before Papa left to settle in Eretz Yisroel, Rabbi Quinn came to say good-bye. Papa had just broken his fast after a long, hot, humid day spent packing his many crates of *seforim* and other belongings.

The telephone rang. It was a police officer calling from an uptown precinct. The officer informed Papa that they were detaining a young man, on a second offense, who had given Papa's name as the one who would bail him out. The bail was set at $100.

Papa telephoned his friend Mr. Brody and asked if he would lend him $100 immediately. When Mr. Brody agreed, Papa arranged to meet him at a specified place in a short while.

As Papa hurried out the door without finishing his meal, Rabbi Quinn asked him, "Why are you going to such trouble to bail out a person you might not even know and who is of such questionable character?"

Papa answered, "This young man is booked on a second offense. If the judge becomes aware that there is no one to help him, the judgment might be harsher."

Papa once told Rabbi Quinn that when a good idea enters

....
nistar: hidden

his mind, it surely stems from the Boss, so he immediately puts it into practice.

When Papa left for Eretz Yisroel, Rabbi Quinn heard Rabbi Shraga Faivel Mendlowitz, *zatzal*, the founder of Mesivta Torah Vodaas, comment, "There is no one to replace Reb Yaakov Yosef in America."

Added note:

Many years later, we were blessed to gain as our daughter-in-law Yehudis Greenbaum, a granddaughter of Rabbi Mendlowitz.

In the issues dated Elul 5726 and Tishrei-Cheshvon 5727 (September and October 1966), the Hebrew monthly *Kol Hashabbath*, printed in Yerusholayim, a two-part article about Papa appeared. It was written by R. M. Rudnitzky, a *talmid* of his. I have translated the following highlights from these articles:

"Happy is the man who feareth Hashem and greatly delights in His commandments" (Psalm 112):

(Mr. Rudnitzky describes the Zichron Moshe *shul*, where *minyonim* are continuous from early dawn until late into the night:)

In every room and corridor of this large *shul*, and even overflowing into the street, hundreds of men come daily to pray. There are also groups of men constantly studying varied religious subjects: *Ein Yaakov, mishnayos, Shulchan Oruch, Gemora*, and a group reciting *tehillim*.

The spiritual leader of the Zichron Moshe *shul* was an old American rabbi, a beloved and interesting Jew, Harav Yaakov Yosef Herman, a godly person. Though he was an old man, he was erect in bearing, handsome of face, immaculately dressed, with a warm smile which endeared him to all. He was a personality—none could compare to him.

My *rebbe,* about whom miracles and wonders are told, guided, influenced and comforted me during the five years I was privileged to have been his *talmid.*

Just as cool waters calm the body, he calmed the soul of many a person who struggled between the *yeitzer hora* and *yeitzer hatov,* the evil and good impulses, and guided them along the stream of Torah.

I would come home from work, eat something, rest for a short while, and then rush to the Zichron Moshe *shul* to be near my *rebbe,* where I joined his *shiurim.* His *shiurim* were different from any others I have ever heard. He never kept only to the subject under discussion, but delved into many other relevant aspects and answered each of our questions patiently. We were spellbound and never felt that time was passing.

When we finished a *masechta,* he prepared a lavish *siyum* and invited many *rabbonim* and poor people. He always insisted on paying for it all.

Once my *rebbe* was told that one of the congregants had many problems of *sholom bayis.* My *rebbe* said, "The main source of trouble in a household comes from *mezuzos* that are not kosher."

He advised the man to check all his *mezuzos.* When the man found some were *posul,* my *rebbe* told him to buy *mezuzos* that are *mehuder* and of a large size. He obeyed, and within a few days, he told my *rebbe* that peace had returned once more to his home. . . .

Once, just before I was ready to make *havdolo,* the top of my wine bottle broke. I was afraid to use the wine because some slivers of glass might have fallen into the bottle. I asked my *rebbe* if it would be permissible to use some other beverage for *havdolo.* He said that I could use a different beverage, but that it is preferable to use wine.

---

masechta: tractate / *sholom bayis*: marital harmony

He suggested that I accompany him to his house, and he would give me a bottle of his own homemade brand. I never tasted such delicious wine. I was told that my *rebbe* makes his own because he is very scrupulous about the *kashrus* of his wine, since it is intended for religious purposes. . . .

I once had a dream and asked my *rebbe* if he could interpret it. He said that he would try, with Hashem's help. I told him that I dreamt I was passing his house with *tefillin* on my head. A broad smile spread over his face, and he said to me, "Come to the *beis medrash*, and I will show you what your dream means." He opened the *gemora Brochos* and read from the chapter *Haroeh* the words of the *tana* Reb Eliezer: "Whoever wears *tefillin* on his head during a dream can expect great things." My *rebbe* added, "Follow in the path of Hashem, and you will have *hatzlocho* in everything you undertake.". . .

I was hurrying to the *beis medrash* one *erev* Simchas Torah, when my *rebbe* met me and invited me to come to his house for *hakofos*. I did not wish to refuse him, but felt a sense of disappointment that I would miss the *hakofos* in the big *shul*. However, as I watched my *rebbe*, dancing with the *sefer Torah*, I was elevated to such a high spiritual degree that it became an experience I shall never forget. . . .

When my *rebbe* lived in America, there was a period when he was extremely wealthy. However, he himself lived frugally, giving much of his income to charity. During the Depression, he lost a great amount of money. His wife, who was a great *tzidkonis*, was asked about her feelings at that time. She answered, "There is no difference in my way of living. When my husband was rich, he gave me ten dollars a week for my household expenses, and I receive the same amount now.". . .

The well-known Irving Trust Company, granted a moratorium to its debtors during the Depression. My *rebbe* also received this privilege. As soon as his financial circumstances improved, he sent his son to the bank director with money for repayment of the debt. The director refused to accept the money and came personally to my *rebbe*'s house to inform him that he had no intention of having this debt repaid. However, my *rebbe* insisted. The director noted that he had never met a man of my *rebbe*'s high moral caliber and honesty in business dealings. He would trust him with millions of dollars. . . .

My *rebbe* once had a trial in court with another businessman. The judge stipulated that my *rebbe* must swear to the facts. My *rebbe* said that he would never swear even for the absolute truth. He lost the case and with it a very large sum of money. . . .

My *rebbe* now lives with his son, as he is weak and ill. When I visited him recently, he came into the corridor and with his pleasant smile and outstretched hands, welcomed me, and asked, "How are you, my *talmid*?"

On the sixteenth of Tammuz, Papa's condition worsened. We called Dr. Halberstat, the lung specialist. He came immediately, took one look at Papa, and said, "My *rebbe*."

His examination was thorough. He motioned for us to come into the dining room. "Your father's condition is serious. He has developed pneumonia. I am prescribing penicillin injections. Do not discuss anything in front of him. He is aware of what is going on."

The doctor stepped back once again into Papa's bedroom, took his hand and said, "Have a *refua shleima*, Rebbe."

Nochum Dovid and Moshe hurried to contact the male nurse to administer the injection. From there, they would go to *shul* to *daven mincha* and *mairiv*. Esther, Bessie, and I decided to return to Kiryat Mattersdorf to prepare the evening meal, since the next day was the fast of Shiva Osor b'Tammuz. We intended to return later in the evening to be with Papa.

As I walked to the door with them, on a sudden impulse I

said, "I will stay with Papa a little longer; I will be over soon."

The doctor had advised us to give Papa as much fluid as possible. Chaye Dube came in from the kitchen with a cool glass of lemonade. I lifted Papa's head, and she spooned the liquid into his mouth. He drank it thirstily.

I sat near Papa holding his hand, quietly saying *tehillim*. Night was approaching. I looked at Papa. His breathing was lighter. His face relaxed.

"Chaye Dube," I called to her in the kitchen, "Papa seems better. The lemonade must have revived him," I said with relief. Every few minutes I gazed at Papa. His chest was not heaving, and his breathing was shallow. His hand became scorchingly hot, as he clutched my hand tightly. Then like a child falling into a deep sleep, his breathing slowly stopped.

I could not move or call out. I was in a trance.

The door opened and the male nurse came in. He walked over to Papa, stared at him, then took his pulse. "Your father is dead."

I cried out, "He was alive this minute. His hand is still hot."

The male nurse released my hand from Papa's death grasp. I gazed at Papa once more. His face was serene. I said softly to him, "I salute you, soldier; you accomplished your mission with honor and distinction; the Boss awaits you in Heaven to bestow upon you your just reward."

It was the night of Shiva Osor b'Tammuz, which starts the three-week period of mourning for the destruction of our Holy Temple. Papa had fasted for over forty years, and he passed away on a day when the entire Jewish nation fasts and cries.

He was eighty-seven years old; in Hebrew letters the number is פז, a word which occurs in Psalms 19:11. Rabbi Samson Raphael Hirsch, in his commentary on Psalms, cites various meanings of the word פז. One of them is the following: "In *Avoda Zara* 11b, Rashi states that the term denotes an extremely rare gem."

An apt description of Papa!

The funeral was a very large one. Though it was a fast day and the weather very hot, his *talmidim* carried the *mitta* with many more hundreds of mourners following, all the way to Har Hamenuchos.

I wanted very much for Papa to be buried on Har Hazeisim near Mama, but the *chevra kadisha* argued that Har Hazeisim was still in a state of disarray after the Six Day War. Therefore, it would not be respectful for Papa to be buried there. (Papa had bought the plot on Har Hamenuchos after the War of Independence, when Har Hazeisim was annexed by Jordan.)

The custom in Yerusholayim is that the children and grandchildren of the *niftar* do not follow the *mitta*. In fact, they do not leave the house during the funeral. Nochum Dovid delivered a moving *hesped* from his porch.

Papa was buried between his beloved son-in-law, Yom Tov Lipman Stern, *zatzal*, and his dear *mechutonim*, Reb Avrohom and Sara Lea Horowitz.

the tombstone

....
mitta: bier

Hundreds of people came to pay condolence calls. Through the days we kept hearing countless stories of Papa's selfless acts of *chesed*.

One *rosh yeshiva* related: "You see these teeth in my mouth? Reb Yaakov Yosef saved my health, physically and emotionally.

"I had a serious inflammation in my gums that necessitated having all my teeth extracted. I had no money to order removable dentures, which were very expensive.

"Your father came to my house to discuss a problem about one of the *talmidim* and noticed that I kept my mouth covered while speaking to him. In answer to his question, I explained that I was very sensitive because of my lack of teeth and had no money to buy false ones.

"Reb Yaakov Yosef said to me, '*Rebbe*, come with me to your dentist.' He ordered these dentures and paid the entire cost. I have blessed him all these years."

After *shiva* there was a large gathering at the Zichron Moshe *shul*, where moving *hespedim* were delivered.

Among the speakers were Rabbi Ben Zion Brook, Rosh Yeshiva of Bais Yosef Novarodok, Rabbi Yisroel Yaakov Fisher, rabbi of the Zichron Moshe *shul* and its surrounding area, Rabbi Sholom Schwadron, Rosh Yeshiva of the Beis Medrash Govoha for Rabbinical Training, my brother, Nochum Dovid, and my nephew, Reb Moshe Aaron Stern.

Rabbi Schwadron began his *hesped* promising to speak concisely. The audience, accustomed to his lengthy speeches, wondered at this change of style.

He explained, "When Reb Yaakov Yosef Herman, *zatzal*, came here in 1939, there was excitement among the Jews of Yerusholayim. I questioned several of them, 'What is all this excitement about?'

"I was told, 'The Chofetz Chaim of America has just arrived.' What more can I add to this statement?"

Nine days after Papa was *niftar*, Yechiel Michel Stern, his great-grandson (Moshe Aaron's son), who was fifteen years old at that time, wrote a heart-warming eulogy about Papa which was printed in the daily Hebrew newspaper, *Hamodia*, dated 26 Tammuz, 5727 (August 3, 1967). Michel began with a quote from Song of Songs (6:2):

"My beloved has gone down into His garden to the beds of spices to feed in the gardens and gather roses." [The Midrash interprets "gathering roses" as an allusion to Hashem "plucking away" the righteous of Israel at the appropriate time.]

My Zeidy was one of these precious roses that Hashem has just plucked to take up with Him to His Garden of Eden.

My Zeidy never sought rabbinical or public office. His only goal was to serve Hashem as a "simple Jew—one of the millions of Hashem's soldiers."

He concerned himself with every problem of *klal Yisroel*. His days were surely blessed, for each day must have been doubled or tripled in time to allow him to accomplish his multitude of religious activities and acts of *chesed*.

My Zeidy never hurried home from *shul* on Friday nights; he waited to see if some person might need a place to eat.

When my Zeidy was questioned about the countless tasks which he performed for the *orchim* that were below his dignity, he answered, "The *orchim* are my children. Is there anything too low or too difficult for a father to do for his sons?"

Someone told my Zeidy that he had seen one of his supposedly poor *orchim* enter a cafeteria and purchase an expensive beverage. Zeidy's reaction was to serve the *orech* that beverage whenever he came to the house. He even apologized to him for not having provided it before.

Another person came to tell him that one of his *orchim* was a vagrant who slept in the street. He immediately cried out, "Why did you not bring him to my house? He is one of Hashem's children."

My Zeidy never closed his ears or his heart to the cry of the distressed. Day after day he was deluged by many people beseeching help. One might think that after a while he would have become calloused to people's troubles and problems. Instead, each cry and sigh from a person in distress touched him to the depths of his heart. It was his own pain.

[Michel ended with the words of the Midrash (Exodus Rabba 6):] "Alas for those that are gone and are no more to be found."

Conclusion

My son-in-law, Elimelech, asked me, "What made Zeidy— Zeidy?" Many others have posed the same question.

How did Papa become the warrior for *yiddishkeit*, the learned man in Torah, the wise sage, who understood the needs of the young and old, and who, above all else, was the "Soldier of the Boss" with an "army" that numbered in the thousands?

Papa's parents maintained that from the time their oldest child was born, they realized that he was a *hechere neshomo*, a lofty soul.

Even as a young lad, his sterling character manifested itself in showing no jealousy, bearing no grudge, using no subterfuge or flattery, righting a wrong immediately. To him truth was like the notes of a violin: he felt each nuance of falsehood.

He had no formal religious education, never attended a yeshiva, and heard no *shiurim* from *gedolei Torah* in his youth. His father was his *rebbe* until his *bar mitzva*.

Zeidy and Bobie Herman left Papa to his own resources as a youth, alone in New York City, when they returned to the Old Country. Instead of succumbing to the slums of the city, where poverty of religion stalked every street, he grew in spiritual stature.

After Papa married, he returned to Torah studies, at the suggestion of his father-in-law. With his brilliant mind and keen desire for learning, he outgrew *rebbe* after *rebbe* until he became the *rebbe* of the little ones, the youth, the young men and the old men, who caught his contagious enthusiasm and zeal for Torah.

He was a raw diamond, who became even more refined through the constant influence of Torah. In time, Papa became the perfect, blue-white diamond, whose sparkles brought light to the dark alleys of those ignorant of Torah and *mitzvos*.

Each Jew was dear to Papa. He felt his loneliness, his pain, his insecurity, his poverty, his need for guidance and advice from someone who cared, and Papa *really cared*.

His *talmidim* were stamped with a permanent seal, which kept them strong and dedicated to the religious principles Papa firmly set in their hearts and minds.

With his singleness of purpose and complete unselfishness, Papa was their tower of strength, the champion and defender of religious education, who imbued his *talmidim* with such spiritual vitality that his fiery words were absorbed by his *talmidim* in every fiber of body and soul.

Papa lives on in the heart and mind of every Jew who was blessed to have known him.

AFTERWORD

During my visit with Papa in 1963, as I sat in his store discussing a variety of subjects, the thought suddenly came to me, "Papa, I should write the story of your life. First of all, I want my children, grandchildren, and all our generations to follow to know who their Zeidy was.

"Secondly, I am sure it would give many people *chizuk* to read about your many accomplishments for *klal Yisroel*, and your love for the Boss."

Papa was silent for a few minutes. Then, pointing his finger at me, he said firmly, "Ruchoma, not in my lifetime." The look he gave me sanctioned my writing his life story after he passed on.

Fifteen years have elapsed since Papa, *zatzal*, was *niftar*. As Rabbi Miller writes so aptly in his Foreword: "The biography of this servant of Hashem is long overdue."

Dearest Papa,

May your *pure* tear that you gave *all for the Boss* be the tear that will overflow the "cup of tears" that stands before the throne of Hashem and bring the final redemption of our Jewish nation, the rebuilding of our Holy Temple, and everlasting peace.

When I first set out to write the story of your life, I knew that you were a soldier of the Boss and a lover of every Jew.

Through writing this book, I have relived my life with you, and I realize that you were far above my limited understanding of your true greatness.

I am doubly blessed to be your daughter.

Ruchoma